Shojo Beat

# La Corda d'Ore

**9**
Story & Art by Yuki Kure

# La Corda d'Oro

## CONTENTS
### Volume 9

## Kahoko Hino
### (General Education School, 2nd year)

The heroine. She knows nothing about music, but she still finds herself participating in the music competition equipped with a magic violin.

## Ryotaro Tsuchiura
### (General Education, 2nd year)

A member of the soccer team who seems to be looking after Kahoko as a fellow Gen Ed student.

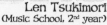

## Len Tsukimori
### (Music School, 2nd year)

A violin major and a cold perfectionist from a musical family of unquestionable talent.

## Kazuki Hihara
### (Music school, 3rd year)

An energetic and friendly trumpet major and a fan of anything fun.

## Keiichi Shimizu
### (Music school, 1st year)

A cello major who walks to the beat of his own drum and is often lost in the world of music. He is also often asleep.

## Azuma Yunoki
### (Music school, 3rd year)

A flute major and the son of a graceful and kind traditional flower arrangement master. He has a dedicated fan club called the "Yunoki Guard."

## Hiroto Kanazawa
### (Music teacher)

The contest coordinator whose lazy demeanor suggests he is avoiding any hassle.

The music fairy Lili, who got Kahoko caught up in this affair. ↓

Our story is set at Seiso Academy, which is split into the General Education School and the Music School. Kahoko, a Gen Ed student, encounters a music fairy named Lili, who gives her a magic violin that anyone can play. Suddenly, Kahoko finds herself in the school's music competition, with good-looking, quirky Music School students as her fellow contestants! Kahoko comes to accept her daunting task and finds herself enjoying music. But on the day of the Third Selection, Lili tells Kahoko that the magic of the violin is fading. Kahoko makes it through her performance, but the violin vanishes, leaving only a single string. At first Kahoko loses faith in herself, but after Lili gives her an ordinary violin she decides to continue to pursue music. Meanwhile, Ryotaro and his ex-girlfriend Mizue go on a double date with Kahoko and Len...

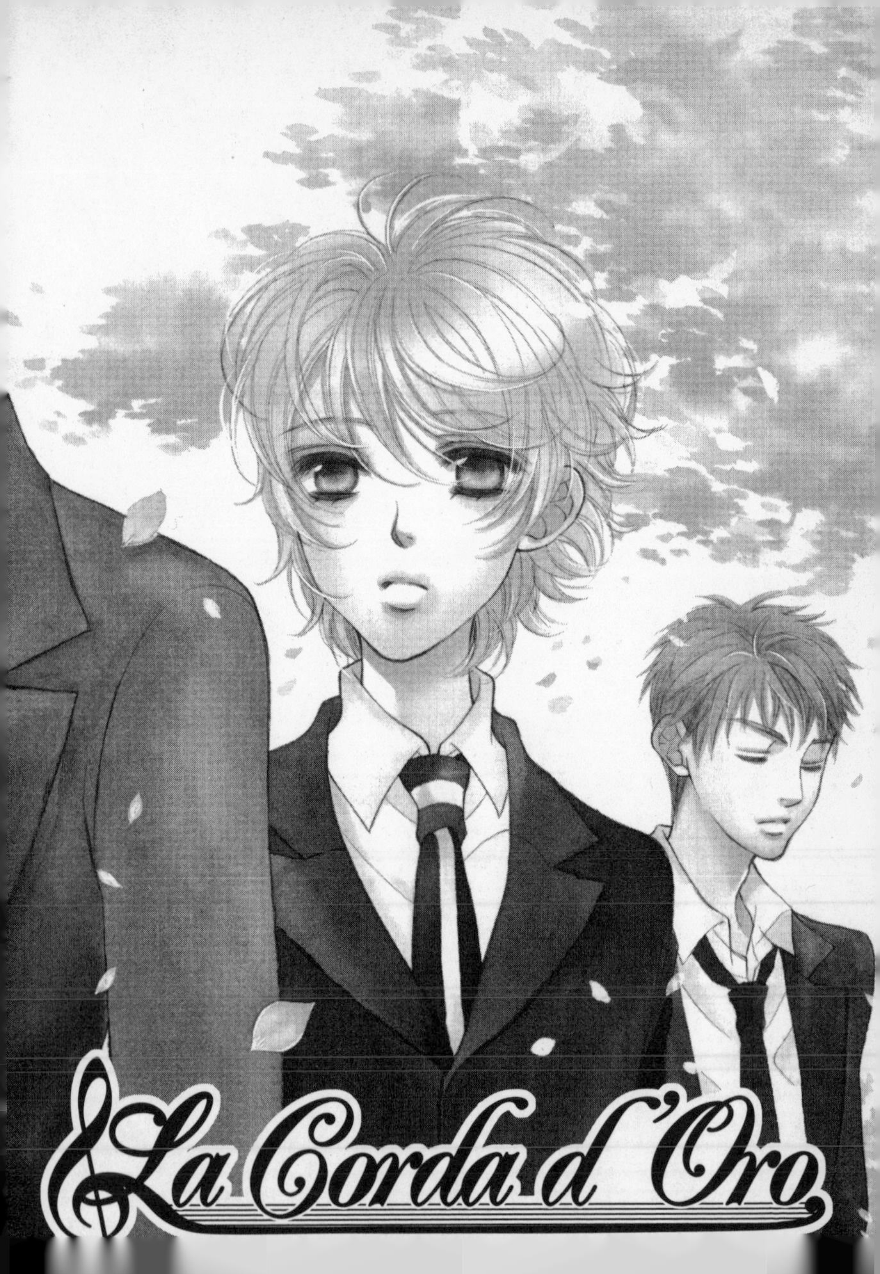
La Corda d'Oro

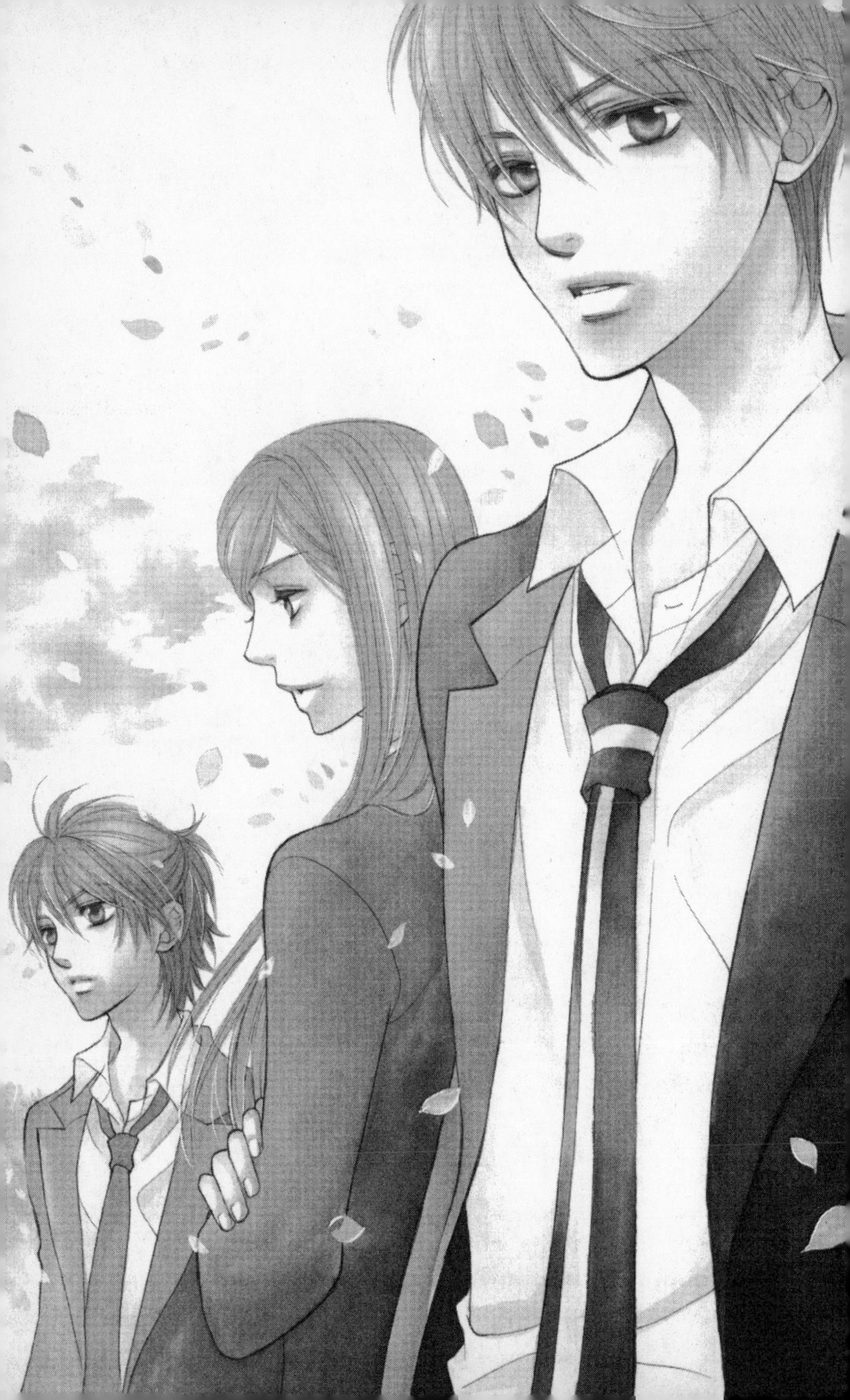

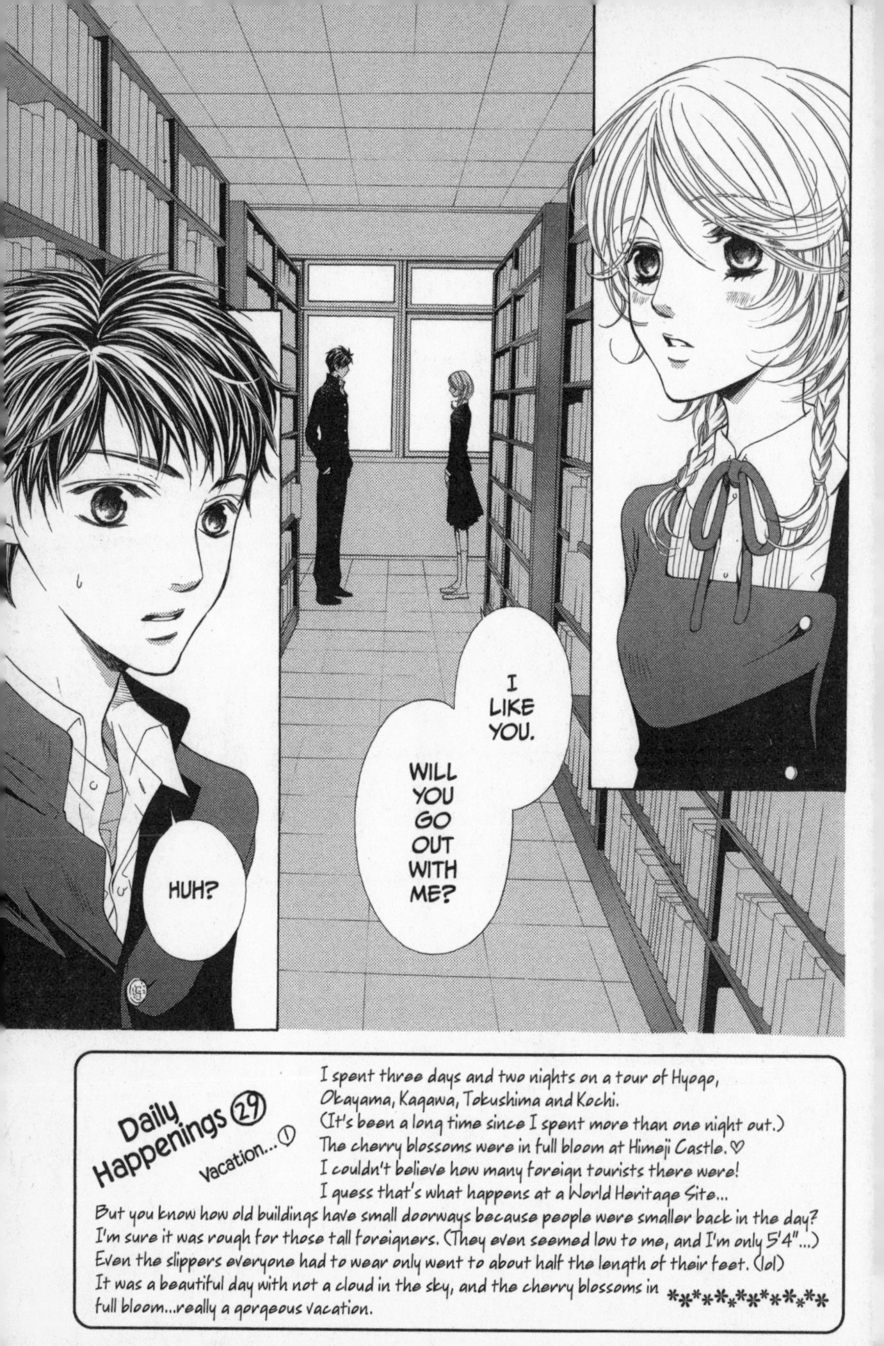
I LIKE YOU.
WILL YOU GO OUT WITH ME?
HUH?

**Daily Happenings ㉙**

**Vacation...①**

I spent three days and two nights on a tour of Hyogo, Okayama, Kagawa, Tokushima and Kochi.
(It's been a long time since I spent more than one night out.)
The cherry blossoms were in full bloom at Himeji Castle. ♡
I couldn't believe how many foreign tourists there were!
I guess that's what happens at a World Heritage Site...
But you know how old buildings have small doorways because people were smaller back in the day?
I'm sure it was rough for those tall foreigners. (They even seemed low to me, and I'm only 5'4"...)
Even the slippers everyone had to wear only went to about half the length of their feet. (lol)
It was a beautiful day with not a cloud in the sky, and the cherry blossoms in full bloom...really a gorgeous vacation.

***********

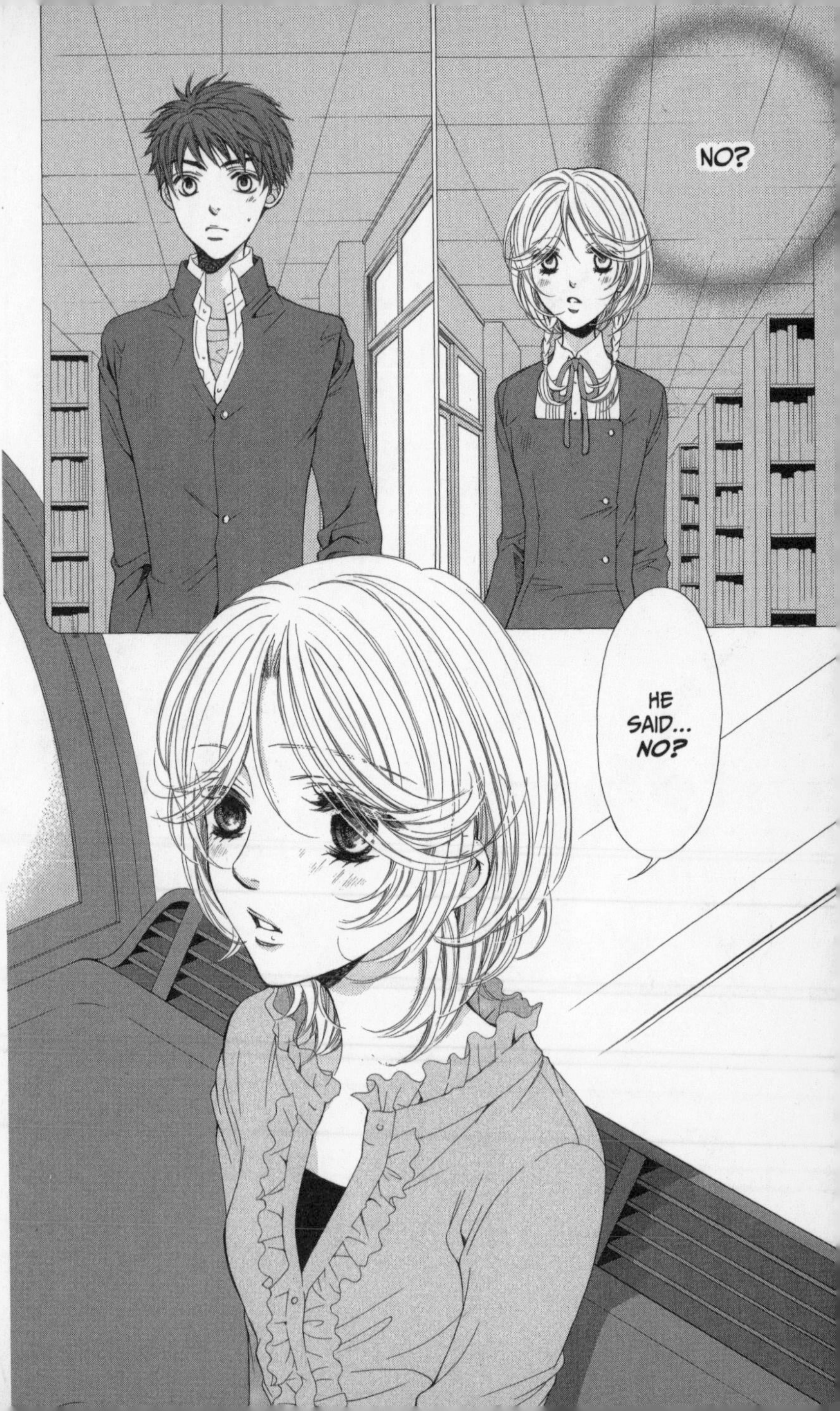
NO?
HE SAID... NO?

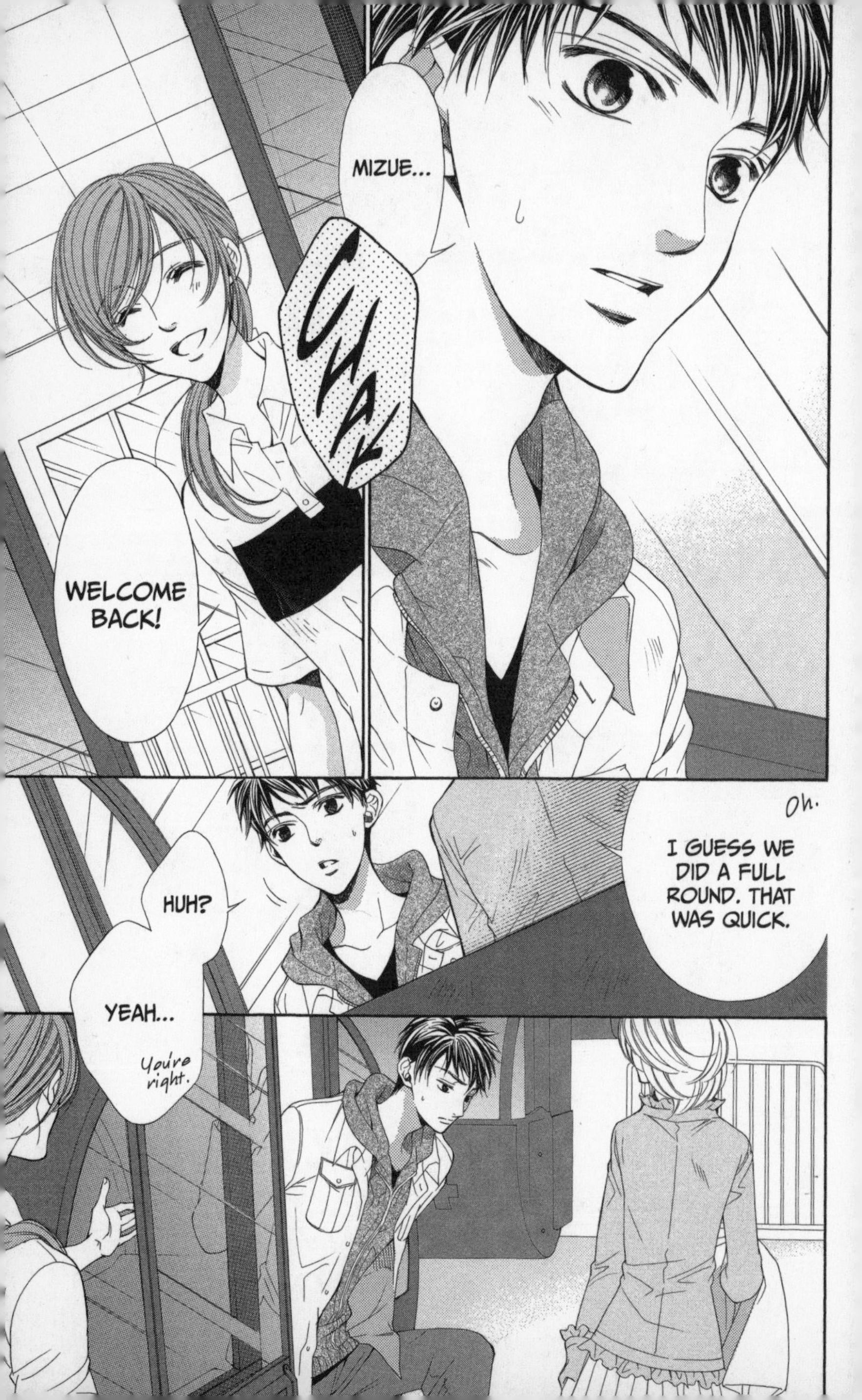
MIZUE...
WELCOME BACK!
Oh.
I GUESS WE DID A FULL ROUND. THAT WAS QUICK.
HUH?
YEAH...
You're right.

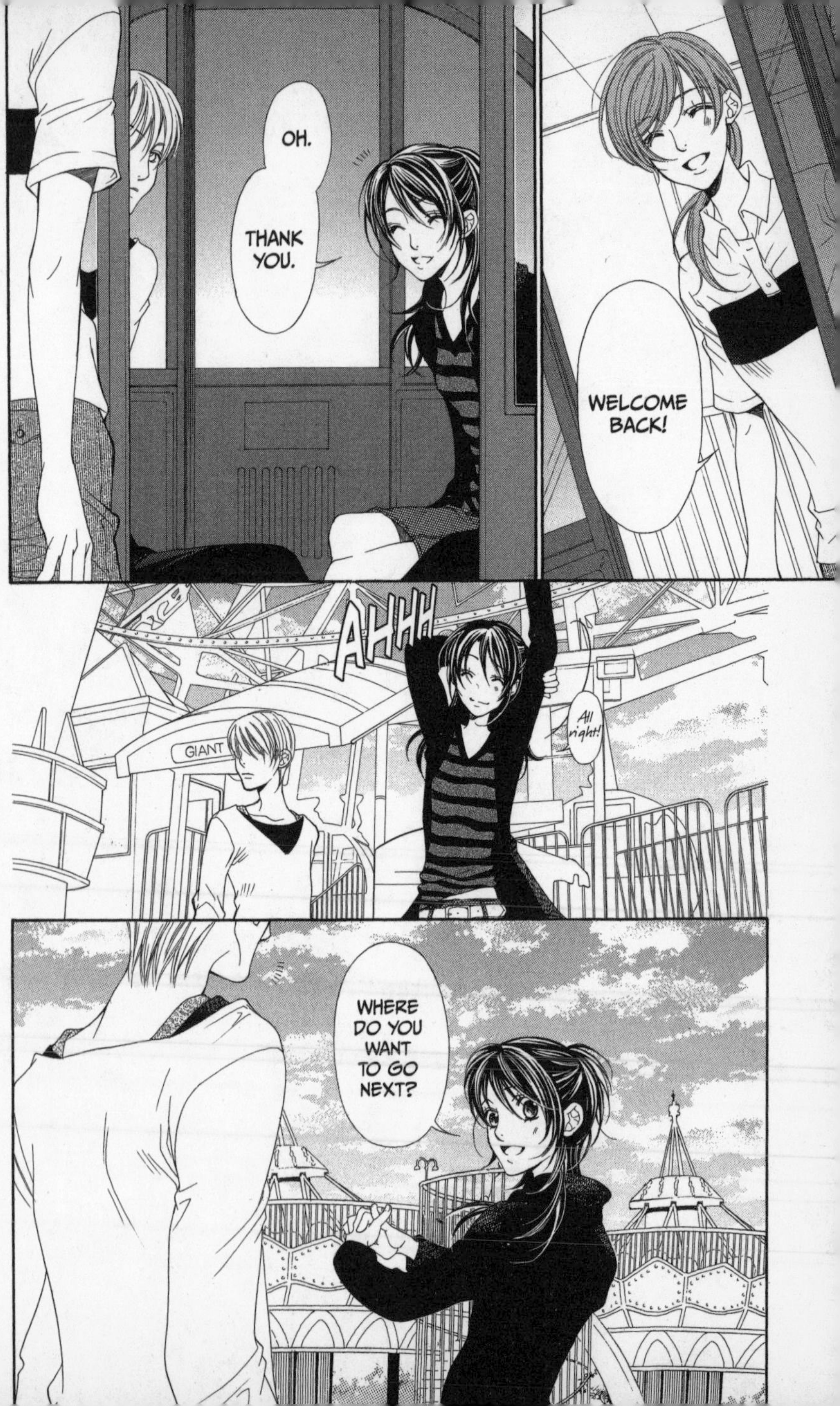
WELCOME BACK!
OH.
THANK YOU.
AHHH
GIANT
All night!
WHERE DO YOU WANT TO GO NEXT?

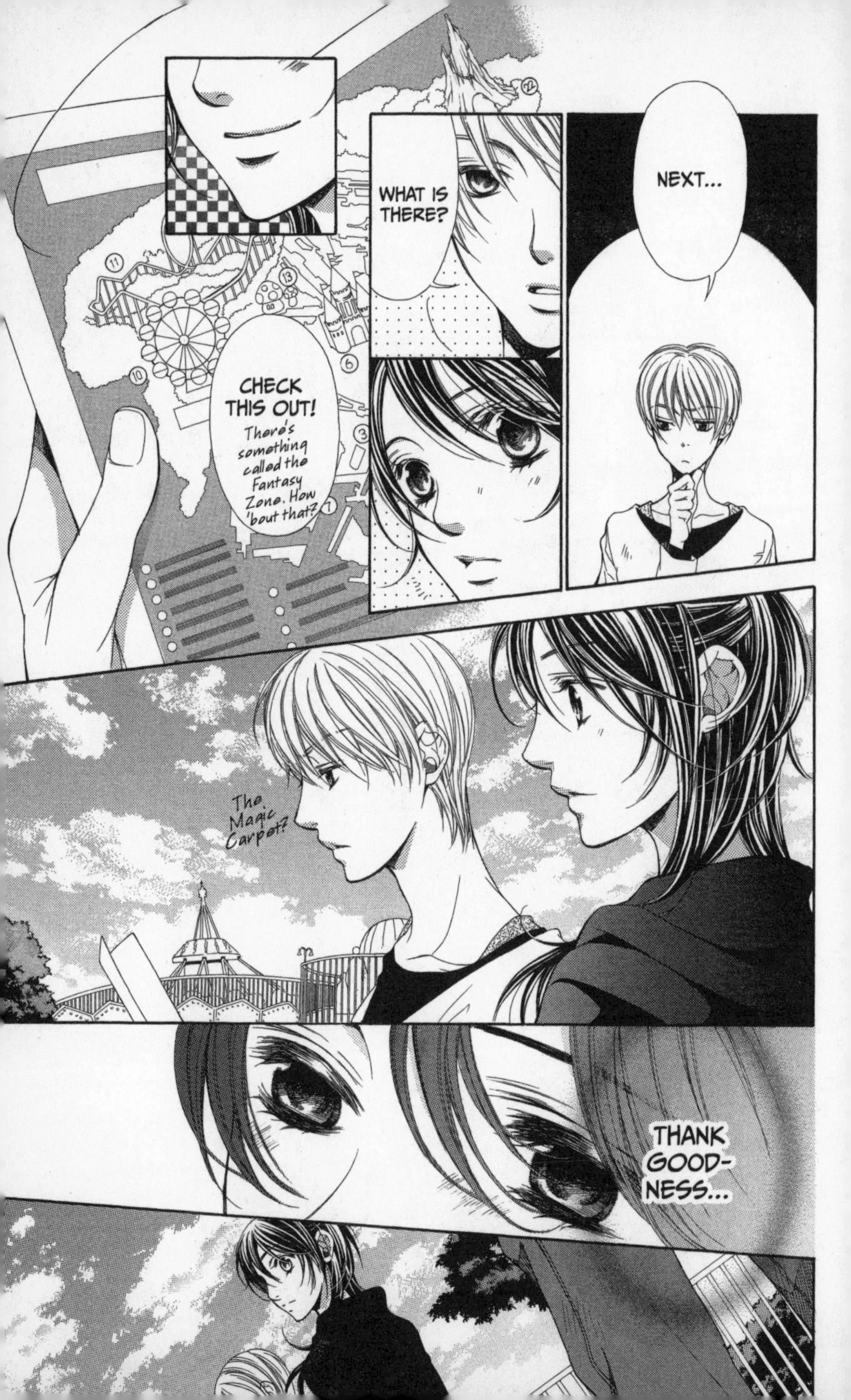
NEXT...
WHAT IS THERE?
CHECK THIS OUT! There's something called the Fantasy Zone. How 'bout that?
The Magic Carpet?
THANK GOOD-NESS...

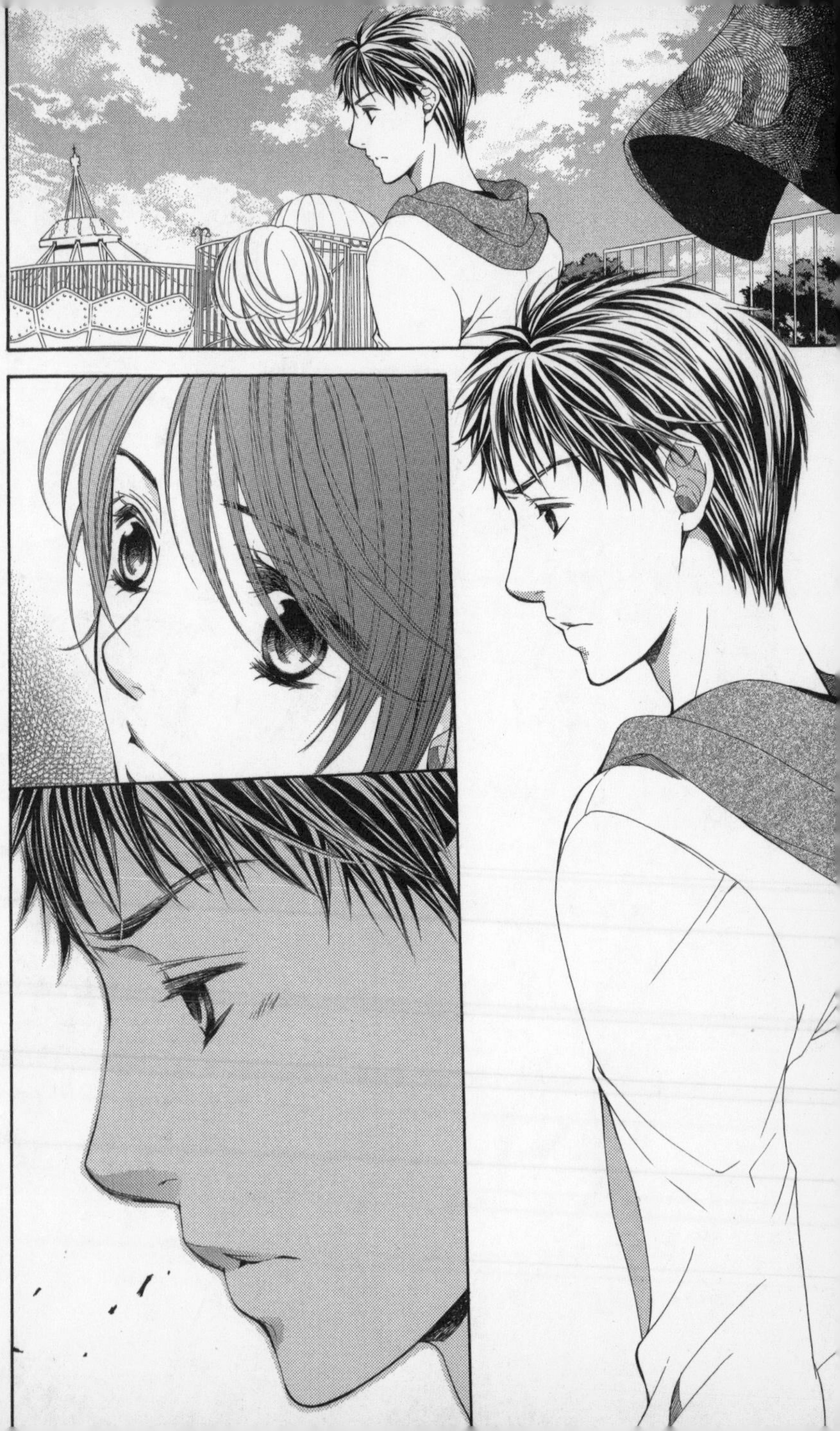

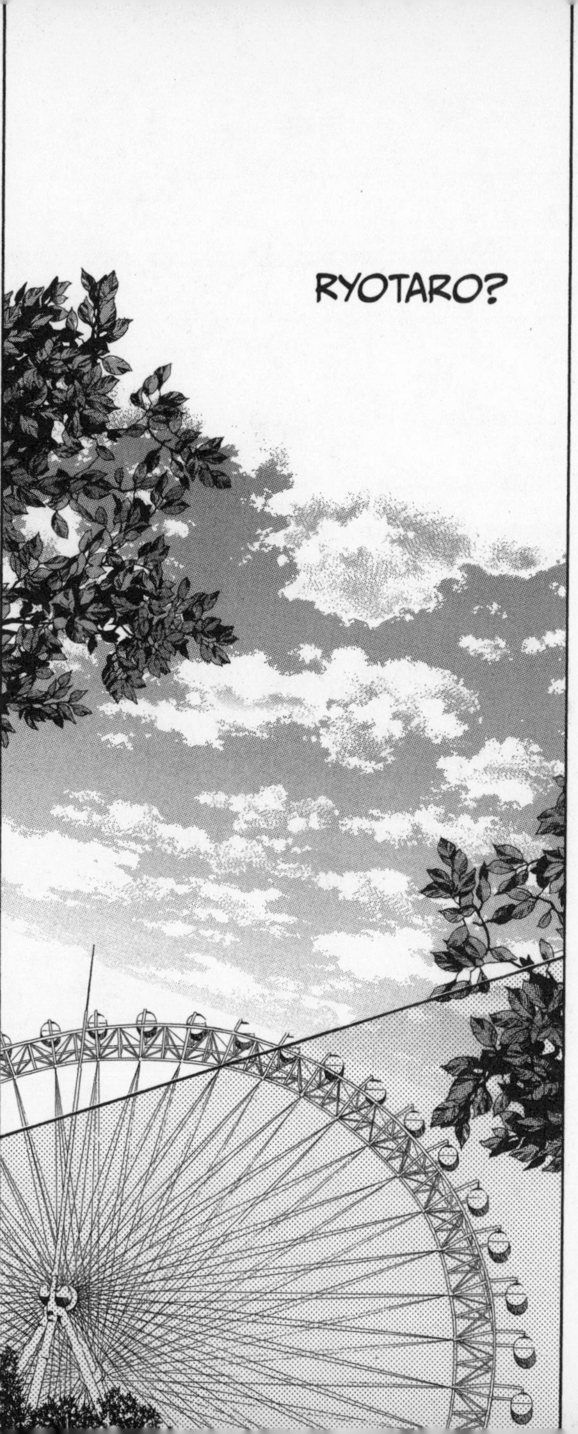
RYOTARO?

**ONE**

Hello.
Long time no see.
Yuki here.
Thank you very much for purchasing volume 9 of *La Corda*.
I hope you enjoy it.

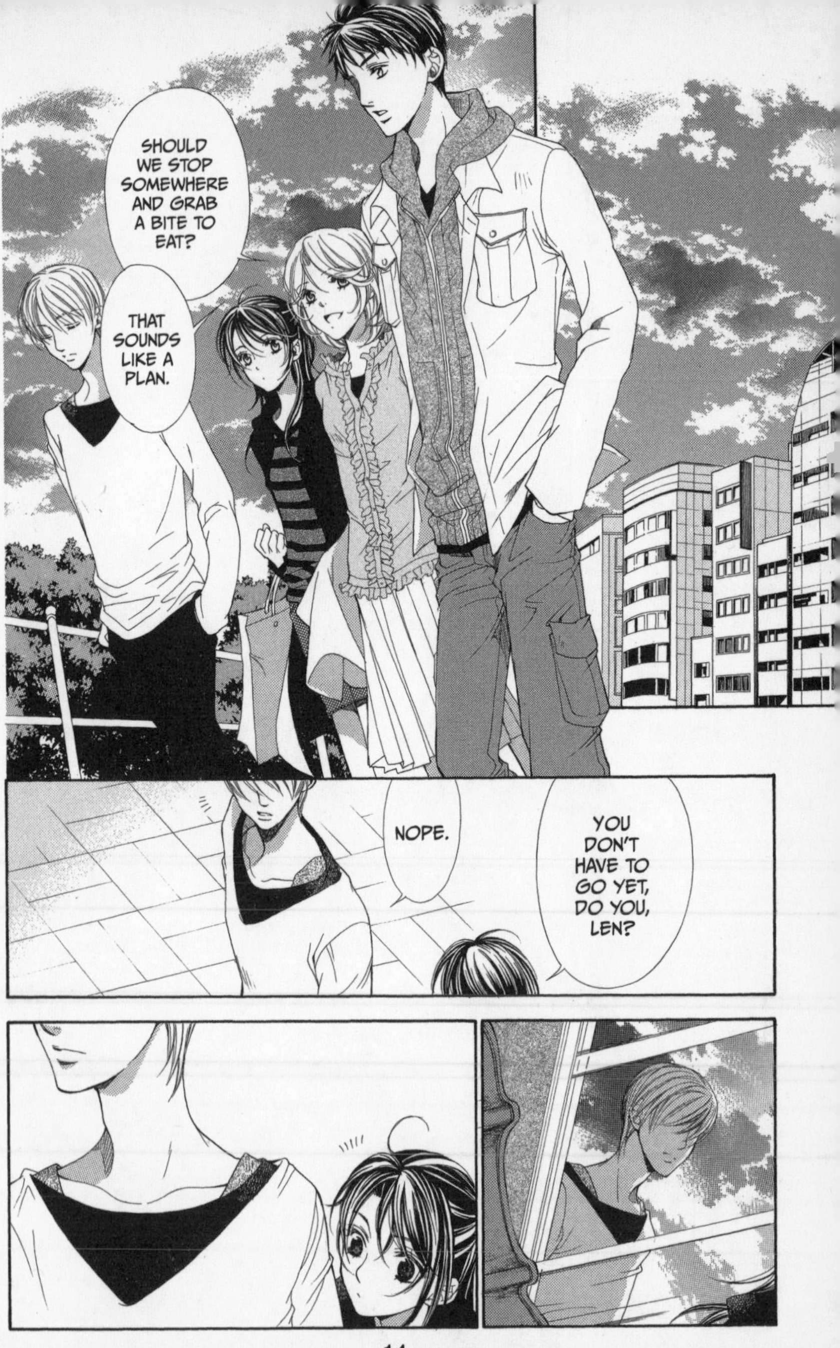
SHOULD WE STOP SOMEWHERE AND GRAB A BITE TO EAT?
THAT SOUNDS LIKE A PLAN.
YOU DON'T HAVE TO GO YET, DO YOU, LEN?
NOPE.

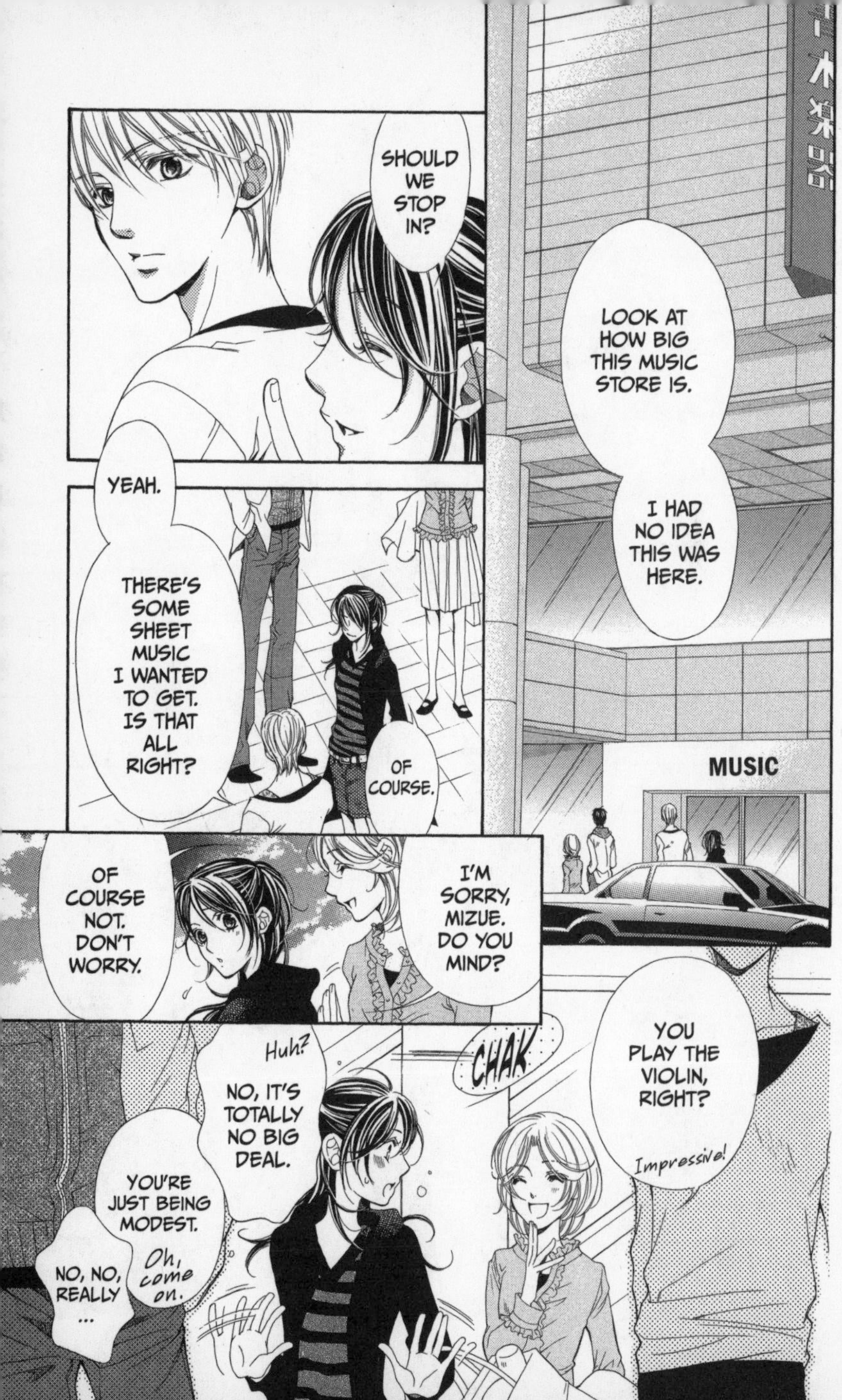
LOOK AT HOW BIG THIS MUSIC STORE IS.
I HAD NO IDEA THIS WAS HERE.
MUSIC
SHOULD WE STOP IN?
YEAH.
THERE'S SOME SHEET MUSIC I WANTED TO GET. IS THAT ALL RIGHT?
OF COURSE.
I'M SORRY, MIZUE. DO YOU MIND?
OF COURSE NOT. DON'T WORRY.
YOU PLAY THE VIOLIN, RIGHT?
Impressive!
CHAK
Huh?
NO, IT'S TOTALLY NO BIG DEAL.
YOU'RE JUST BEING MODEST.
Oh, come on.
NO, NO, REALLY ...

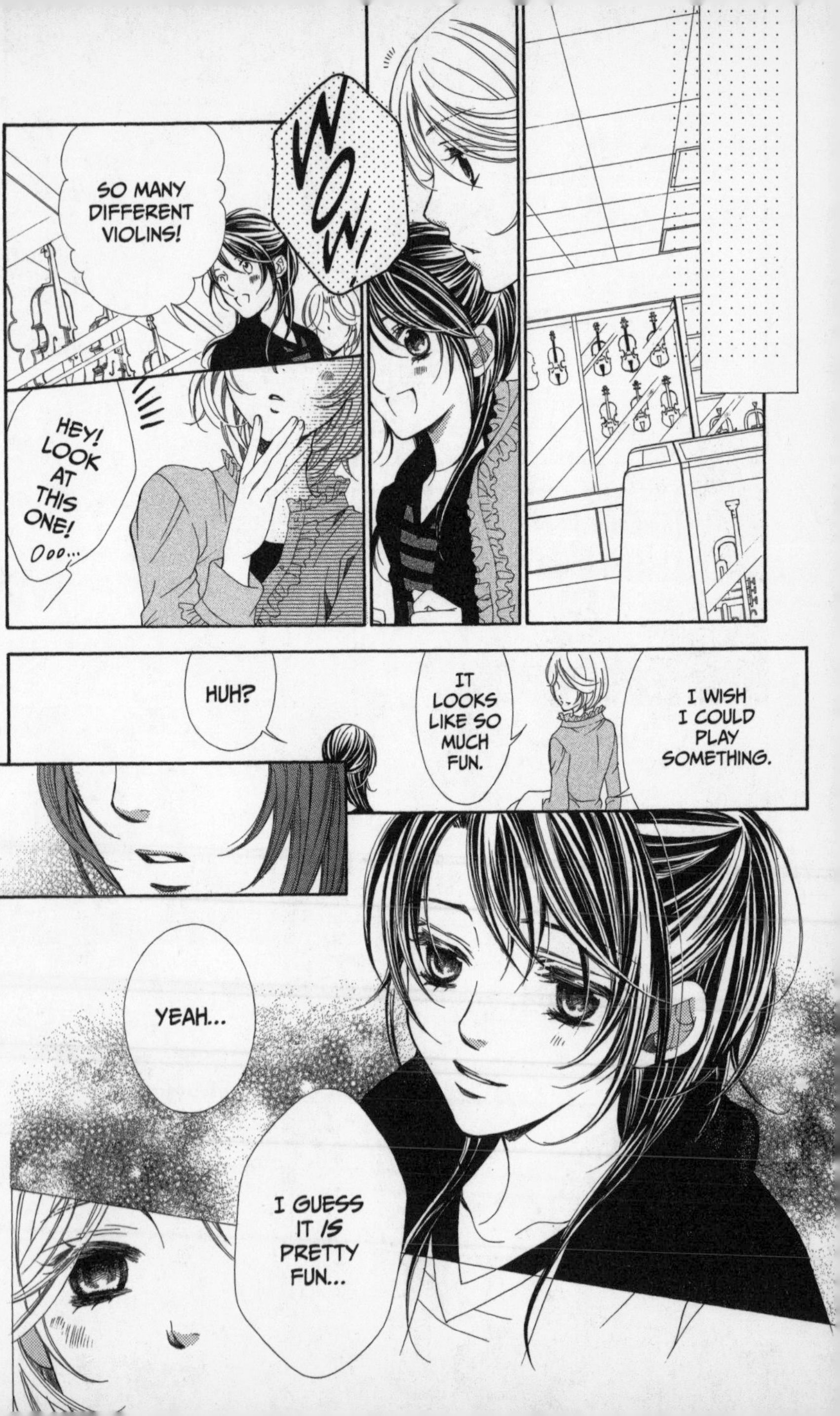
WOW!
SO MANY DIFFERENT VIOLINS!
HEY! LOOK AT THIS ONE! Ooo...
I WISH I COULD PLAY SOMETHING.
IT LOOKS LIKE SO MUCH FUN.
HUH?
YEAH...
I GUESS IT *IS* PRETTY FUN...

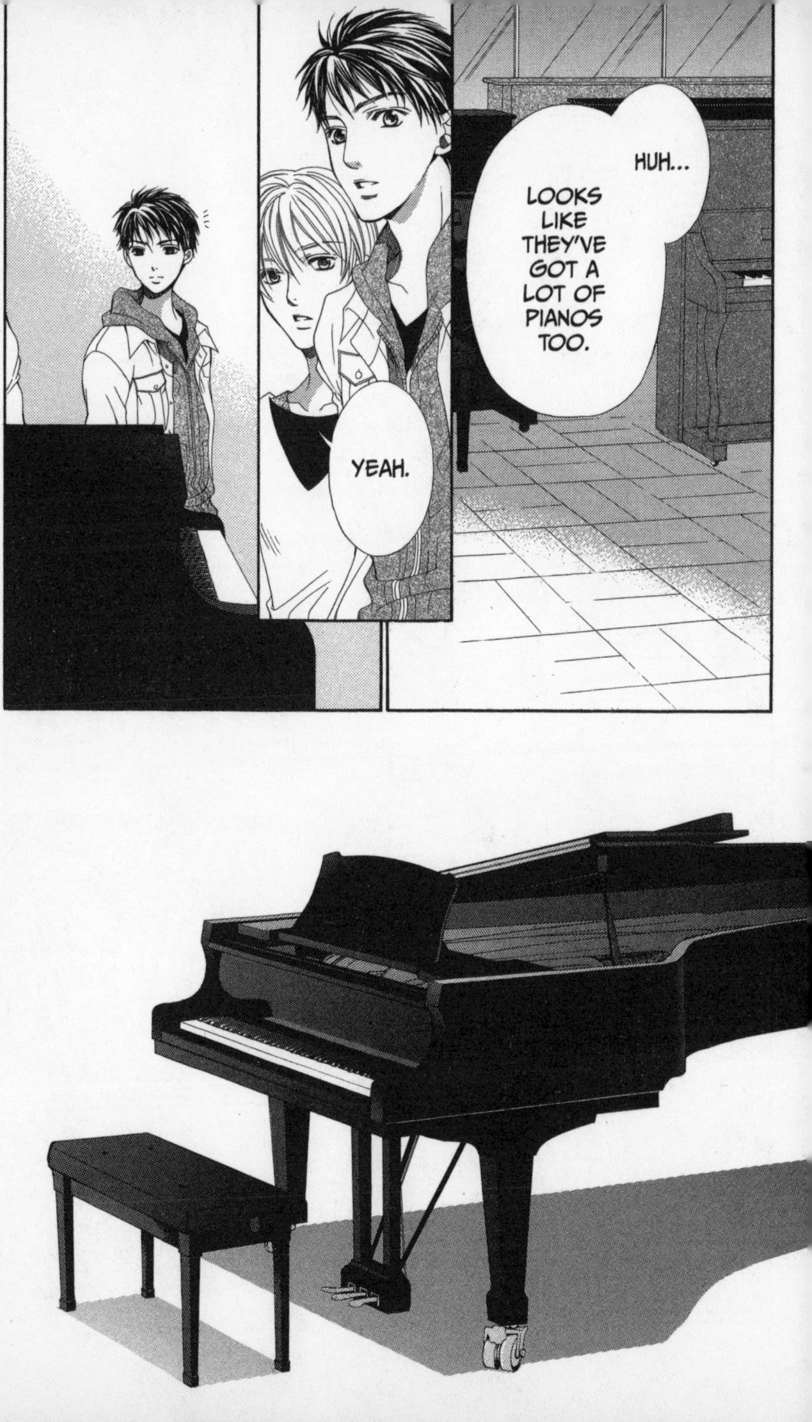
HUH...
LOOKS LIKE THEY'VE GOT A LOT OF PIANOS TOO.
YEAH.

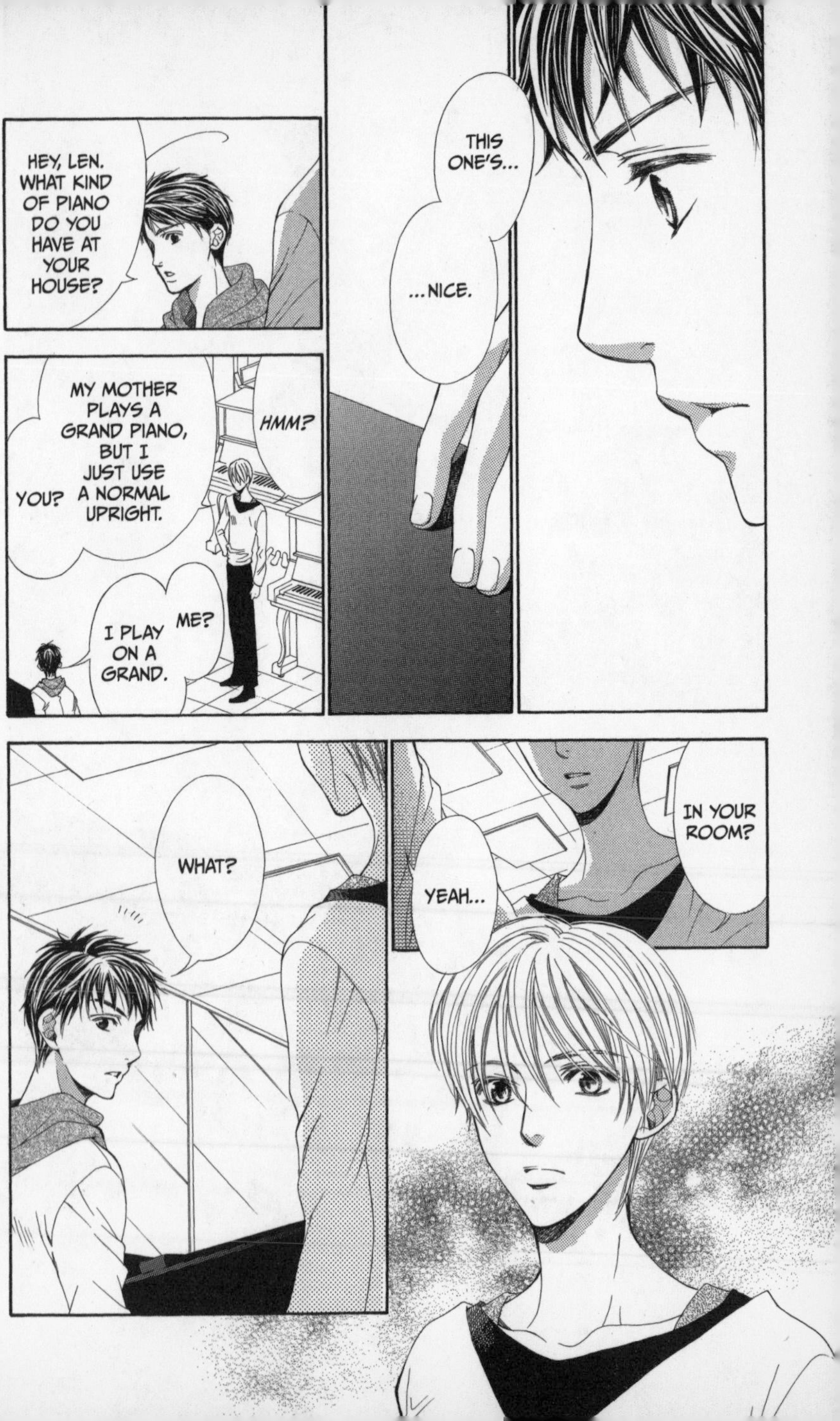
THIS ONE'S...
...NICE.
HEY, LEN. WHAT KIND OF PIANO DO YOU HAVE AT YOUR HOUSE?
HMM?
MY MOTHER PLAYS A GRAND PIANO, BUT I JUST USE A NORMAL UPRIGHT.
YOU?
ME?
I PLAY ON A GRAND.
IN YOUR ROOM?
YEAH...
WHAT?

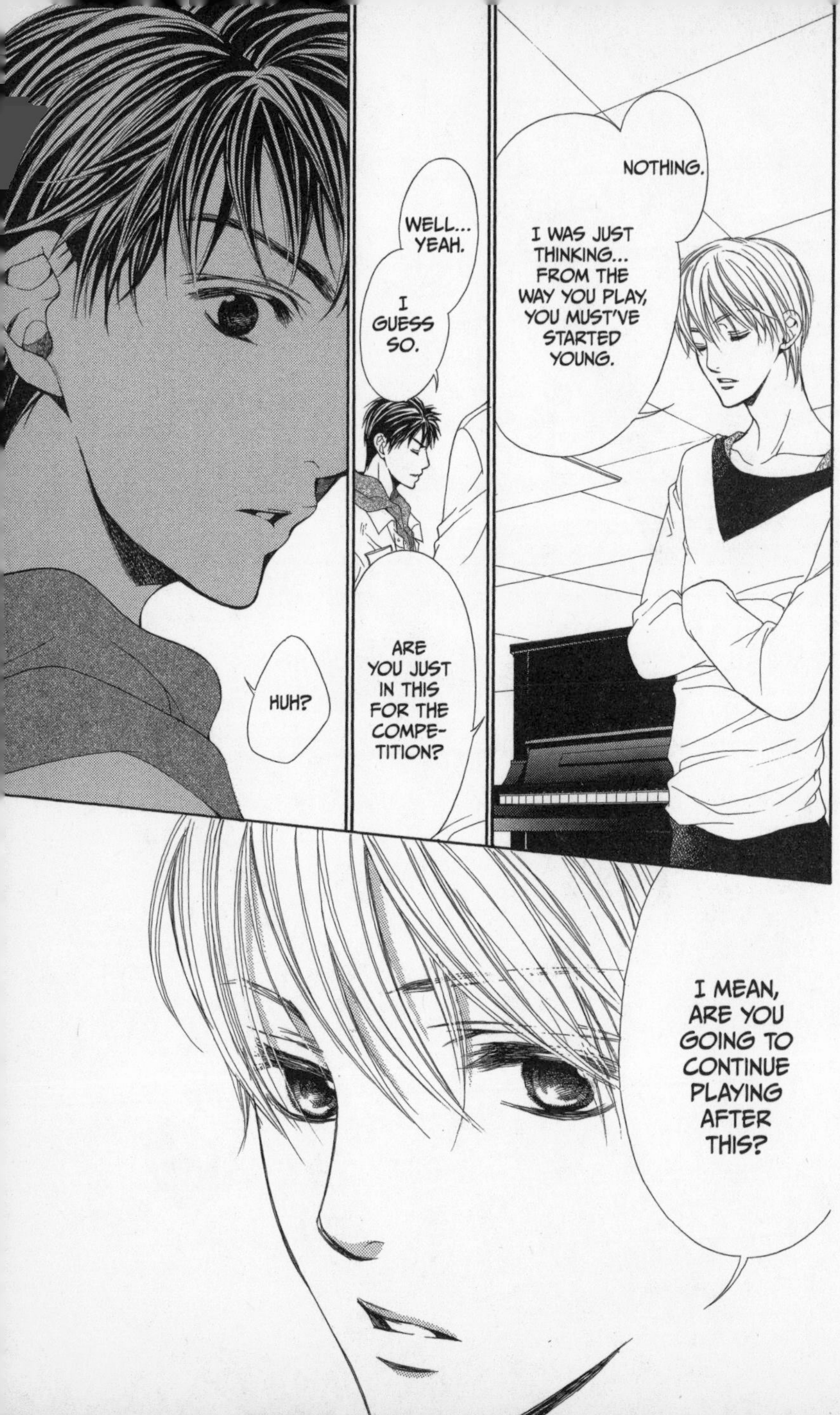
NOTHING.
I WAS JUST THINKING... FROM THE WAY YOU PLAY, YOU MUST'VE STARTED YOUNG.
WELL... YEAH.
I GUESS SO.
ARE YOU JUST IN THIS FOR THE COMPETITION?
HUH?
I MEAN, ARE YOU GOING TO CONTINUE PLAYING AFTER THIS?

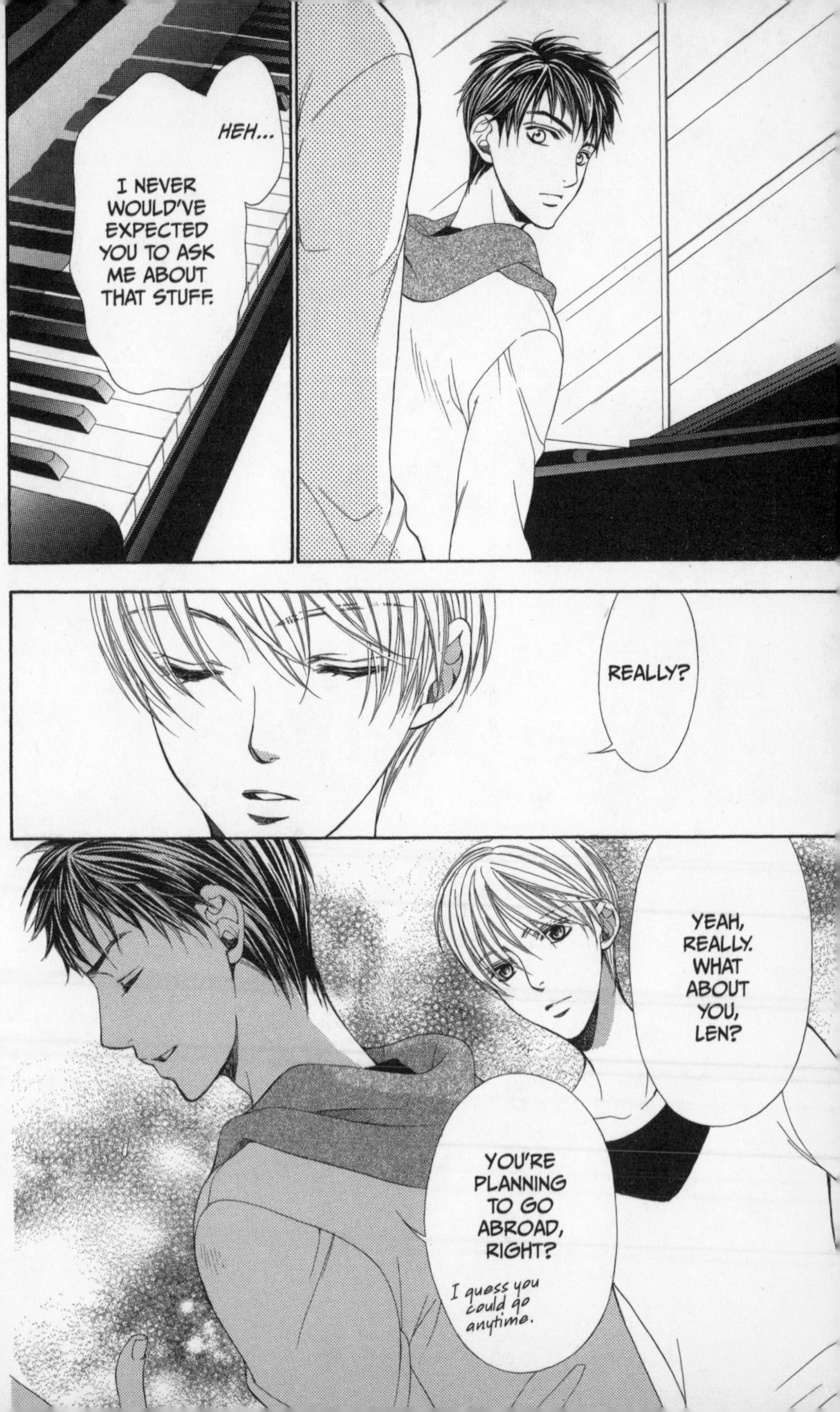
HEH...
I NEVER WOULD'VE EXPECTED YOU TO ASK ME ABOUT THAT STUFF.
REALLY?
YEAH, REALLY. WHAT ABOUT YOU, LEN?
YOU'RE PLANNING TO GO ABROAD, RIGHT?
I guess you could go anytime.

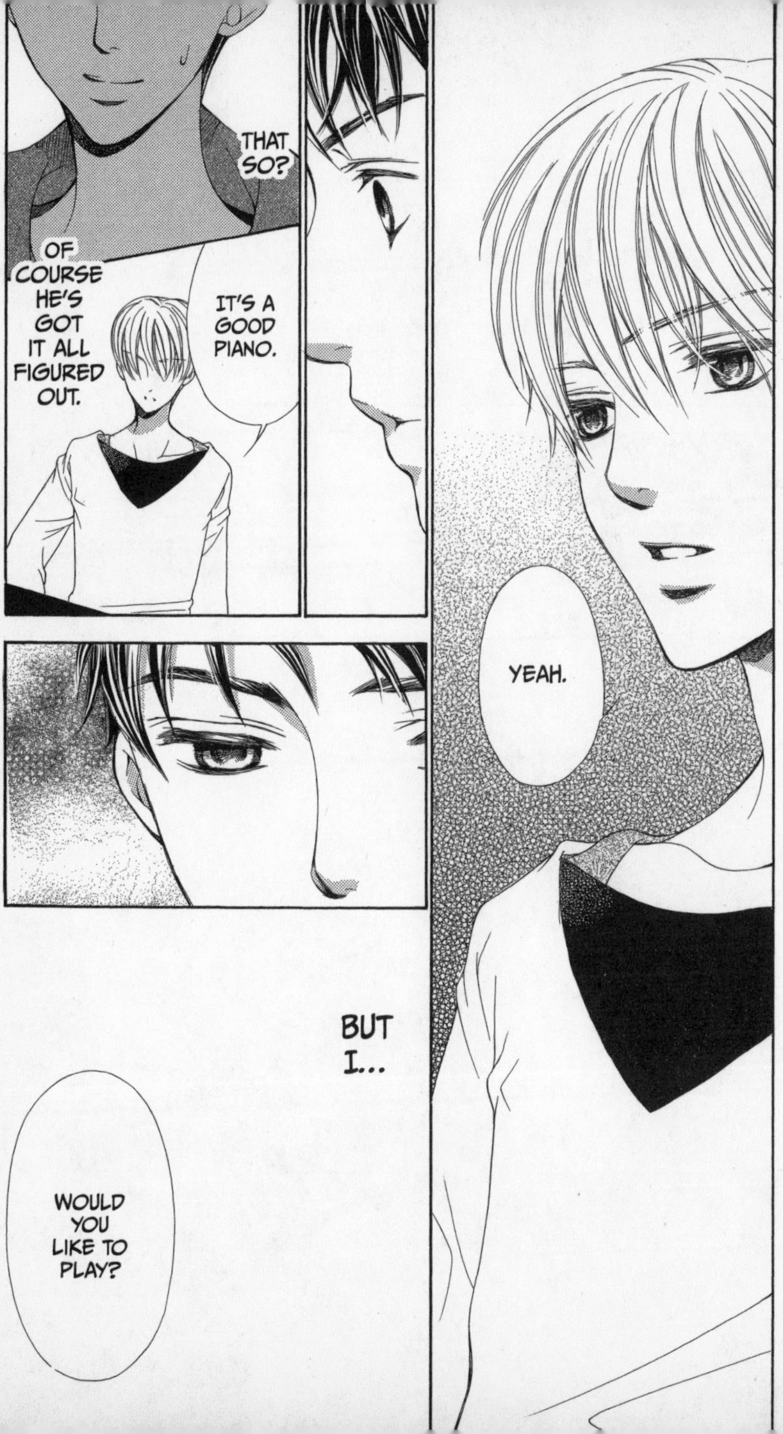
YEAH.
IT'S A GOOD PIANO.
THAT SO?
OF COURSE HE'S GOT IT ALL FIGURED OUT.
BUT I...
WOULD YOU LIKE TO PLAY?

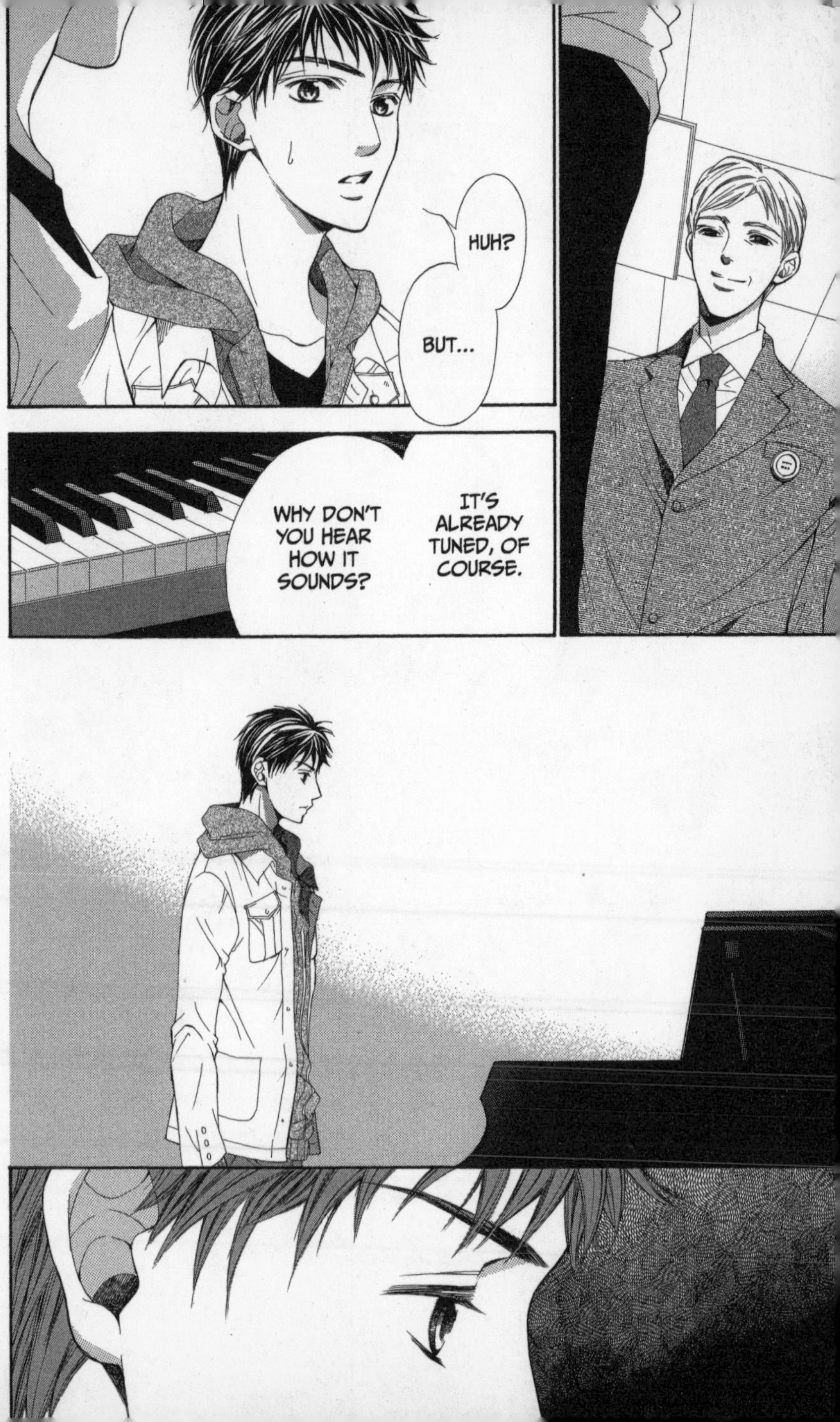
HUH?
BUT...
IT'S ALREADY TUNED, OF COURSE.
WHY DON'T YOU HEAR HOW IT SOUNDS?

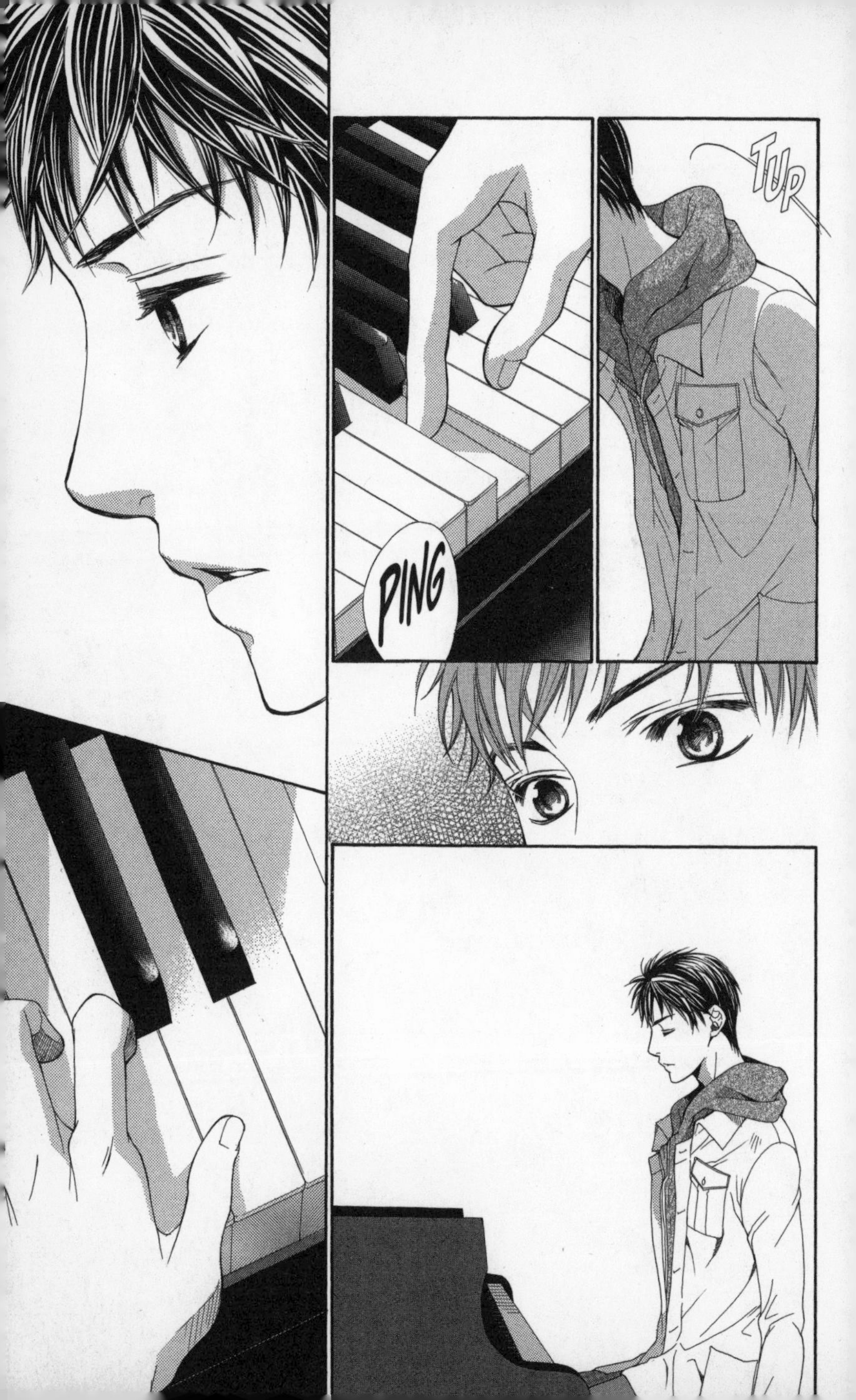
TUP
PING

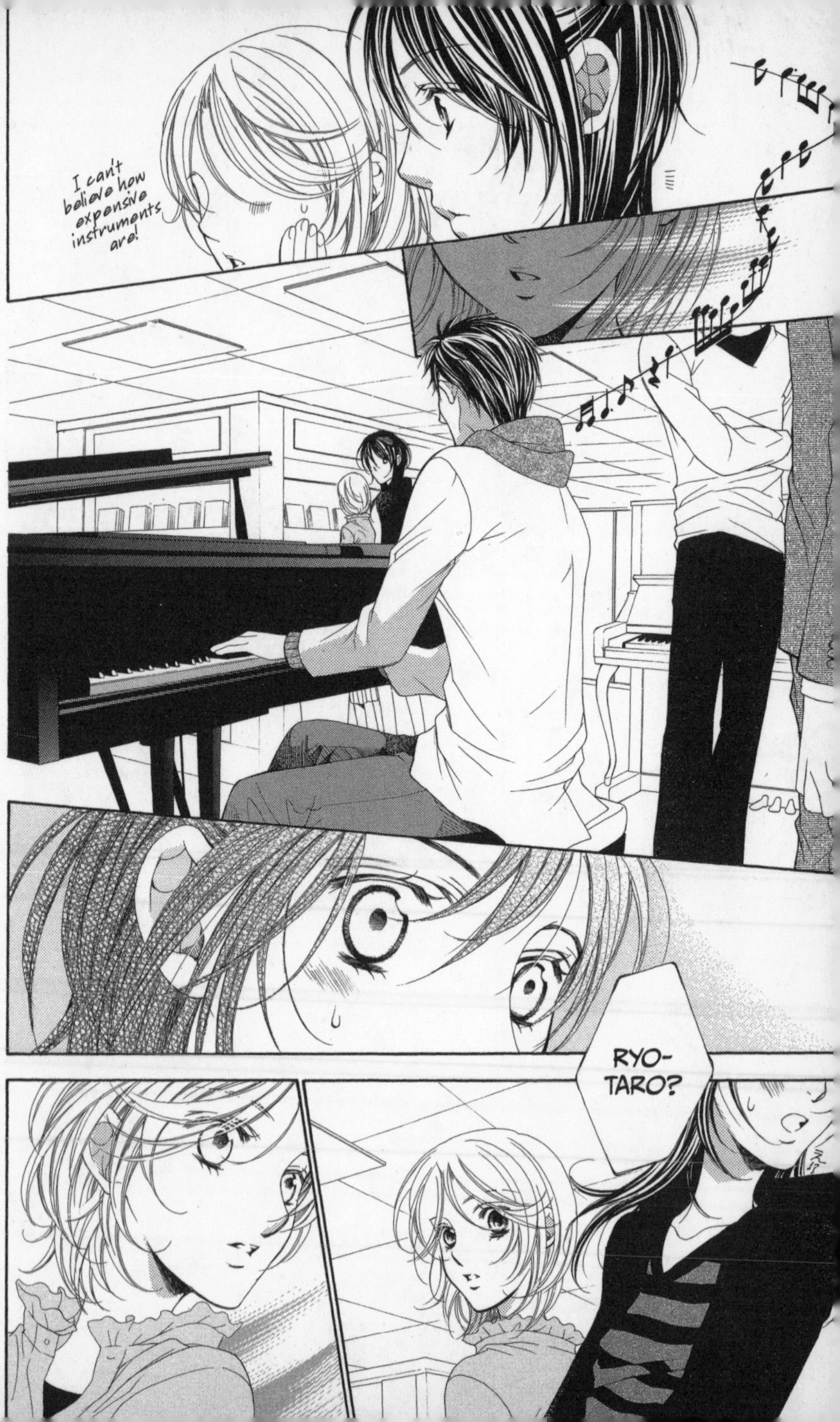
I can't believe how expensive instruments are!
RYO-TARO?

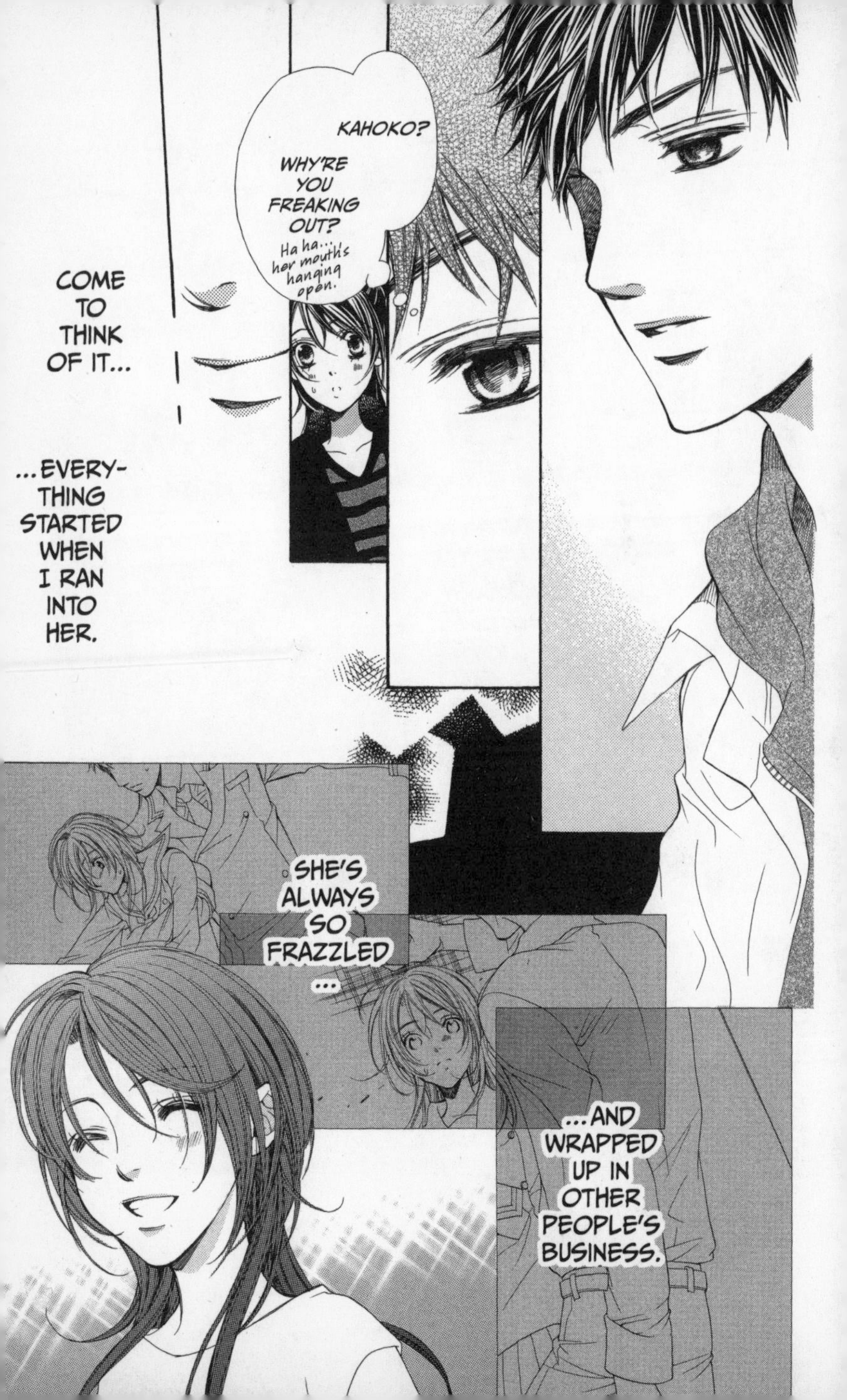
KAHOKO?
WHY'RE YOU FREAKING OUT?
Ha ha... her mouth's hanging open.
COME TO THINK OF IT...
...EVERYTHING STARTED WHEN I RAN INTO HER.
SHE'S ALWAYS SO FRAZZLED...
...AND WRAPPED UP IN OTHER PEOPLE'S BUSINESS.

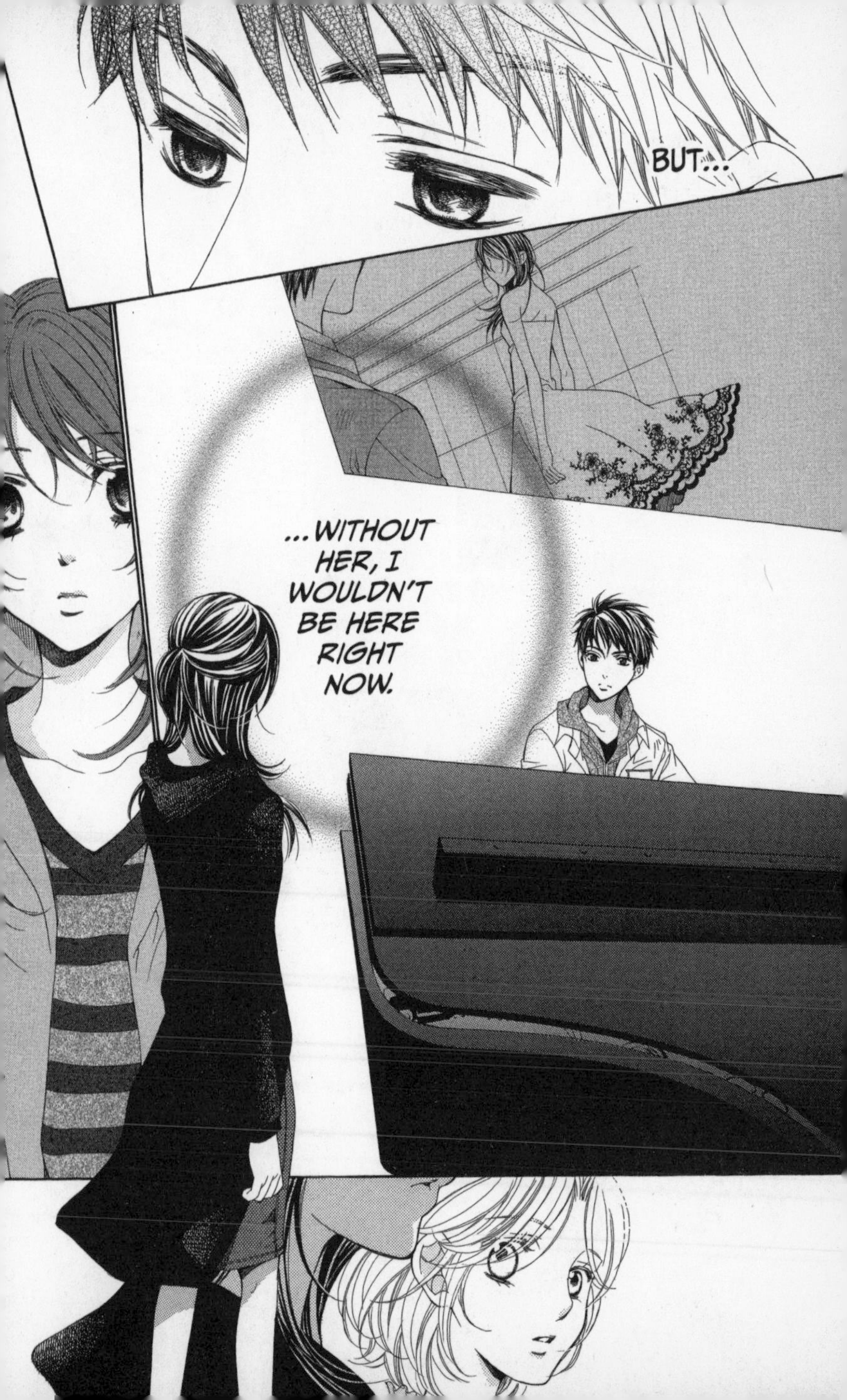
BUT...
...WITHOUT HER, I WOULDN'T BE HERE RIGHT NOW.

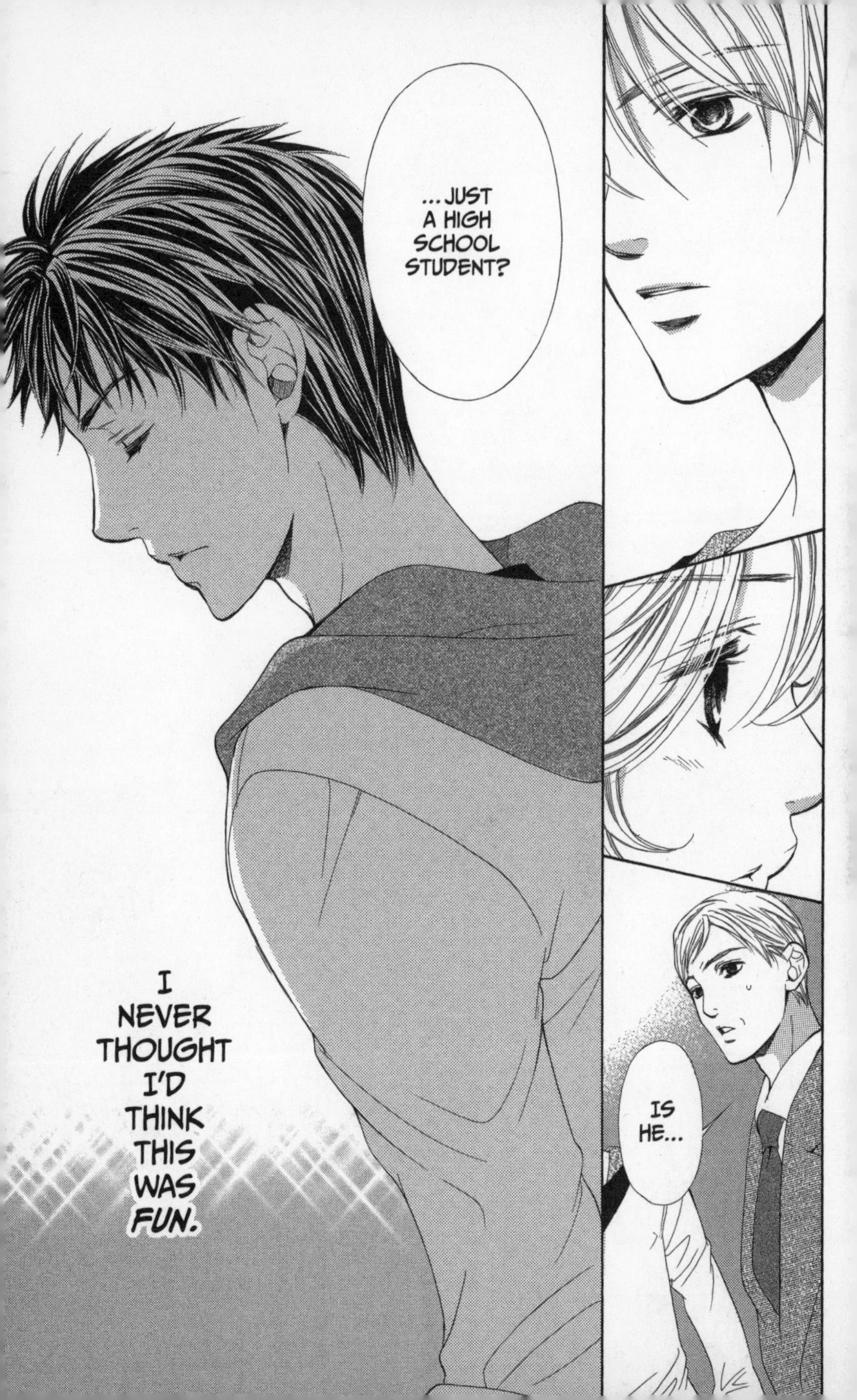
IS HE...
...JUST A HIGH SCHOOL STUDENT?
I NEVER THOUGHT I'D THINK THIS WAS *FUN.*

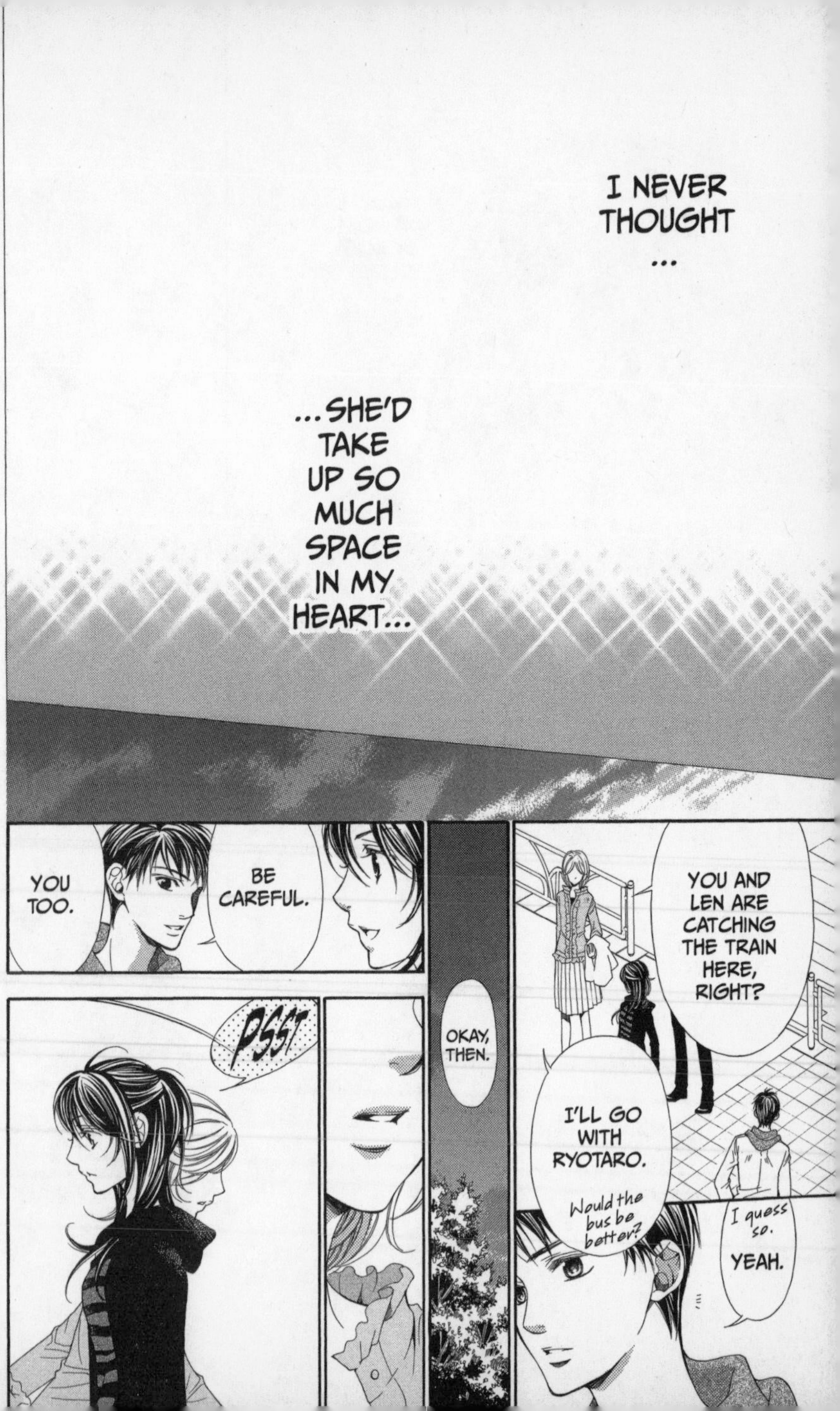

I NEVER THOUGHT ...
...SHE'D TAKE UP SO MUCH SPACE IN MY HEART...
YOU AND LEN ARE CATCHING THE TRAIN HERE, RIGHT?
I'LL GO WITH RYOTARO.
Would the bus be better?
I guess so.
YEAH.
OKAY, THEN.
BE CAREFUL.
YOU TOO.
PSST

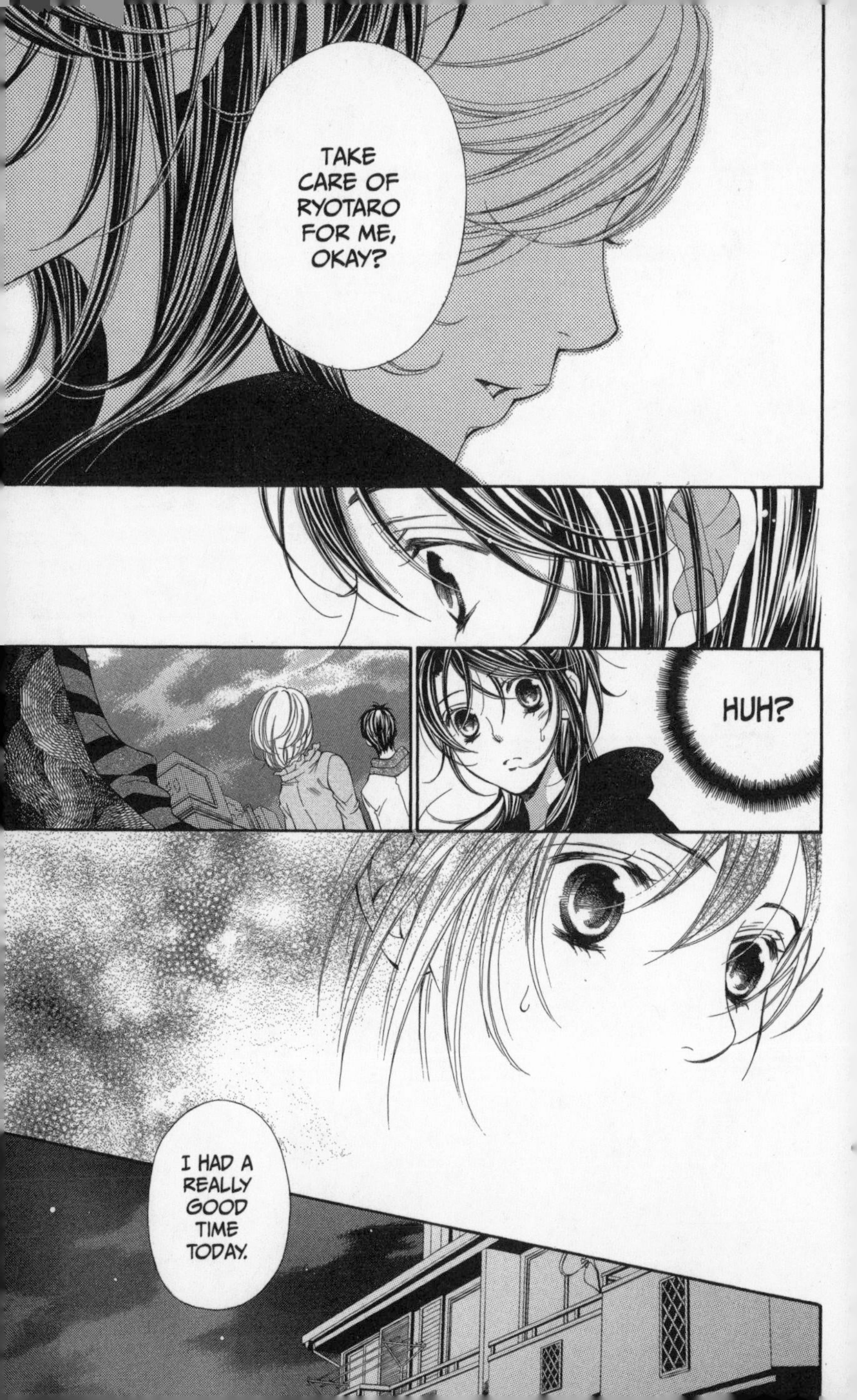
TAKE CARE OF RYOTARO FOR ME, OKAY?
HUH?
I HAD A REALLY GOOD TIME TODAY.

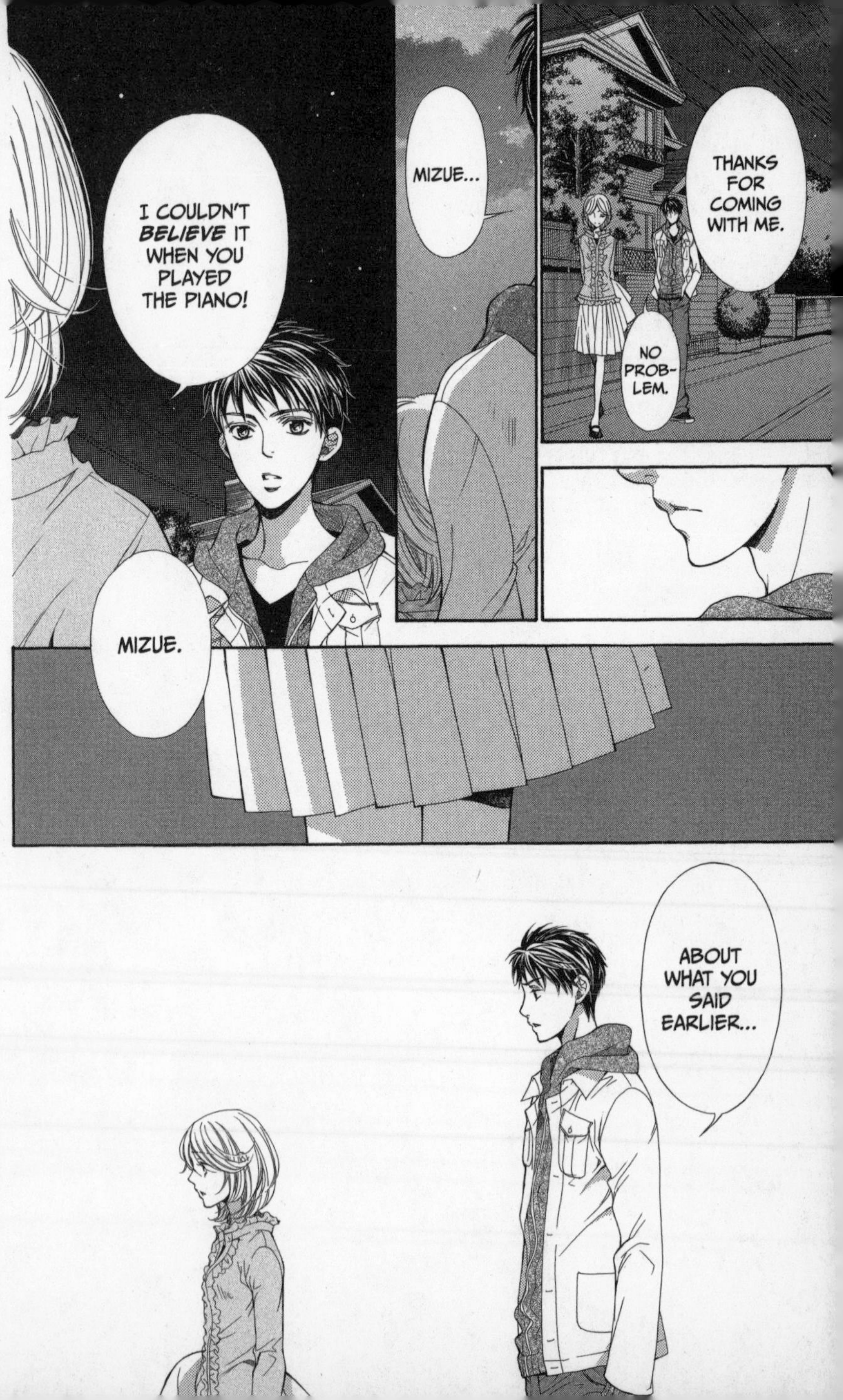
THANKS FOR COMING WITH ME.
NO PROB-LEM.
MIZUE...
I COULDN'T *BELIEVE* IT WHEN YOU PLAYED THE PIANO!
MIZUE.
ABOUT WHAT YOU SAID EARLIER...

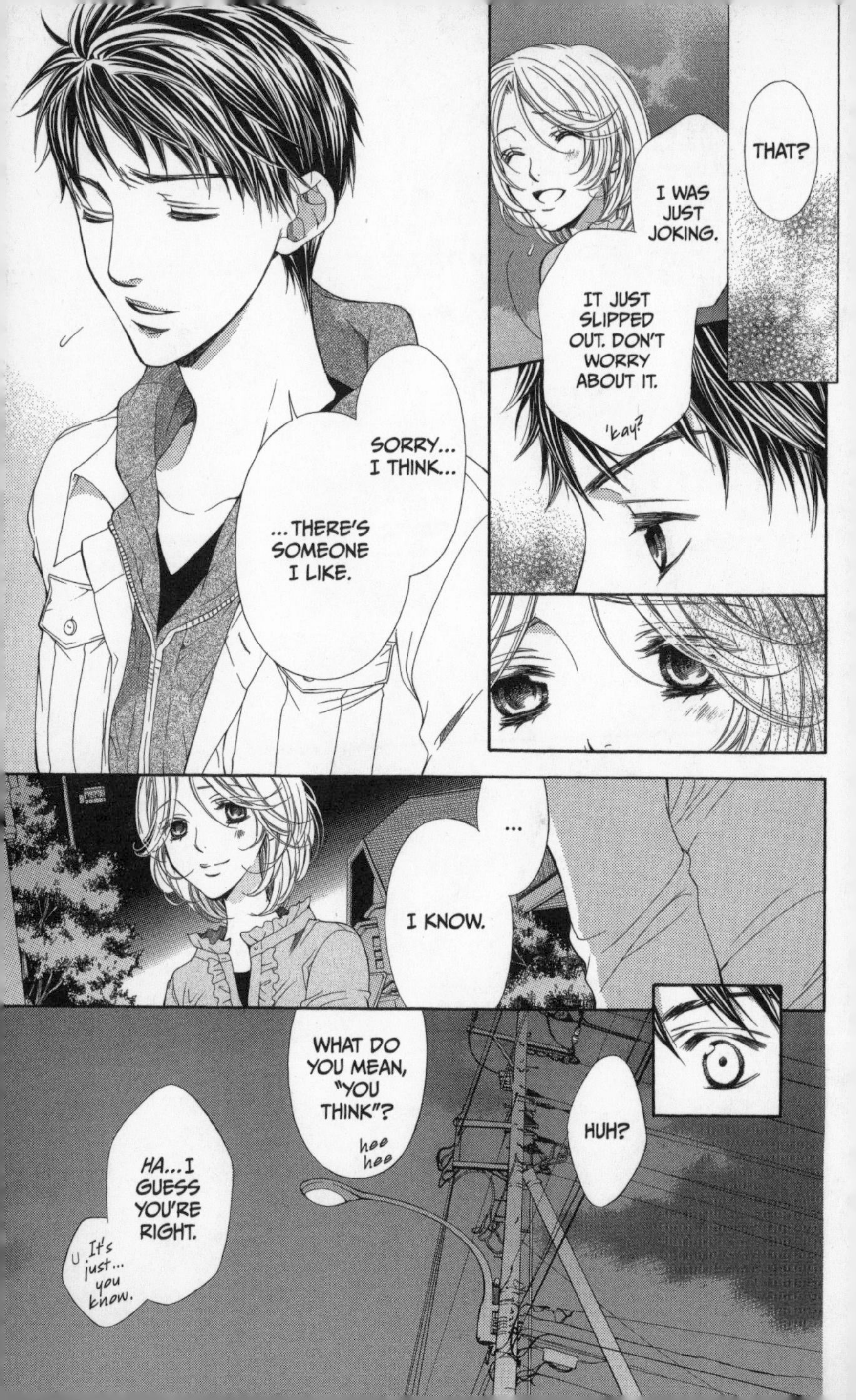
THAT?
I WAS JUST JOKING.
IT JUST SLIPPED OUT. DON'T WORRY ABOUT IT.
'kay?
SORRY... I THINK...
...THERE'S SOMEONE I LIKE.
...
I KNOW.
HUH?
WHAT DO YOU MEAN, "YOU THINK"?
hee hee
HA...I GUESS YOU'RE RIGHT.
It's just... you know.

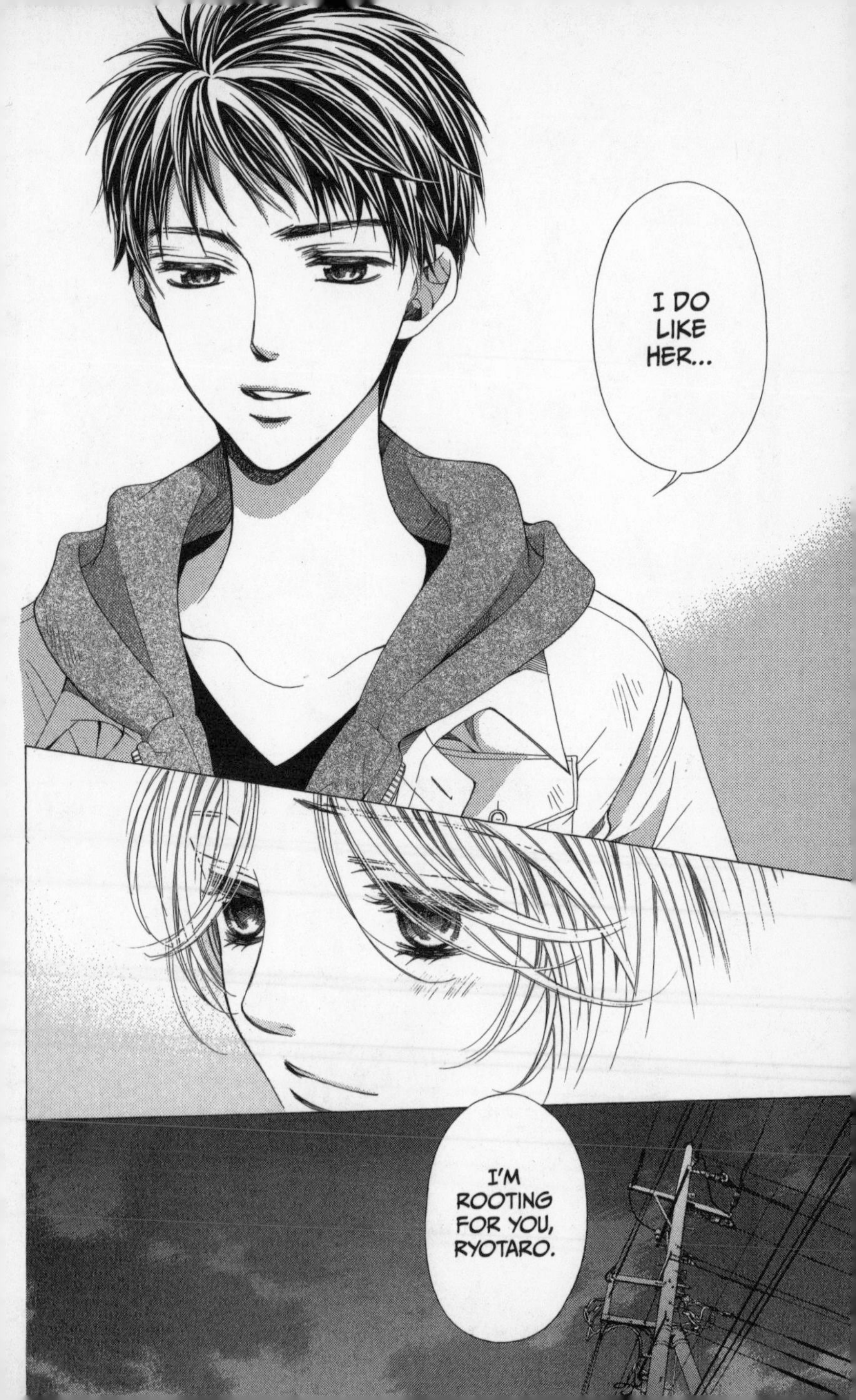
I DO LIKE HER...
I'M ROOTING FOR YOU, RYOTARO.

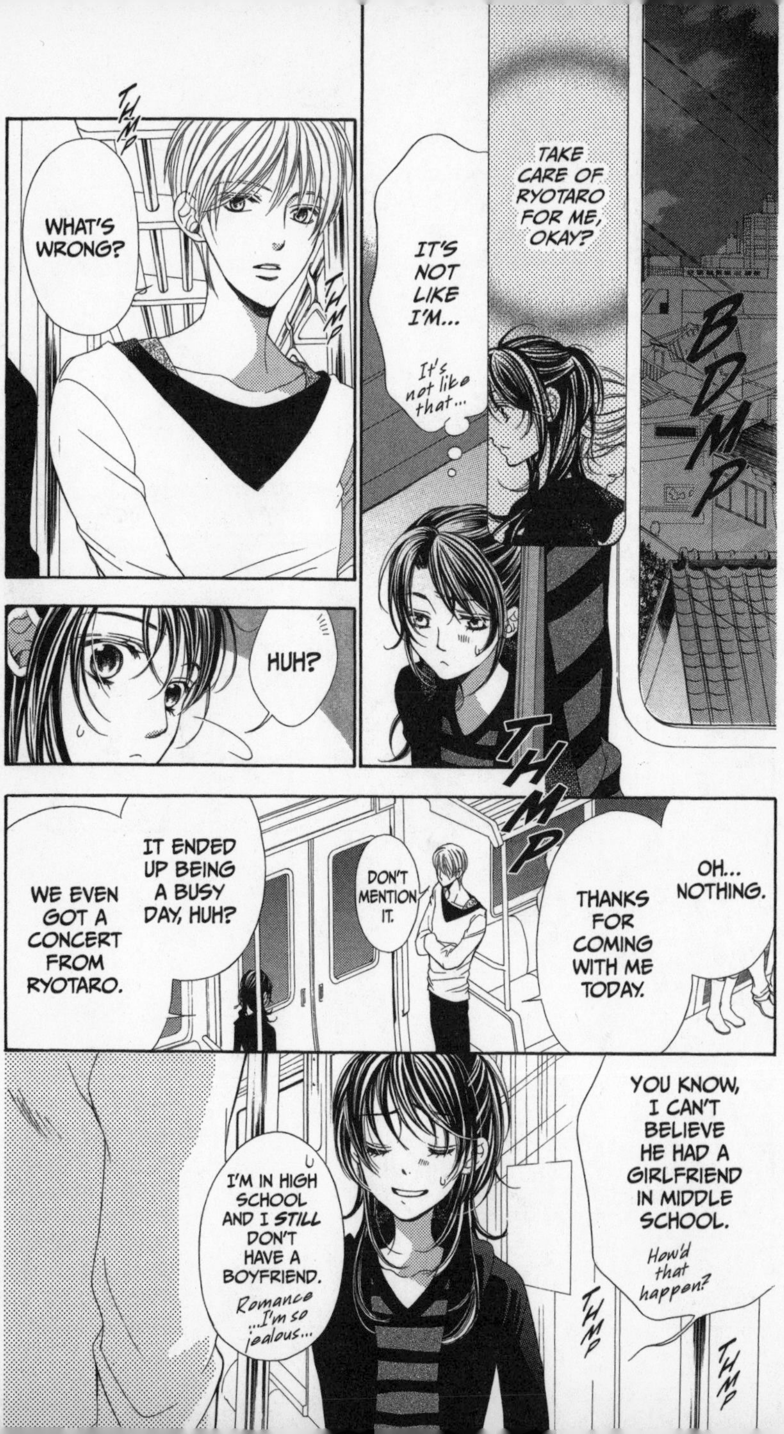
BDMP
TAKE CARE OF RYOTARO FOR ME, OKAY?
IT'S NOT LIKE I'M...
It's not like that...
THMP
WHAT'S WRONG?
THMP
THMP
HUH?
OH... NOTHING.
THANKS FOR COMING WITH ME TODAY.
DON'T MENTION IT.
IT ENDED UP BEING A BUSY DAY, HUH?
WE EVEN GOT A CONCERT FROM RYOTARO.
YOU KNOW, I CAN'T BELIEVE HE HAD A GIRLFRIEND IN MIDDLE SCHOOL.
How'd that happen?
THMP
THMP
I'M IN HIGH SCHOOL AND I STILL DON'T HAVE A BOYFRIEND.
Romance ...I'm so jealous...

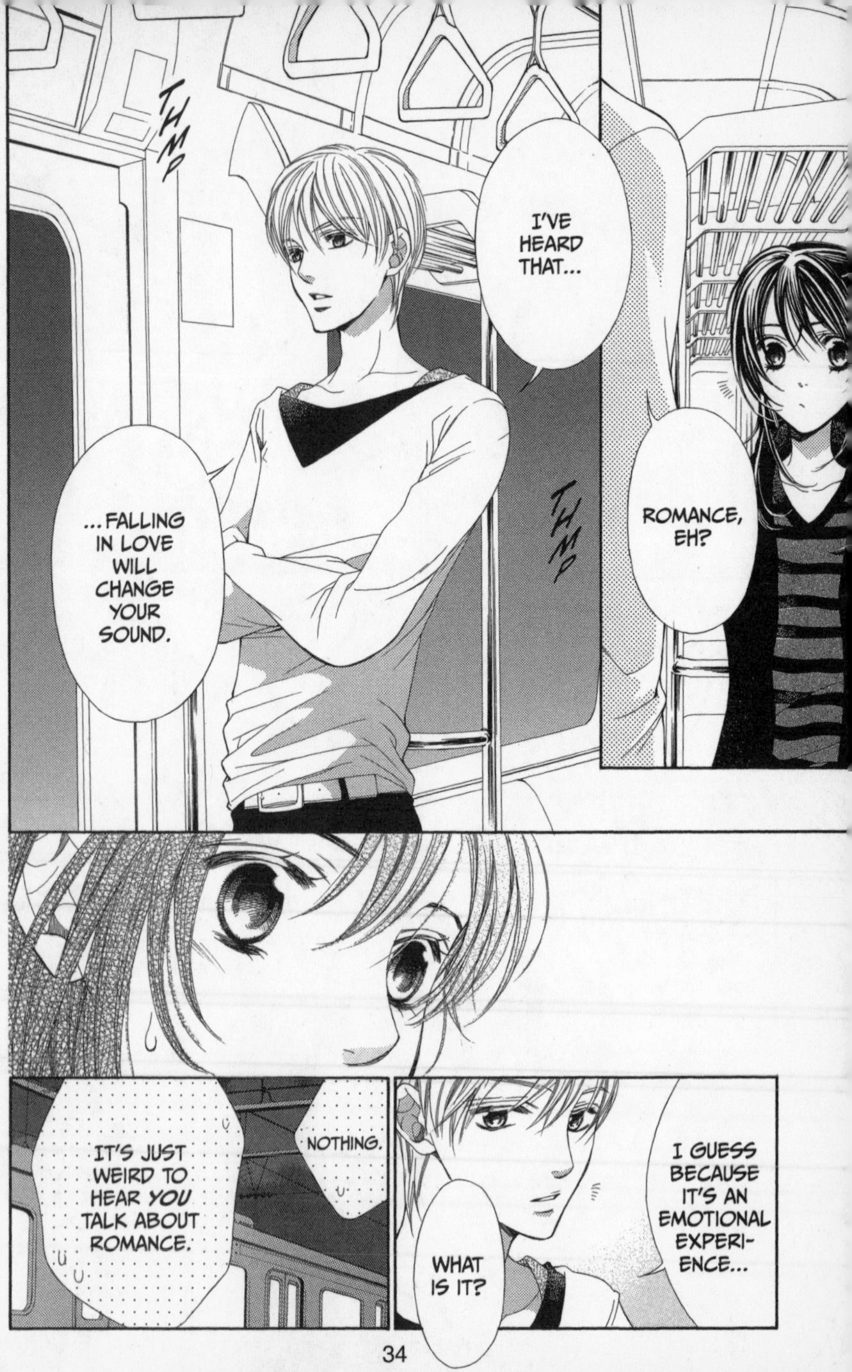
ROMANCE, EH?
THMP
I'VE HEARD THAT...
THMP
...FALLING IN LOVE WILL CHANGE YOUR SOUND.
I GUESS BECAUSE IT'S AN EMOTIONAL EXPERIENCE...
WHAT IS IT?
NOTHING.
IT'S JUST WEIRD TO HEAR *YOU* TALK ABOUT ROMANCE.

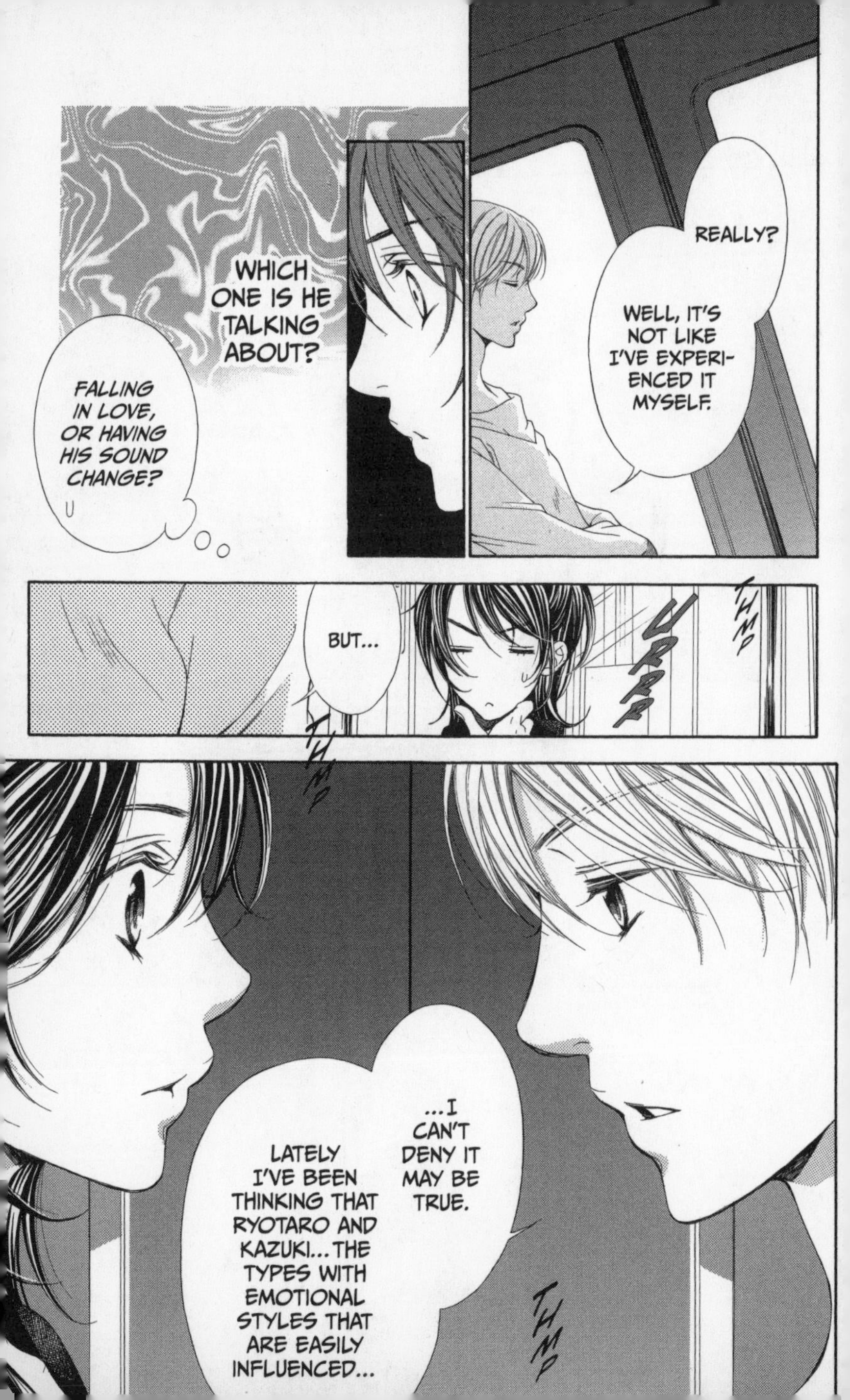
REALLY?
WELL, IT'S NOT LIKE I'VE EXPERIENCED IT MYSELF.
WHICH ONE IS HE TALKING ABOUT?
FALLING IN LOVE, OR HAVING HIS SOUND CHANGE?
THMP
URRRR
BUT...
THMP
...I CAN'T DENY IT MAY BE TRUE.
LATELY I'VE BEEN THINKING THAT RYOTARO AND KAZUKI... THE TYPES WITH EMOTIONAL STYLES THAT ARE EASILY INFLUENCED...
THMP

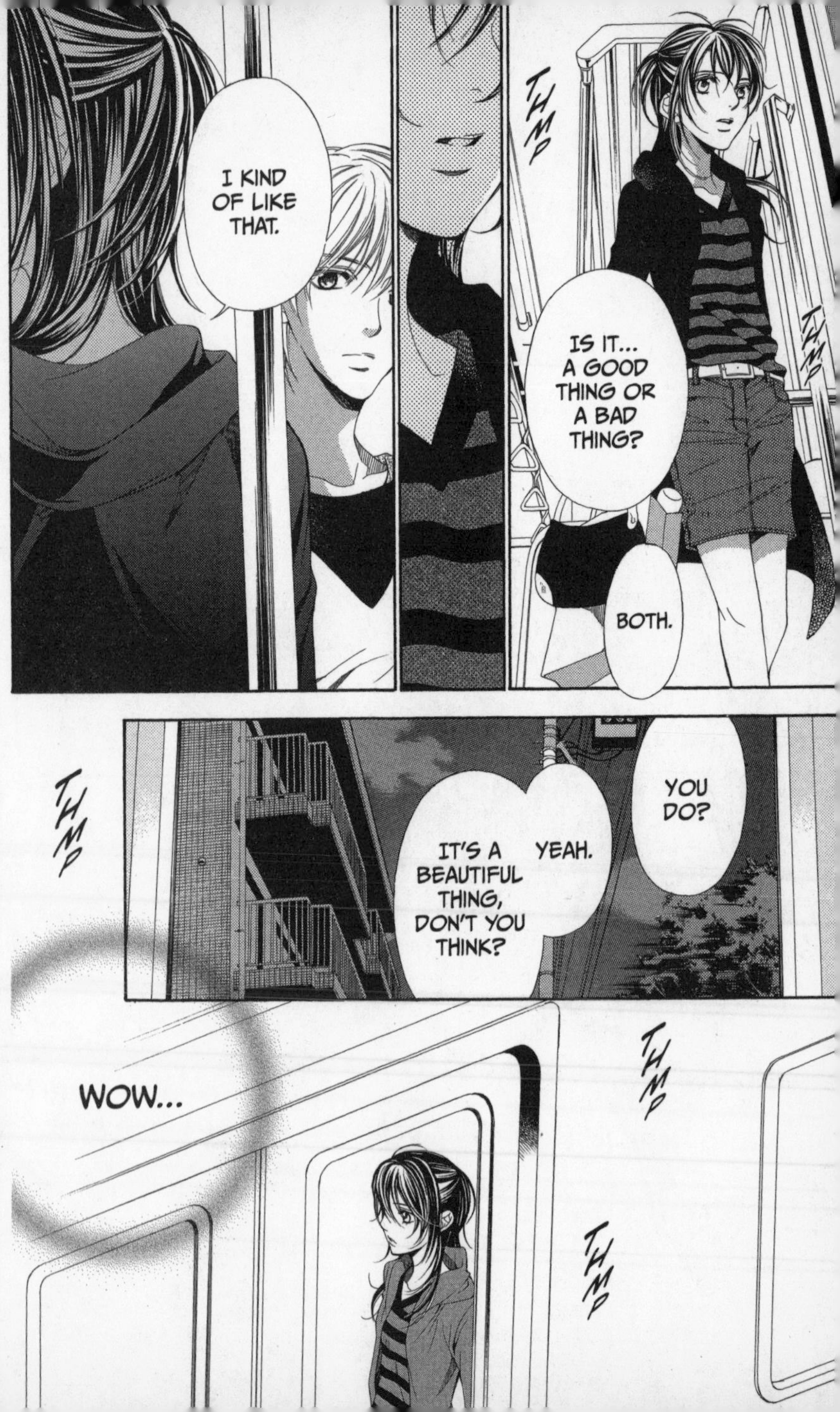
THMP
IS IT... A GOOD THING OR A BAD THING?
THMP
BOTH.
I KIND OF LIKE THAT.
YOU DO?
YEAH. IT'S A BEAUTIFUL THING, DON'T YOU THINK?
THMP
THMP
THMP
WOW...

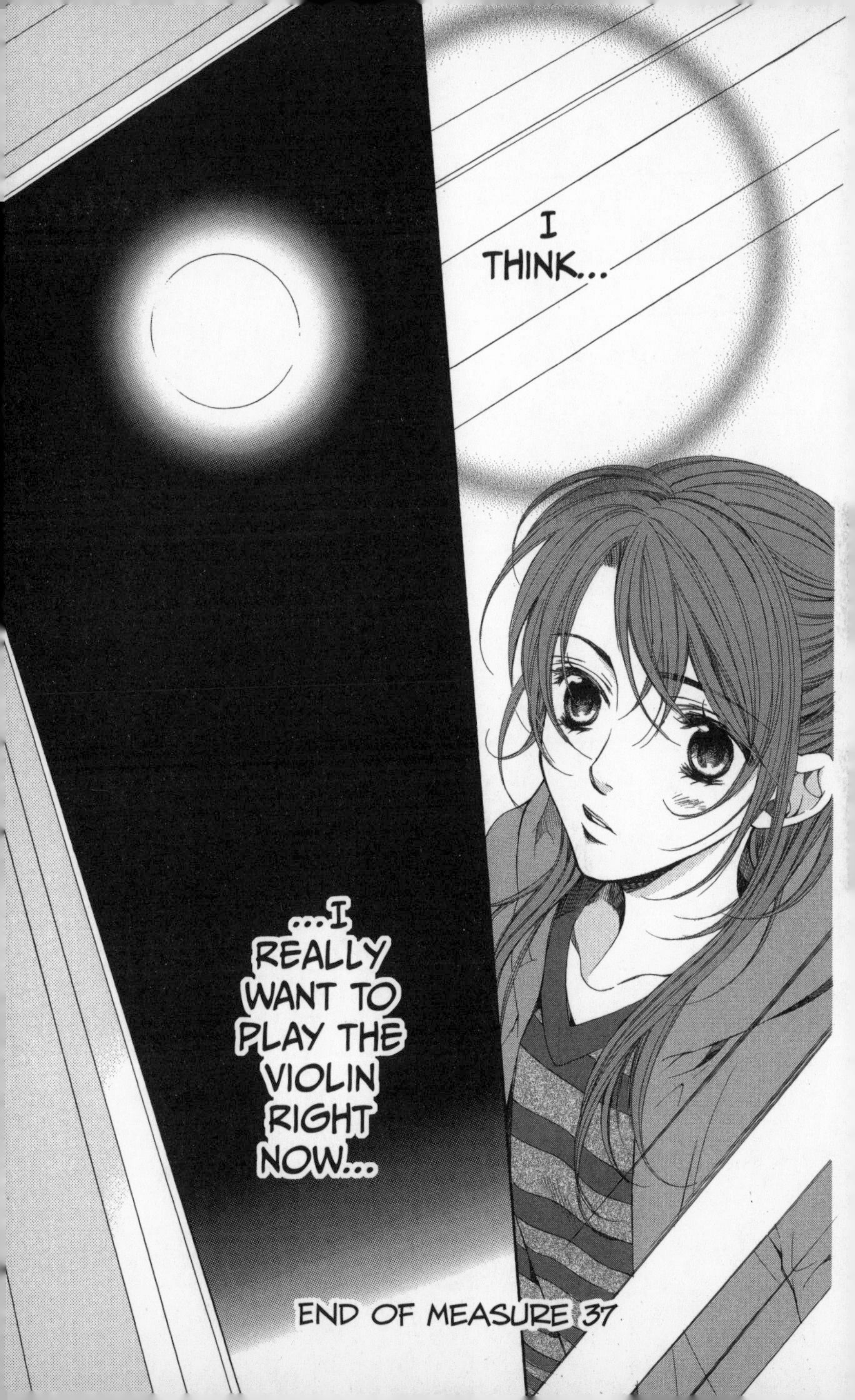
I THINK...
...I REALLY WANT TO PLAY THE VIOLIN RIGHT NOW...
END OF MEASURE 37

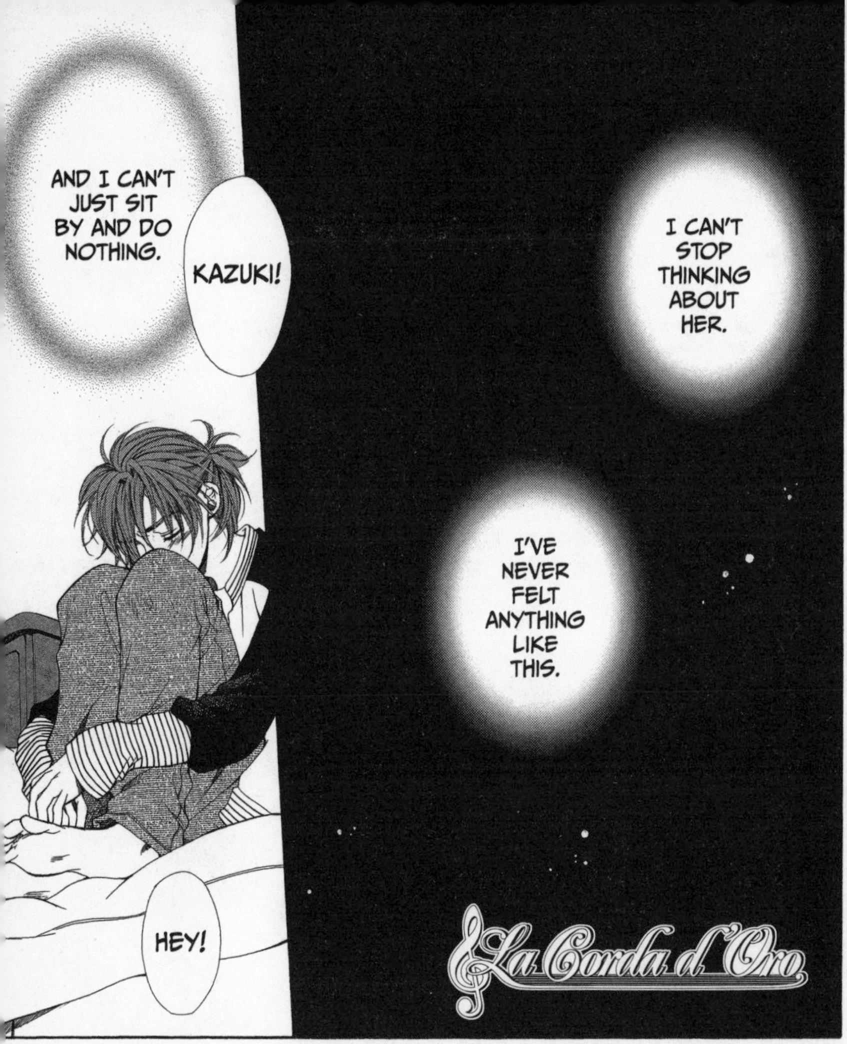
I CAN'T STOP THINKING ABOUT HER.
I'VE NEVER FELT ANYTHING LIKE THIS.
La Corda d'Oro
KAZUKI!
AND I CAN'T JUST SIT BY AND DO NOTHING.
HEY!

**Daily Happenings 30**
**Vacation... 2**

So the express train from Kagawa to Kochi was awesome. ♡
It's an express train, but it's on a single track.
And there were only three cars. (Wait, maybe only two...)
I was all excited to be by myself. (lol)
The view was great (although there were a lot of tunnels through the mountains) and I would definitely go back. But as a Chiba girl, It's not like I can get out there all the time. Arrgh... On the local line between Himeji and Okayama, some high school students were talking about "that university in Tokyo." They said they liked going from Okayama to Kagawa because you have to cross the ocean... It was hard to explain...

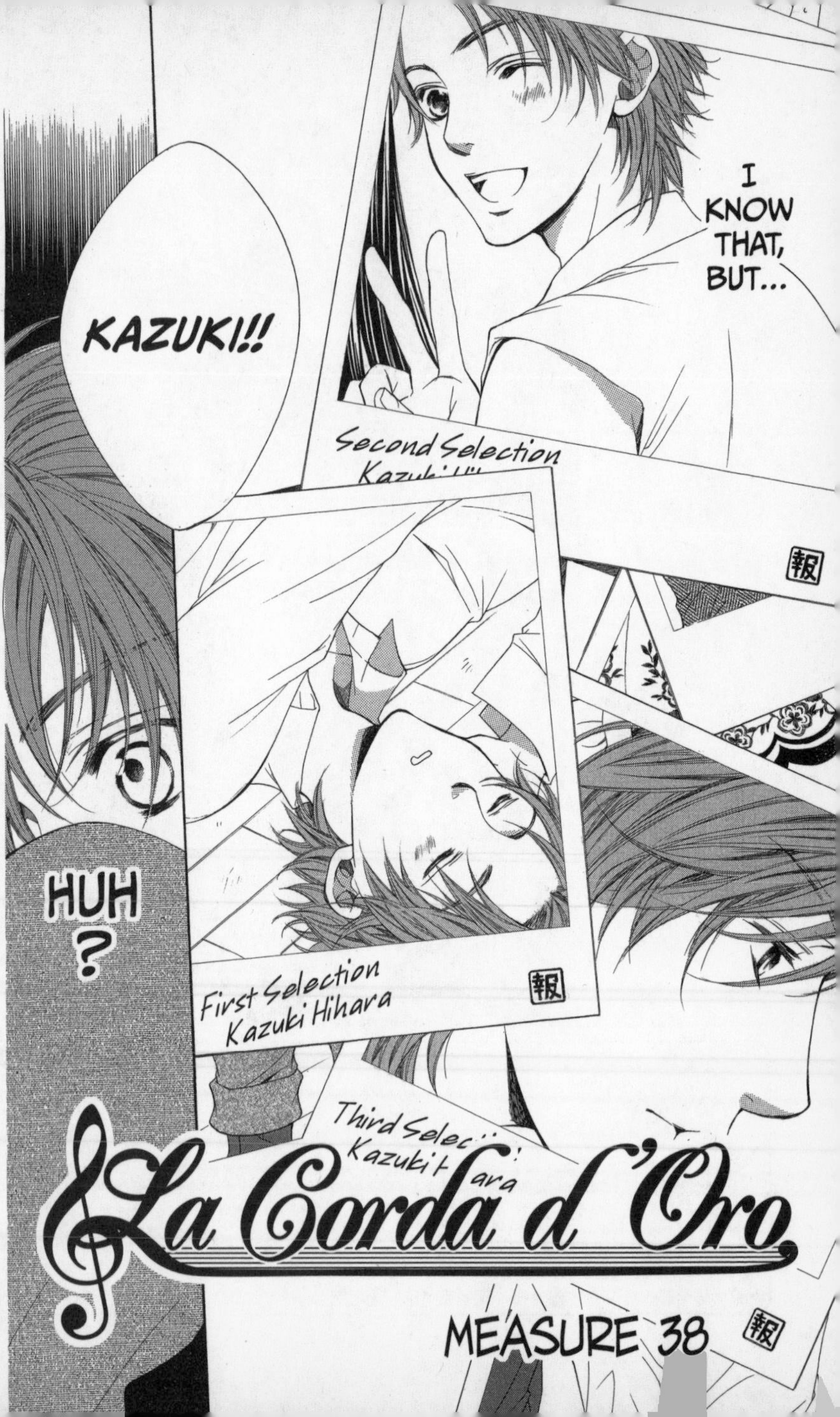
I KNOW THAT, BUT...
KAZUKI!!
Second Selection
First Selection
Kazuki Hihara
HUH?
La Corda d'Oro
MEASURE 38

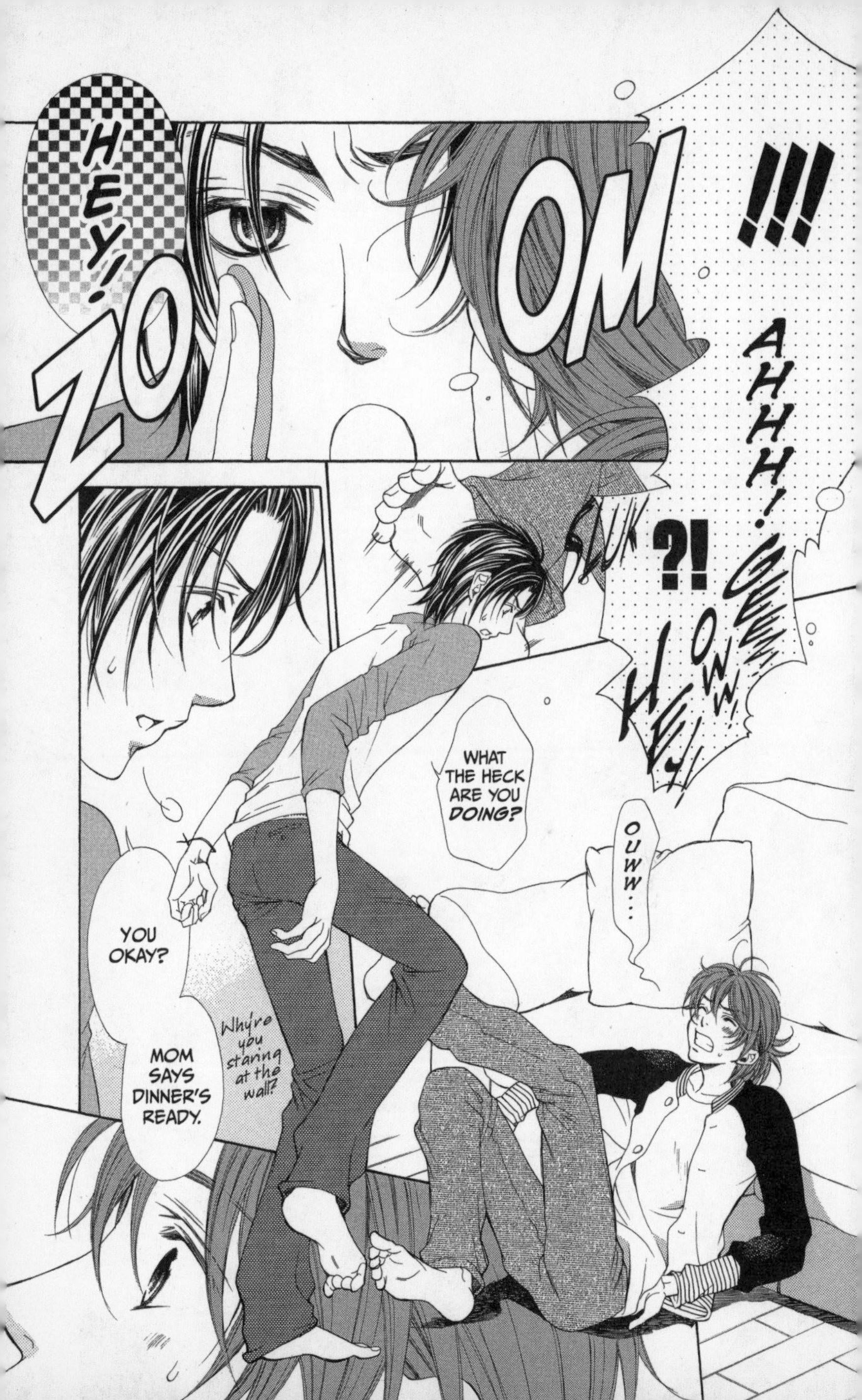

AHHH! OUWW
HEY! OWW
HEY!
ZOOM!!!
?!
WHAT THE HECK ARE YOU DOING?
OUWW...
YOU OKAY?
Why're you staring at the wall?
MOM SAYS DINNER'S READY.

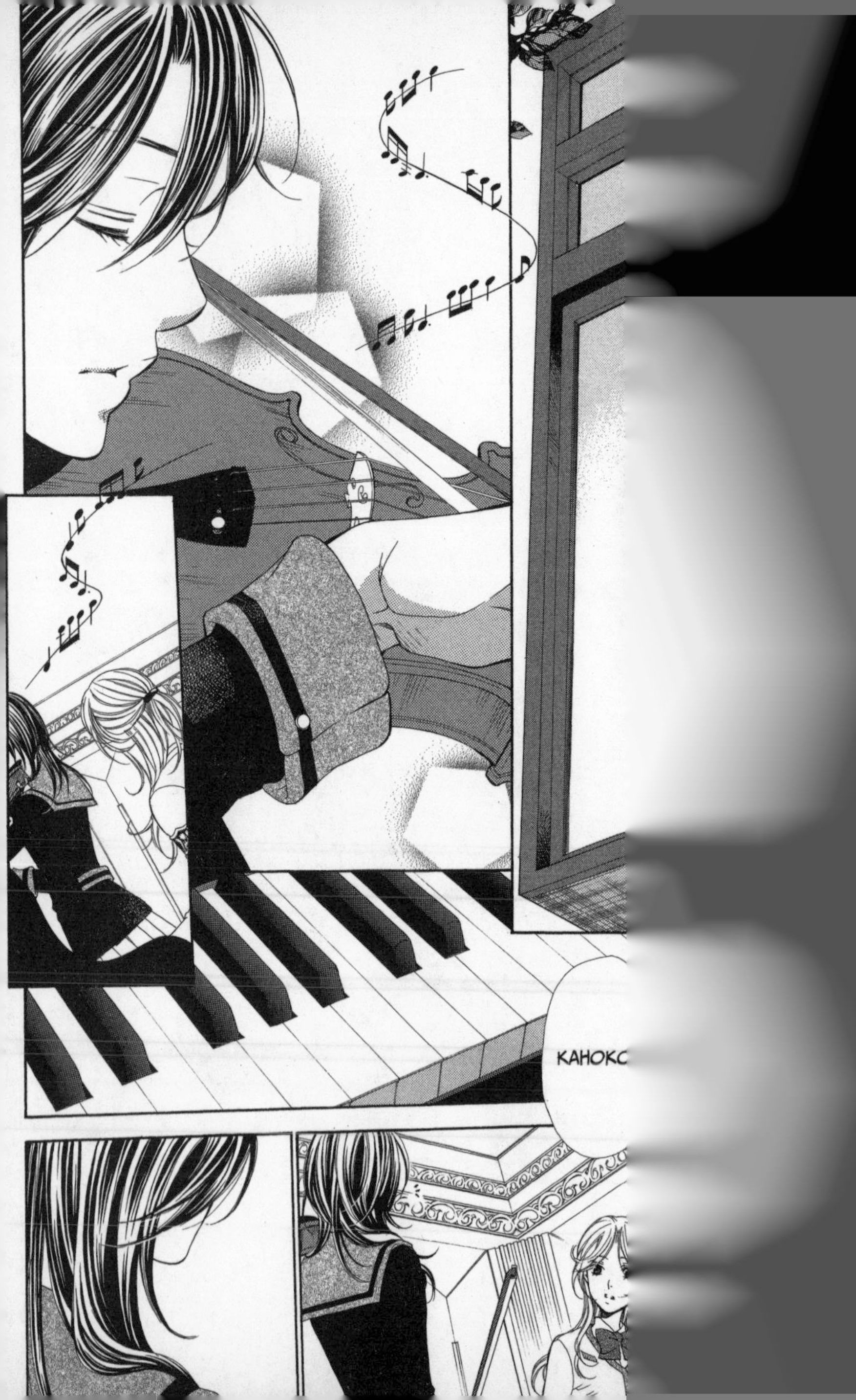
KAHOKO

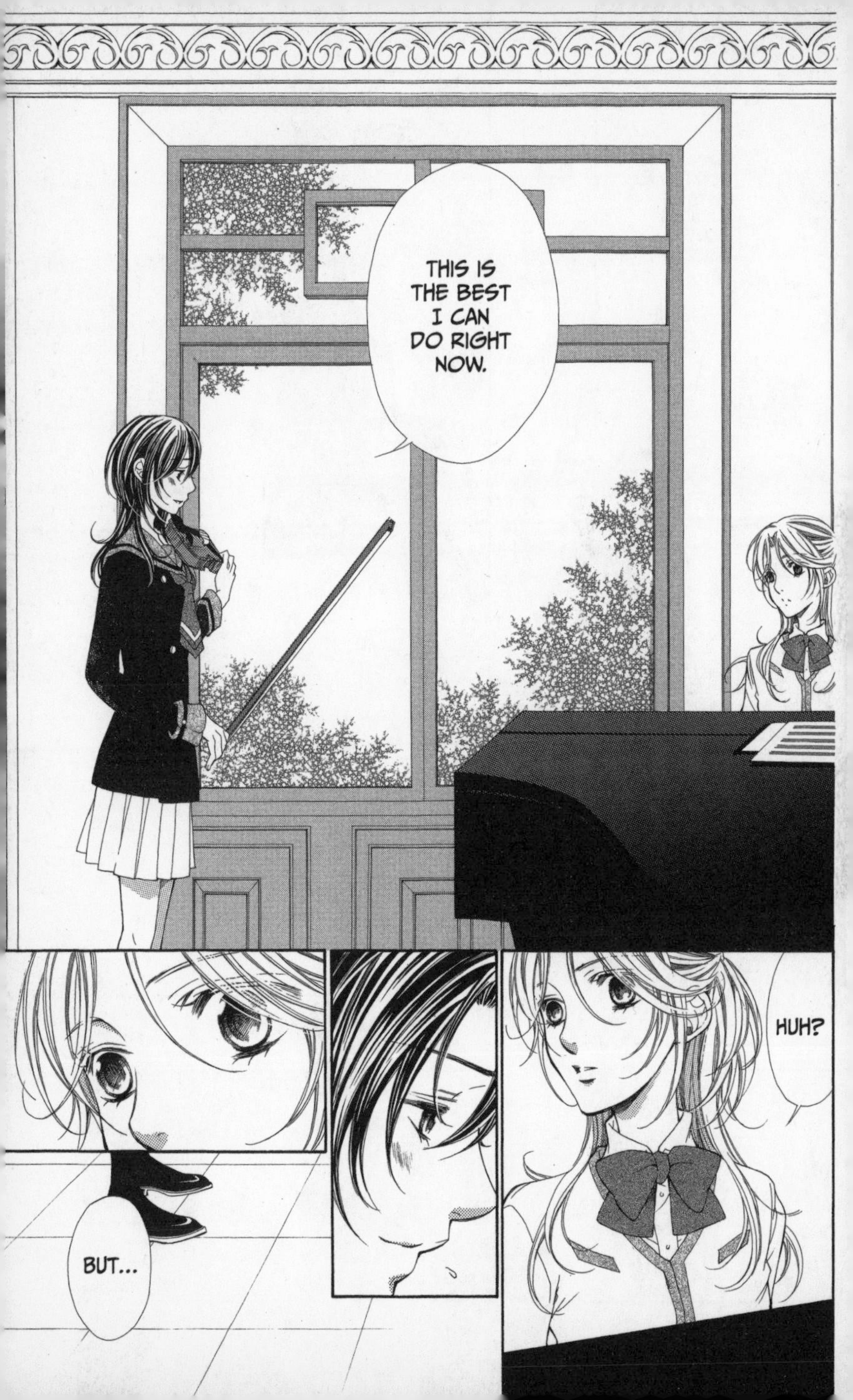
THIS IS THE BEST I CAN DO RIGHT NOW.
HUH?
BUT...

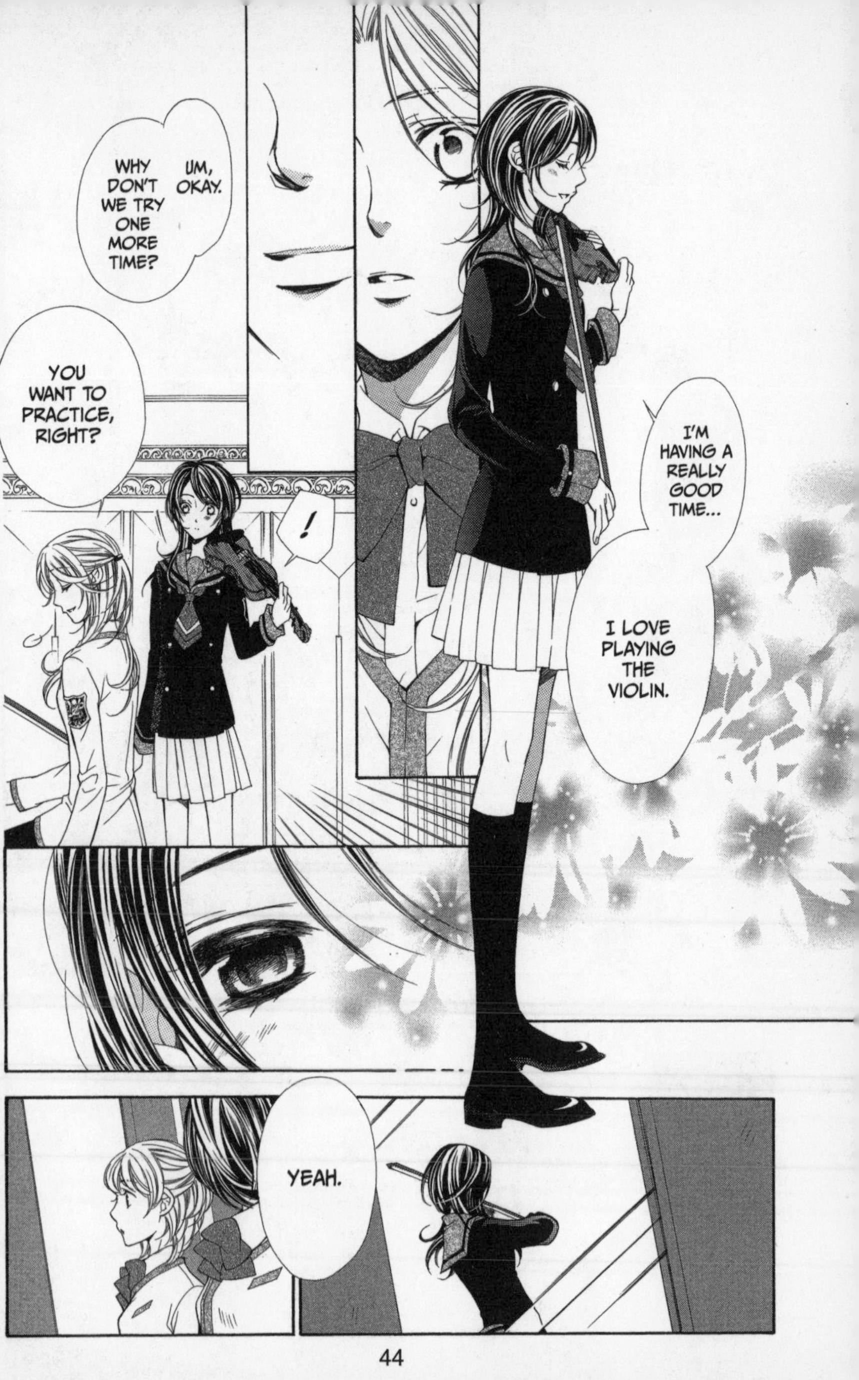
I'M HAVING A REALLY GOOD TIME...
I LOVE PLAYING THE VIOLIN.
WHY DON'T WE TRY ONE MORE TIME?
UM, OKAY.
YOU WANT TO PRACTICE, RIGHT?
!
YEAH.

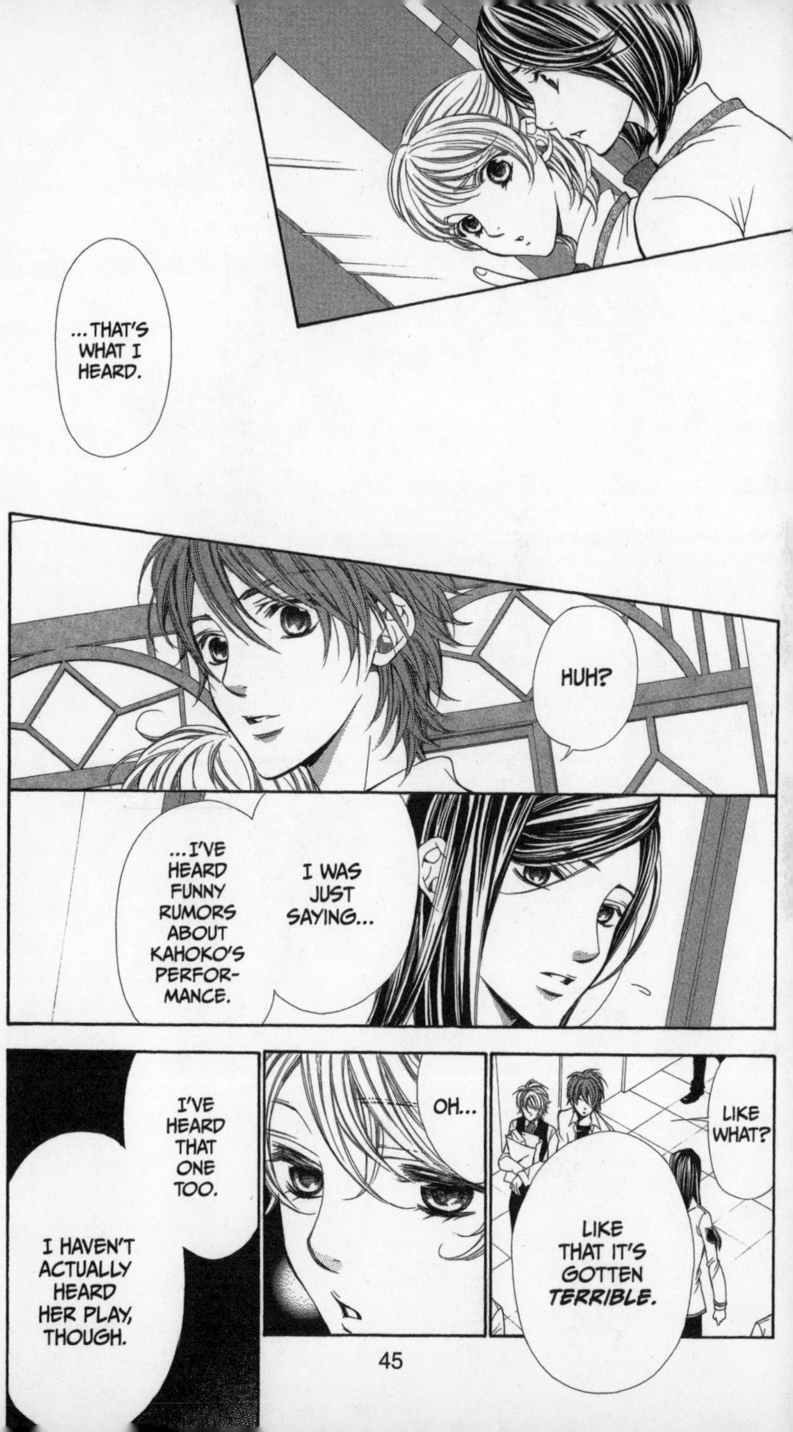
...THAT'S WHAT I HEARD.
HUH?
I WAS JUST SAYING...
...I'VE HEARD FUNNY RUMORS ABOUT KAHOKO'S PERFORMANCE.
LIKE WHAT?
LIKE THAT IT'S GOTTEN *TERRIBLE.*
OH...
I'VE HEARD THAT ONE TOO.
I HAVEN'T ACTUALLY HEARD HER PLAY, THOUGH.

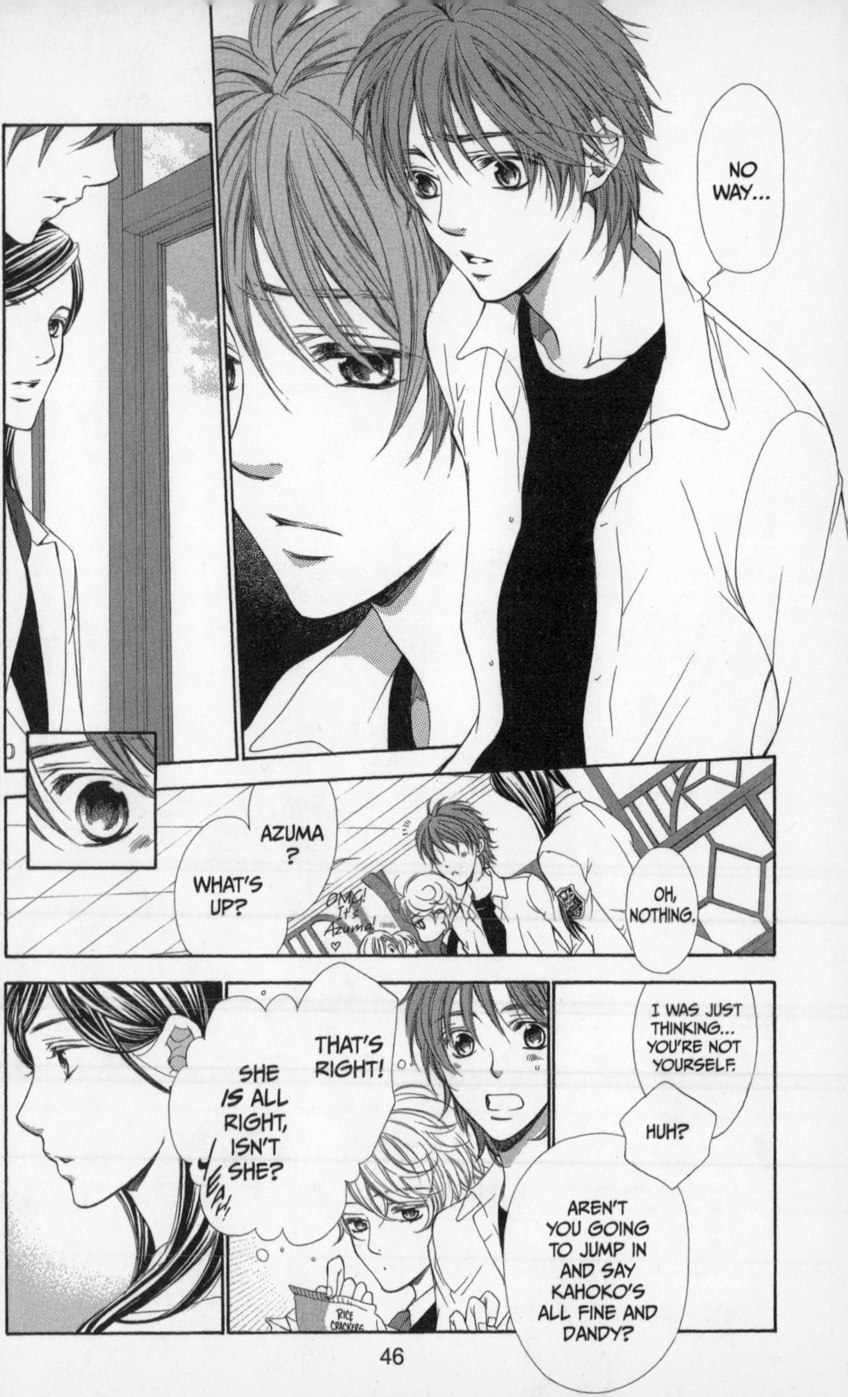
NO WAY...
AZUMA? WHAT'S UP?
OMG! It's Azuma! ♡
OH, NOTHING.
I WAS JUST THINKING... YOU'RE NOT YOURSELF.
HUH?
AREN'T YOU GOING TO JUMP IN AND SAY KAHOKO'S ALL FINE AND DANDY?
THAT'S RIGHT!
SHE IS ALL RIGHT, ISN'T SHE?
RICE CRACKERS

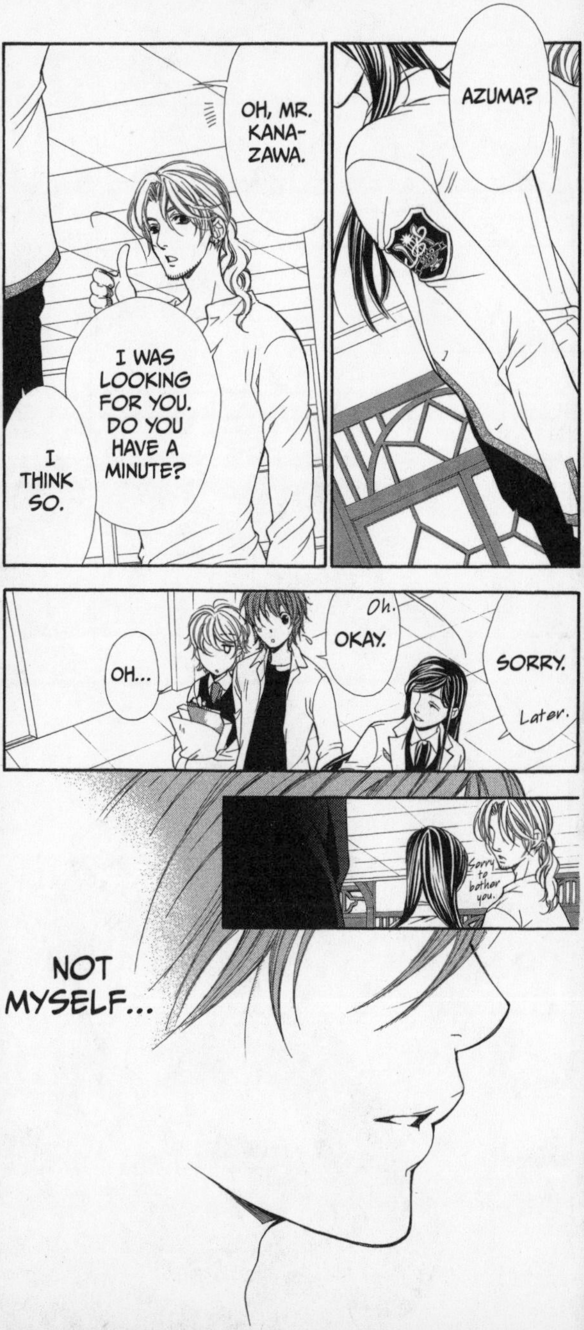
AZUMA?
OH, MR. KANA-ZAWA.
I WAS LOOKING FOR YOU. DO YOU HAVE A MINUTE?
I THINK SO.
SORRY.
Later.
Oh.
OKAY.
OH...
Sorry to bother you.
NOT MYSELF...

## TWO

I had the privilege of doing the cover for *LaLa* magazine when Measure 37 came out, but when I got the assignment, it said...

"Azuma as a celebrity."

I couldn't believe my eyes. I had to ask, "Huh? Azuma?" and make sure that was who they really wanted.

Even when I was drawing it, I doubted whether it would turn out okay. I was afraid they weren't going to sell a lot of copies! (lol) When all was said and done, I made him look more like a well-dressed concierge than a celebrity...

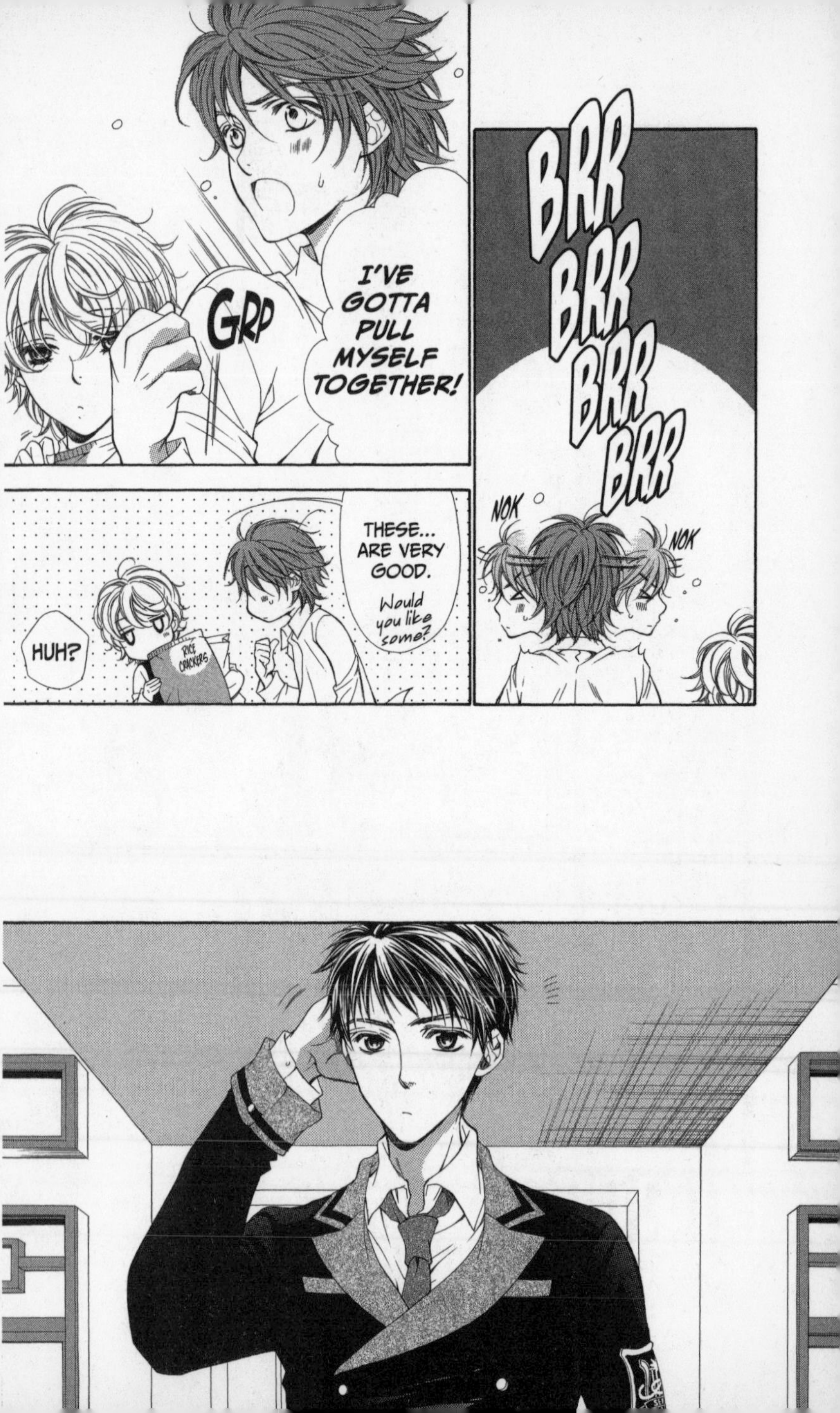
BRR BRR BRR BRR BRR
NOK
NOK
GRP
I'VE GOTTA PULL MYSELF TOGETHER!
THESE... ARE VERY GOOD.
Would you like some?
RICE CRACKERS
HUH?

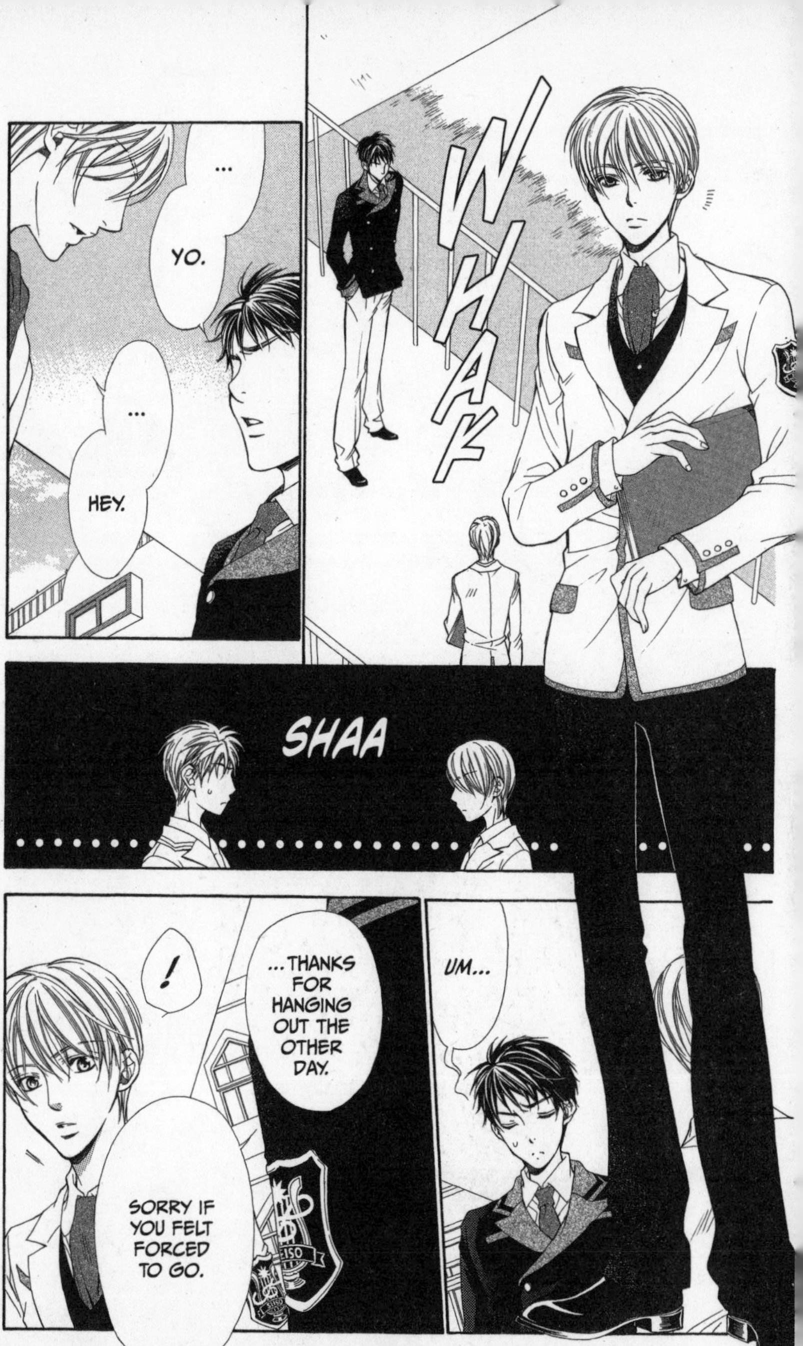
WHAK
...
YO.
...
HEY.
SHAA
UM...
...THANKS FOR HANGING OUT THE OTHER DAY.
!
SORRY IF YOU FELT FORCED TO GO.

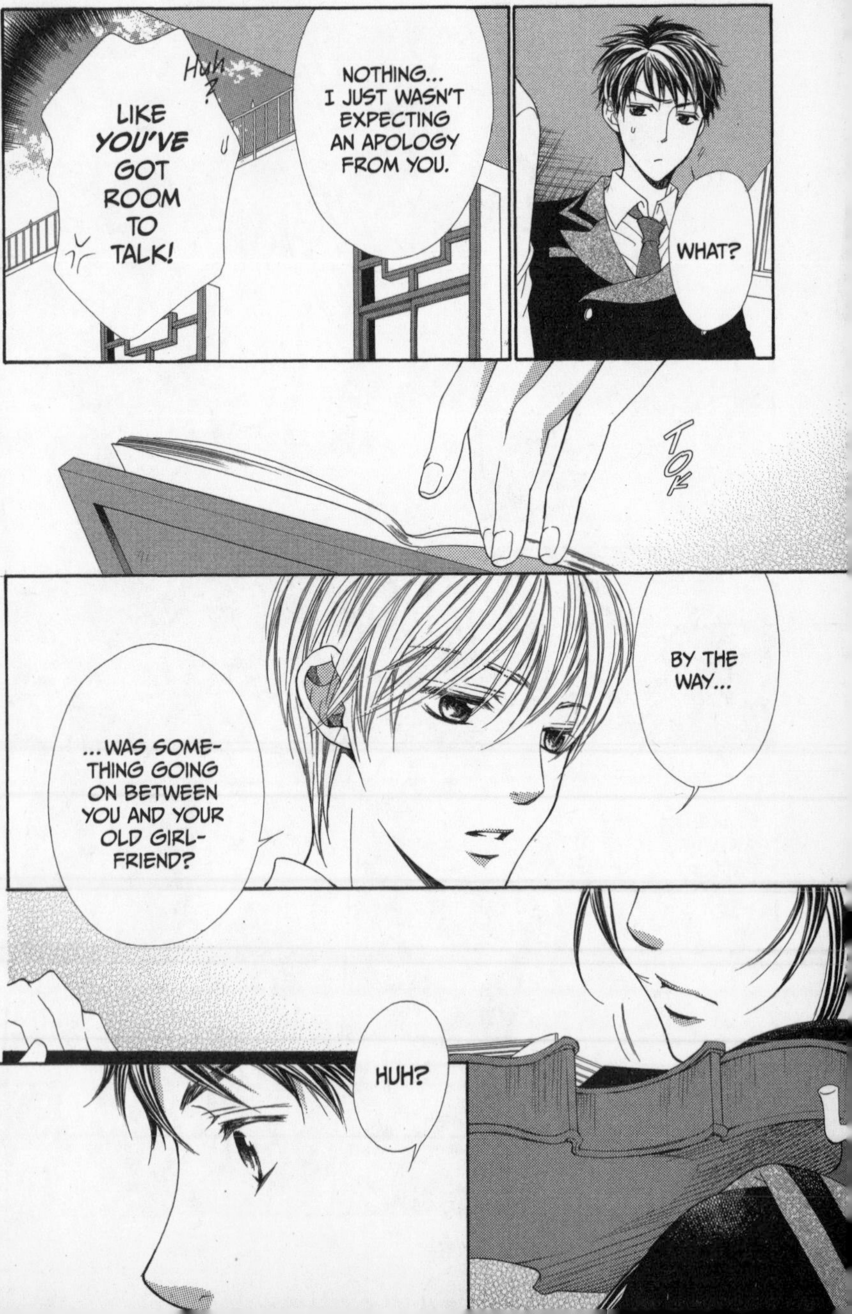
WHAT?
NOTHING... I JUST WASN'T EXPECTING AN APOLOGY FROM YOU.
Huh?
LIKE *YOU'VE* GOT ROOM TO TALK!
TOK
BY THE WAY...
...WAS SOME-THING GOING ON BETWEEN YOU AND YOUR OLD GIRL-FRIEND?
HUH?

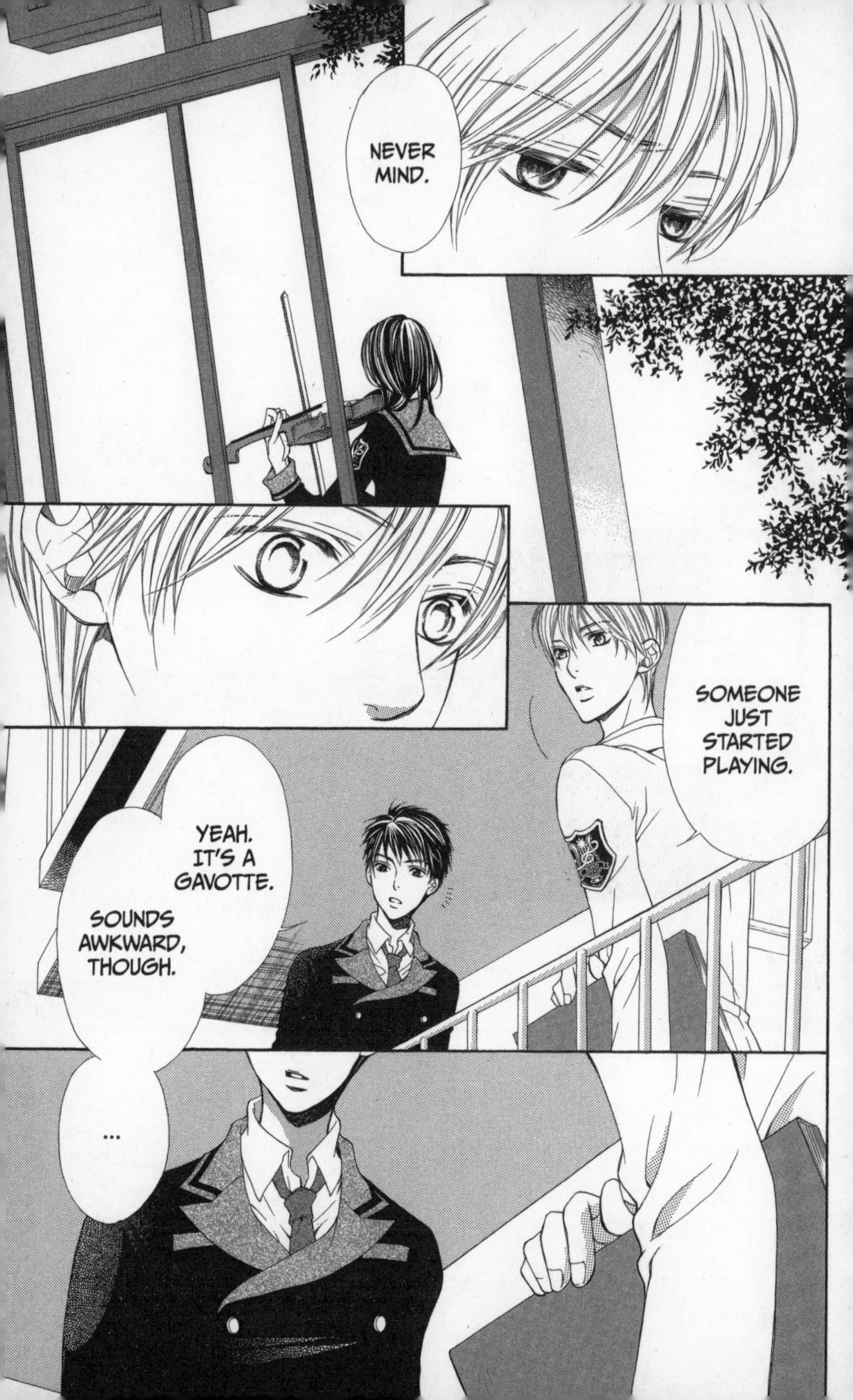
NEVER MIND.
SOMEONE JUST STARTED PLAYING.
YEAH. IT'S A GAVOTTE.
SOUNDS AWKWARD, THOUGH.
...

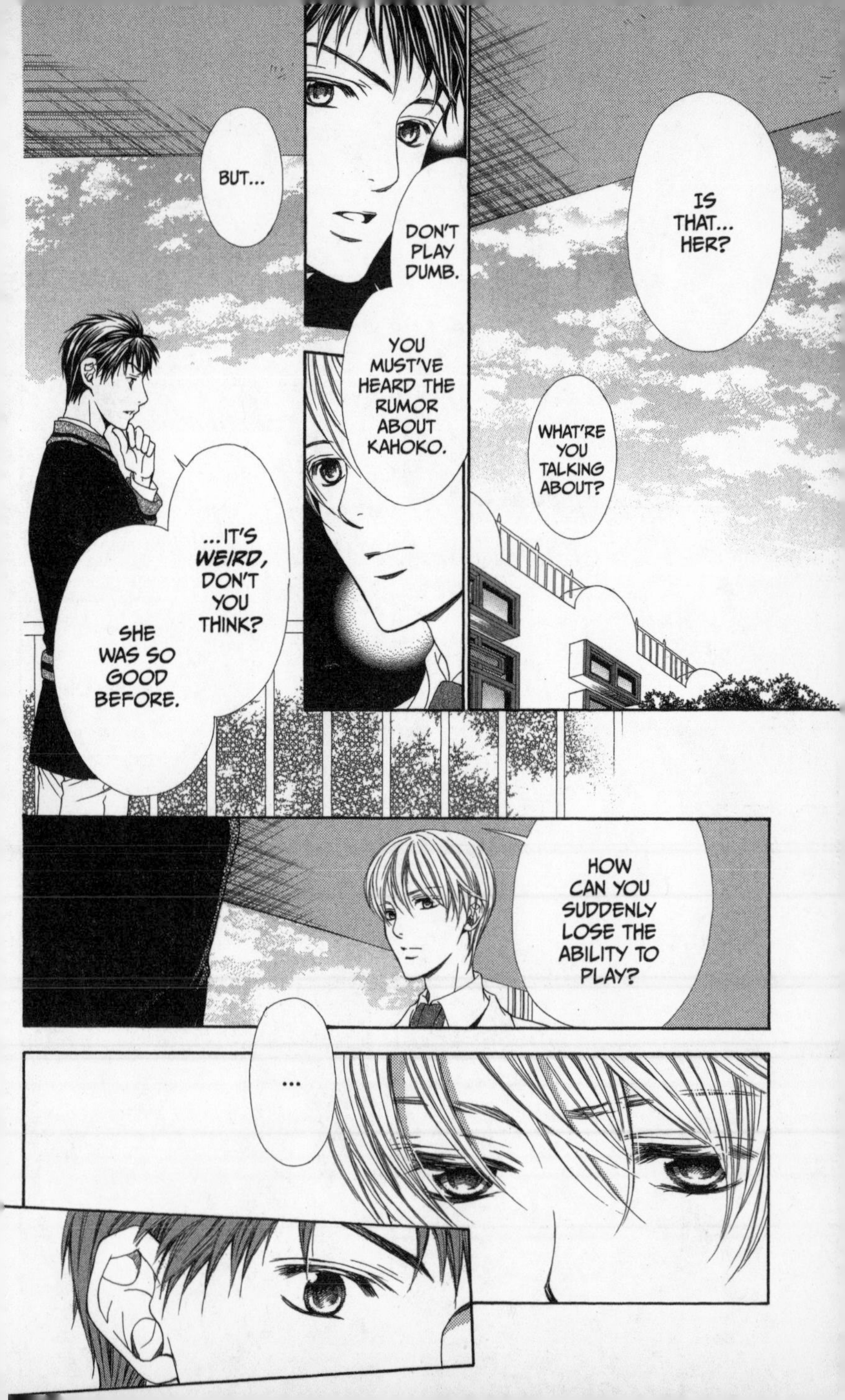
IS THAT... HER?
WHAT'RE YOU TALKING ABOUT?
DON'T PLAY DUMB.
YOU MUST'VE HEARD THE RUMOR ABOUT KAHOKO.
BUT...
...IT'S *WEIRD,* DON'T YOU THINK?
SHE WAS SO GOOD BEFORE.
HOW CAN YOU SUDDENLY LOSE THE ABILITY TO PLAY?
...

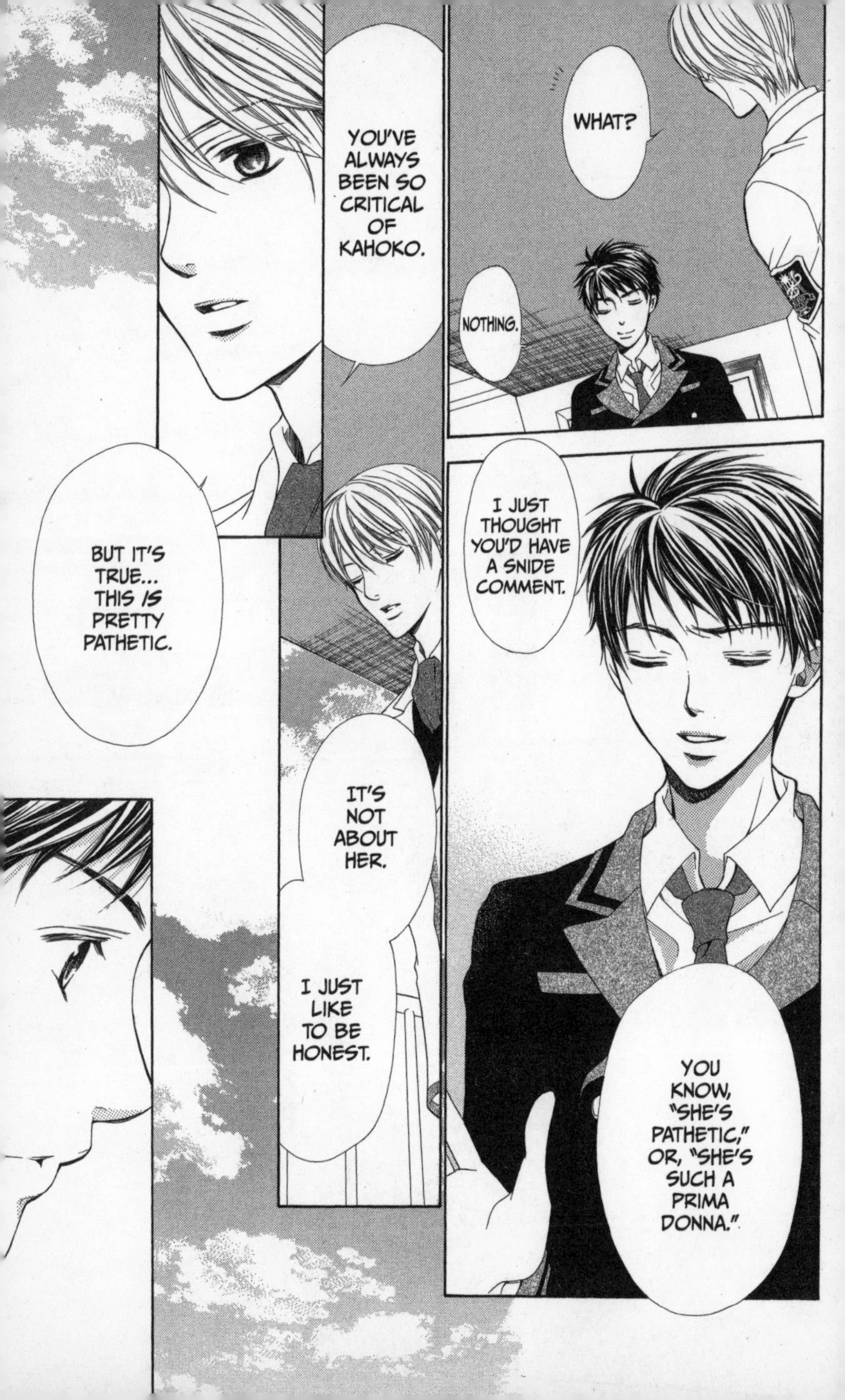
WHAT?
NOTHING.
YOU'VE ALWAYS BEEN SO CRITICAL OF KAHOKO.
I JUST THOUGHT YOU'D HAVE A SNIDE COMMENT.
YOU KNOW, "SHE'S PATHETIC," OR, "SHE'S SUCH A PRIMA DONNA."
IT'S NOT ABOUT HER.
I JUST LIKE TO BE HONEST.
BUT IT'S TRUE... THIS *IS* PRETTY PATHETIC.

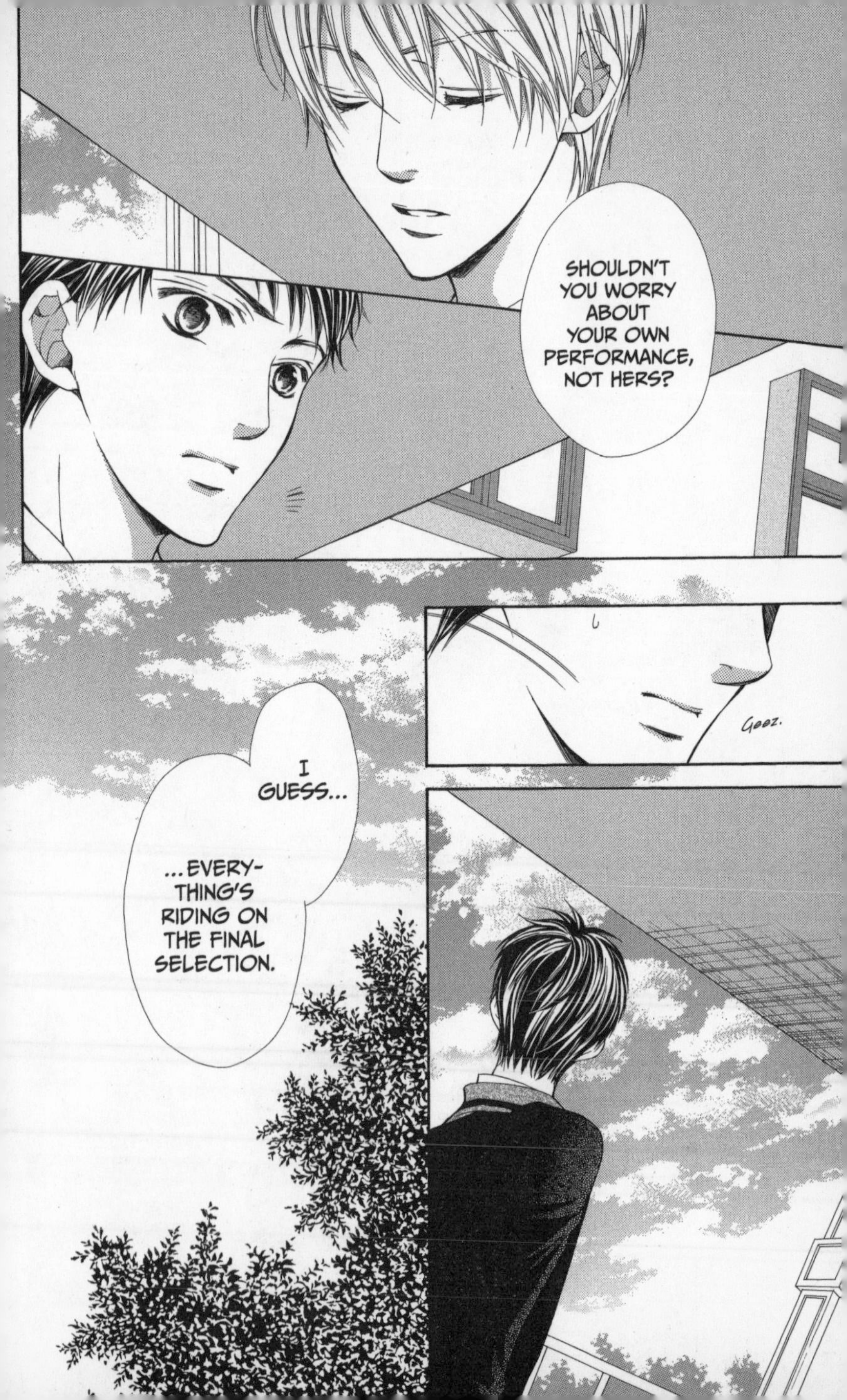
SHOULDN'T YOU WORRY ABOUT YOUR OWN PERFORMANCE, NOT HERS?
Geez.
I GUESS...
...EVERY-THING'S RIDING ON THE FINAL SELECTION.

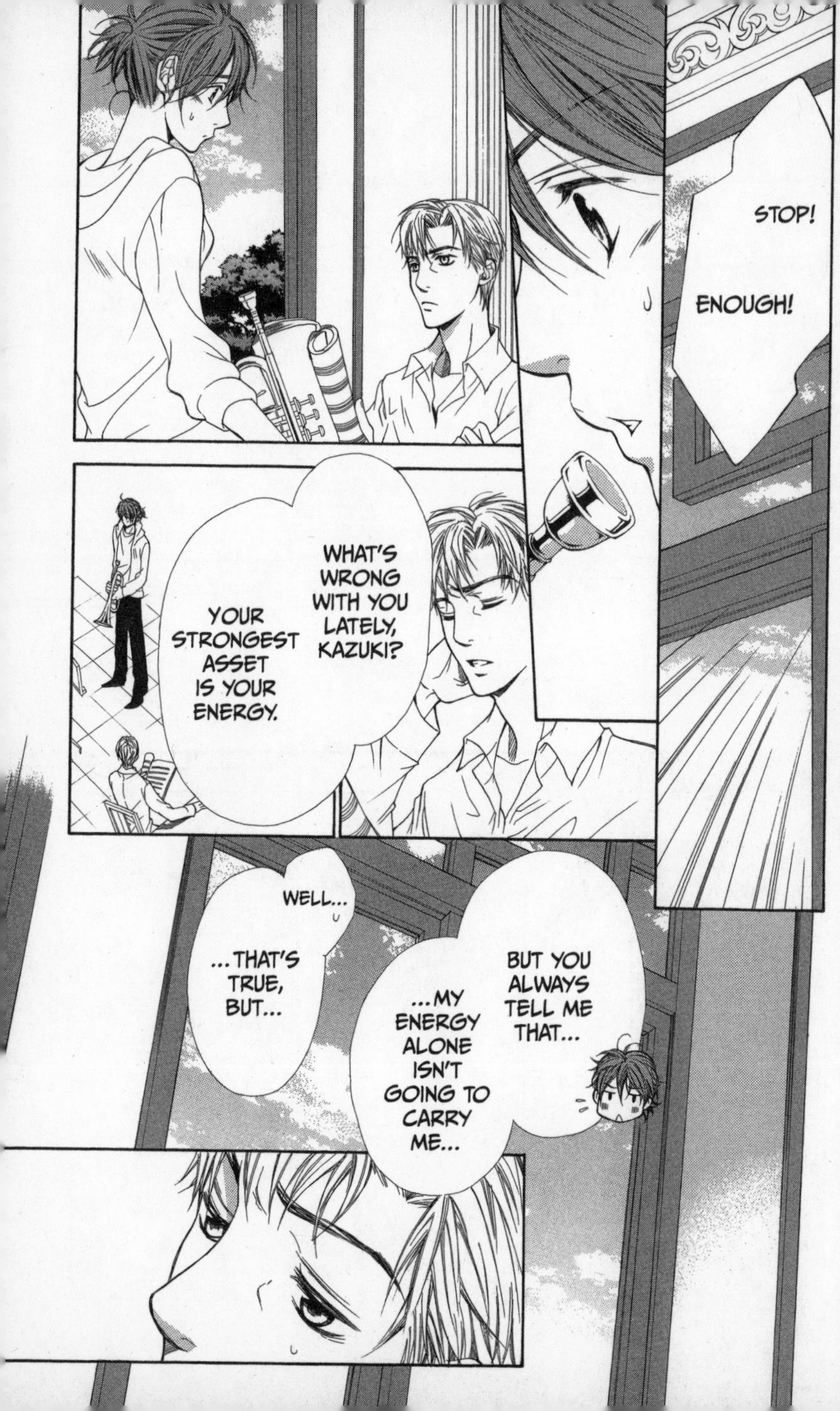
STOP!
ENOUGH!
WHAT'S WRONG WITH YOU LATELY, KAZUKI?
YOUR STRONGEST ASSET IS YOUR ENERGY.
BUT YOU ALWAYS TELL ME THAT...
...MY ENERGY ALONE ISN'T GOING TO CARRY ME...
WELL...
...THAT'S TRUE, BUT...

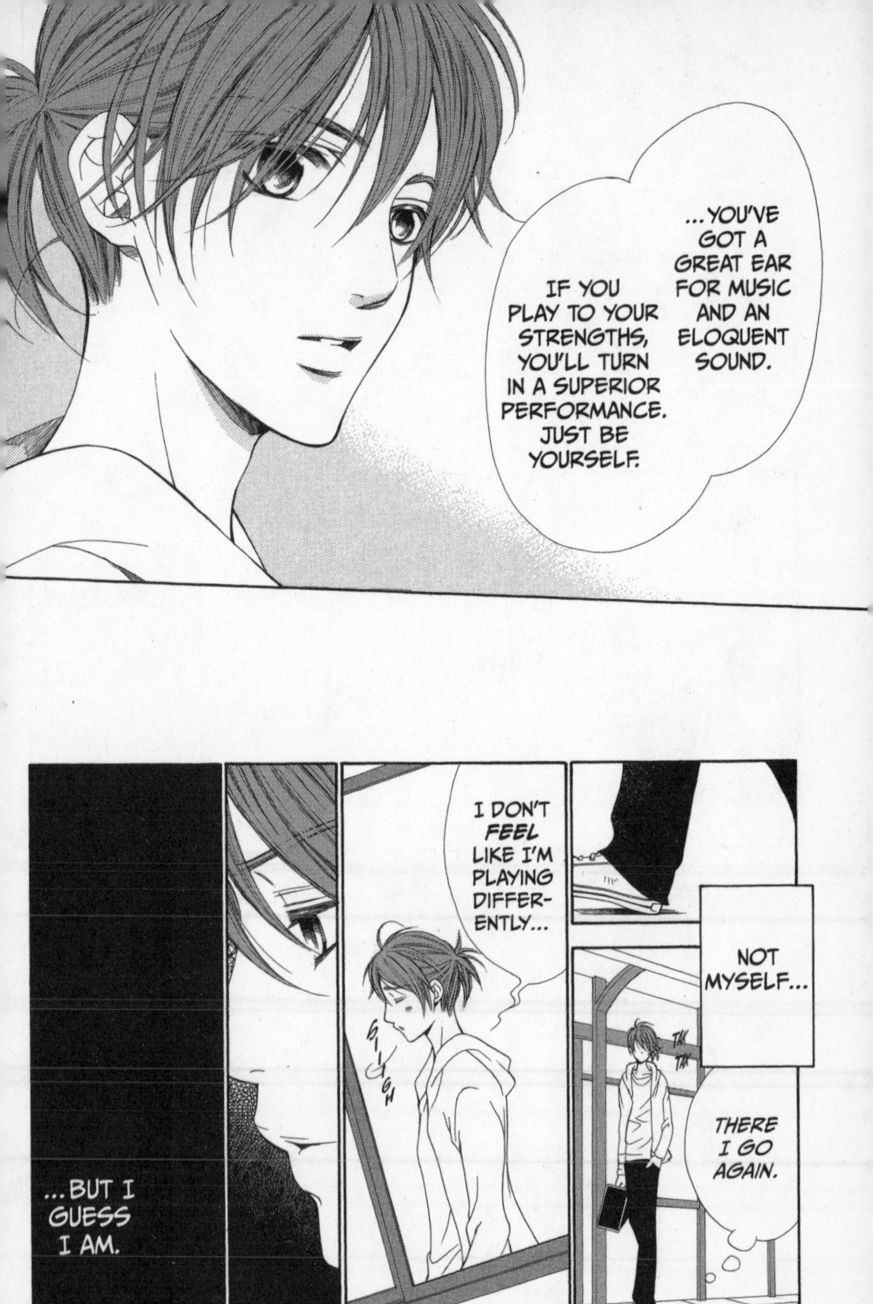
...YOU'VE GOT A GREAT EAR FOR MUSIC AND AN ELOQUENT SOUND.
IF YOU PLAY TO YOUR STRENGTHS, YOU'LL TURN IN A SUPERIOR PERFORMANCE. JUST BE YOURSELF.
NOT MYSELF...
TAK TAK
THERE I GO AGAIN.
I DON'T *FEEL* LIKE I'M PLAYING DIFFER-ENTLY...
SIIIGH
...BUT I GUESS I AM.

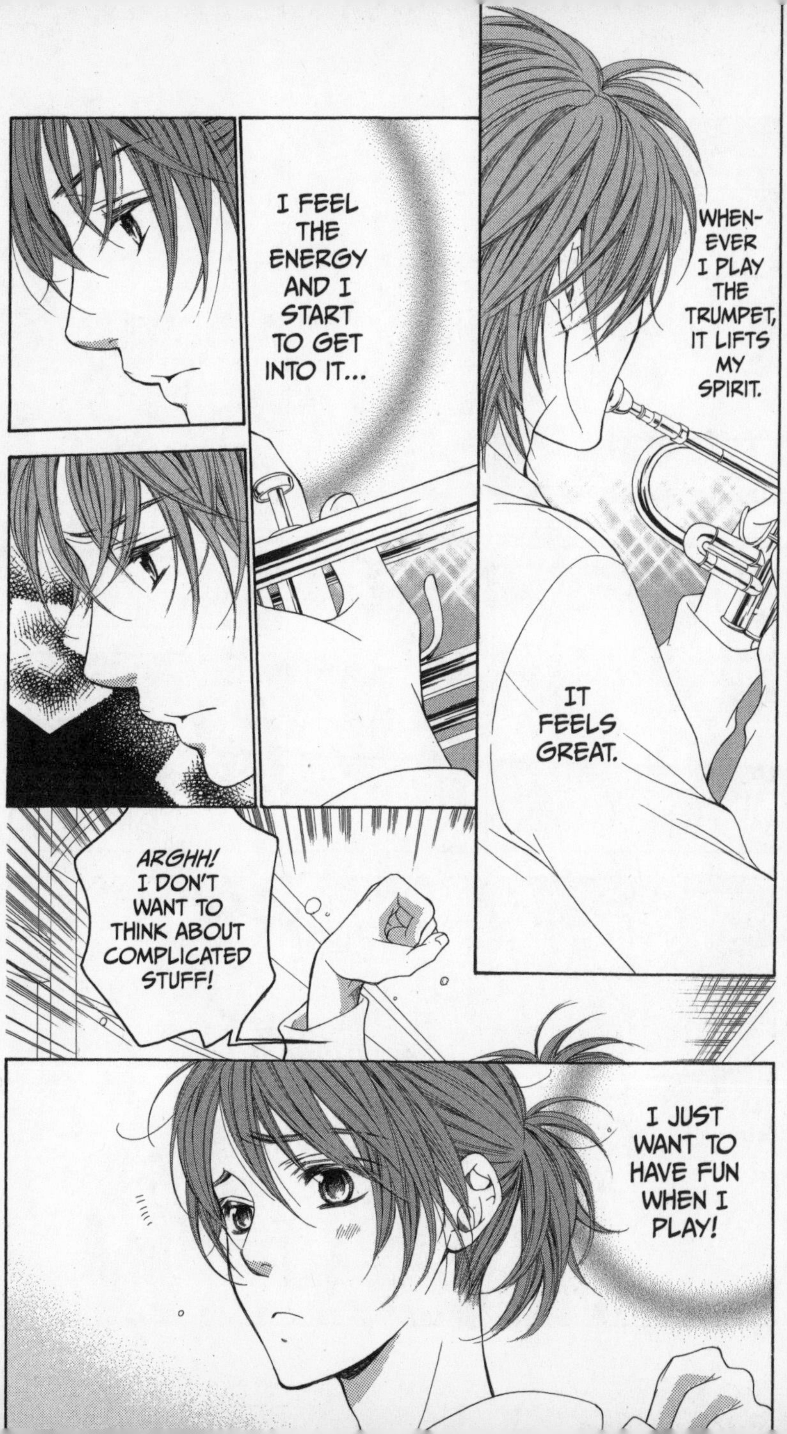
WHEN-EVER I PLAY THE TRUMPET, IT LIFTS MY SPIRIT.
IT FEELS GREAT.
I FEEL THE ENERGY AND I START TO GET INTO IT...
ARGHH! I DON'T WANT TO THINK ABOUT COMPLICATED STUFF!
I JUST WANT TO HAVE FUN WHEN I PLAY!

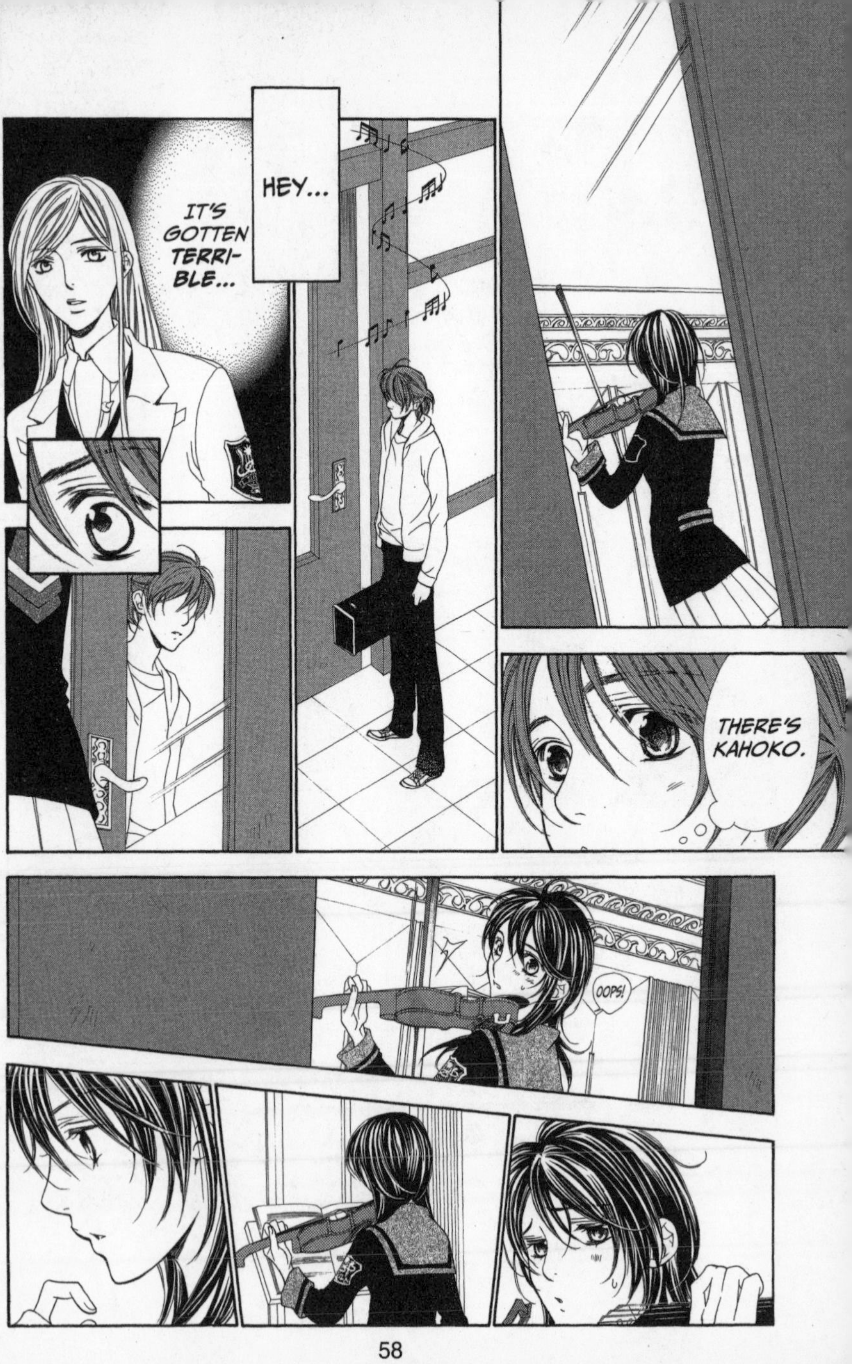
THERE'S KAHOKO.
HEY...
IT'S GOTTEN TERRI-BLE...
OOPS!

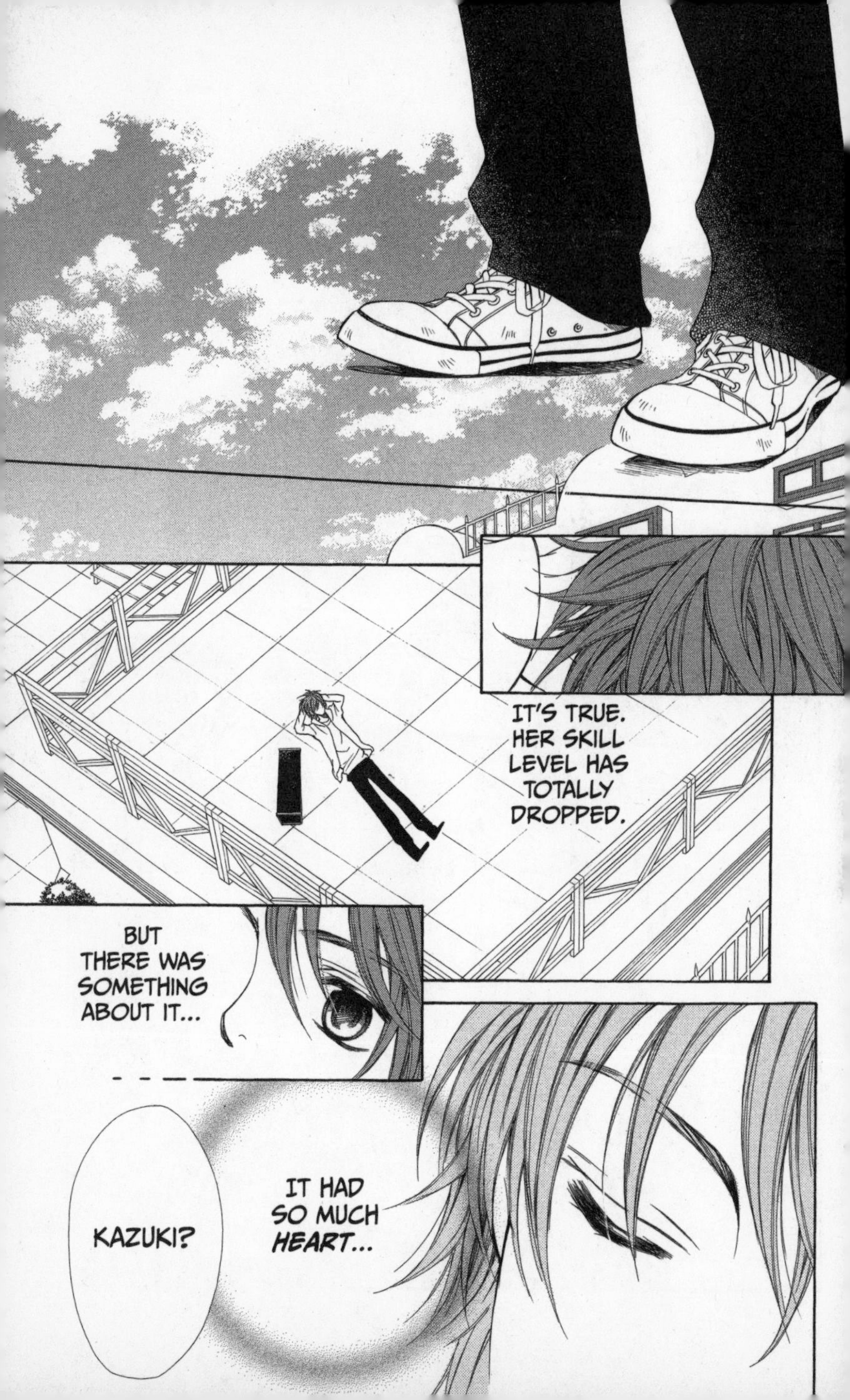
IT'S TRUE. HER SKILL LEVEL HAS TOTALLY DROPPED.
BUT THERE WAS SOMETHING ABOUT IT...
IT HAD SO MUCH *HEART*...
KAZUKI?

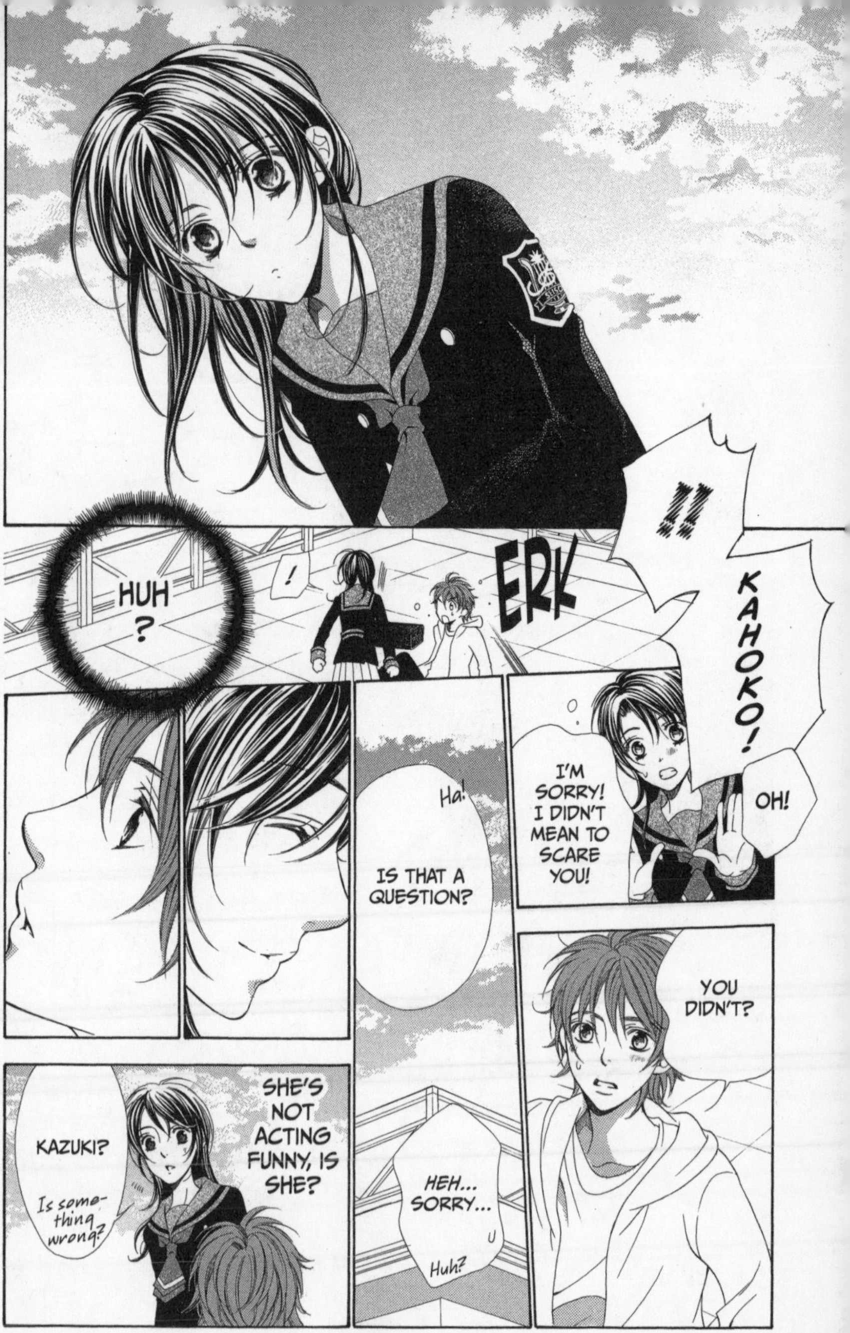
!!
KAHOKO!
ERK
!
HUH?
OH!
I'M SORRY! I DIDN'T MEAN TO SCARE YOU!
Ha!
IS THAT A QUESTION?
YOU DIDN'T?
HEH... SORRY...
Huh?
SHE'S NOT ACTING FUNNY, IS SHE?
KAZUKI?
Is something wrong?

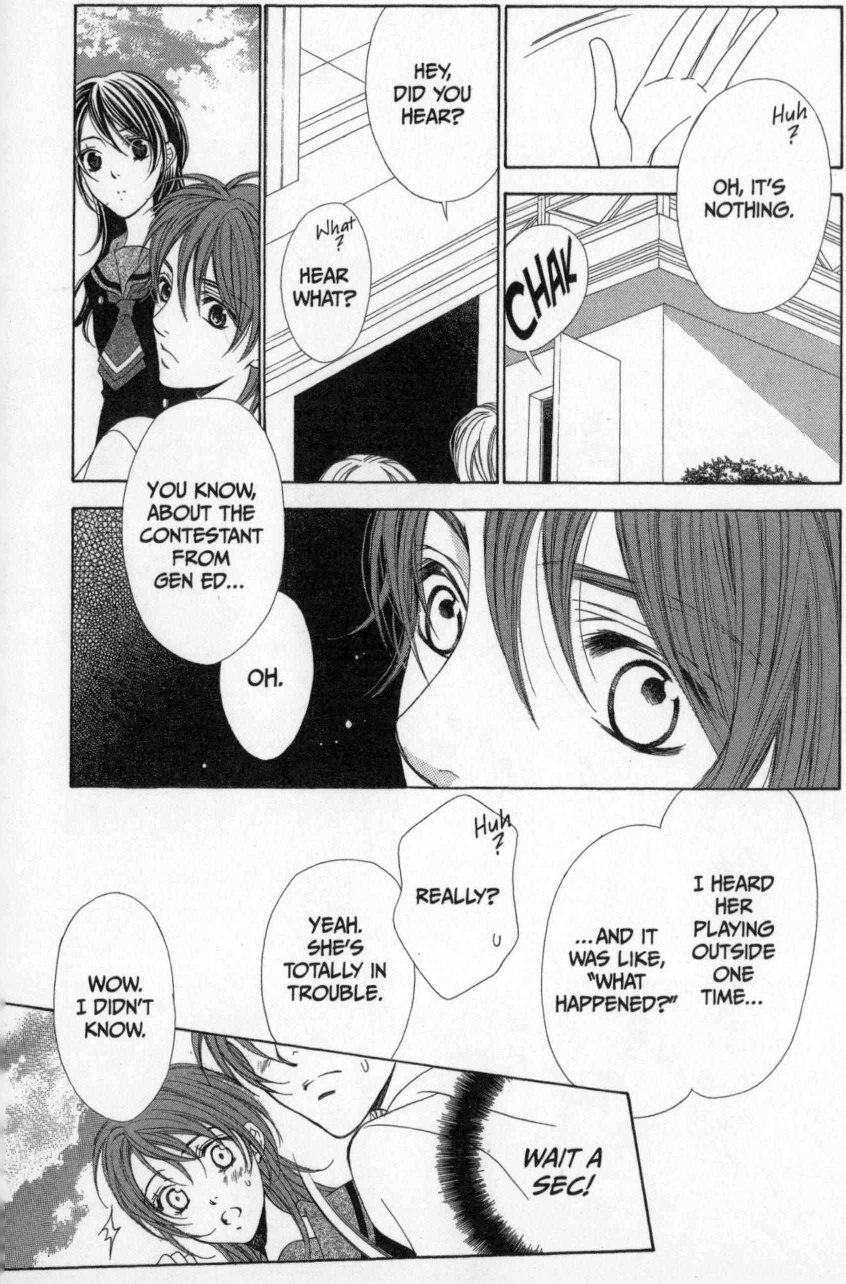
Huh?
OH, IT'S NOTHING.
CHAK
HEY, DID YOU HEAR?
What?
HEAR WHAT?
YOU KNOW, ABOUT THE CONTESTANT FROM GEN ED...
OH.
I HEARD HER PLAYING OUTSIDE ONE TIME...
...AND IT WAS LIKE, "WHAT HAPPENED?"
Huh?
REALLY?
YEAH. SHE'S TOTALLY IN TROUBLE.
WOW. I DIDN'T KNOW.
WAIT A SEC!

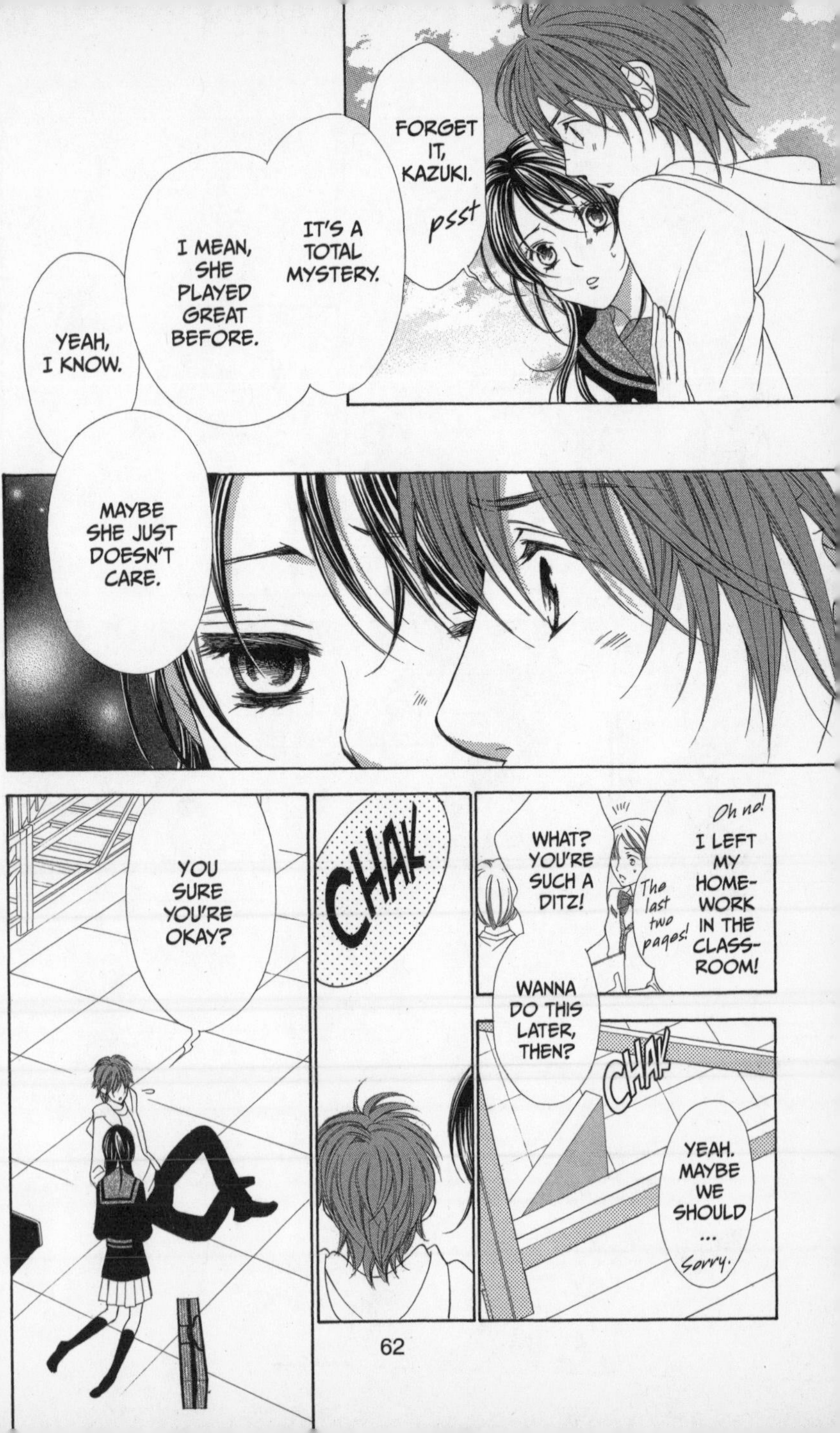
FORGET IT, KAZUKI.
psst
IT'S A TOTAL MYSTERY.
I MEAN, SHE PLAYED GREAT BEFORE.
YEAH, I KNOW.
MAYBE SHE JUST DOESN'T CARE.
Oh no!
I LEFT MY HOMEWORK IN THE CLASSROOM!
The last two pages!
WHAT? YOU'RE SUCH A DITZ!
CHAK
WANNA DO THIS LATER, THEN?
YEAH. MAYBE WE SHOULD...
Sorry.
CHAK
YOU SURE YOU'RE OKAY?

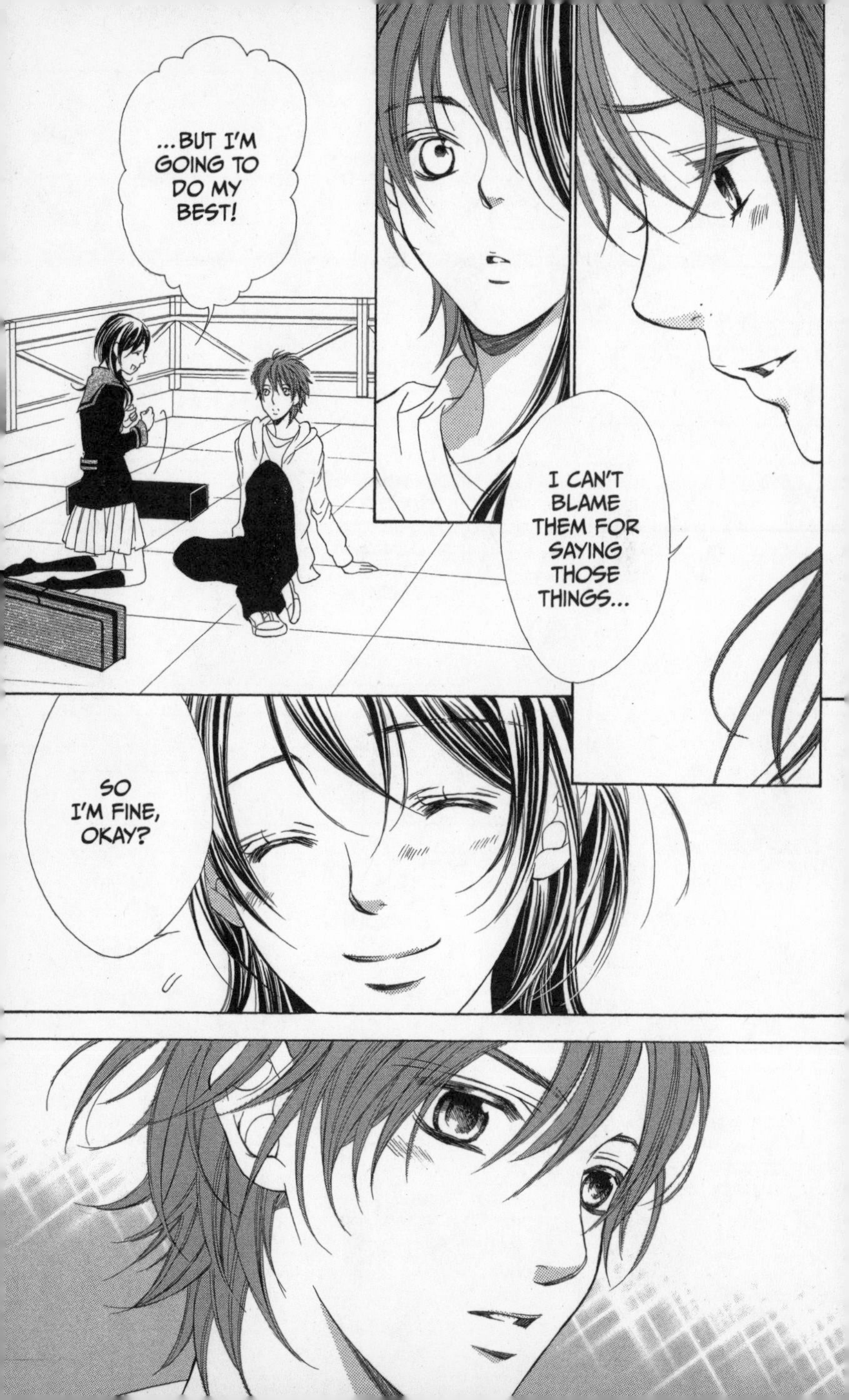
I CAN'T BLAME THEM FOR SAYING THOSE THINGS...
...BUT I'M GOING TO DO MY BEST!
SO I'M FINE, OKAY?

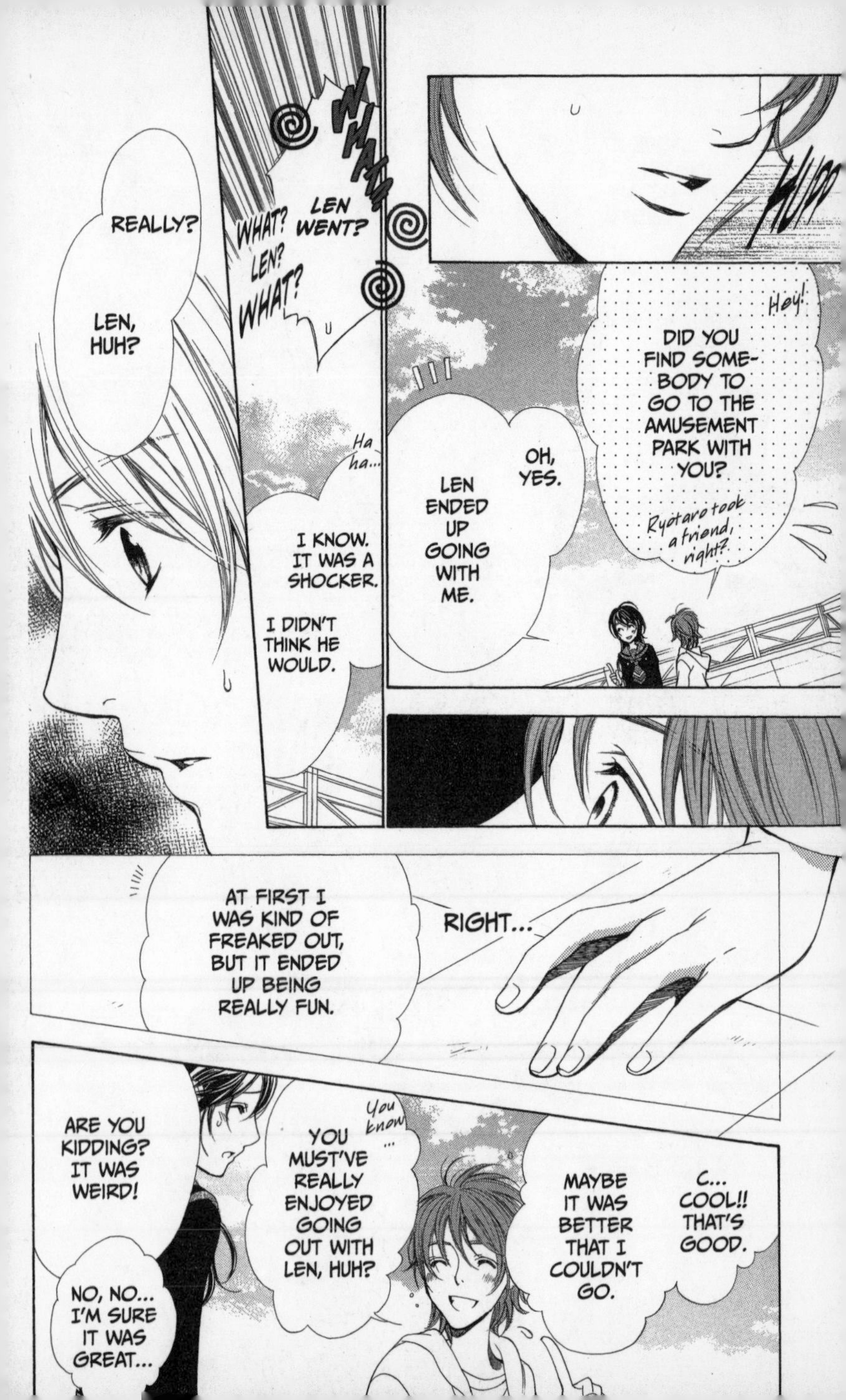
HUFF
Hey!
DID YOU FIND SOME-BODY TO GO TO THE AMUSEMENT PARK WITH YOU?
Ryotaro took a friend, right?
OH, YES.
LEN ENDED UP GOING WITH ME.
WHAM
LEN WENT?
WHAT? LEN? WHAT?
Ha ha...
I KNOW. IT WAS A SHOCKER.
I DIDN'T THINK HE WOULD.
REALLY?
LEN, HUH?
RIGHT...
AT FIRST I WAS KIND OF FREAKED OUT, BUT IT ENDED UP BEING REALLY FUN.
C... COOL!! THAT'S GOOD.
MAYBE IT WAS BETTER THAT I COULDN'T GO.
You know...
YOU MUST'VE REALLY ENJOYED GOING OUT WITH LEN, HUH?
ARE YOU KIDDING? IT WAS WEIRD!
NO, NO... I'M SURE IT WAS GREAT...

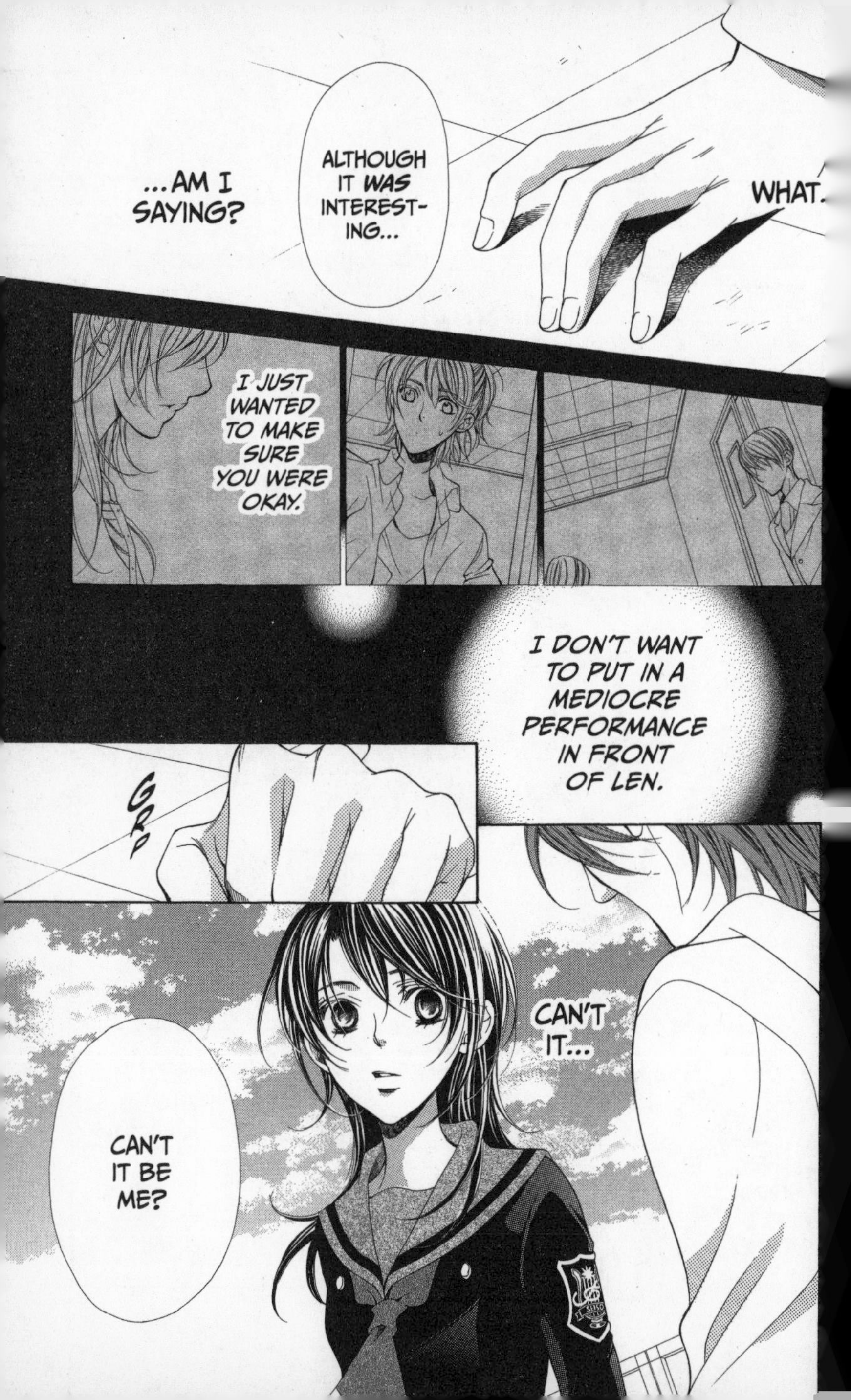
WHAT.
ALTHOUGH IT WAS INTERESTING...
...AM I SAYING?
I JUST WANTED TO MAKE SURE YOU WERE OKAY.
I DON'T WANT TO PUT IN A MEDIOCRE PERFORMANCE IN FRONT OF LEN.
GRP
CAN'T IT...
CAN'T IT BE ME?

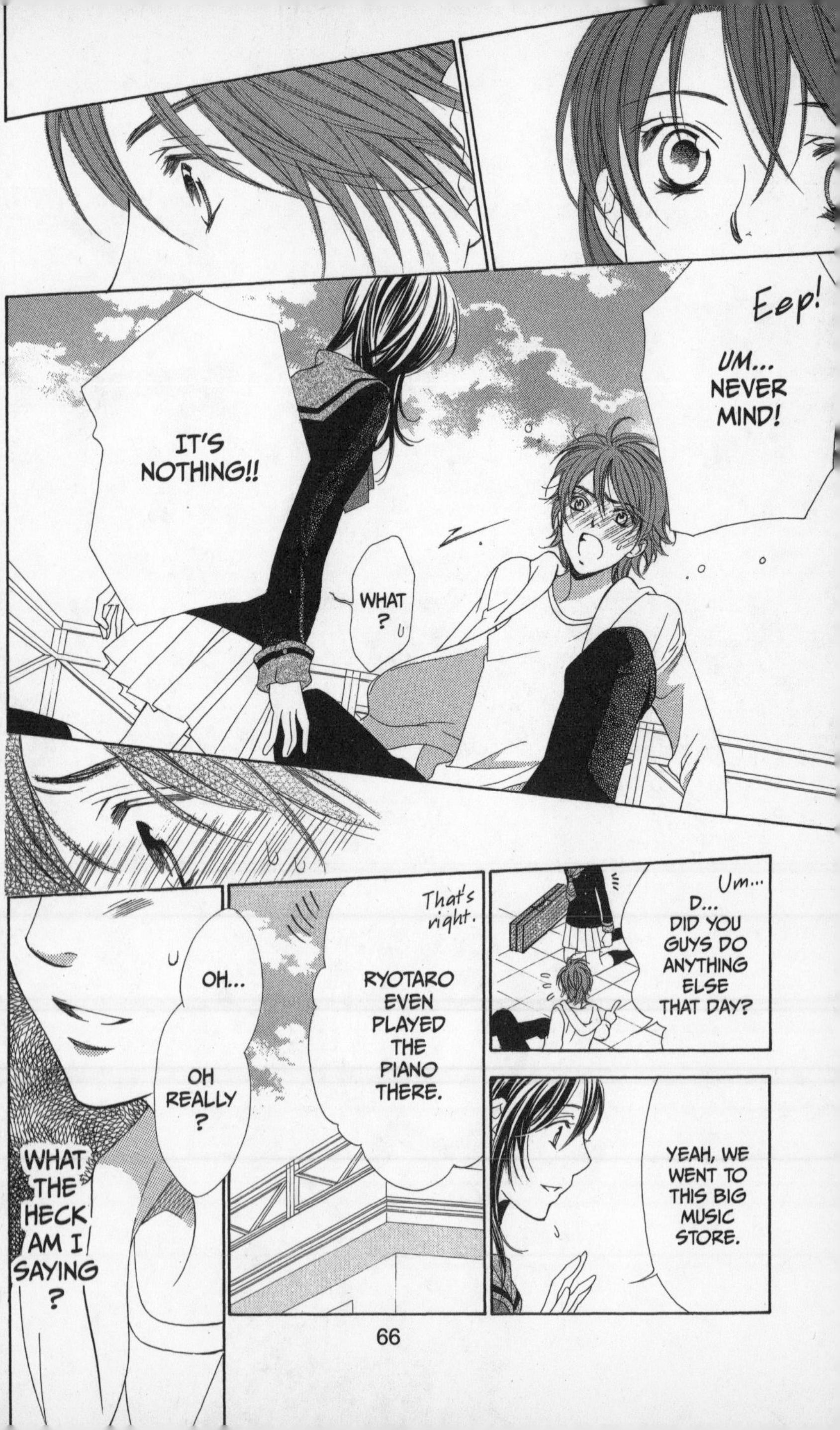
Eep!
UM... NEVER MIND!
WHAT?
IT'S NOTHING!!
Um...
D... DID YOU GUYS DO ANYTHING ELSE THAT DAY?
YEAH, WE WENT TO THIS BIG MUSIC STORE.
That's right.
RYOTARO EVEN PLAYED THE PIANO THERE.
OH...
OH REALLY?
WHAT THE HECK AM I SAYING?

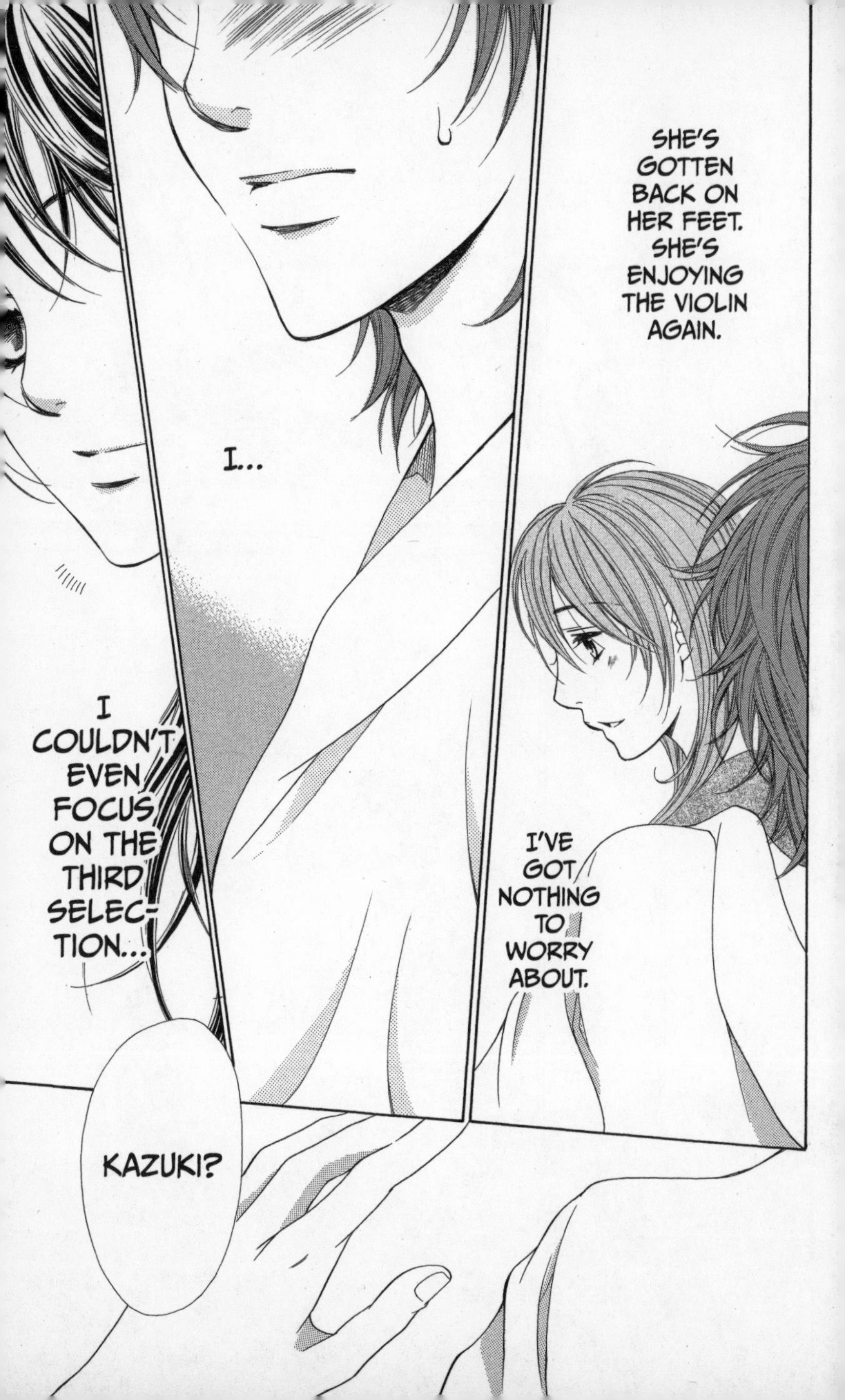
SHE'S GOTTEN BACK ON HER FEET. SHE'S ENJOYING THE VIOLIN AGAIN.
I'VE GOT NOTHING TO WORRY ABOUT.
I...
I COULDN'T EVEN FOCUS ON THE THIRD SELECTION...
KAZUKI?

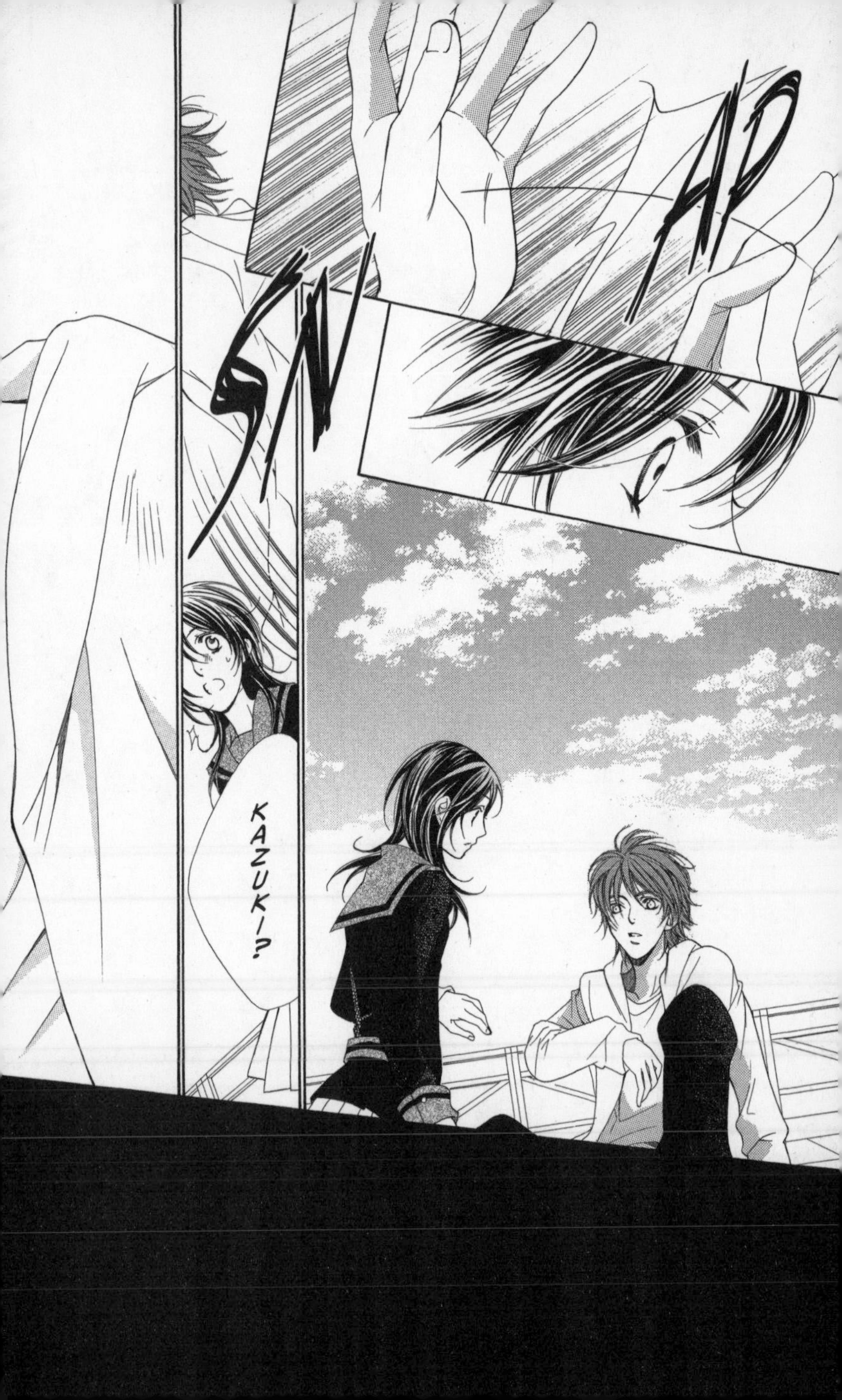
SNAP
KAZUKI?

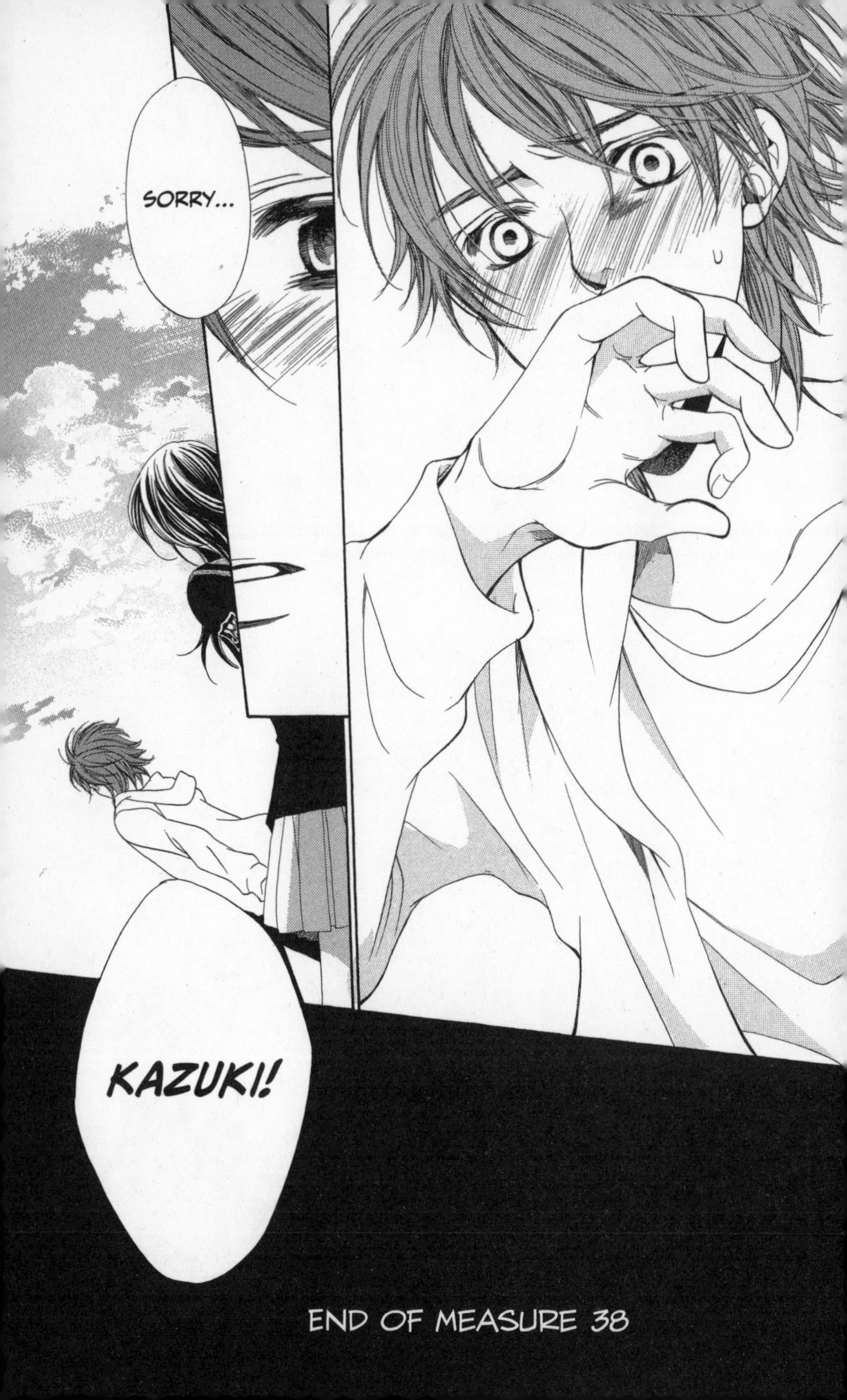
SORRY...
KAZUKI!
END OF MEASURE 38

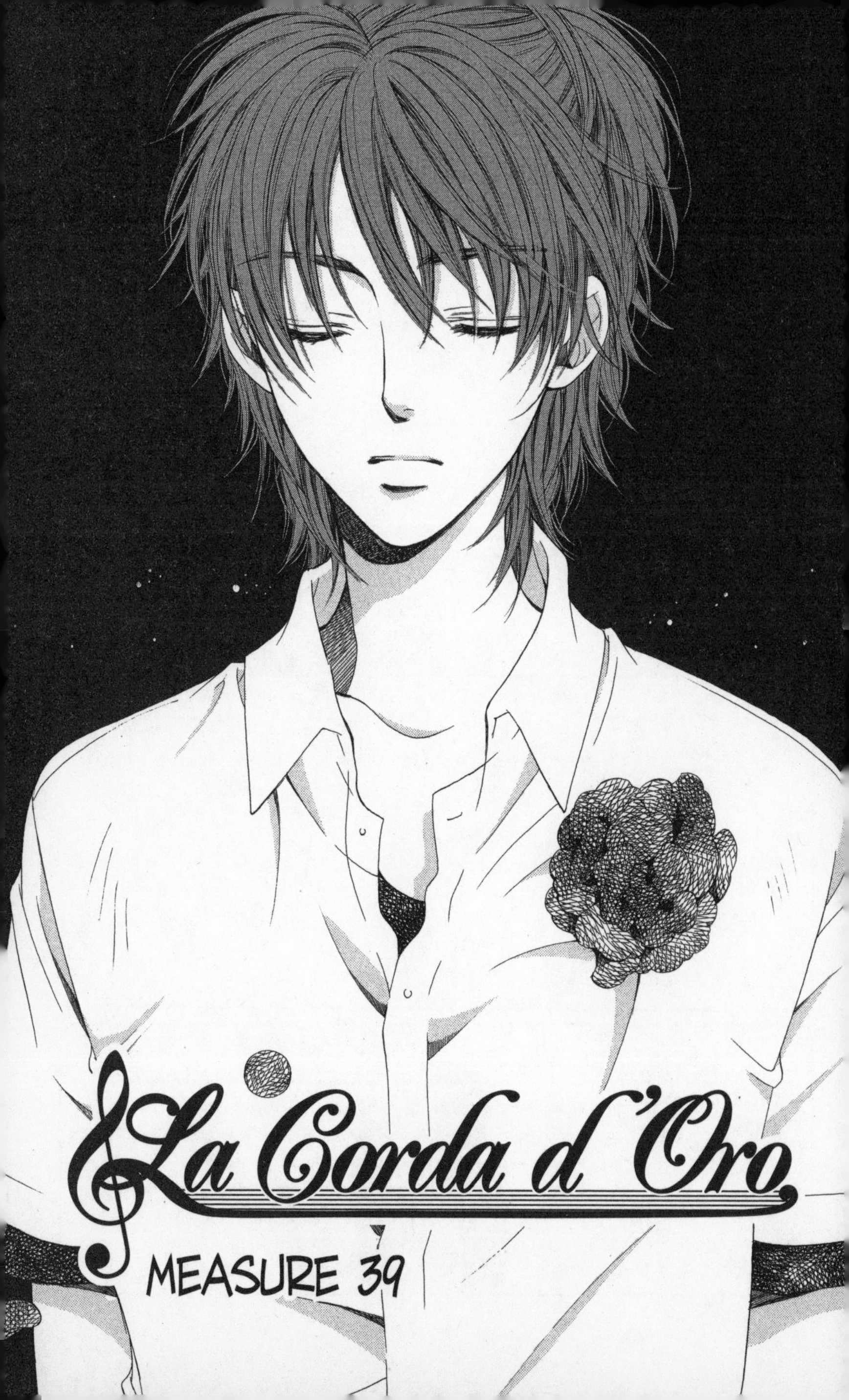
La Corda d'Oro
MEASURE 39

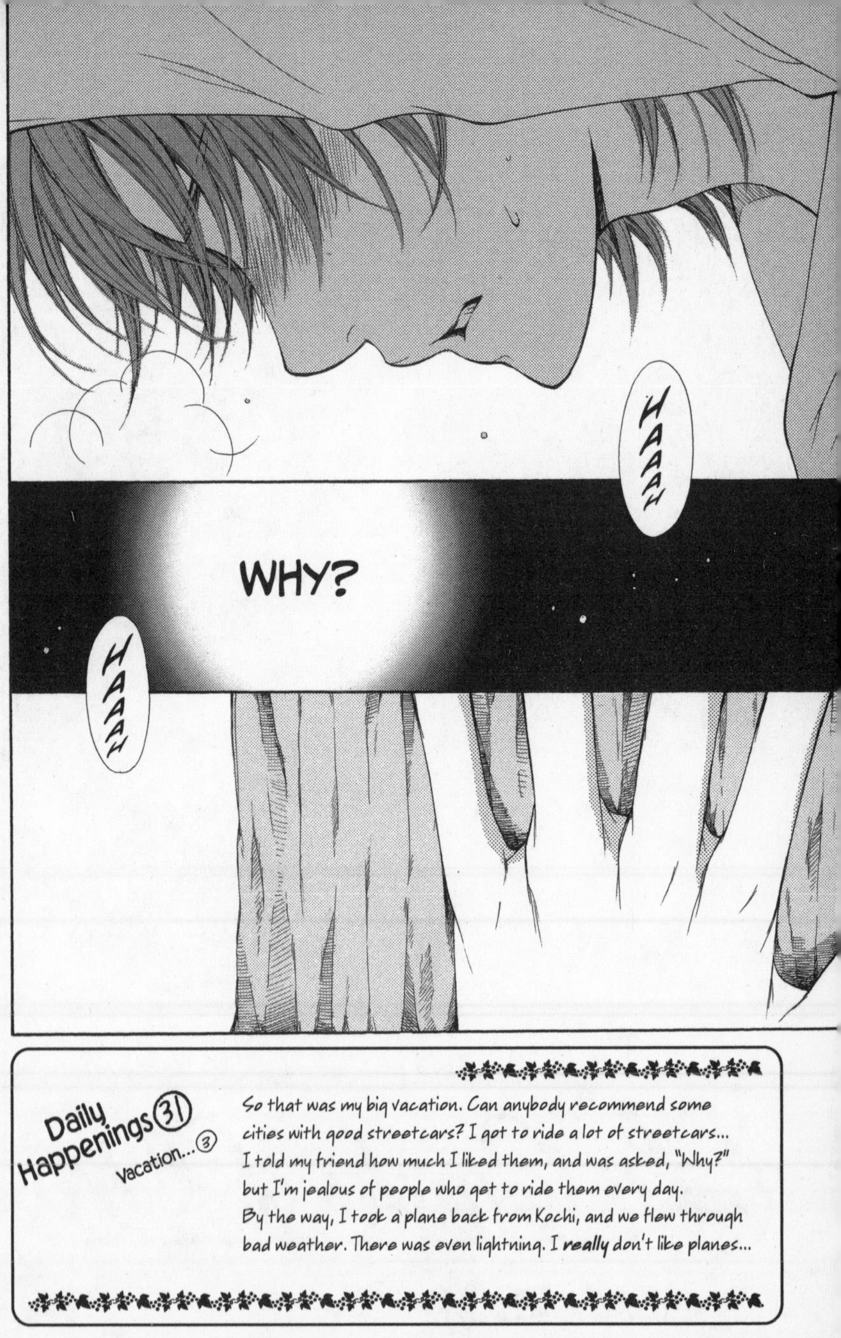
HAAAH
WHY?
HAAAH

**Daily Happenings 31**
*Vacation... 3*

So that was my big vacation. Can anybody recommend some cities with good streetcars? I got to ride a lot of streetcars... I told my friend how much I liked them, and was asked, "Why?" but I'm jealous of people who get to ride them every day.
By the way, I took a plane back from Kochi, and we flew through bad weather. There was even lightning. I **really** don't like planes...

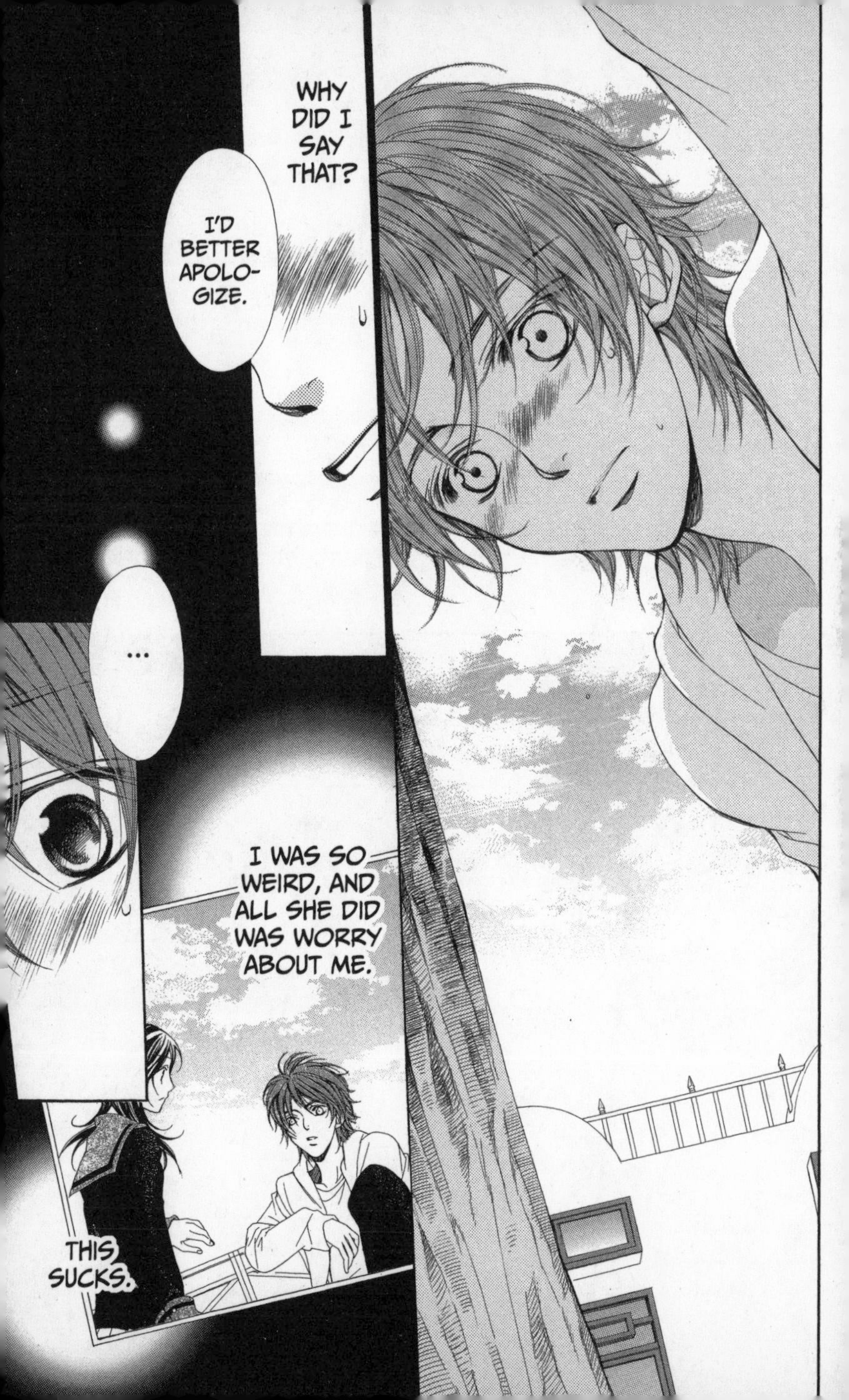
WHY DID I SAY THAT?
I'D BETTER APOLOGIZE.
...
I WAS SO WEIRD, AND ALL SHE DID WAS WORRY ABOUT ME.
THIS SUCKS.

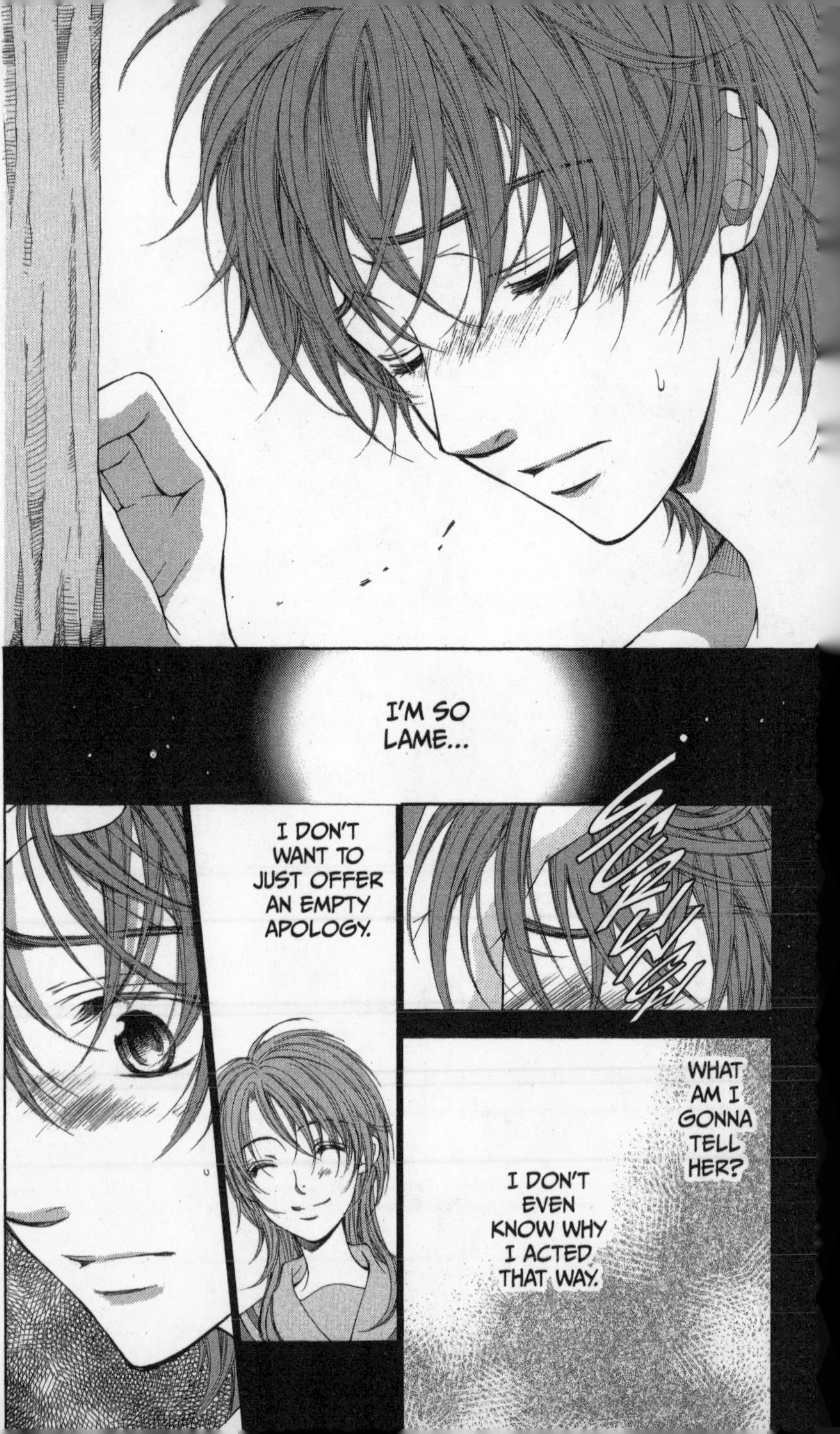
I'M SO LAME...
WHAT AM I GONNA TELL HER?
I DON'T EVEN KNOW WHY I ACTED THAT WAY.
I DON'T WANT TO JUST OFFER AN EMPTY APOLOGY.

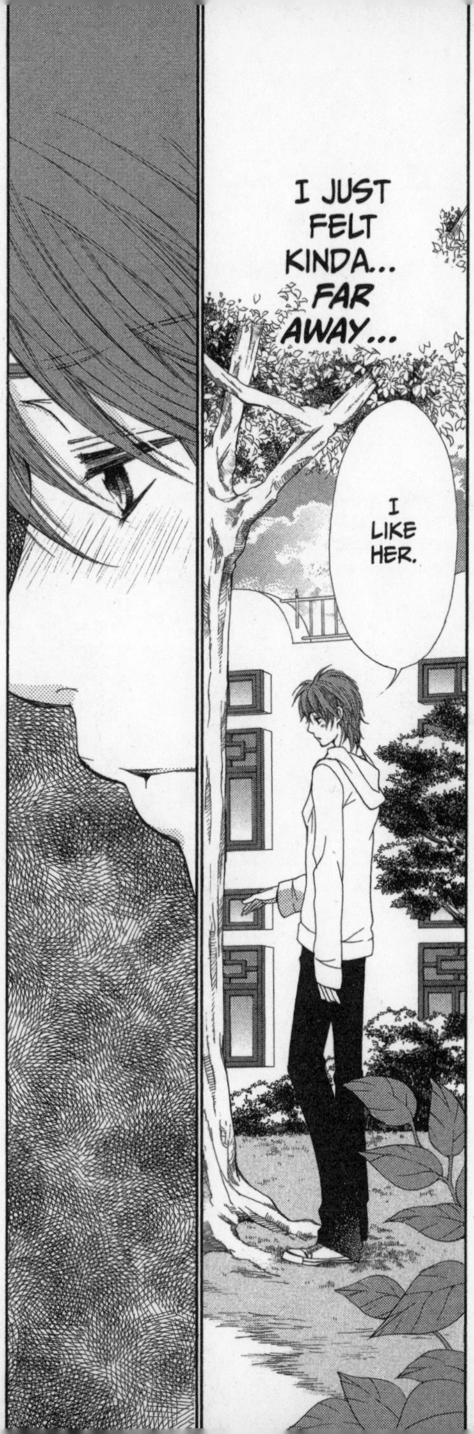
I JUST FELT KINDA... FAR AWAY...
I LIKE HER.

WHAT AM I...

...TO HER?

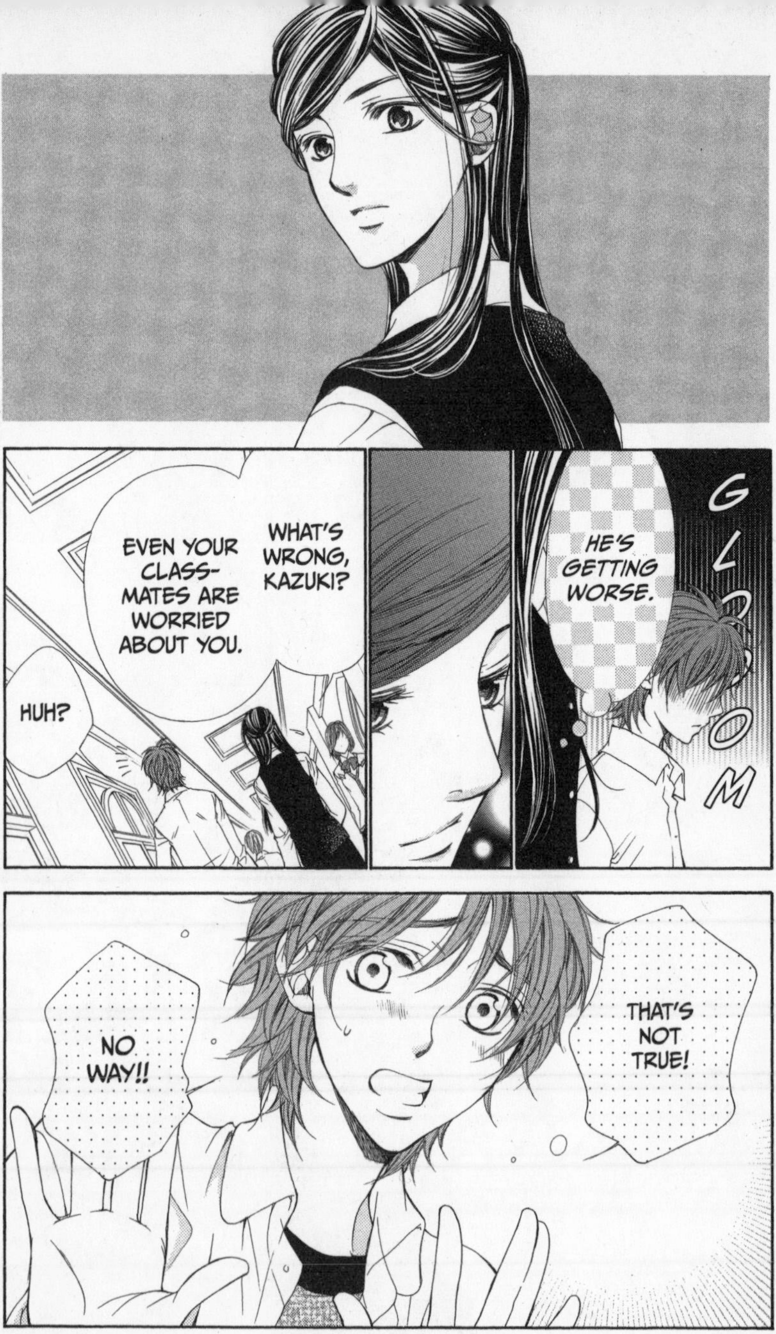
GLOOM
HE'S GETTING WORSE.
WHAT'S WRONG, KAZUKI?
EVEN YOUR CLASS-MATES ARE WORRIED ABOUT YOU.
HUH?
THAT'S NOT TRUE!
NO WAY!!

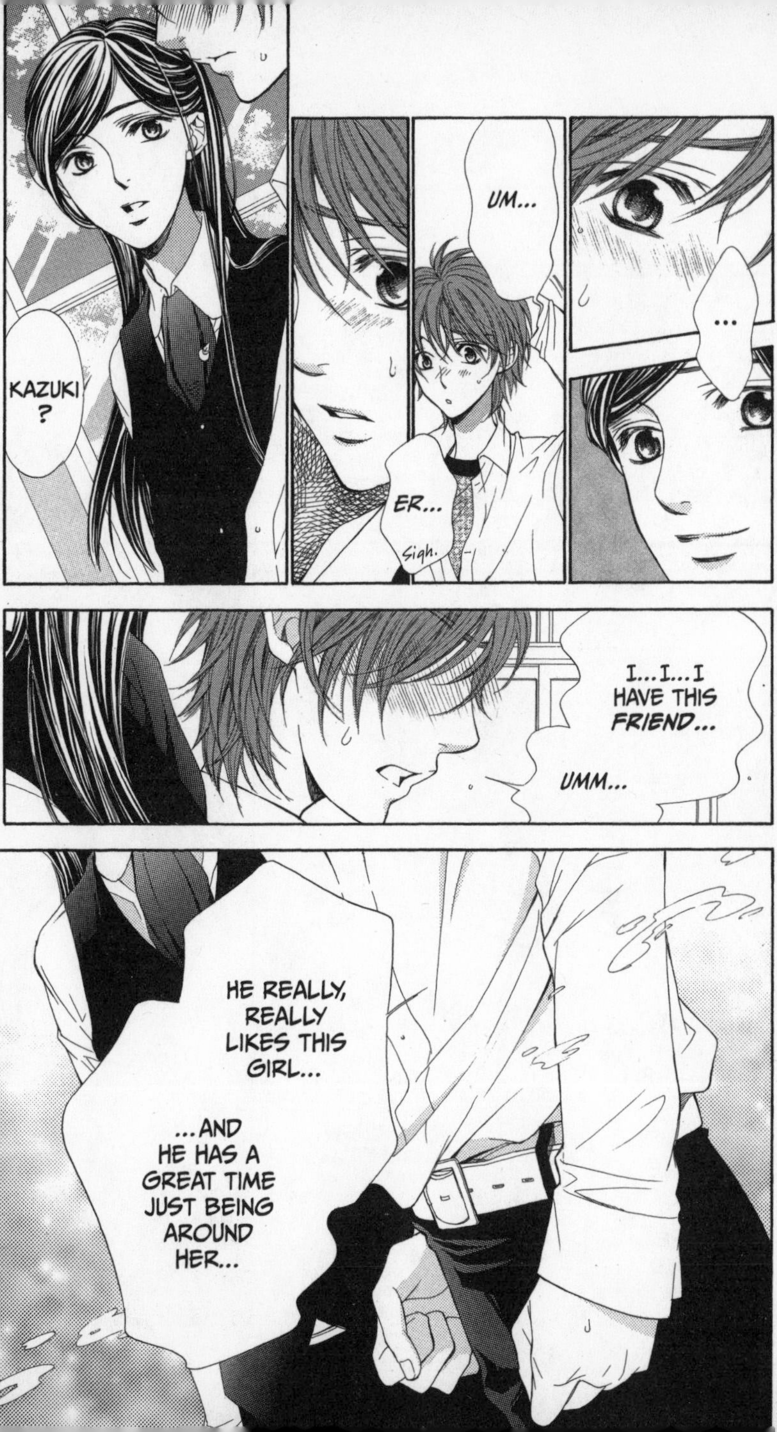
...
UM...
ER...
Sigh.
KAZUKI ?
I...I...I HAVE THIS FRIEND...
UMM...
HE REALLY, REALLY LIKES THIS GIRL...
...AND HE HAS A GREAT TIME JUST BEING AROUND HER...

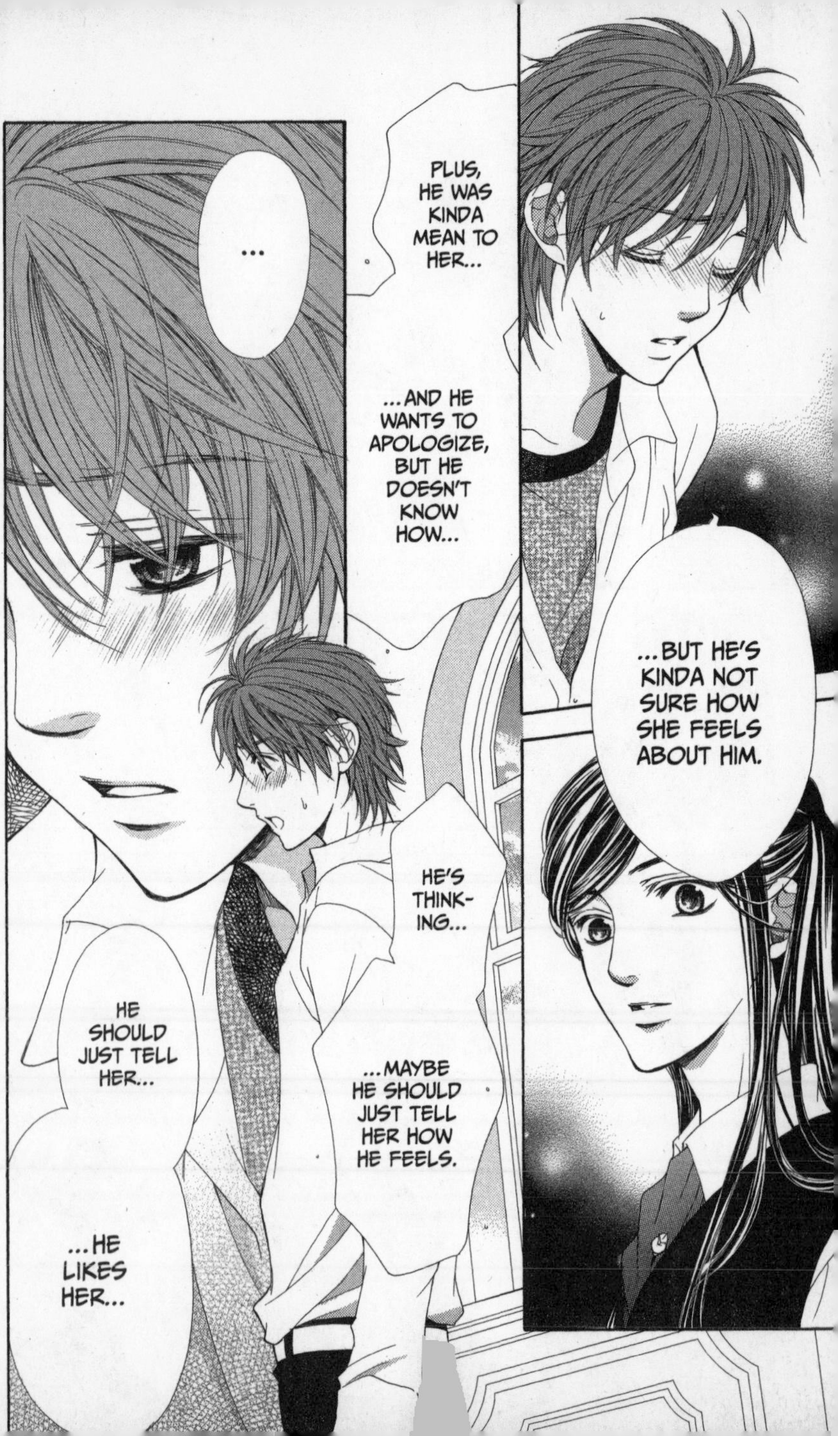
PLUS, HE WAS KINDA MEAN TO HER...
...AND HE WANTS TO APOLOGIZE, BUT HE DOESN'T KNOW HOW...
...BUT HE'S KINDA NOT SURE HOW SHE FEELS ABOUT HIM.
HE'S THINKING...
...MAYBE HE SHOULD JUST TELL HER HOW HE FEELS.
...
HE SHOULD JUST TELL HER...
...HE LIKES HER...

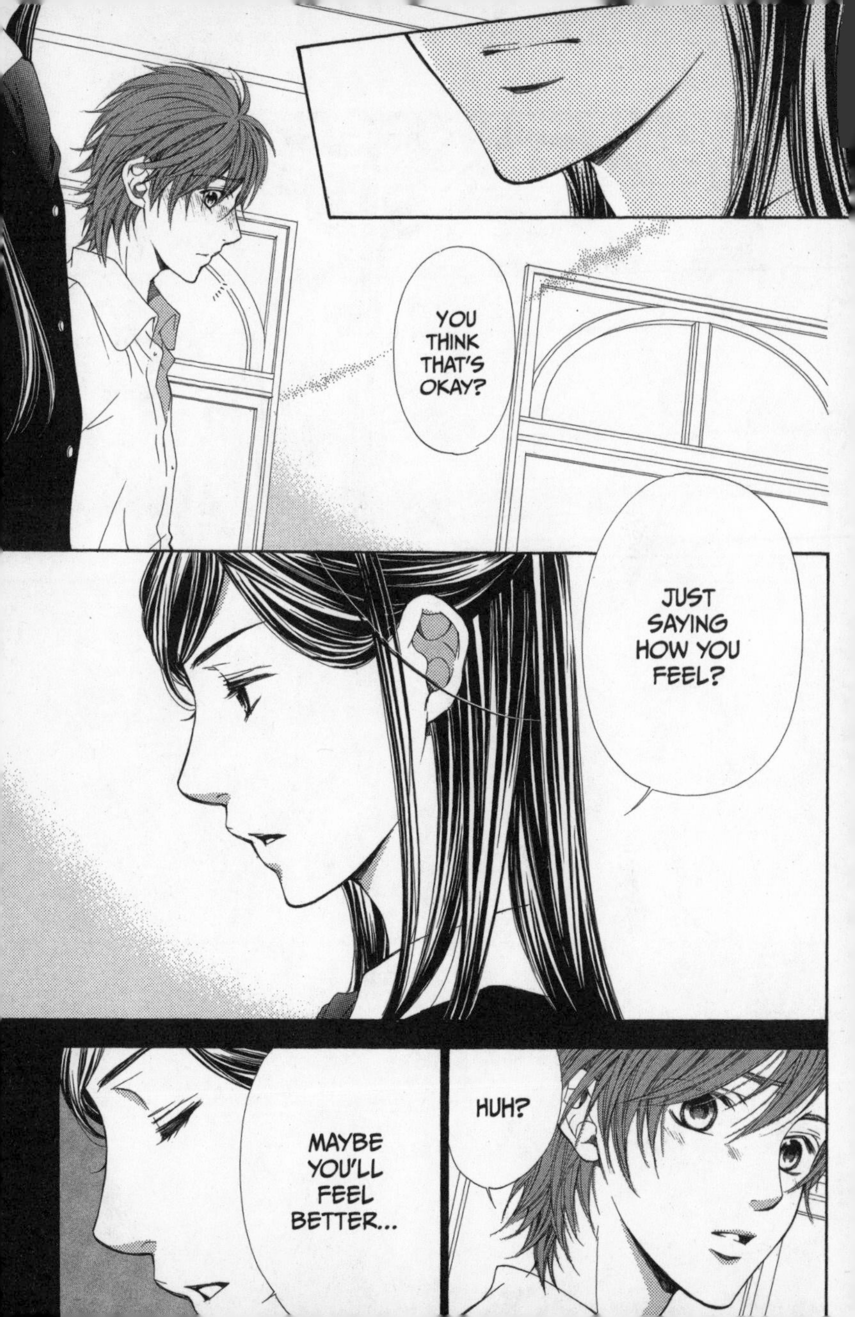
YOU THINK THAT'S OKAY?
JUST SAYING HOW YOU FEEL?
HUH?
MAYBE YOU'LL FEEL BETTER...

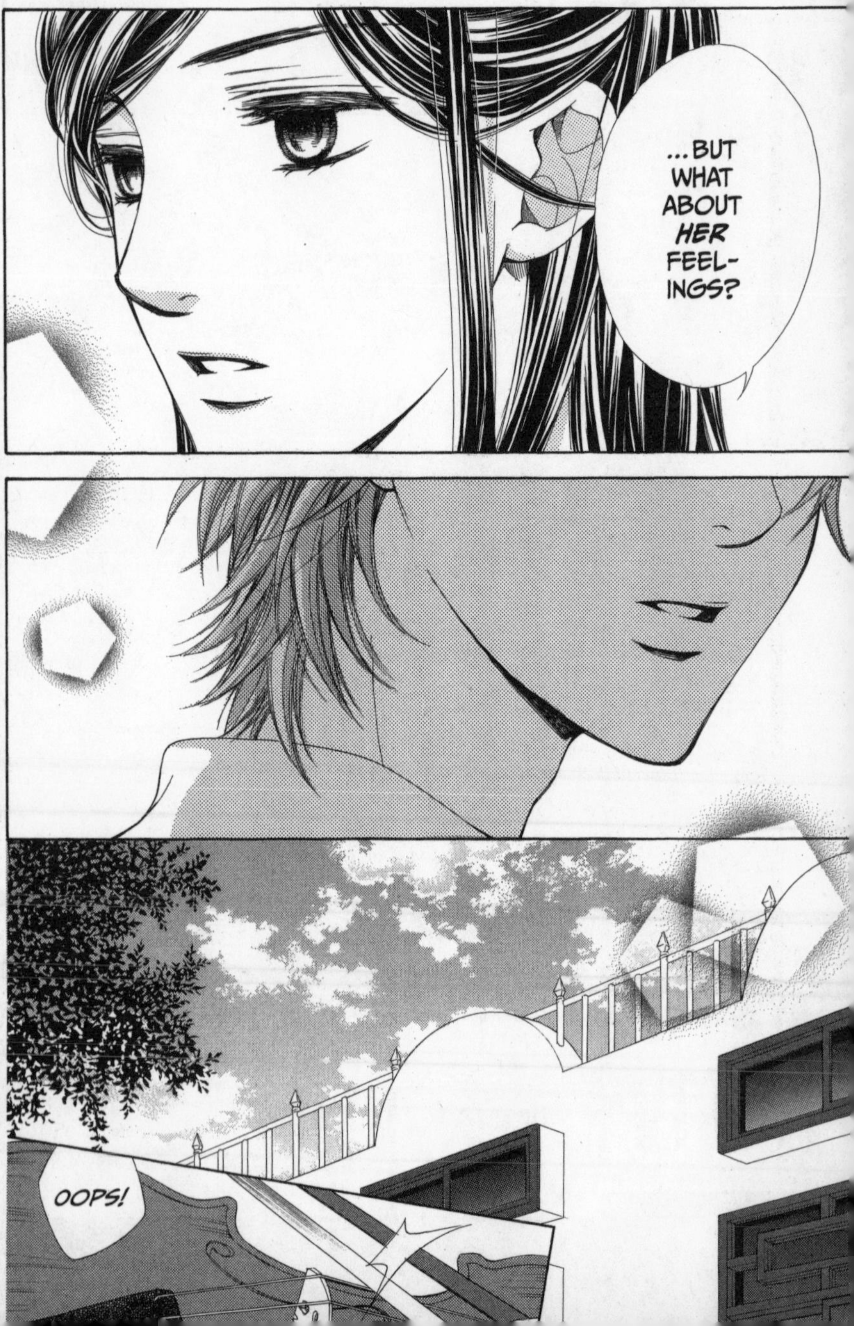
...BUT WHAT ABOUT HER FEEL- INGS?
OOPS!

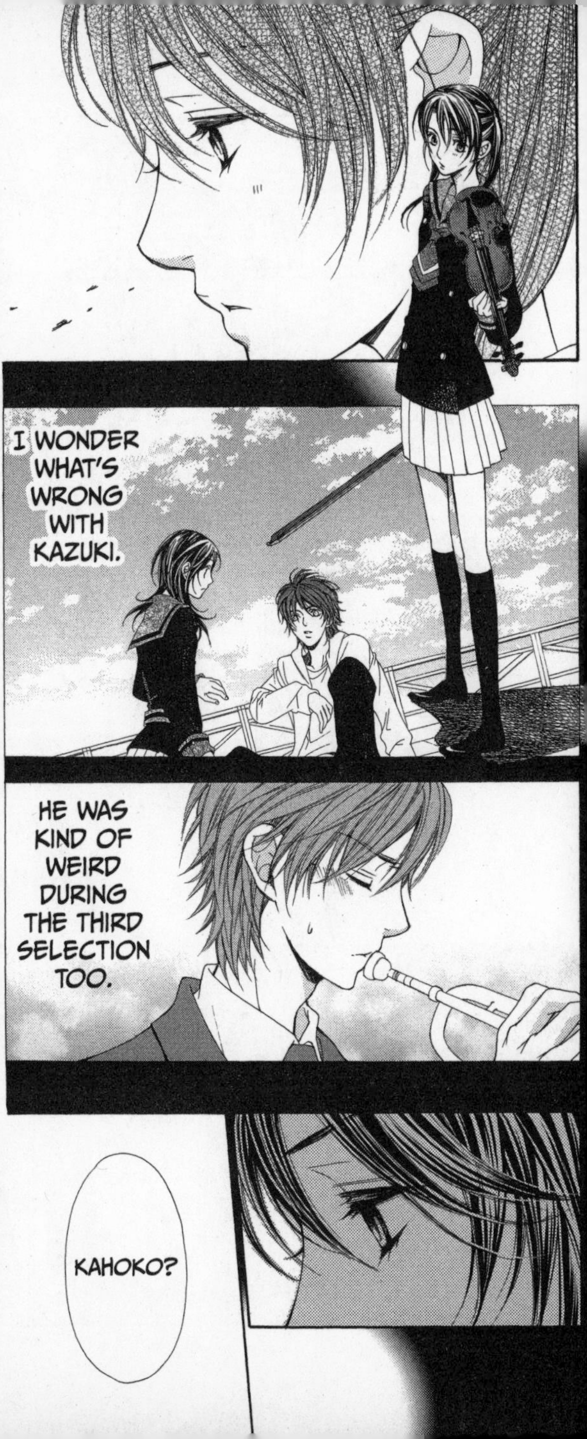
I WONDER WHAT'S WRONG WITH KAZUKI.
HE WAS KIND OF WEIRD DURING THE THIRD SELECTION TOO.
KAHOKO?

**THREE**

Kazuki's been depressed for two whole chapters, and I feel like I need to cheer him up!

And my assistants really don't like the scripts where Kazuki appears a lot. It takes forever to lay the screen-tone we have to use for his hair. Even something as simple as finishing the hair tips turns into a big deal. (lol)
By the way, it's screentone SE-72.←Totally useless infor-mation...

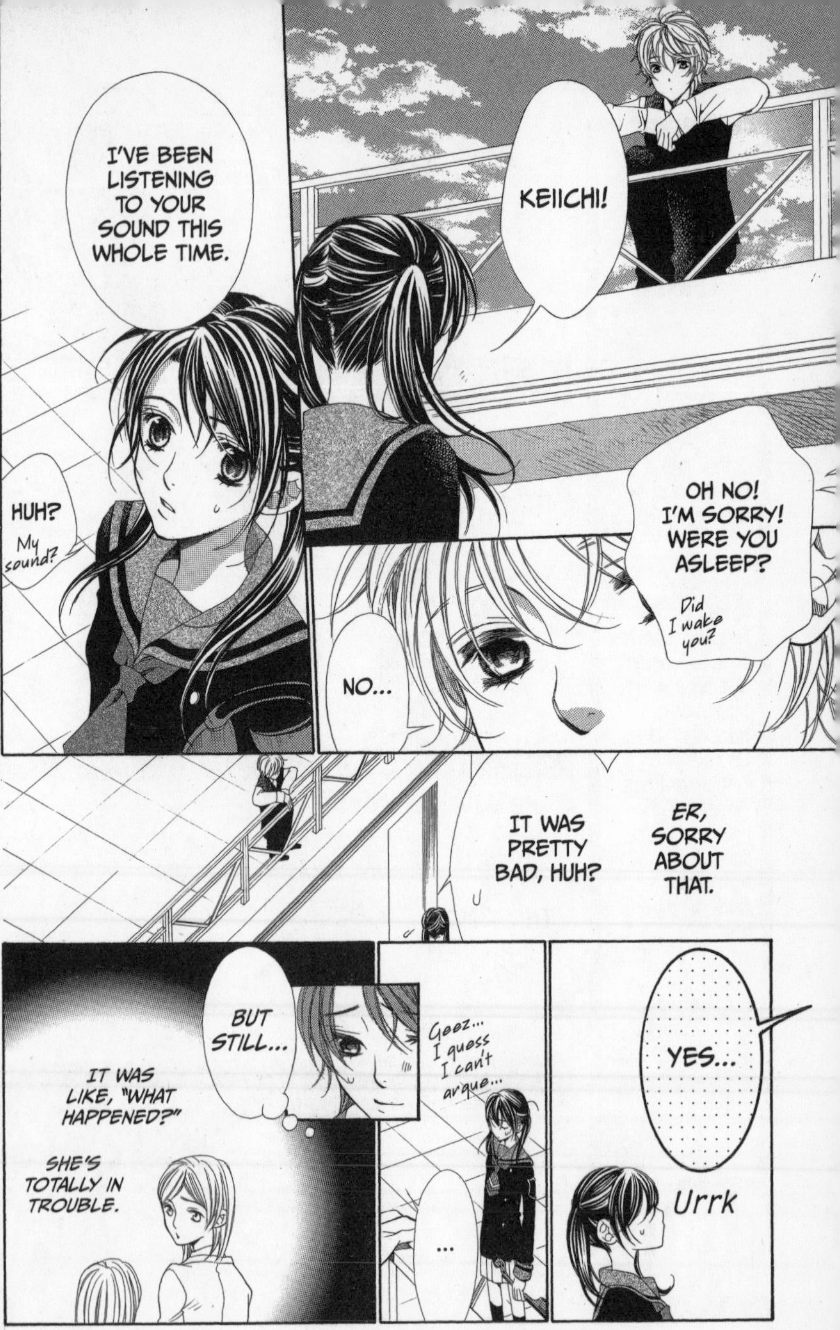
KEIICHI!
OH NO! I'M SORRY! WERE YOU ASLEEP?
Did I wake you?
NO...
I'VE BEEN LISTENING TO YOUR SOUND THIS WHOLE TIME.
HUH?
My sound?
ER, SORRY ABOUT THAT.
IT WAS PRETTY BAD, HUH?
YES...
Urrk
Geez... I guess I can't argue...
...
BUT STILL...
IT WAS LIKE, "WHAT HAPPENED?"
SHE'S TOTALLY IN TROUBLE.

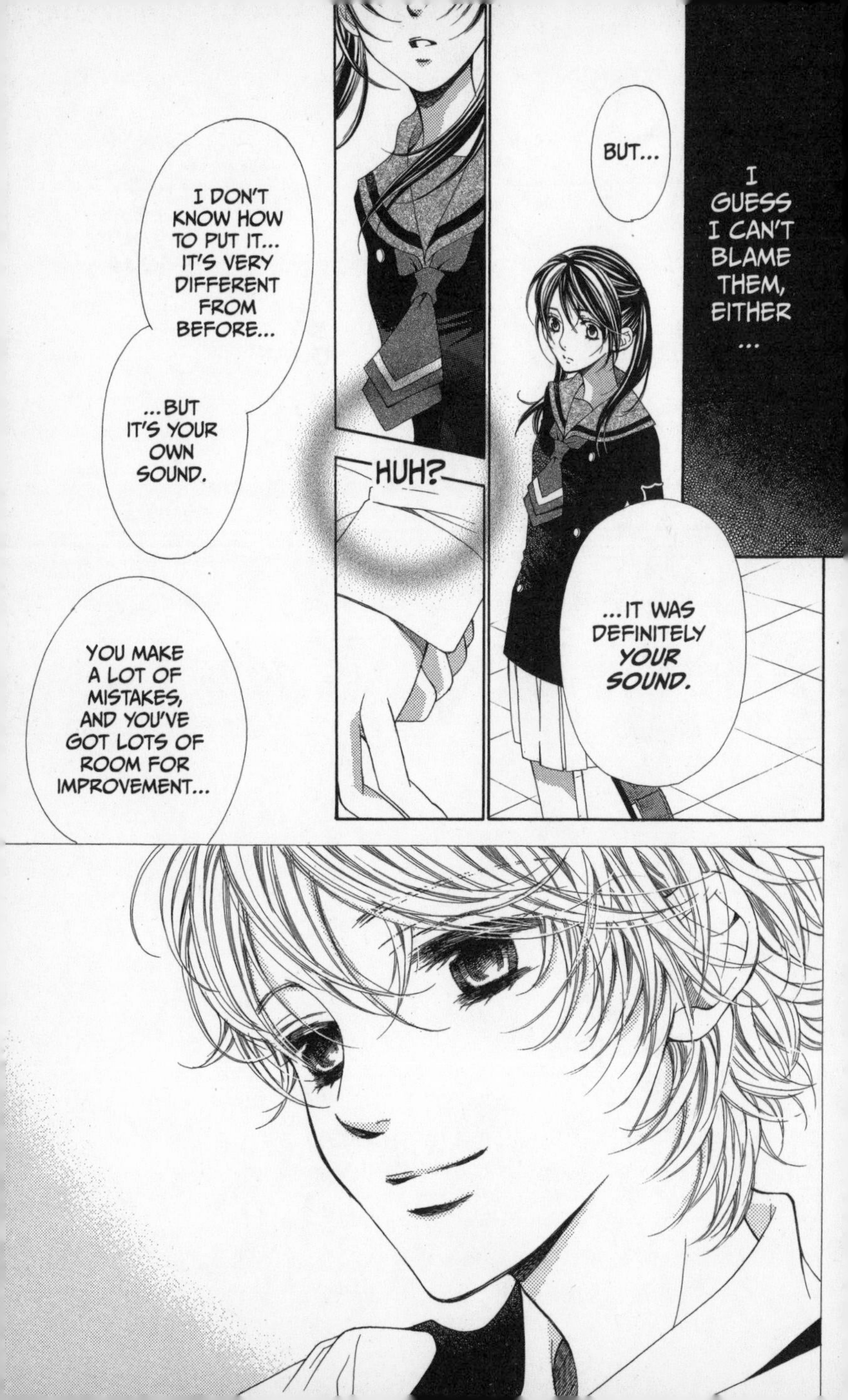
I GUESS I CAN'T BLAME THEM, EITHER...
BUT...
...IT WAS DEFINITELY *YOUR SOUND.*
HUH?
I DON'T KNOW HOW TO PUT IT... IT'S VERY DIFFERENT FROM BEFORE...
...BUT IT'S YOUR OWN SOUND.
YOU MAKE A LOT OF MISTAKES, AND YOU'VE GOT LOTS OF ROOM FOR IMPROVEMENT...

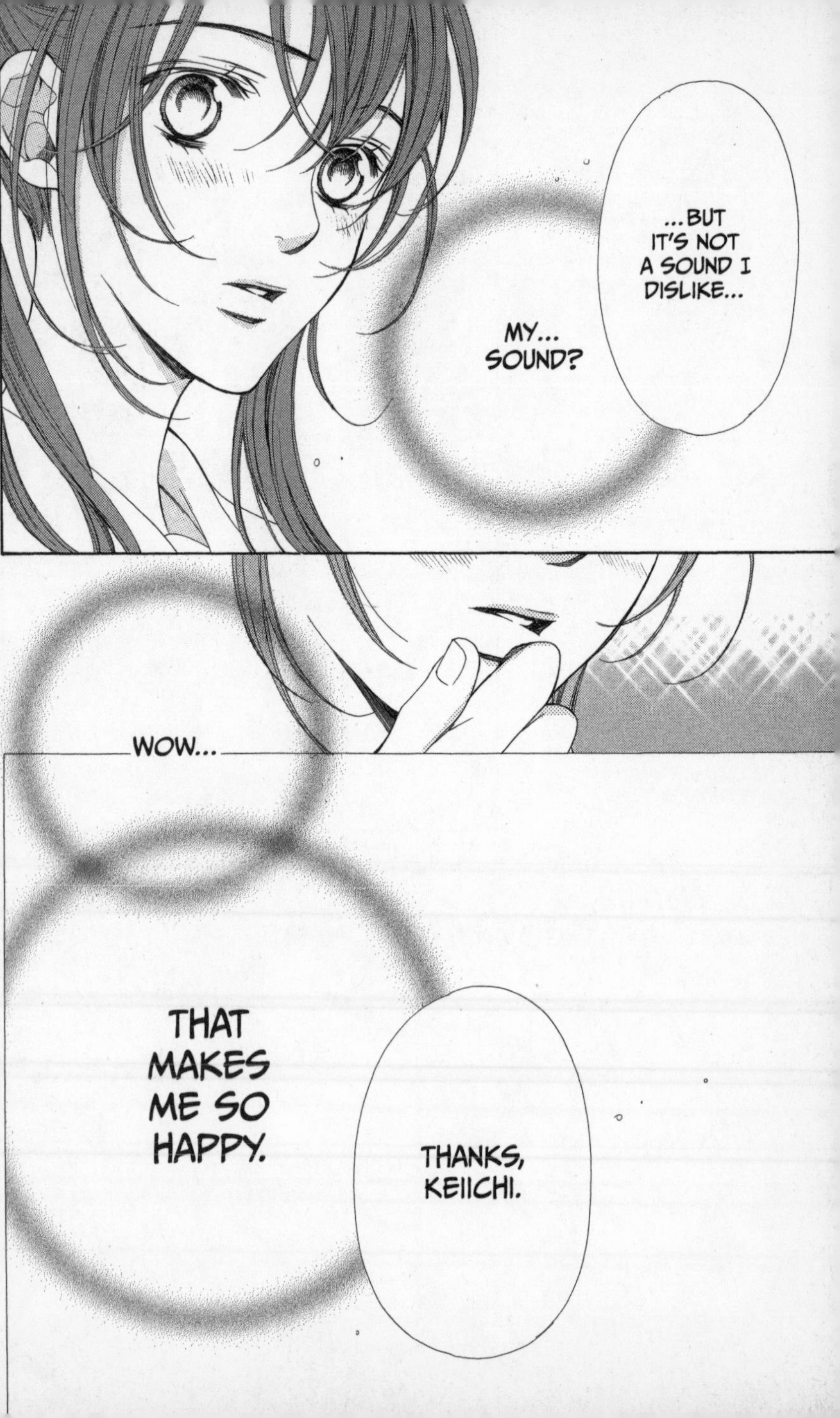
...BUT IT'S NOT A SOUND I DISLIKE...
MY... SOUND?
WOW...
THANKS, KEIICHI.
THAT MAKES ME SO HAPPY.

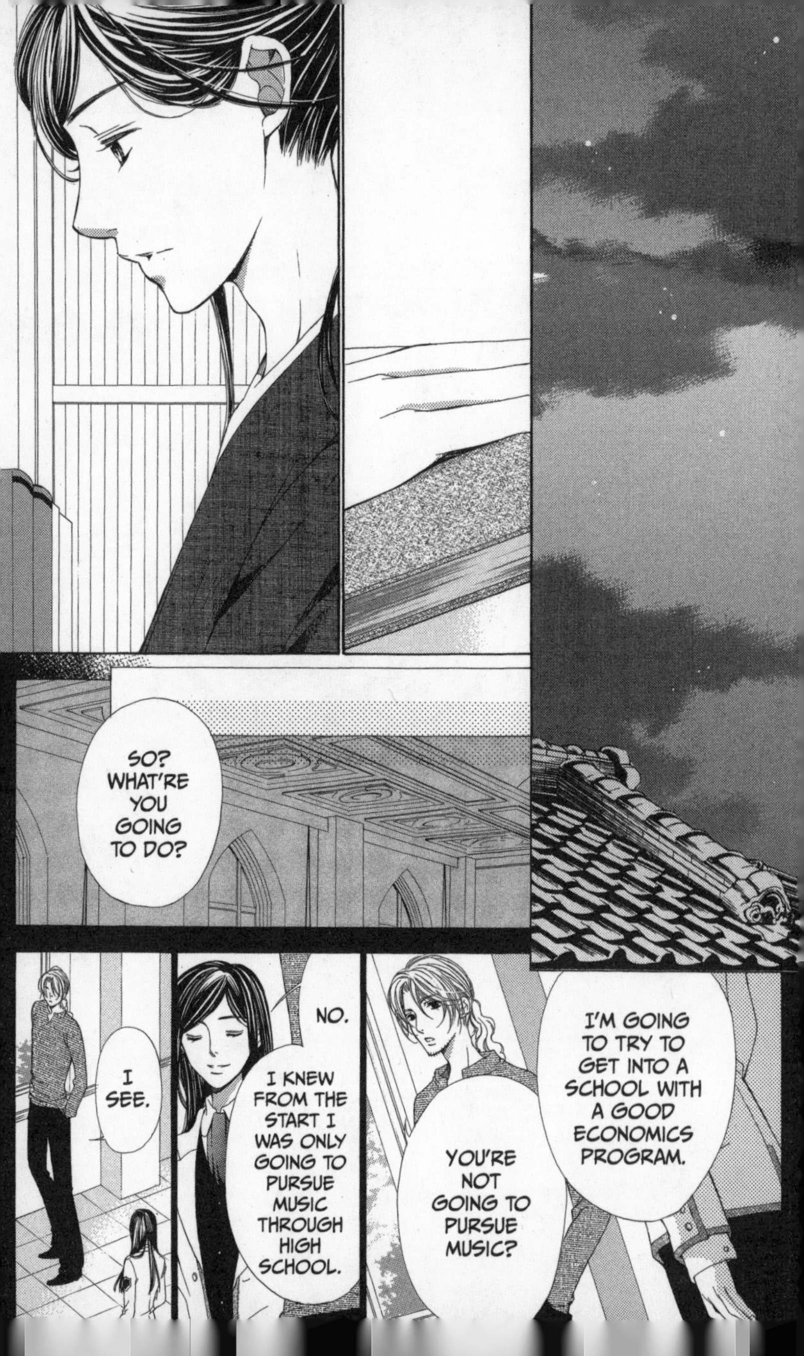
SO? WHAT'RE YOU GOING TO DO?
I'M GOING TO TRY TO GET INTO A SCHOOL WITH A GOOD ECONOMICS PROGRAM.
YOU'RE NOT GOING TO PURSUE MUSIC?
NO.
I KNEW FROM THE START I WAS ONLY GOING TO PURSUE MUSIC THROUGH HIGH SCHOOL.
I SEE.

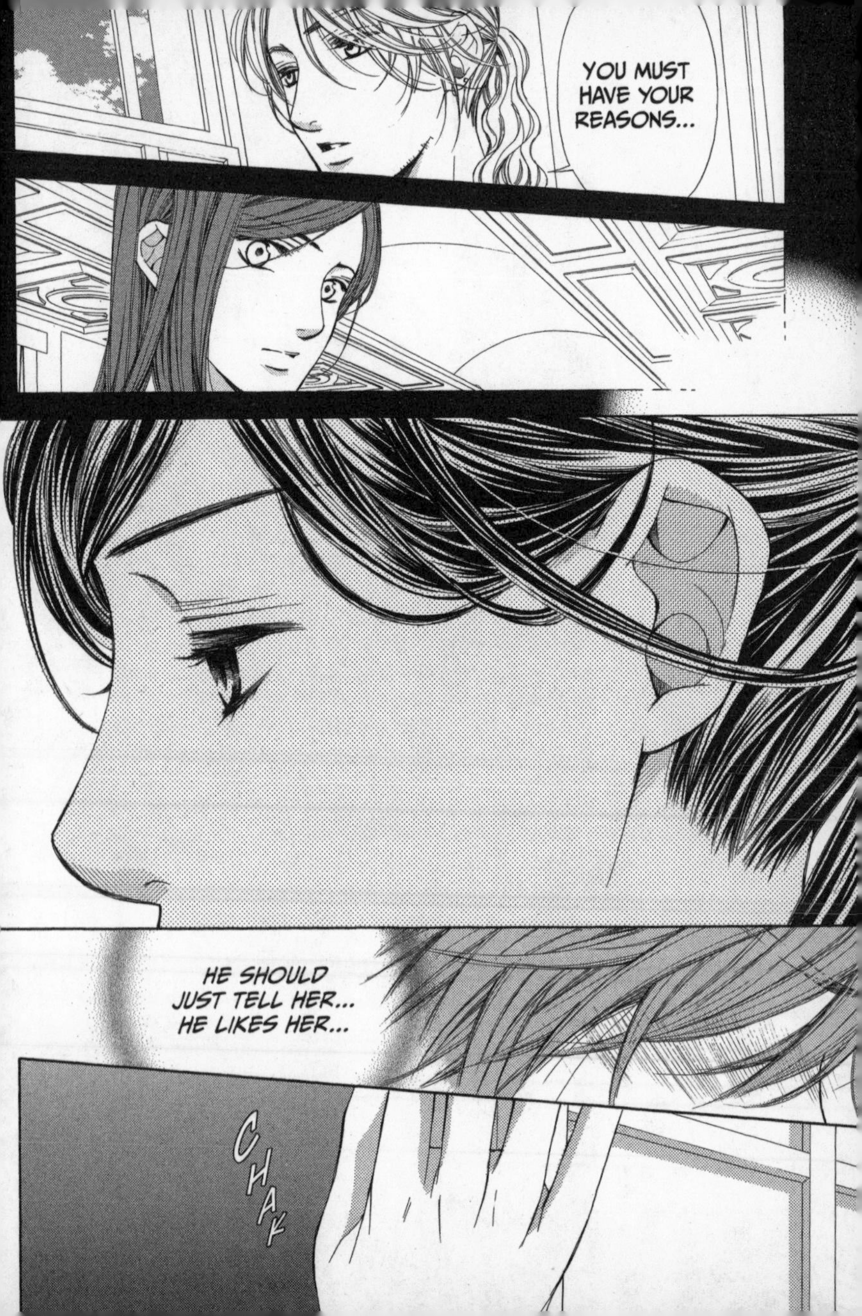
YOU MUST HAVE YOUR REASONS...
HE SHOULD JUST TELL HER... HE LIKES HER...
CHAK

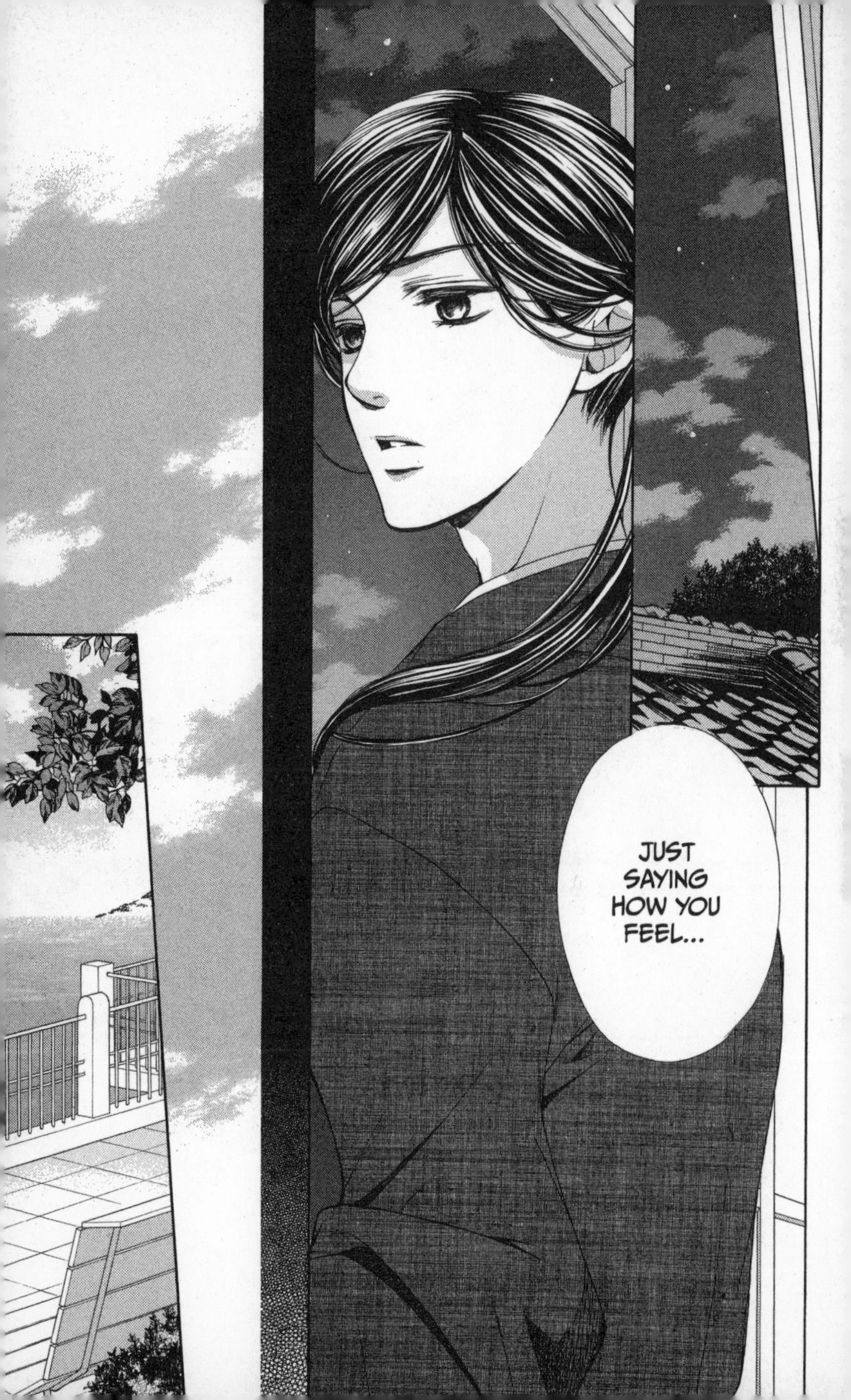
JUST SAYING HOW YOU FEEL...

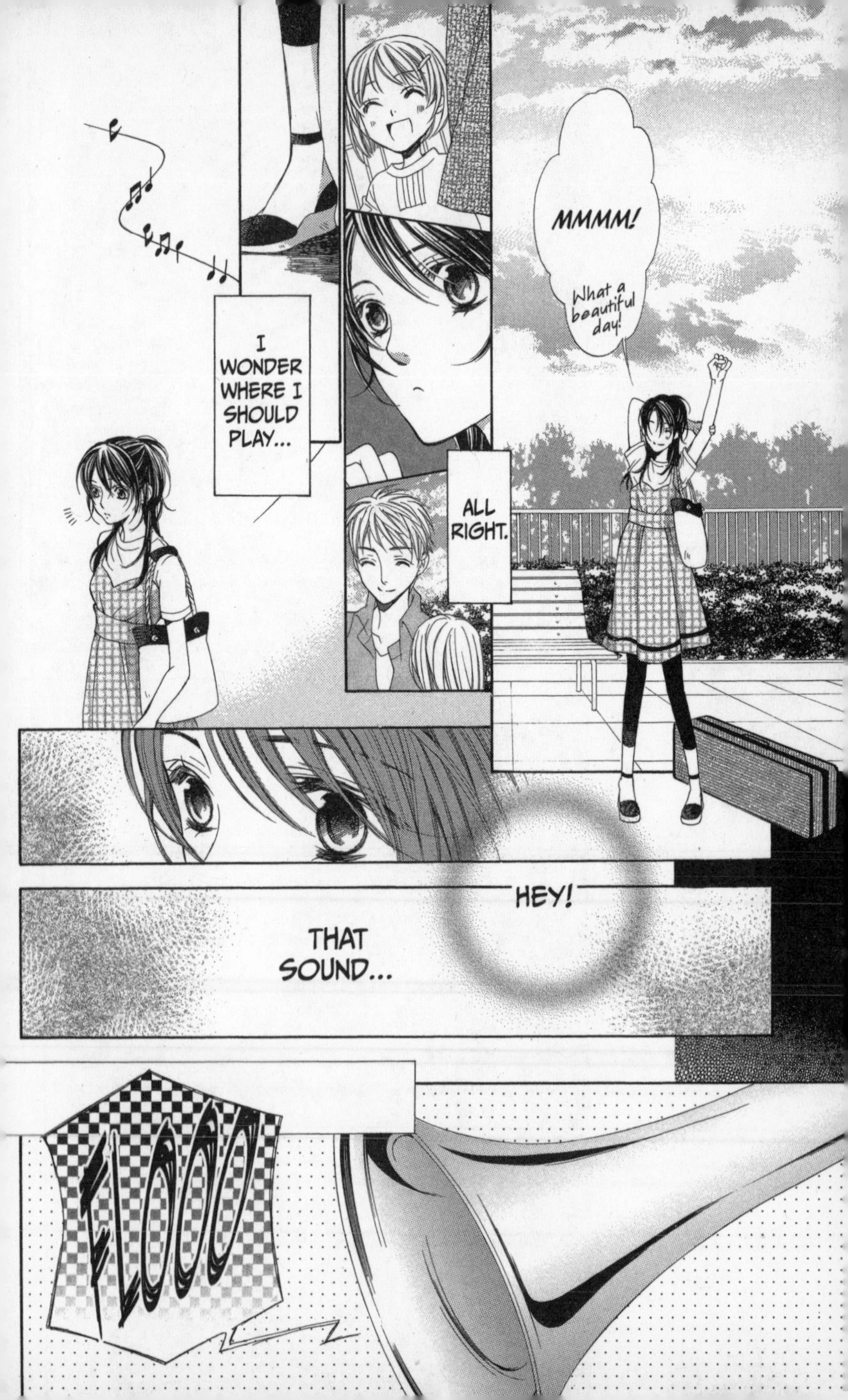
MMMM!
What a beautiful day!
ALL RIGHT.
I WONDER WHERE I SHOULD PLAY...
HEY!
THAT SOUND...
FLOOO!

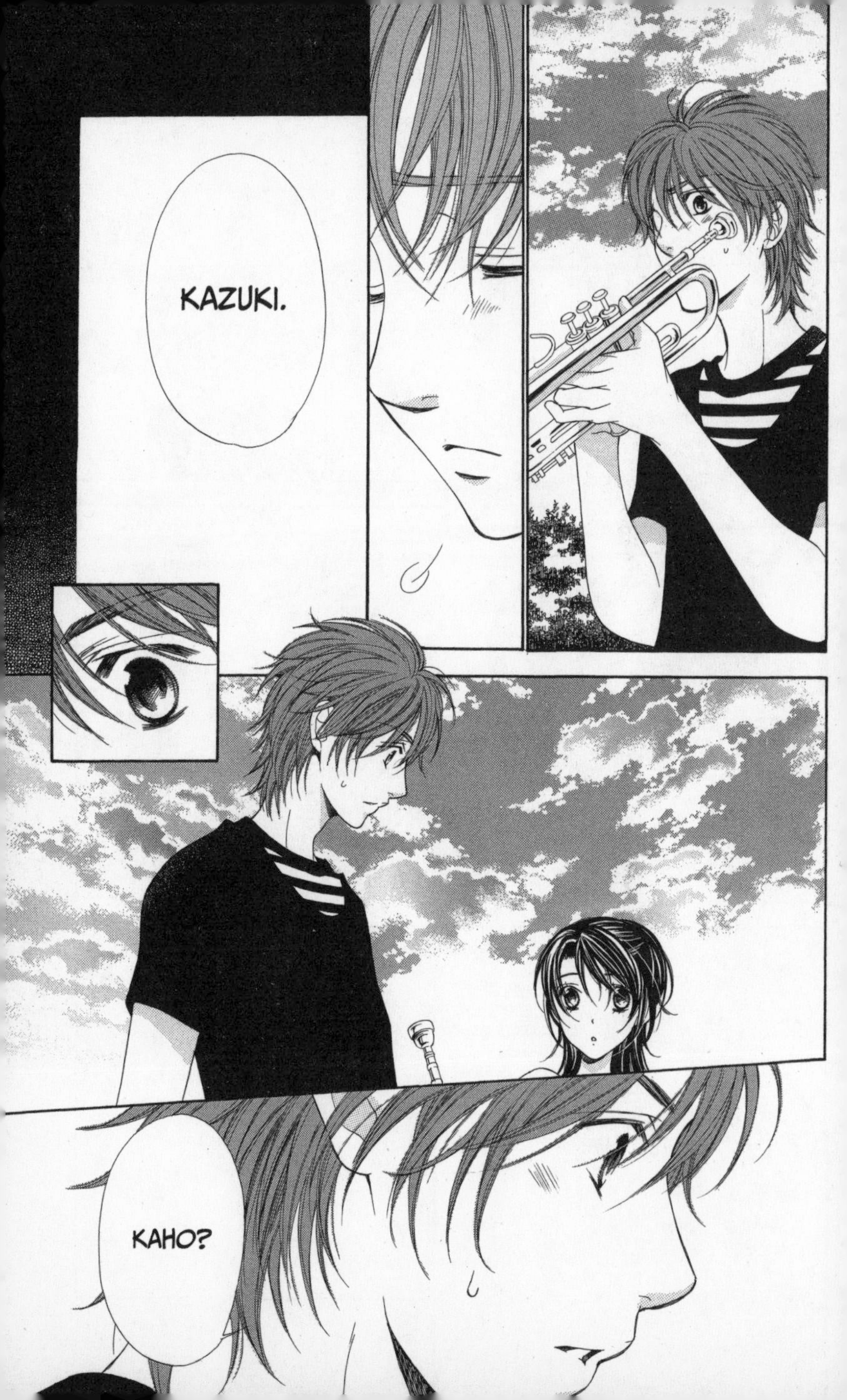
KAZUKI.
KAHO?

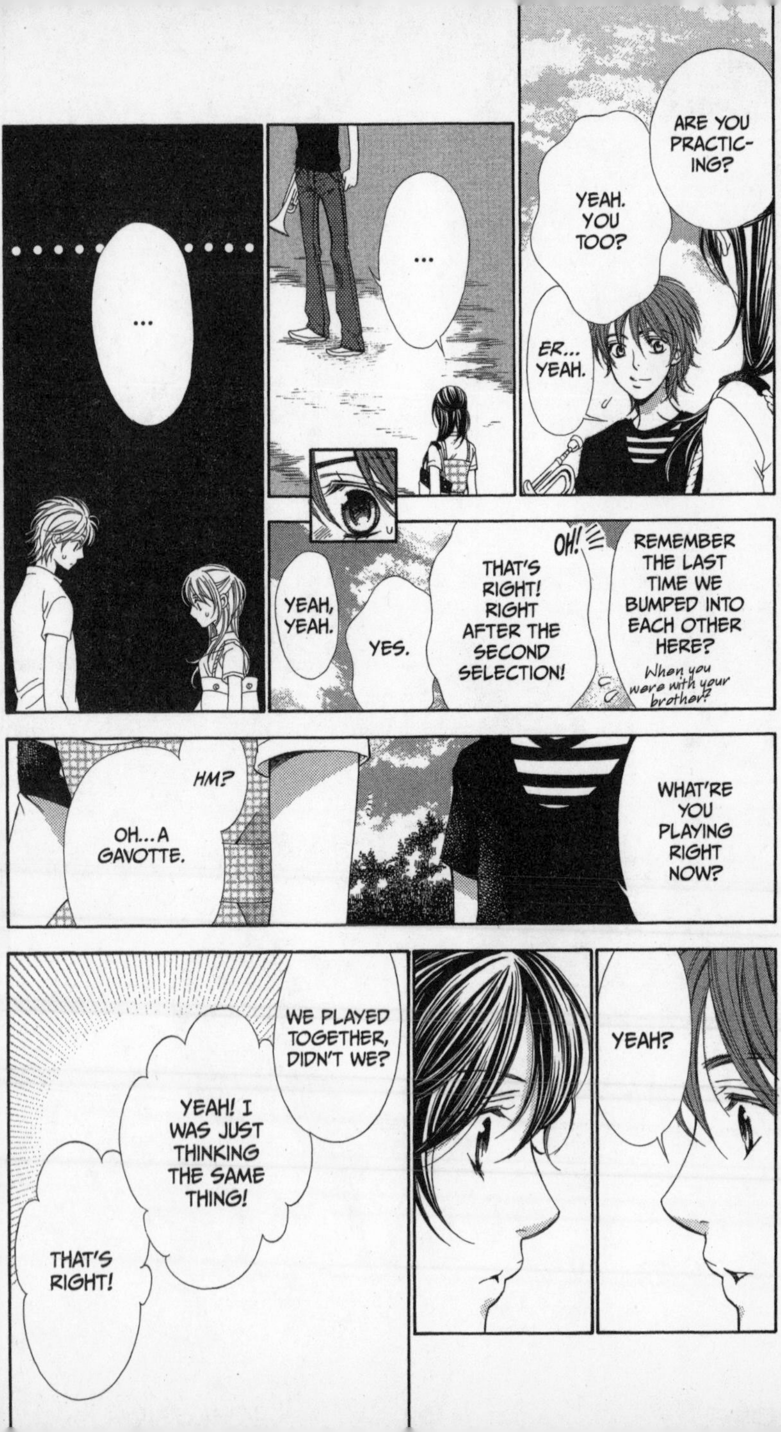
ARE YOU PRACTICING?
YEAH. YOU TOO?
ER... YEAH.
...
REMEMBER THE LAST TIME WE BUMPED INTO EACH OTHER HERE?
When you were with your brother?
OH!
THAT'S RIGHT! RIGHT AFTER THE SECOND SELECTION!
YES.
YEAH, YEAH.
...
WHAT'RE YOU PLAYING RIGHT NOW?
HM?
OH...A GAVOTTE.
YEAH?
WE PLAYED TOGETHER, DIDN'T WE?
YEAH! I WAS JUST THINKING THE SAME THING!
THAT'S RIGHT!

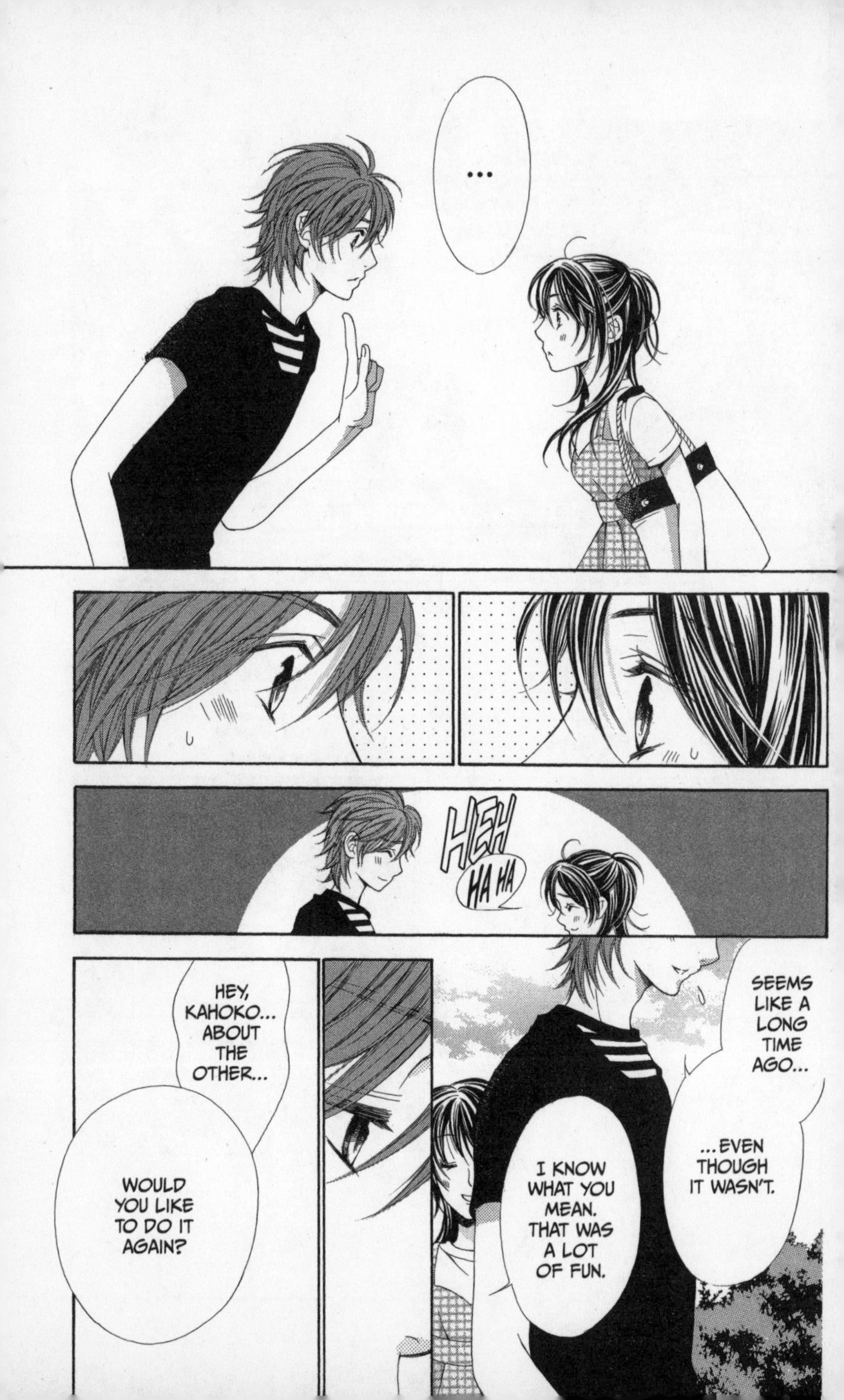
...
HEH
HA HA
SEEMS LIKE A LONG TIME AGO...
...EVEN THOUGH IT WASN'T.
I KNOW WHAT YOU MEAN. THAT WAS A LOT OF FUN.
HEY, KAHOKO... ABOUT THE OTHER...
WOULD YOU LIKE TO DO IT AGAIN?

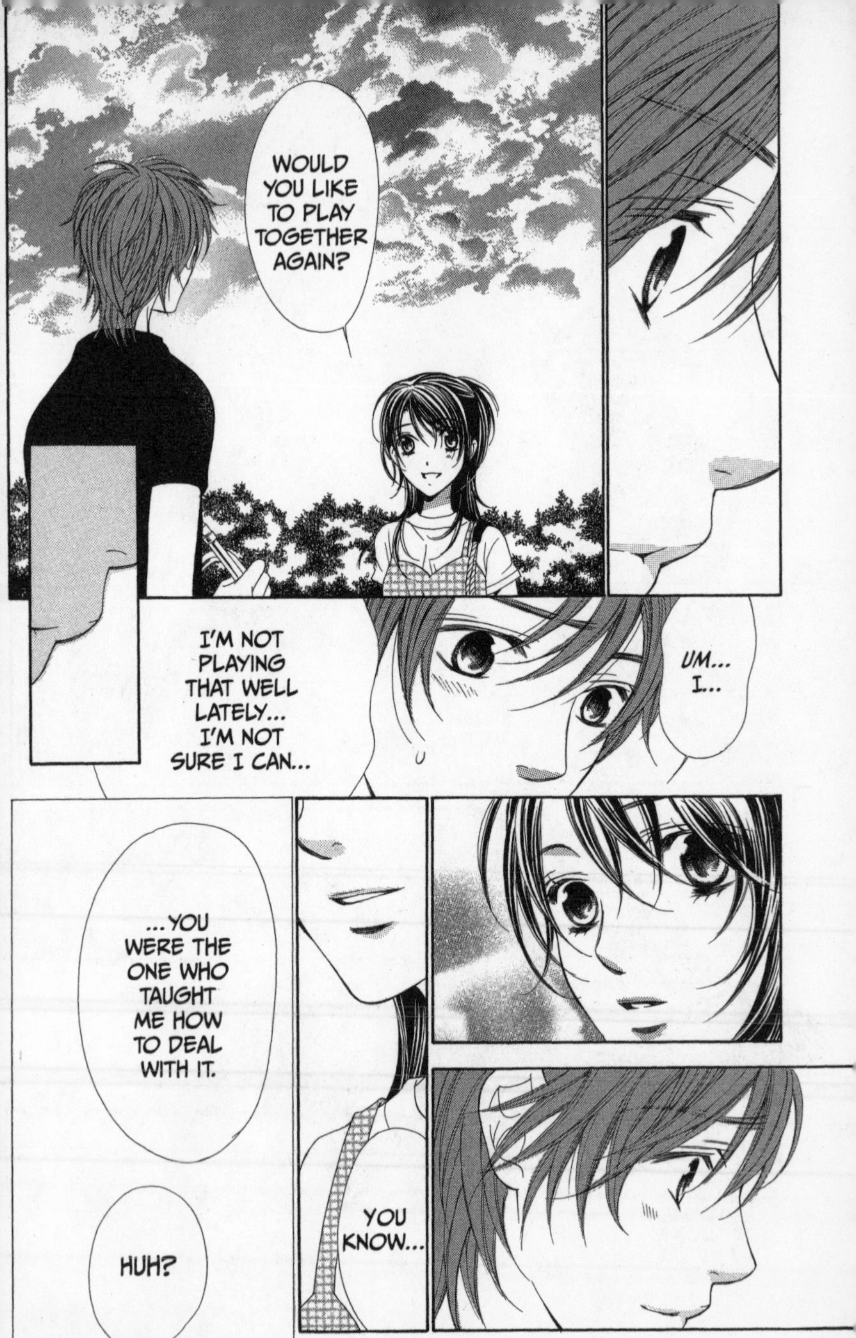
WOULD YOU LIKE TO PLAY TOGETHER AGAIN?
UM... I...
I'M NOT PLAYING THAT WELL LATELY... I'M NOT SURE I CAN...
YOU KNOW...
...YOU WERE THE ONE WHO TAUGHT ME HOW TO DEAL WITH IT.
HUH?

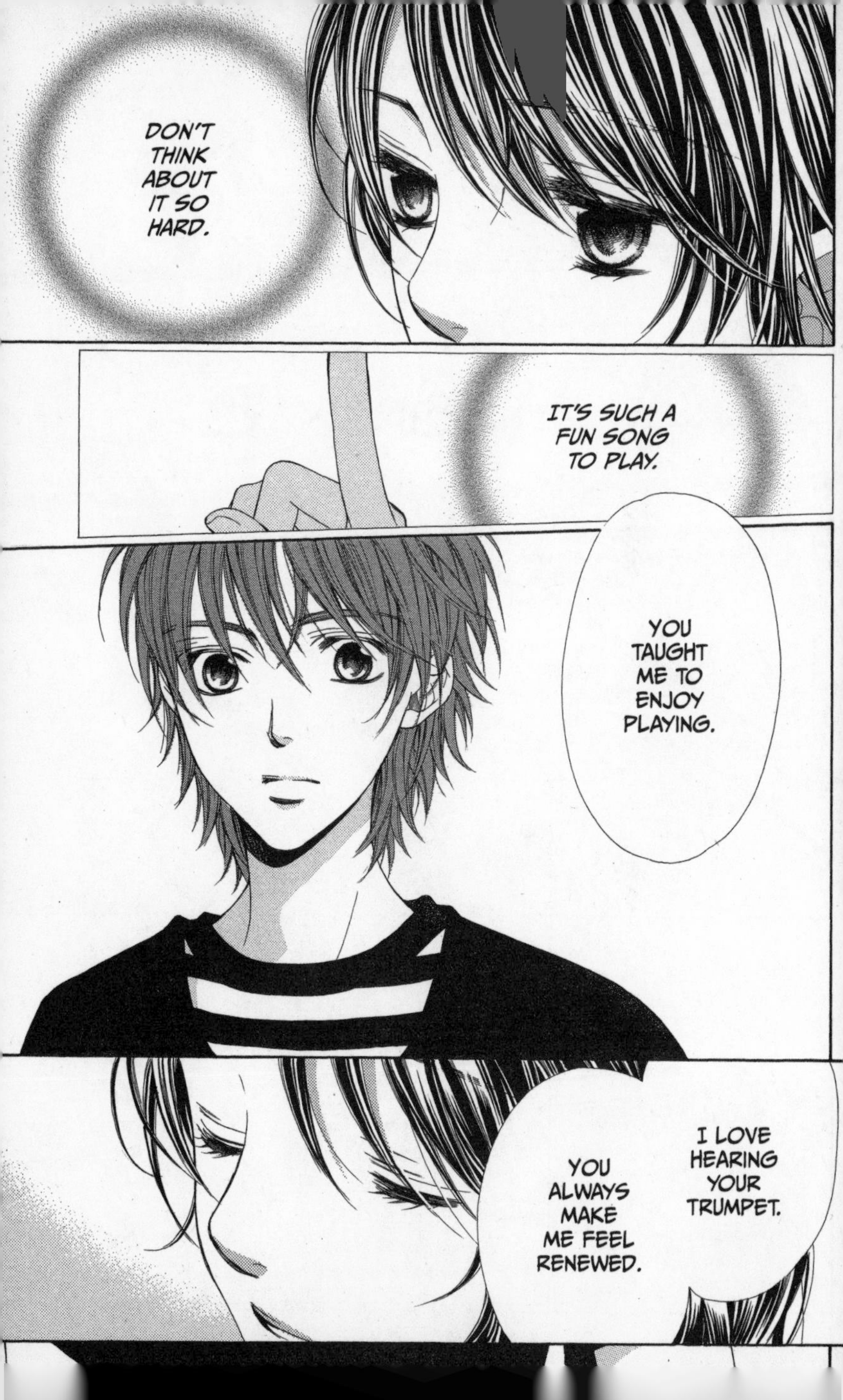
DON'T THINK ABOUT IT SO HARD.
IT'S SUCH A FUN SONG TO PLAY.
YOU TAUGHT ME TO ENJOY PLAYING.
I LOVE HEARING YOUR TRUMPET.
YOU ALWAYS MAKE ME FEEL RENEWED.

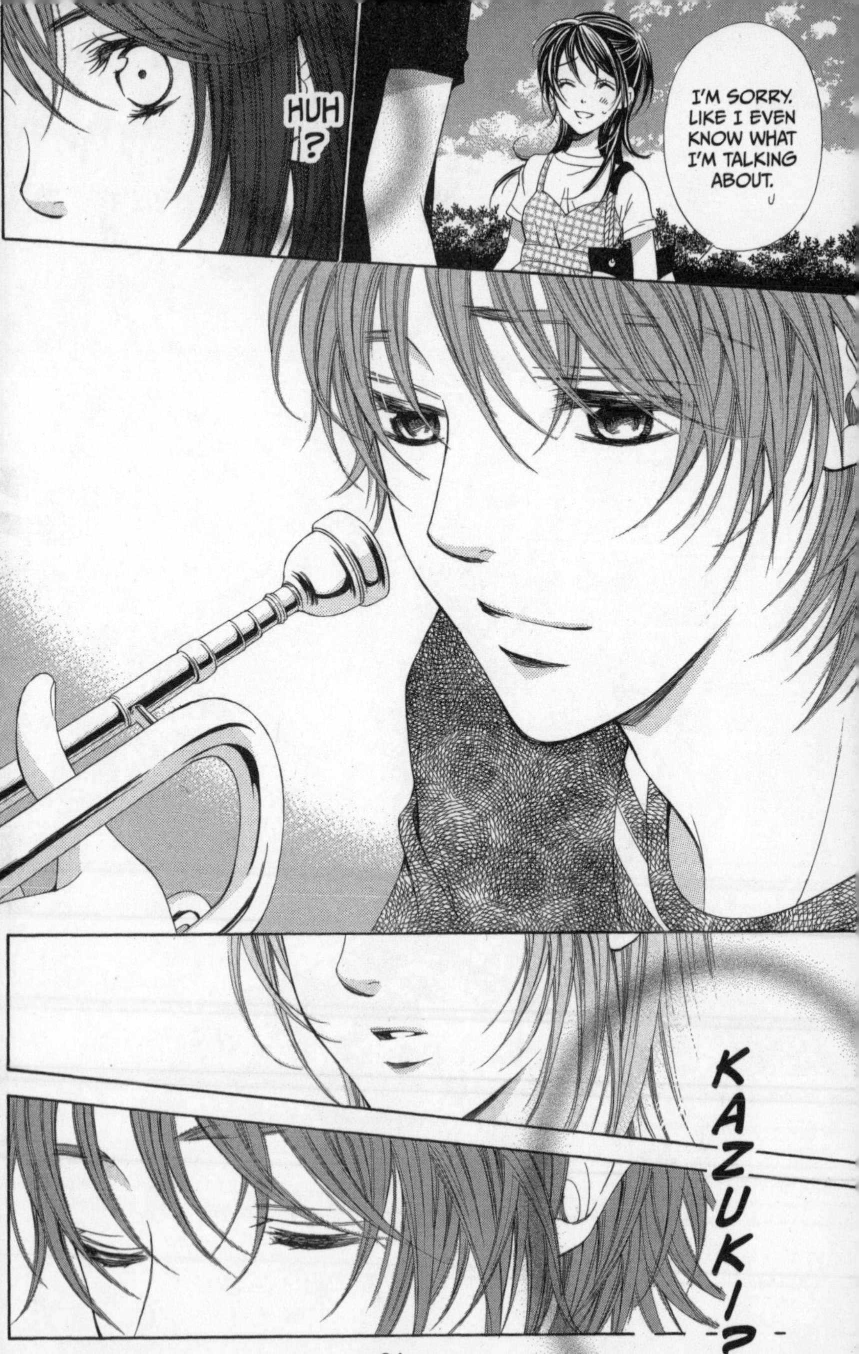
I'M SORRY. LIKE I EVEN KNOW WHAT I'M TALKING ABOUT.
HUH ?
KAZUKI!?

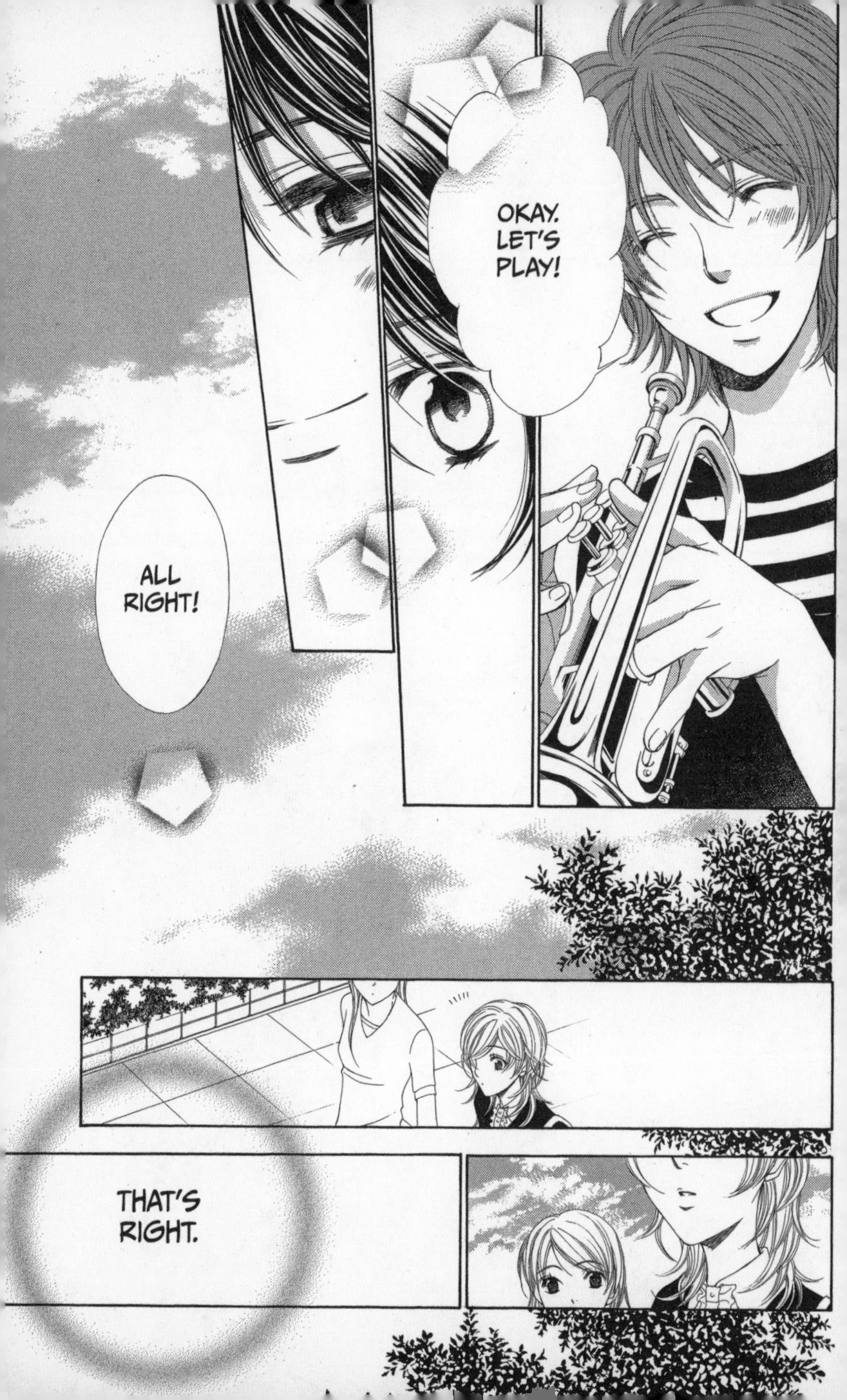
OKAY. LET'S PLAY!
ALL RIGHT!
THAT'S RIGHT.

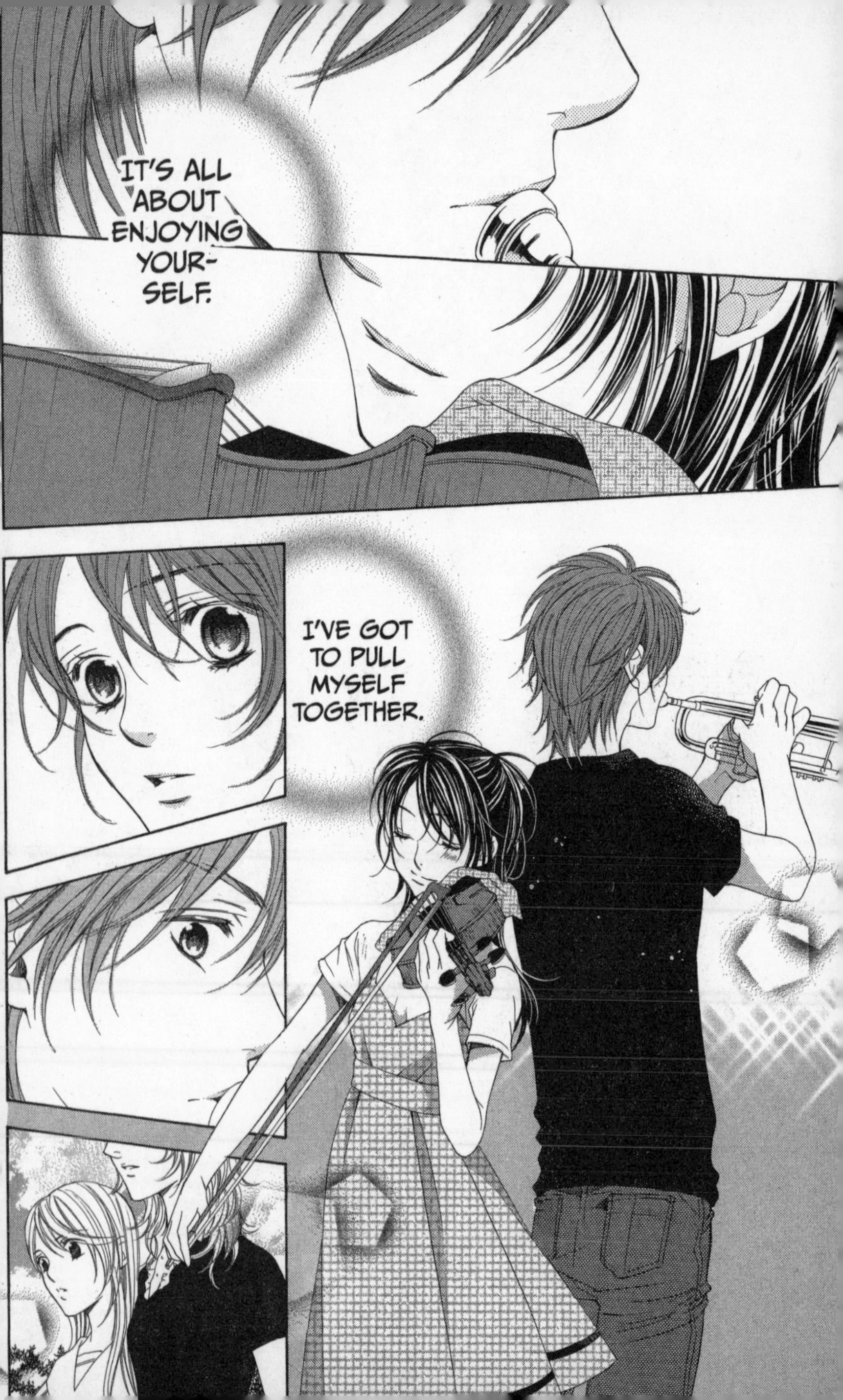
IT'S ALL ABOUT ENJOYING YOUR-SELF.
I'VE GOT TO PULL MYSELF TOGETHER.

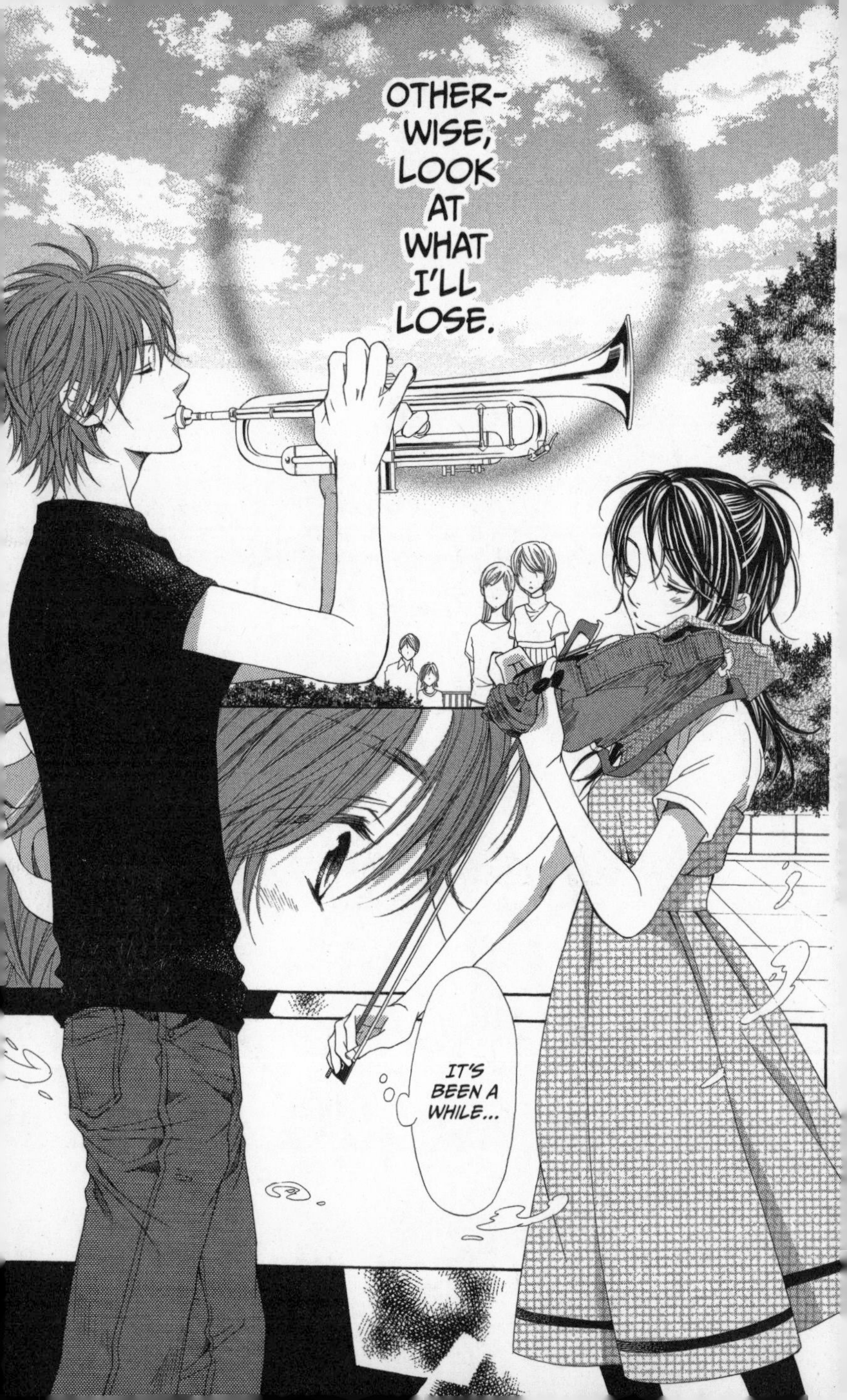
OTHER-WISE, LOOK AT WHAT I'LL LOSE.
IT'S BEEN A WHILE...

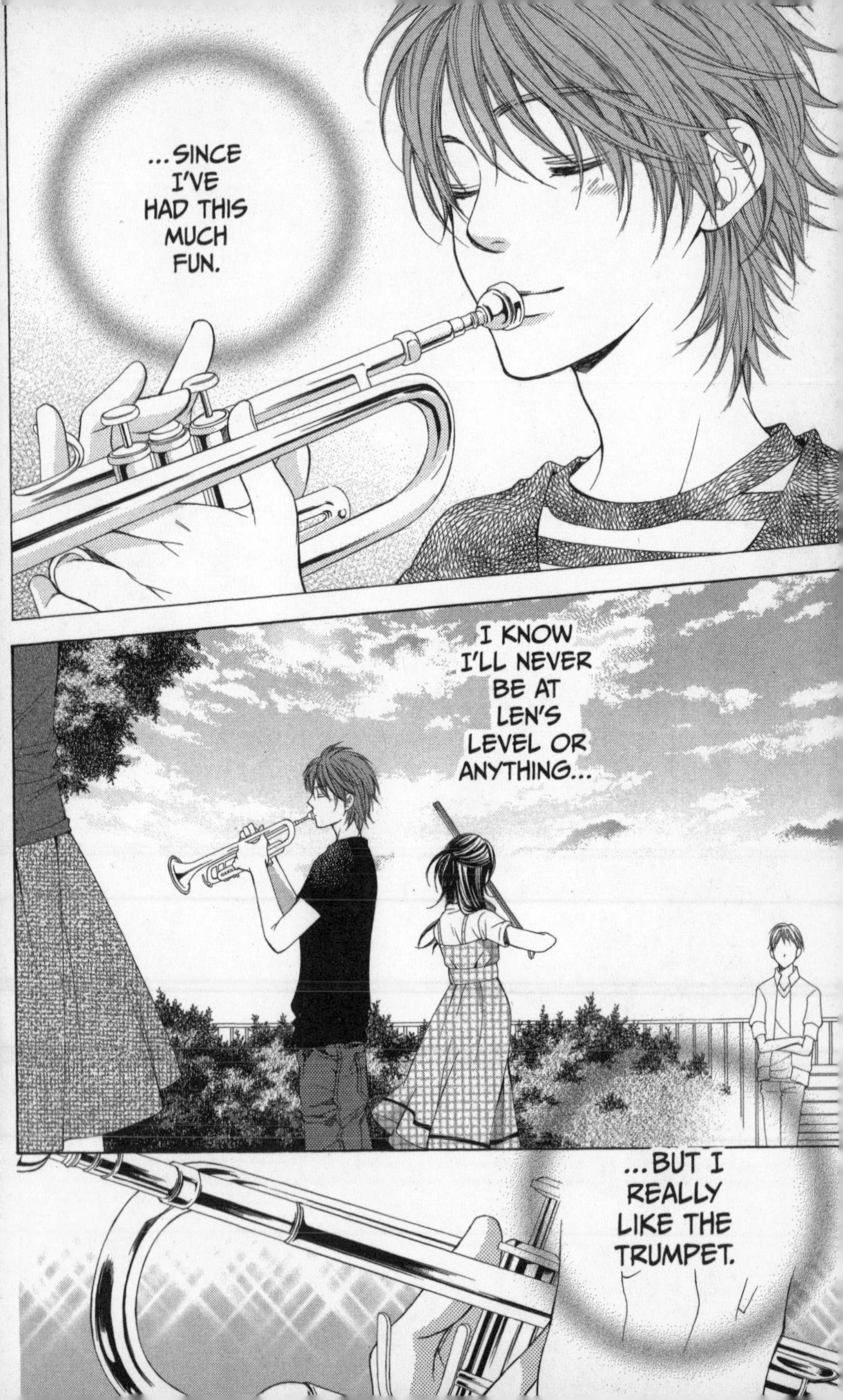
...SINCE I'VE HAD THIS MUCH FUN.
I KNOW I'LL NEVER BE AT LEN'S LEVEL OR ANYTHING...
...BUT I REALLY LIKE THE TRUMPET.

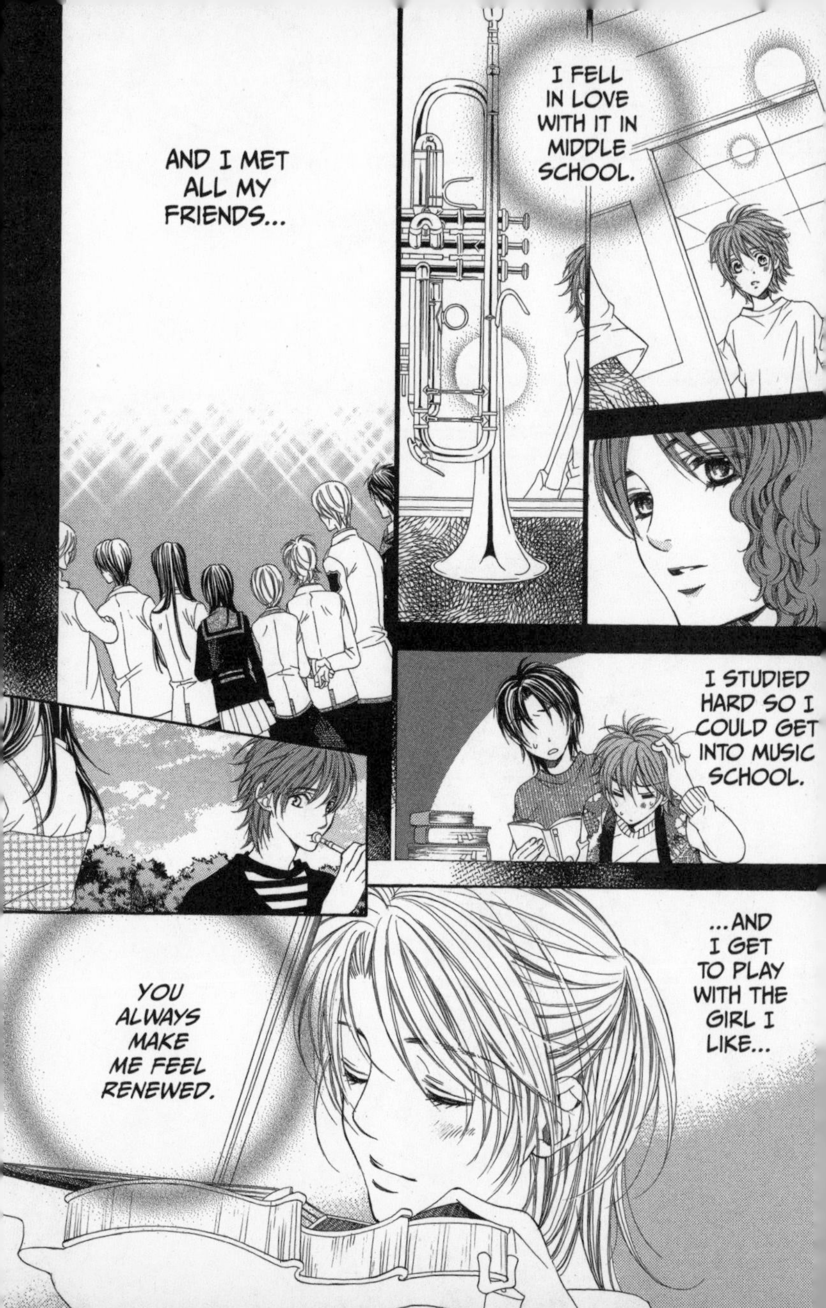
I FELL IN LOVE WITH IT IN MIDDLE SCHOOL.
I STUDIED HARD SO I COULD GET INTO MUSIC SCHOOL.
AND I MET ALL MY FRIENDS...
...AND I GET TO PLAY WITH THE GIRL I LIKE...
YOU ALWAYS MAKE ME FEEL RENEWED.

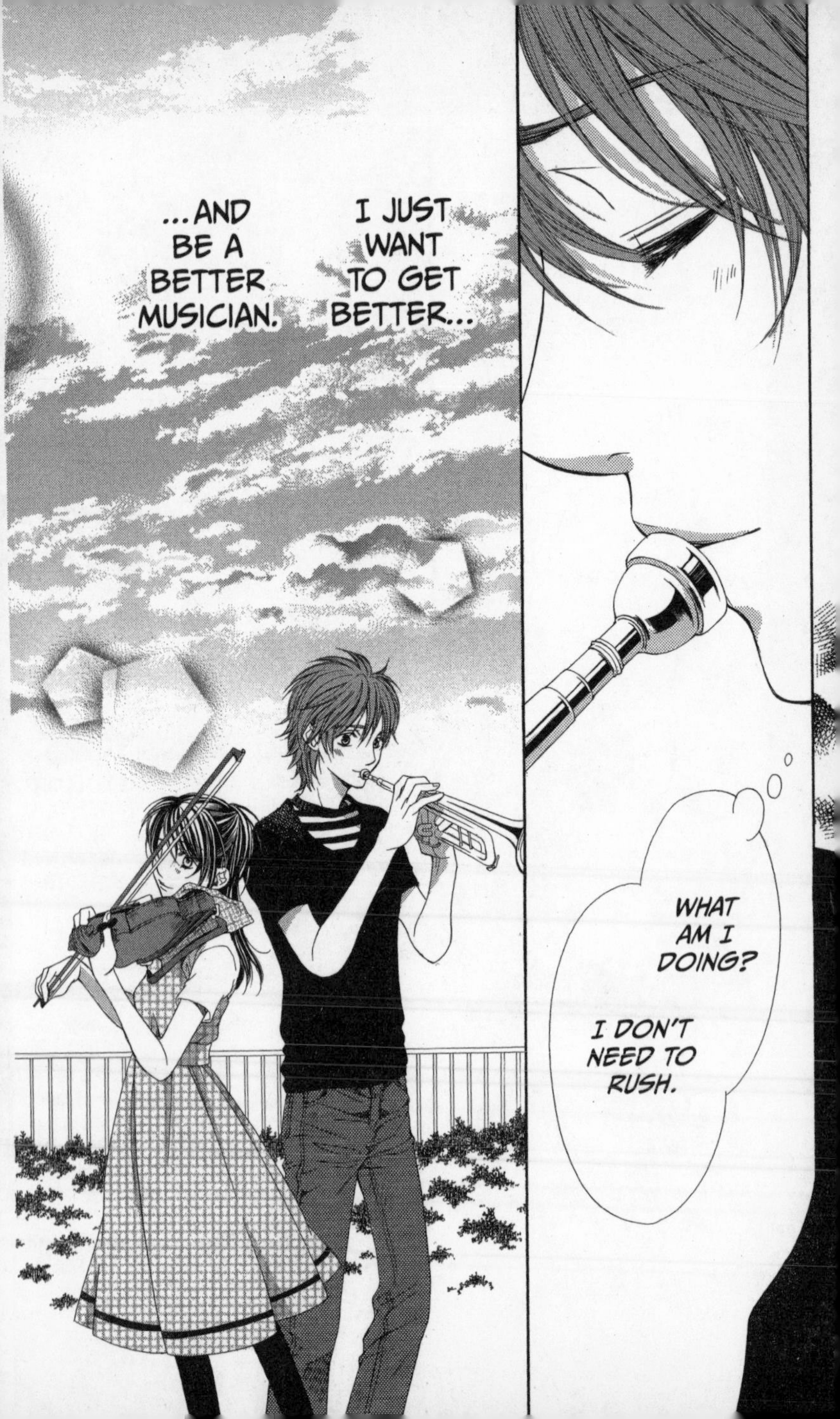
WHAT AM I DOING?
I DON'T NEED TO RUSH.
I JUST WANT TO GET BETTER...
...AND BE A BETTER MUSICIAN.

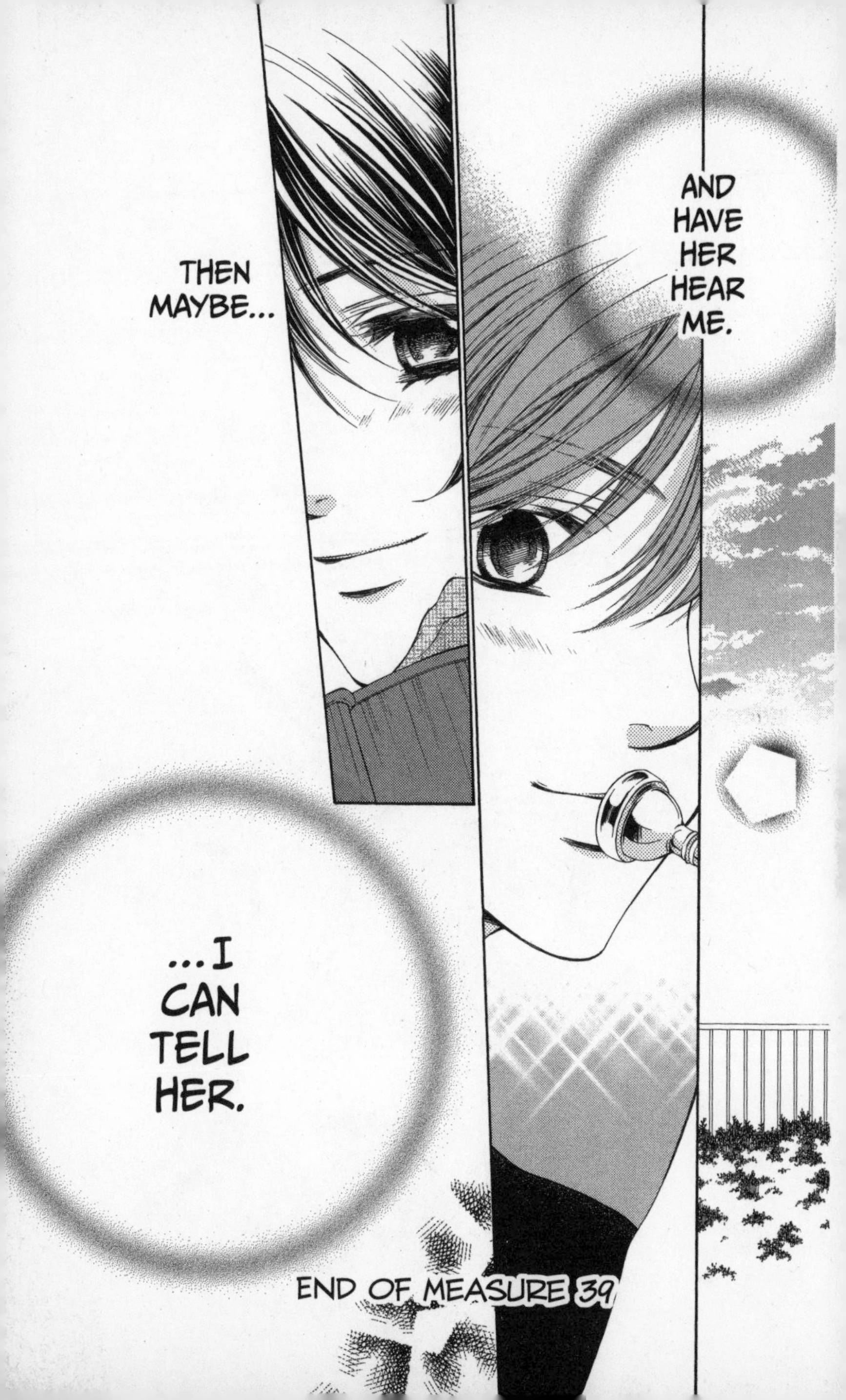
THEN MAYBE...
...I CAN TELL HER.
AND HAVE HER HEAR ME.
END OF MEASURE 39

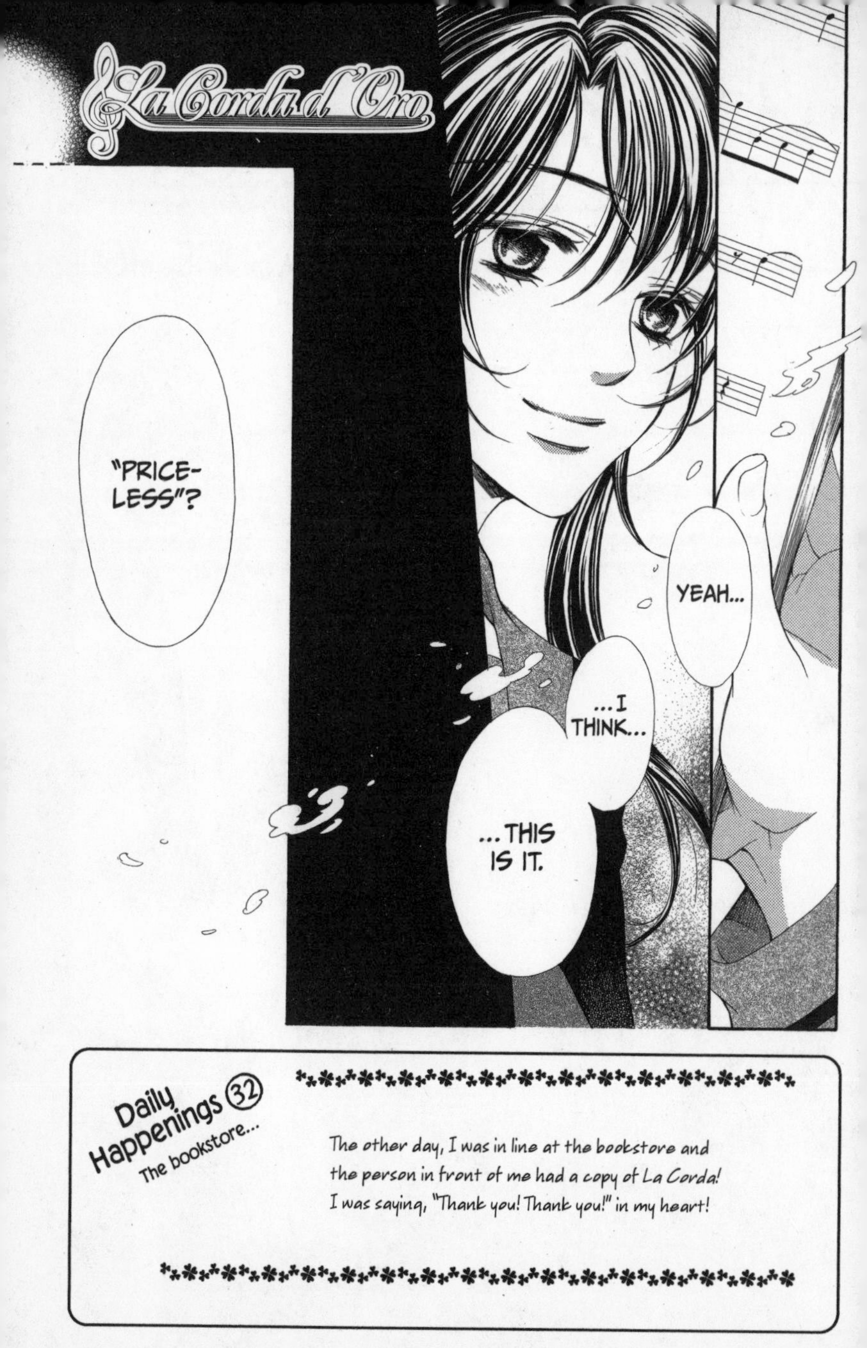
YEAH...
...I THINK...
...THIS IS IT.
"PRICE-LESS"?

**Daily Happenings ㉜**
**The bookstore...**

The other day, I was in line at the bookstore and the person in front of me had a copy of La Corda! I was saying, "Thank you! Thank you!" in my heart!

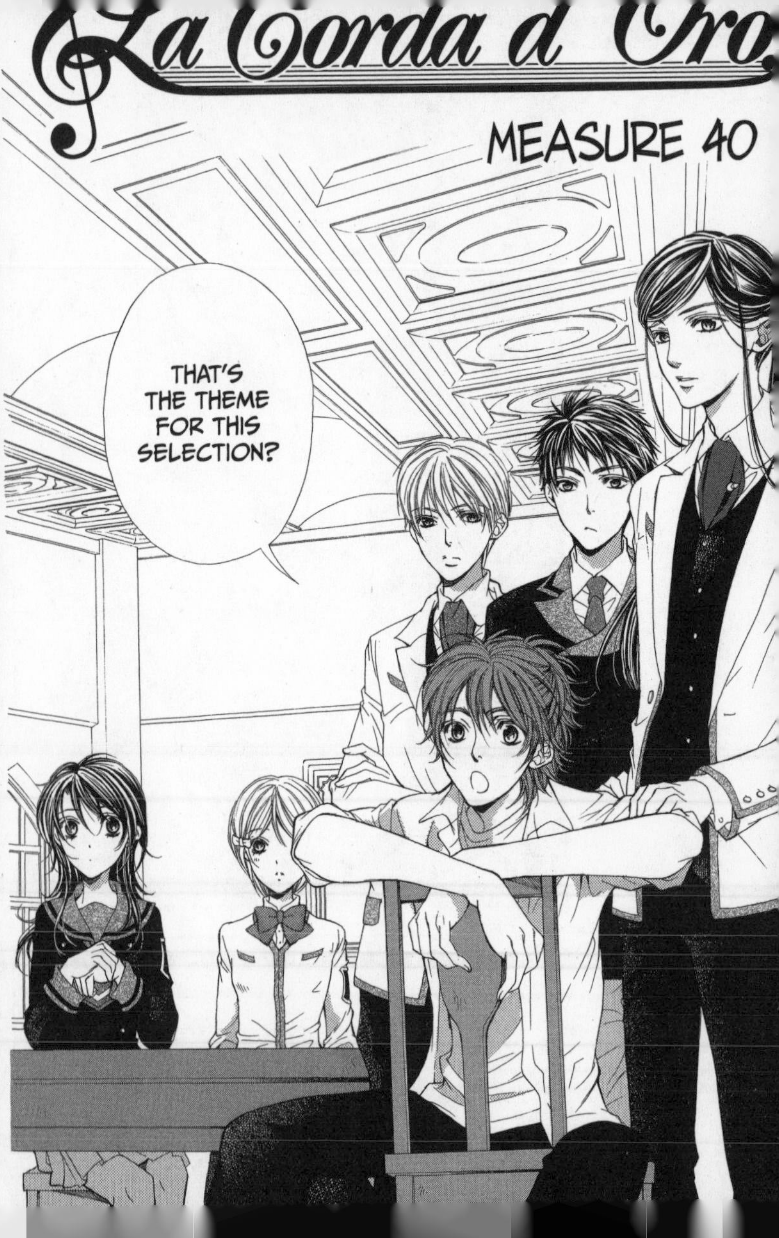
La Corda d'Oro
MEASURE 40
THAT'S THE THEME FOR THIS SELECTION?

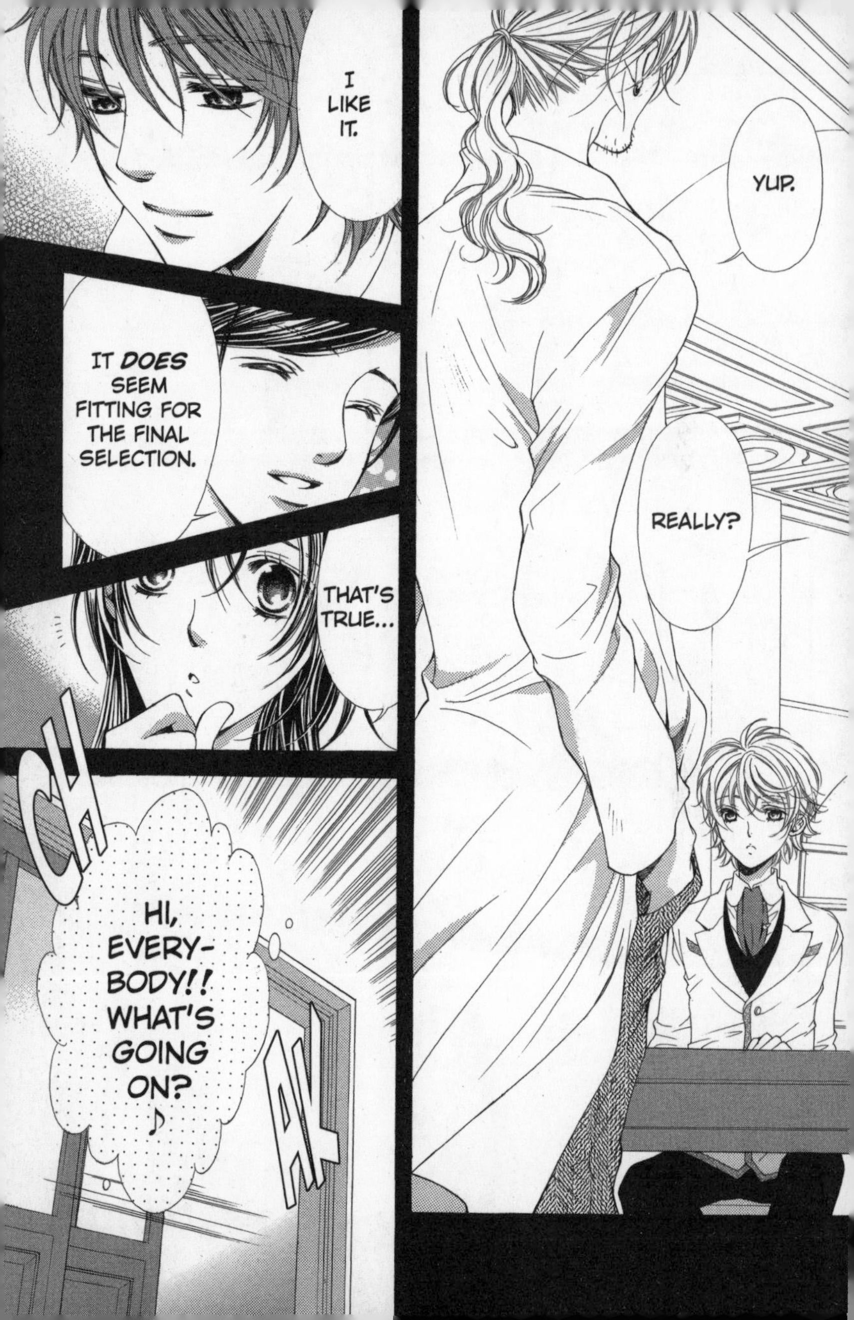
YUP.
REALLY?
I LIKE IT.
IT *DOES* SEEM FITTING FOR THE FINAL SELECTION.
THAT'S TRUE...
CH
HI, EVERY-BODY!! WHAT'S GOING ON? ♪
A

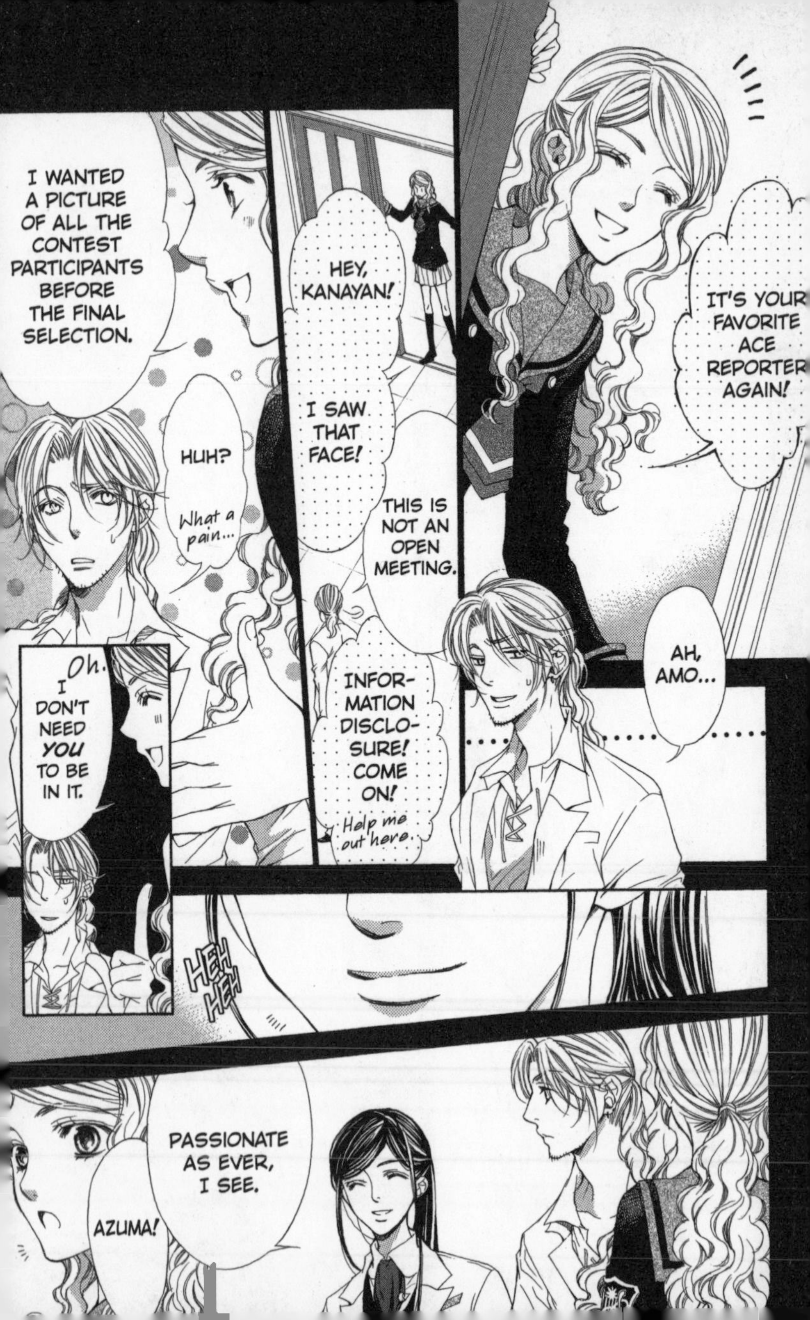
IT'S YOUR FAVORITE ACE REPORTER AGAIN!
AH, AMO...
HEY, KANAYAN!
I SAW THAT FACE!
THIS IS NOT AN OPEN MEETING.
INFORMATION DISCLOSURE! COME ON!
Help me out here.
I WANTED A PICTURE OF ALL THE CONTEST PARTICIPANTS BEFORE THE FINAL SELECTION.
HUH?
What a pain...
Oh.
I DON'T NEED YOU TO BE IN IT.
HEH HEH
PASSIONATE AS EVER, I SEE.
AZUMA!

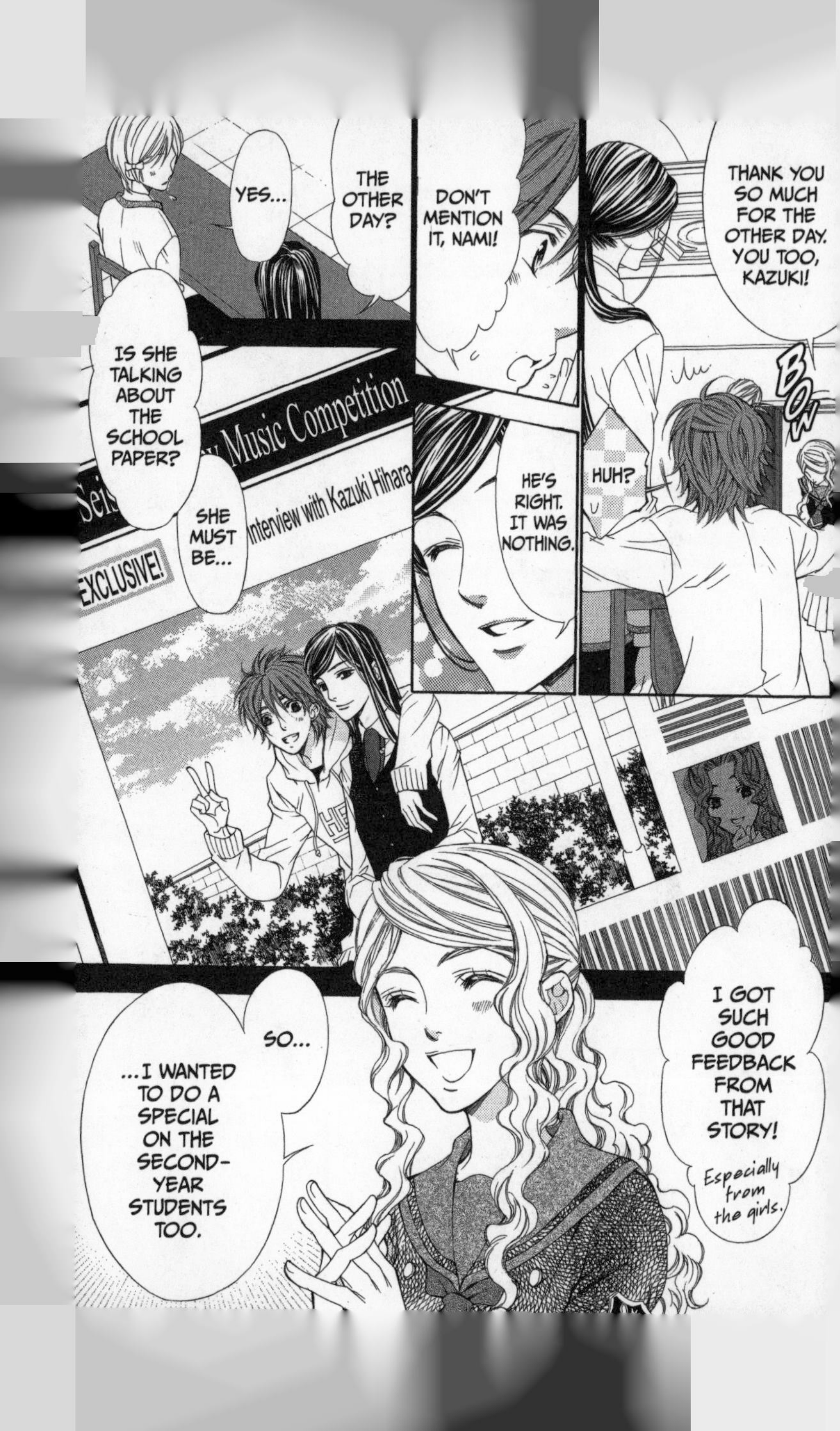
THANK YOU SO MUCH FOR THE OTHER DAY. YOU TOO, KAZUKI!
BOW
HUH?
DON'T MENTION IT, NAMI!
HE'S RIGHT. IT WAS NOTHING.
THE OTHER DAY?
YES...
IS SHE TALKING ABOUT THE SCHOOL PAPER?
SHE MUST BE...
Music Competition
Interview with Kazuki Hihara
EXCLUSIVE!
I GOT SUCH GOOD FEEDBACK FROM THAT STORY!
Especially from the girls.
SO...
...I WANTED TO DO A SPECIAL ON THE SECOND-YEAR STUDENTS TOO.

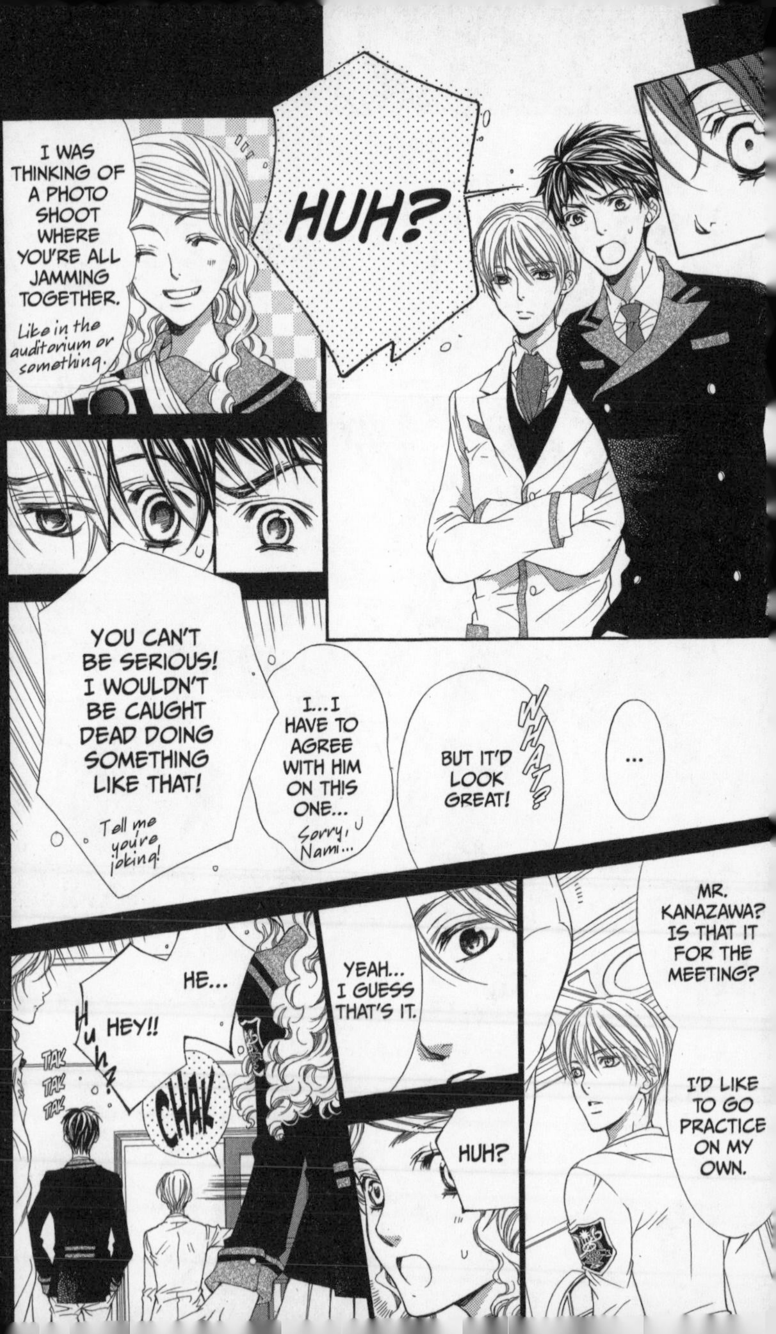
HUH?
I WAS THINKING OF A PHOTO SHOOT WHERE YOU'RE ALL JAMMING TOGETHER.
Like in the auditorium or something.
...
WHAT?
BUT IT'D LOOK GREAT!
I...I HAVE TO AGREE WITH HIM ON THIS ONE...
Sorry, Nami...
YOU CAN'T BE SERIOUS! I WOULDN'T BE CAUGHT DEAD DOING SOMETHING LIKE THAT!
Tell me you're joking!
MR. KANAZAWA? IS THAT IT FOR THE MEETING?
I'D LIKE TO GO PRACTICE ON MY OWN.
YEAH... I GUESS THAT'S IT.
HUH?
HE...
HEY!!
CHAK
TAK TAK TAK

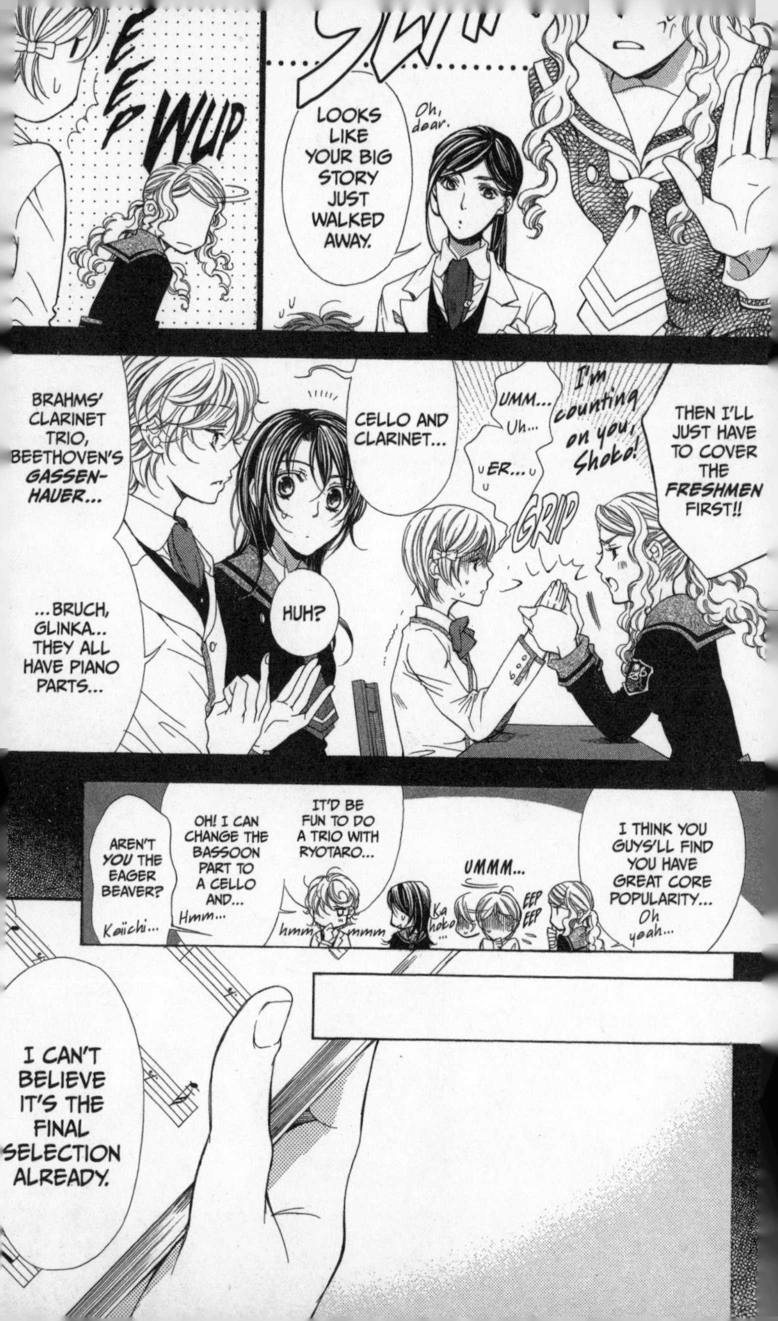
LOOKS LIKE YOUR BIG STORY JUST WALKED AWAY.
Oh, dear.
EEEP
WUP
THEN I'LL JUST HAVE TO COVER THE FRESHMEN FIRST!!
I'm counting on you, Shoko!
GRIP
UMM...
Uh...
ER...
CELLO AND CLARINET...
HUH?
BRAHMS' CLARINET TRIO, BEETHOVEN'S GASSEN-HAUER...
...BRUCH, GLINKA... THEY ALL HAVE PIANO PARTS...
I THINK YOU GUYS'LL FIND YOU HAVE GREAT CORE POPULARITY...
Oh yeah...
EEP EEP
Kahoko...
UMMM...
IT'D BE FUN TO DO A TRIO WITH RYOTARO...
hmm mmm
OH! I CAN CHANGE THE BASSOON PART TO A CELLO AND...
Hmm...
AREN'T YOU THE EAGER BEAVER?
Keiichi...
I CAN'T BELIEVE IT'S THE FINAL SELECTION ALREADY.

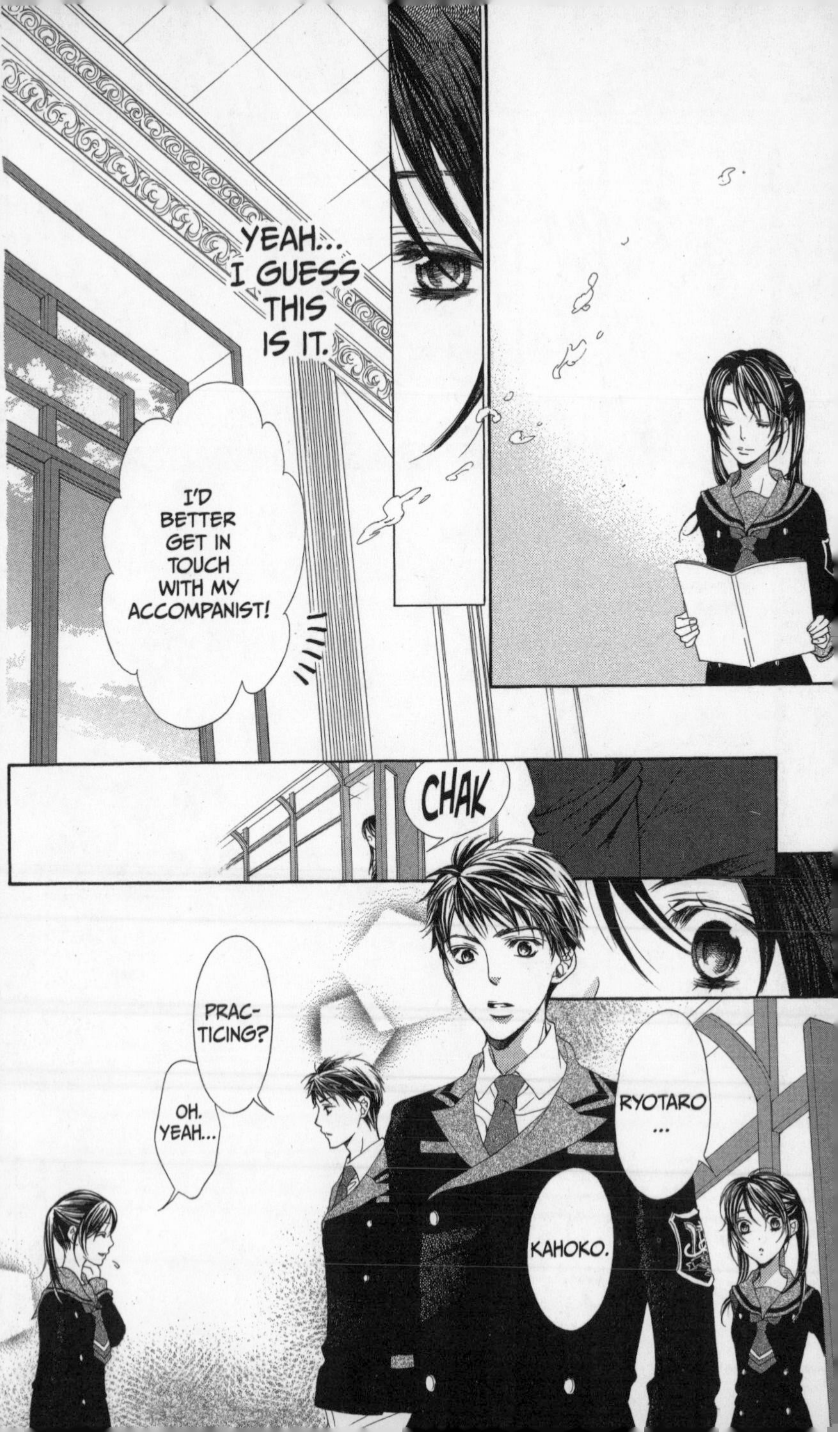
YEAH... I GUESS THIS IS IT.
I'D BETTER GET IN TOUCH WITH MY ACCOMPANIST!
CHAK
RYOTARO ...
KAHOKO.
PRAC-TICING?
OH. YEAH...

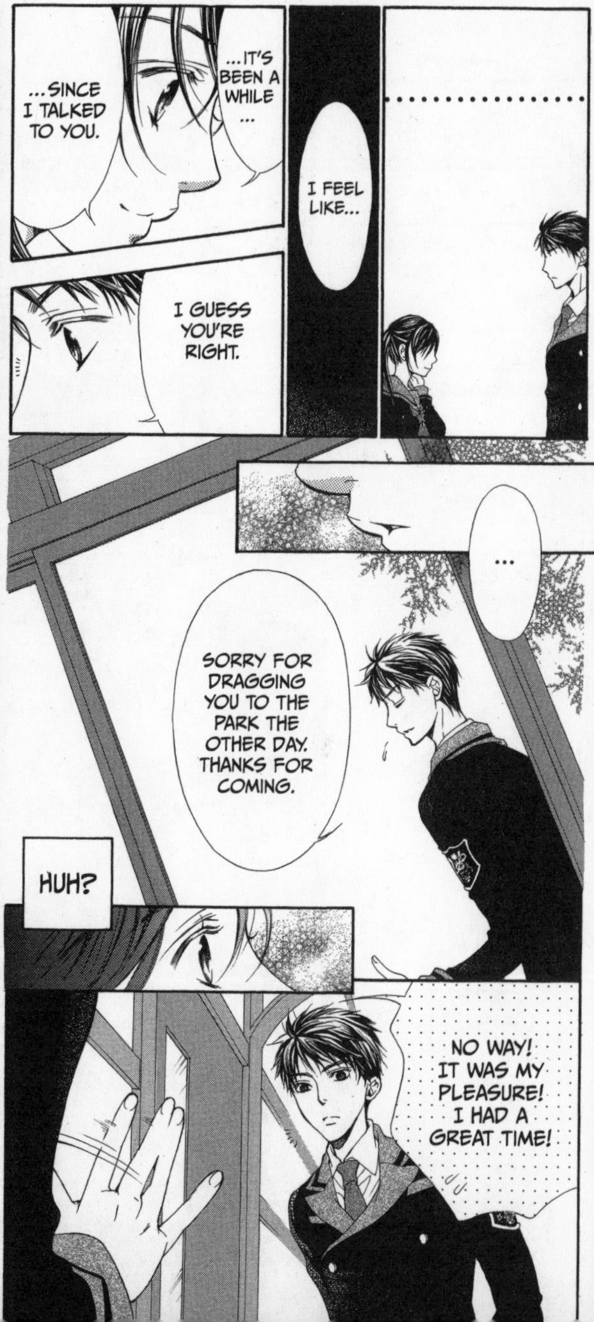

..........
I FEEL LIKE...
...IT'S BEEN A WHILE ...
...SINCE I TALKED TO YOU.
I GUESS YOU'RE RIGHT.
...
SORRY FOR DRAGGING YOU TO THE PARK THE OTHER DAY. THANKS FOR COMING.
HUH?
NO WAY! IT WAS MY PLEASURE! I HAD A GREAT TIME!


## FOUR

The Final Selection... I remember when I started this manga, I never thought I'd really get this far... (lol) Len's accompanist is a new character from the *La Corda d'Oro 2* video game. He looks completely different in the anime, though.

Still... I really like drawing him.

I plan on incorporating other characters from *La Corda d'Oro 2* in Volume 10, so please stay tuned!

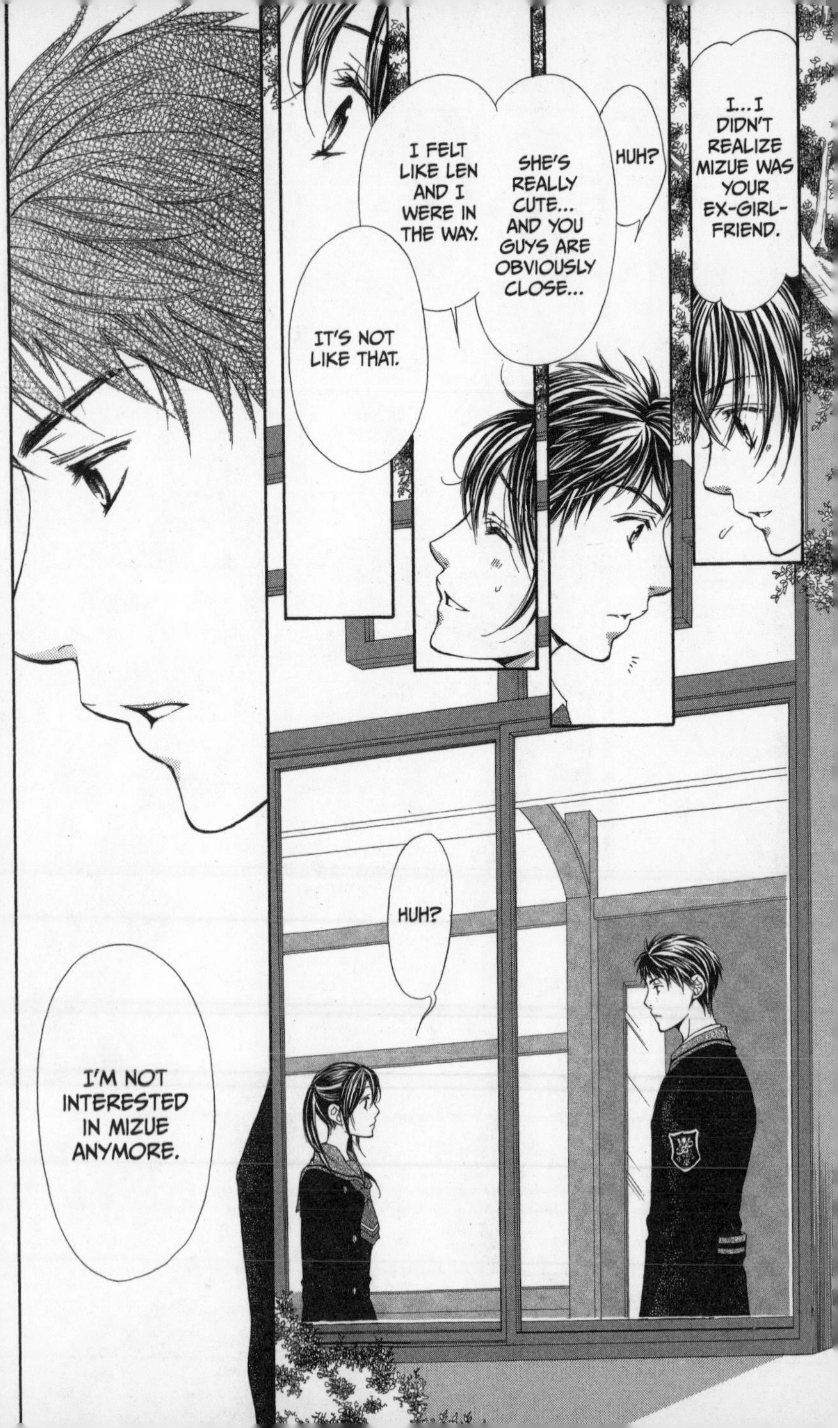
I...I DIDN'T REALIZE MIZUE WAS YOUR EX-GIRL-FRIEND.
HUH?
SHE'S REALLY CUTE... AND YOU GUYS ARE OBVIOUSLY CLOSE...
I FELT LIKE LEN AND I WERE IN THE WAY.
IT'S NOT LIKE THAT.
HUH?
I'M NOT INTERESTED IN MIZUE ANYMORE.

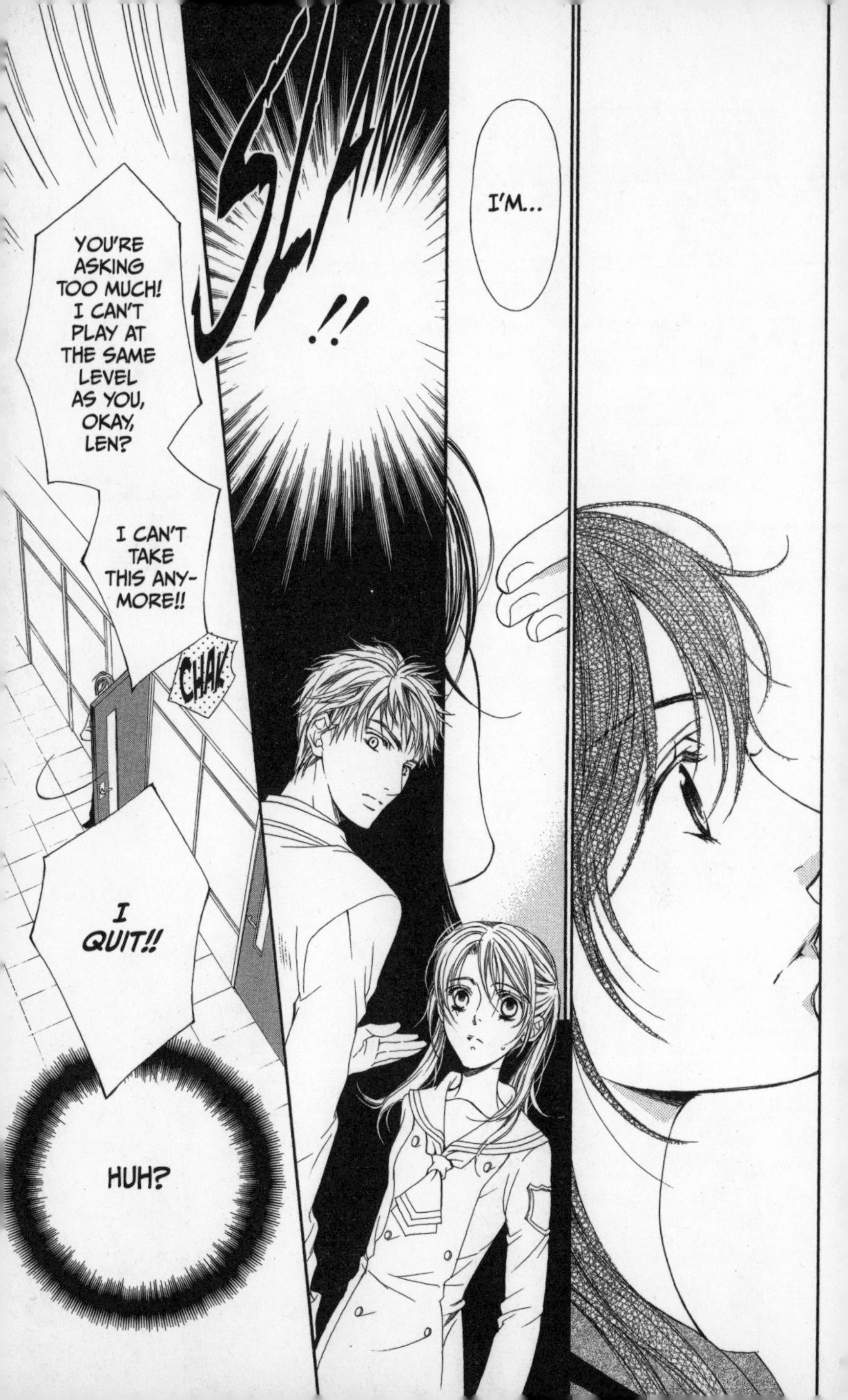
I'M...
!!
YOU'RE ASKING TOO MUCH! I CAN'T PLAY AT THE SAME LEVEL AS YOU, OKAY, LEN?
I CAN'T TAKE THIS ANY-MORE!!
CHAK
I QUIT!!
HUH?

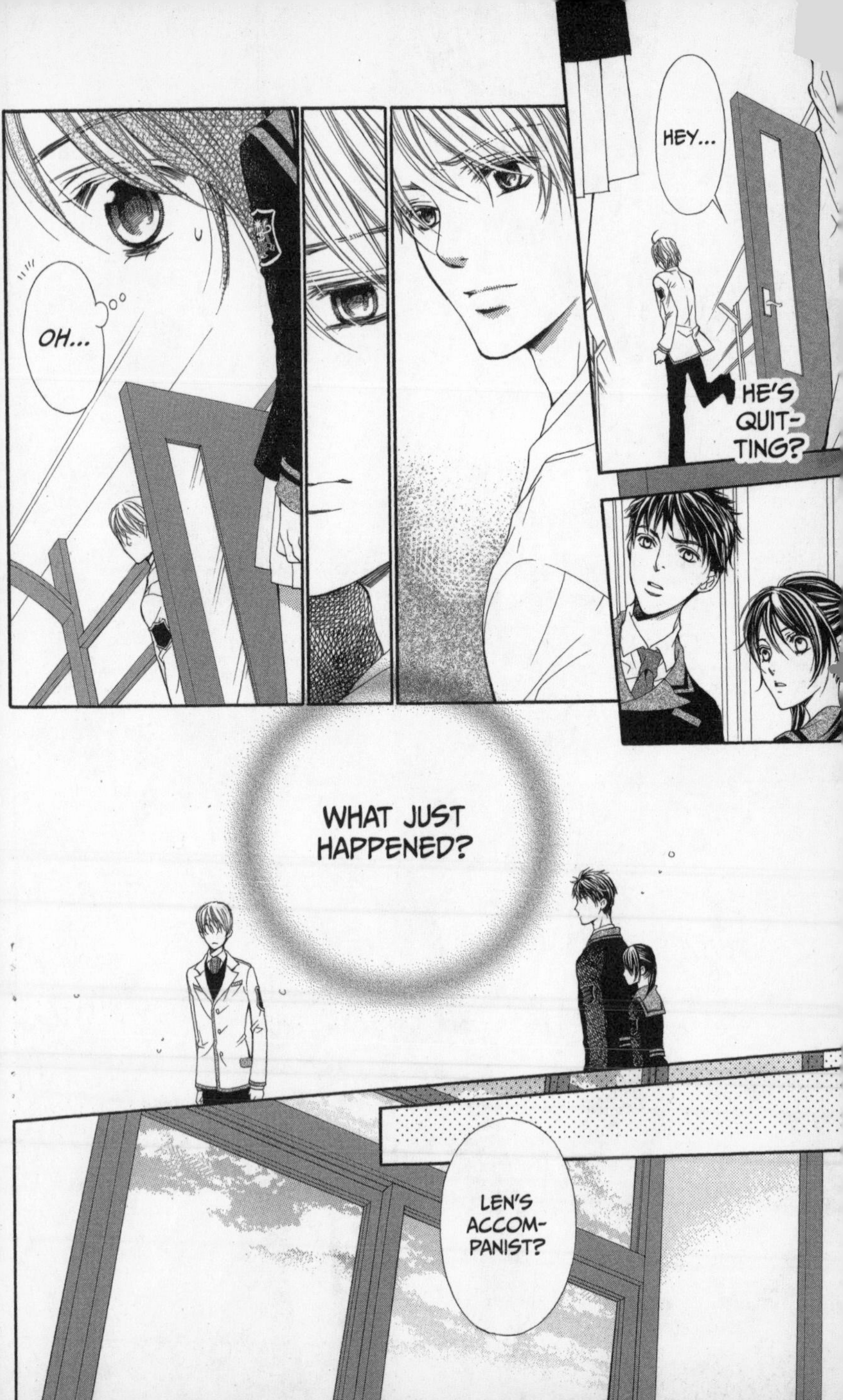
HEY...
HE'S QUIT-TING?
OH...
WHAT JUST HAPPENED?
LEN'S ACCOM-PANIST?

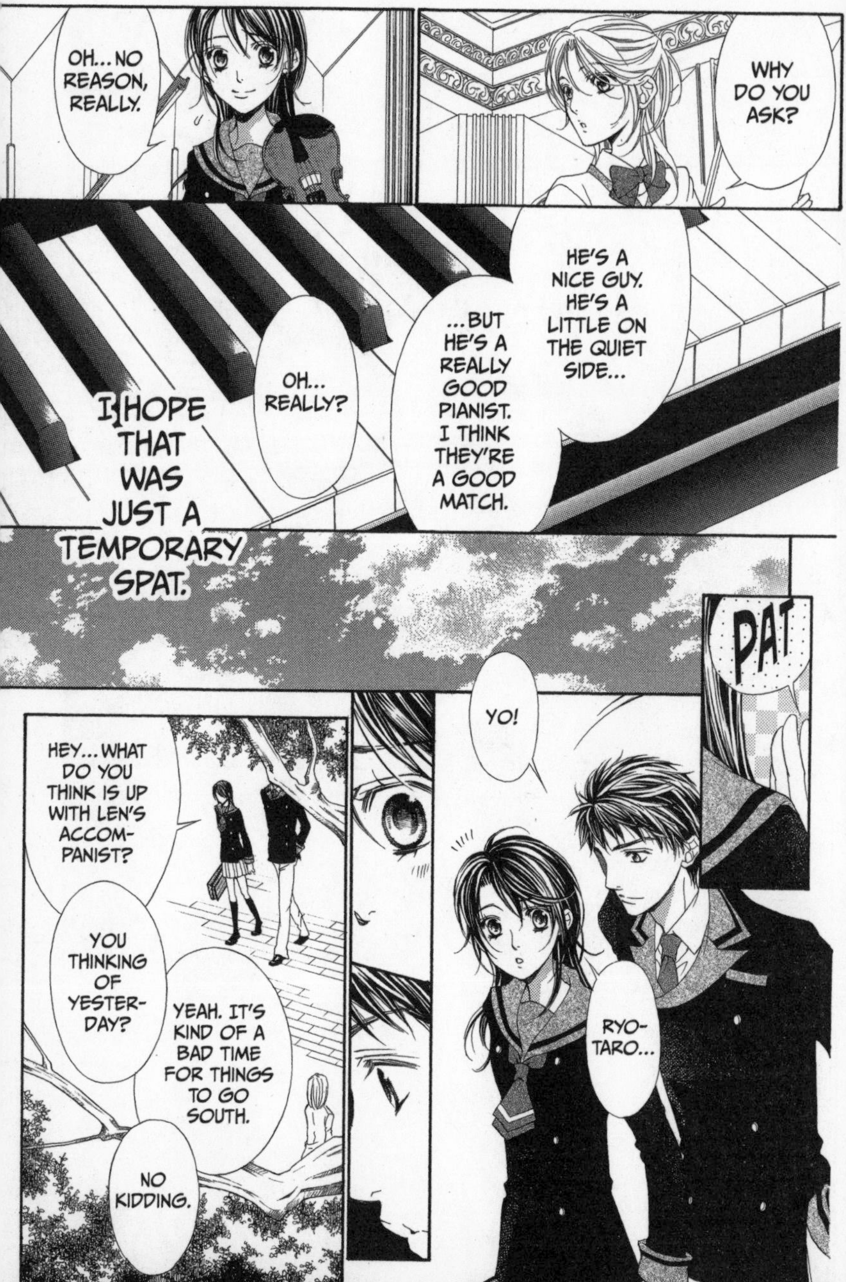
WHY DO YOU ASK?
OH... NO REASON, REALLY.
HE'S A NICE GUY. HE'S A LITTLE ON THE QUIET SIDE...
...BUT HE'S A REALLY GOOD PIANIST. I THINK THEY'RE A GOOD MATCH.
OH... REALLY?
I HOPE THAT WAS JUST A TEMPORARY SPAT.
PAT
YO!
RYO-TARO...
HEY... WHAT DO YOU THINK IS UP WITH LEN'S ACCOM-PANIST?
YOU THINKING OF YESTER-DAY?
YEAH. IT'S KIND OF A BAD TIME FOR THINGS TO GO SOUTH.
NO KIDDING.

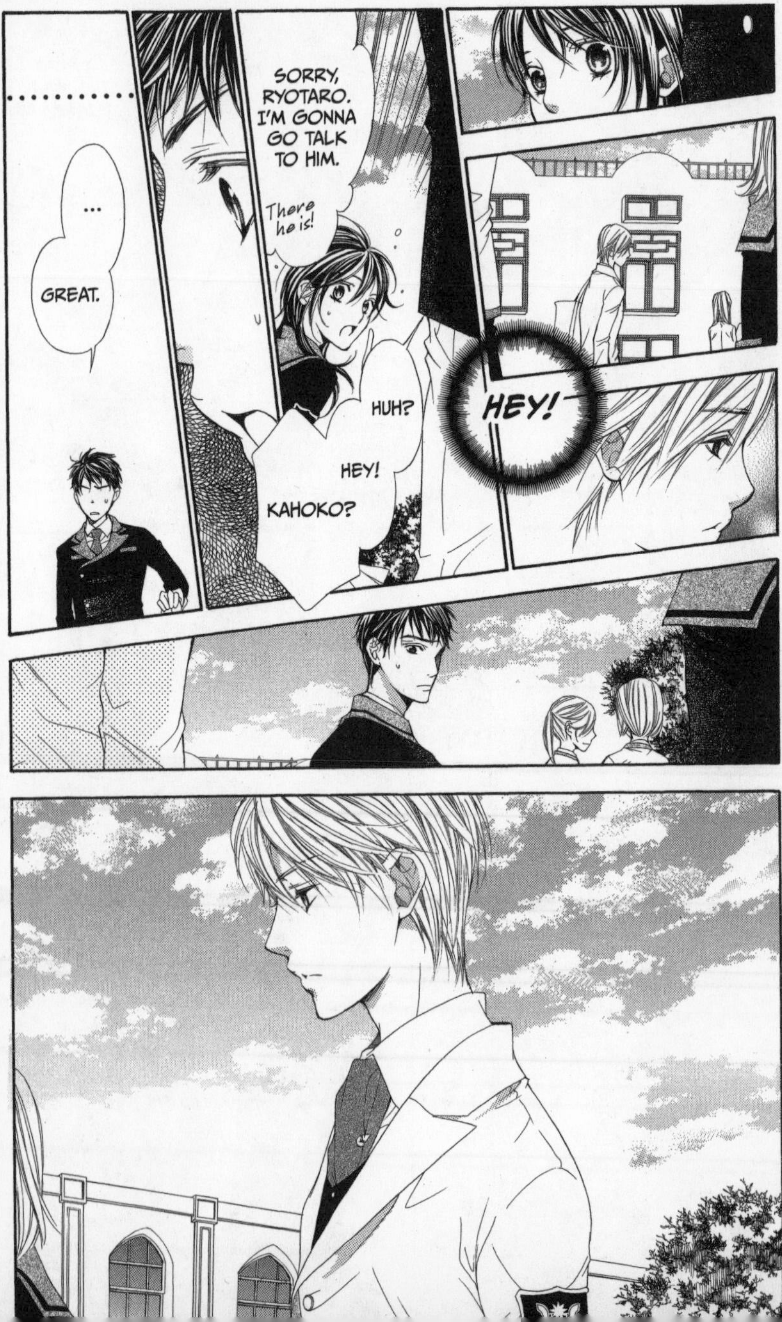
HEY!
SORRY, RYOTARO. I'M GONNA GO TALK TO HIM.
There he is!
HUH?
HEY!
KAHOKO?
........
...
GREAT.

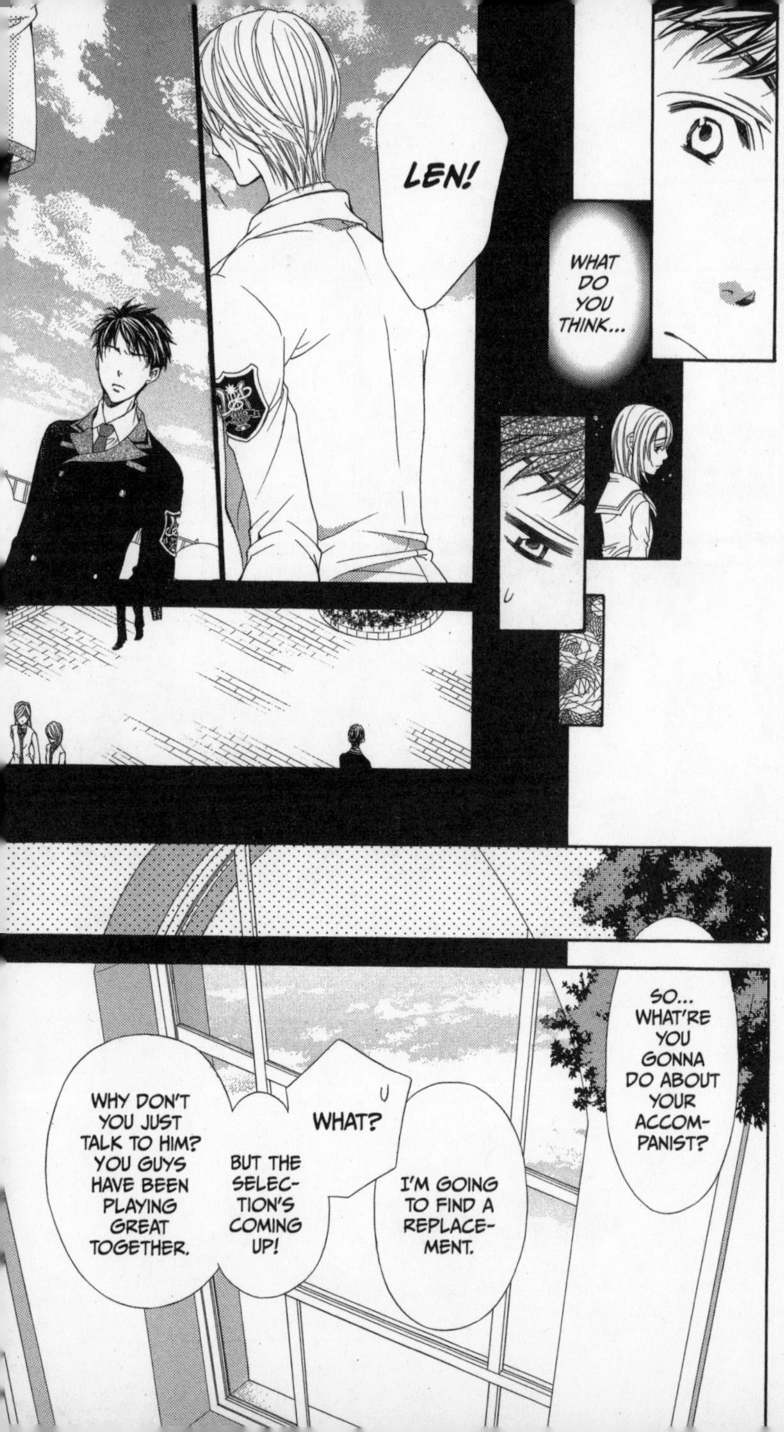
LEN!
WHAT DO YOU THINK...
SO... WHAT'RE YOU GONNA DO ABOUT YOUR ACCOM-PANIST?
I'M GOING TO FIND A REPLACE-MENT.
WHAT?
BUT THE SELEC-TION'S COMING UP!
WHY DON'T YOU JUST TALK TO HIM? YOU GUYS HAVE BEEN PLAYING GREAT TOGETHER.

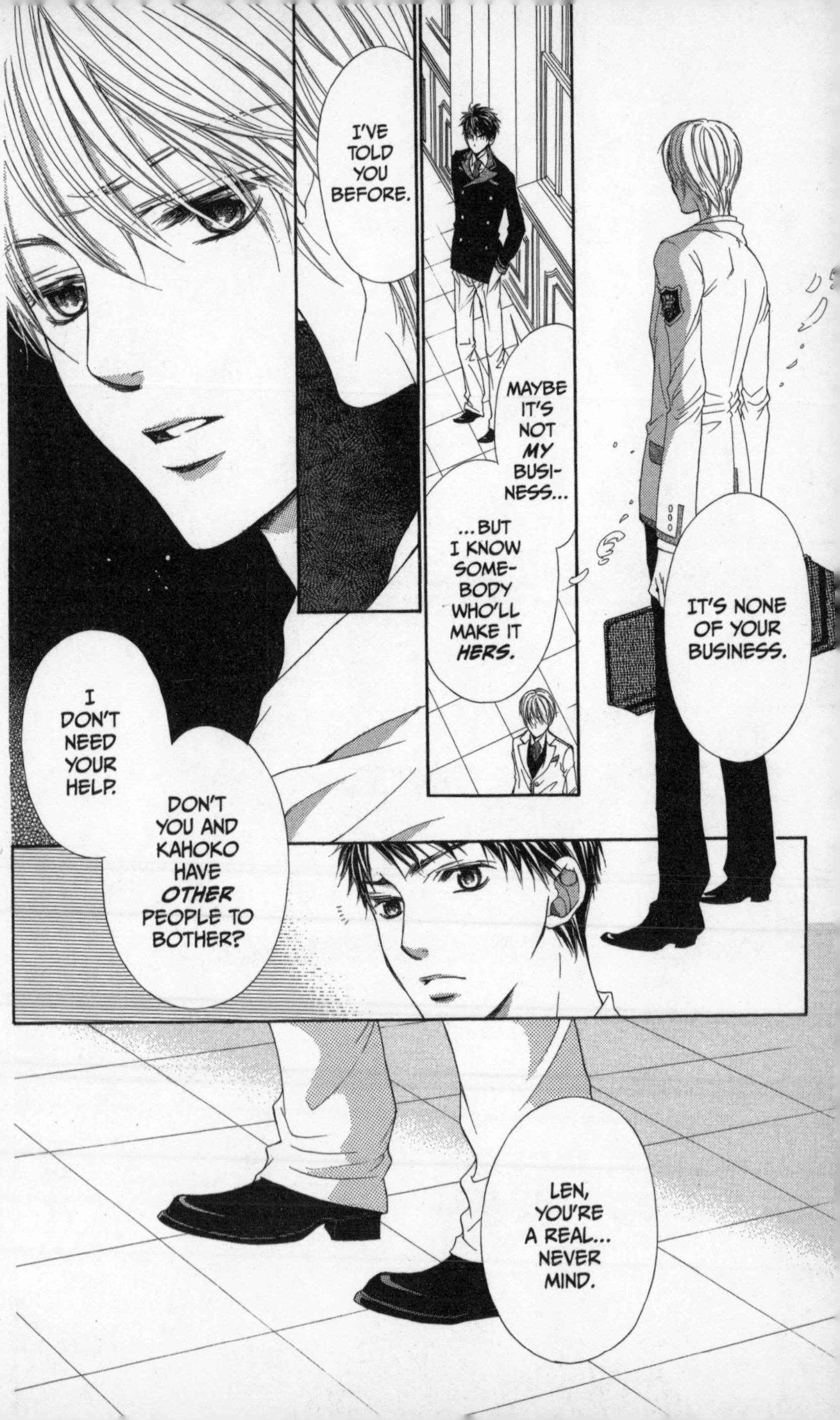
IT'S NONE OF YOUR BUSINESS.
MAYBE IT'S NOT *MY* BUSINESS...
...BUT I KNOW SOMEBODY WHO'LL MAKE IT ***HERS.***
I'VE TOLD YOU BEFORE.
I DON'T NEED YOUR HELP.
DON'T YOU AND KAHOKO HAVE *OTHER* PEOPLE TO BOTHER?
LEN, YOU'RE A REAL... NEVER MIND.

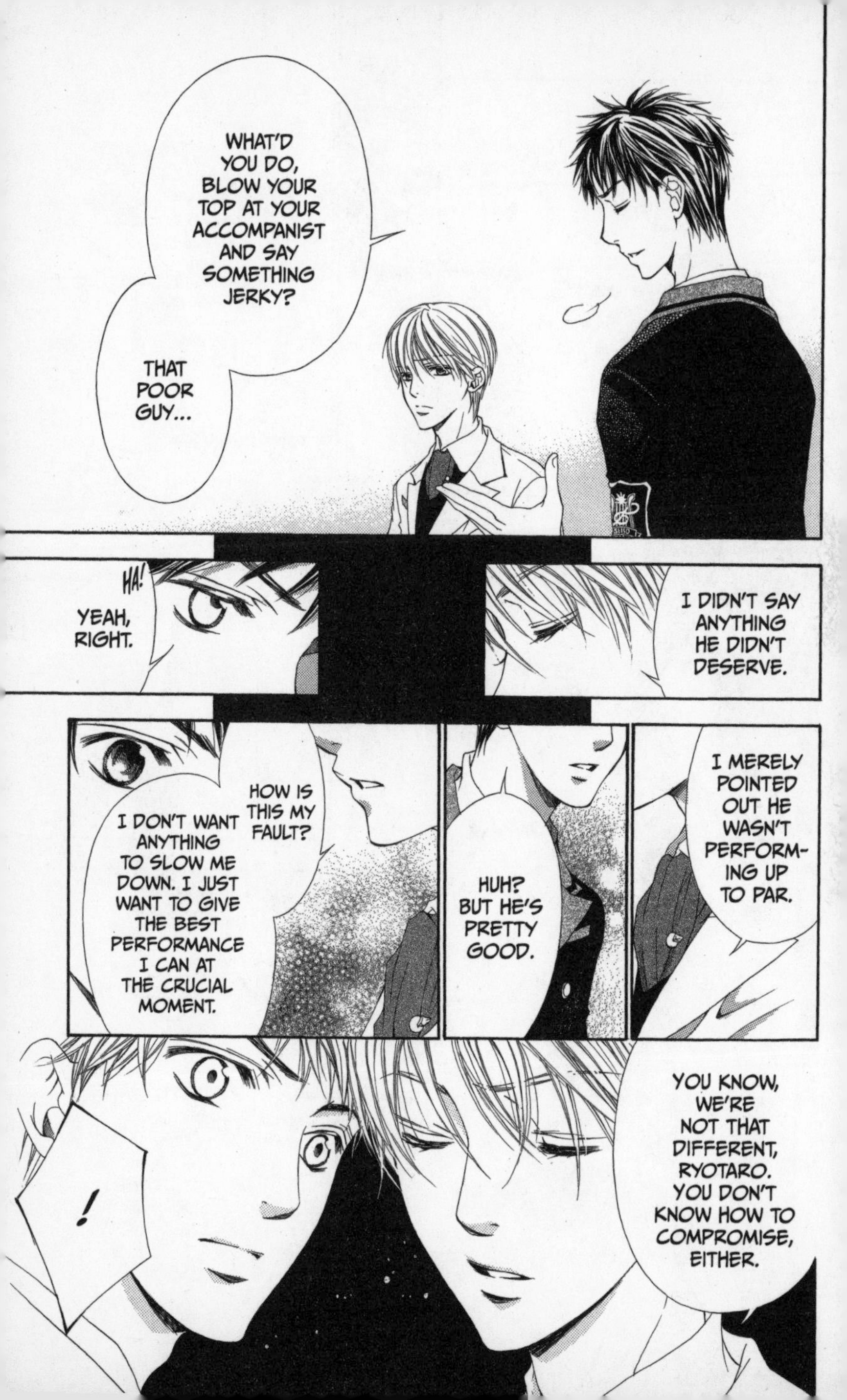
WHAT'D YOU DO, BLOW YOUR TOP AT YOUR ACCOMPANIST AND SAY SOMETHING JERKY?
THAT POOR GUY...
I DIDN'T SAY ANYTHING HE DIDN'T DESERVE.
HA!
YEAH, RIGHT.
I MERELY POINTED OUT HE WASN'T PERFORMING UP TO PAR.
HUH? BUT HE'S PRETTY GOOD.
HOW IS THIS MY FAULT?
I DON'T WANT ANYTHING TO SLOW ME DOWN. I JUST WANT TO GIVE THE BEST PERFORMANCE I CAN AT THE CRUCIAL MOMENT.
YOU KNOW, WE'RE NOT THAT DIFFERENT, RYOTARO. YOU DON'T KNOW HOW TO COMPROMISE, EITHER.
!

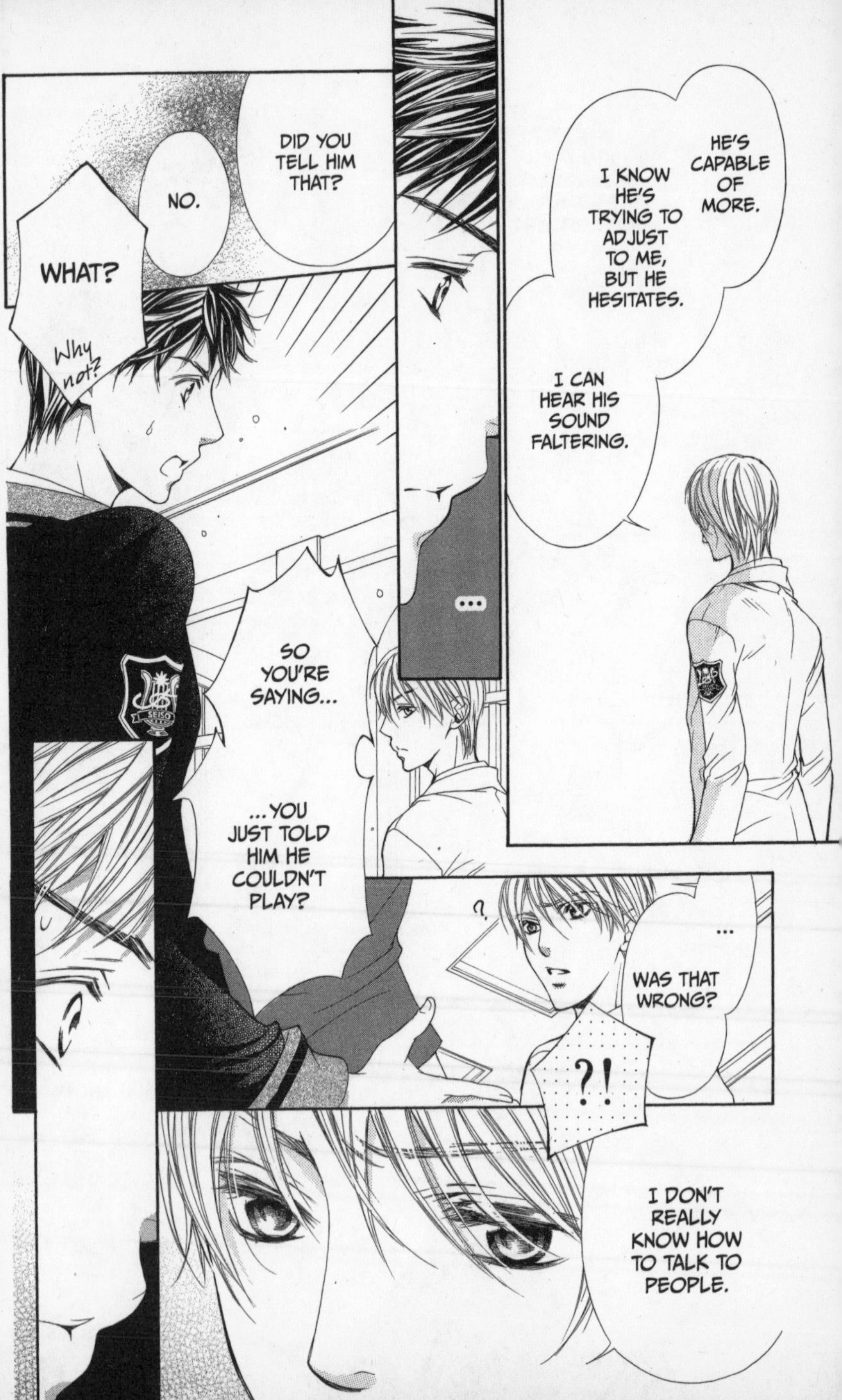
HE'S CAPABLE OF MORE.
I KNOW HE'S TRYING TO ADJUST TO ME, BUT HE HESITATES.
I CAN HEAR HIS SOUND FALTERING.
...
DID YOU TELL HIM THAT?
NO.
WHAT?
Why not?
SO YOU'RE SAYING...
...YOU JUST TOLD HIM HE COULDN'T PLAY?
?
... WAS THAT WRONG?
?!
I DON'T REALLY KNOW HOW TO TALK TO PEOPLE.

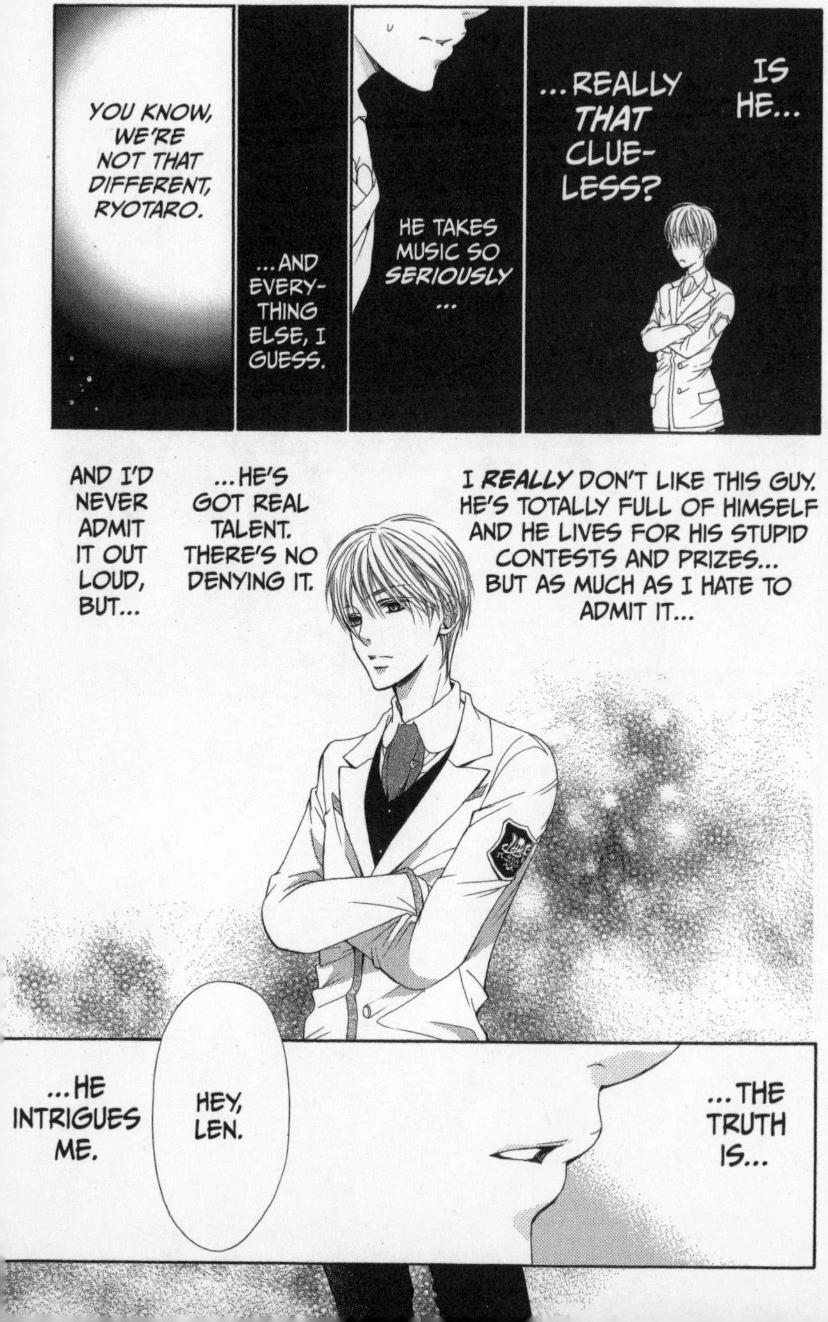
IS HE...
...REALLY THAT CLUE-LESS?
HE TAKES MUSIC SO SERIOUSLY ...
...AND EVERY-THING ELSE, I GUESS.
YOU KNOW, WE'RE NOT THAT DIFFERENT, RYOTARO.
I REALLY DON'T LIKE THIS GUY. HE'S TOTALLY FULL OF HIMSELF AND HE LIVES FOR HIS STUPID CONTESTS AND PRIZES... BUT AS MUCH AS I HATE TO ADMIT IT...
...HE'S GOT REAL TALENT. THERE'S NO DENYING IT.
AND I'D NEVER ADMIT IT OUT LOUD, BUT...
...THE TRUTH IS...
HEY, LEN.
...HE INTRIGUES ME.

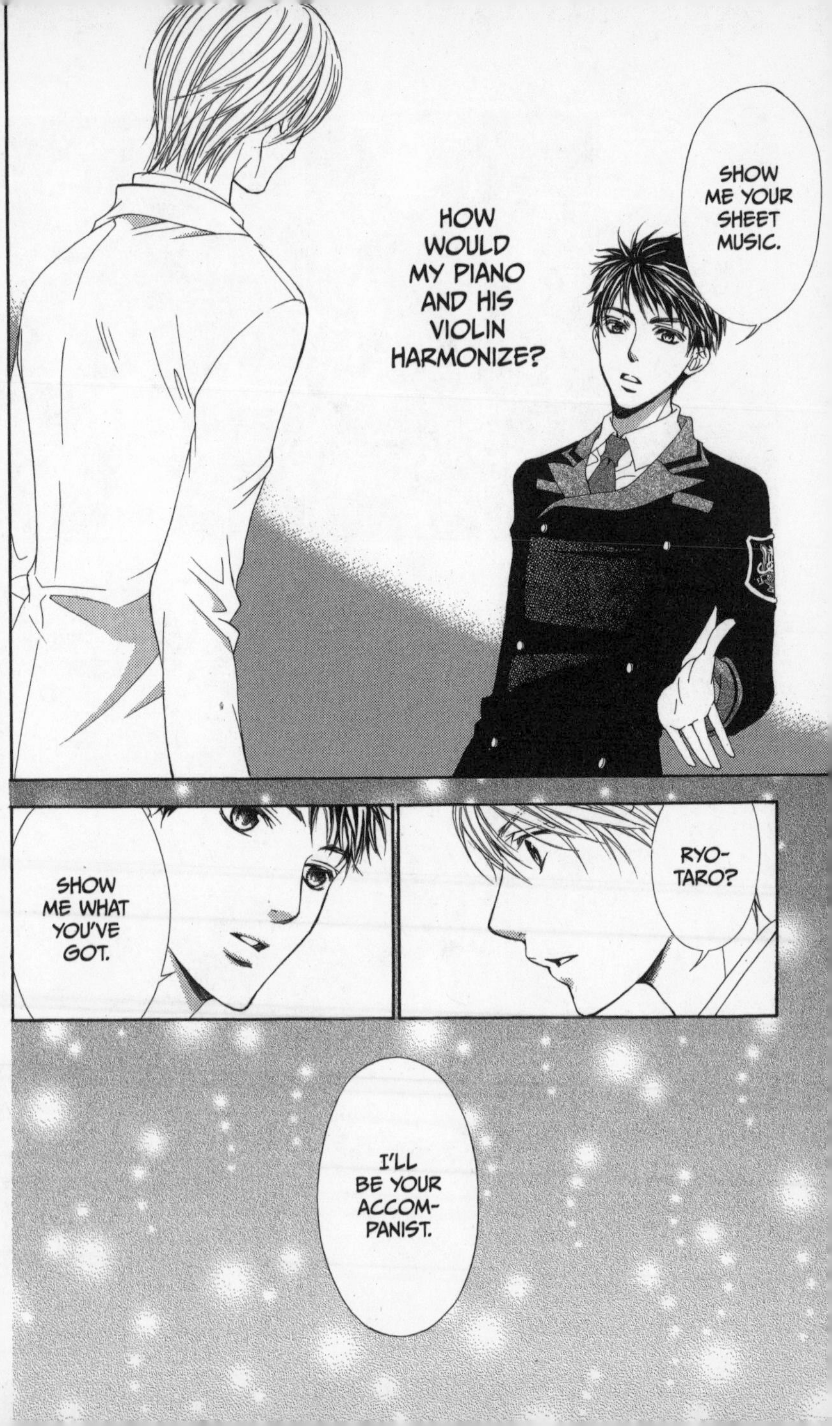
SHOW ME YOUR SHEET MUSIC.
HOW WOULD MY PIANO AND HIS VIOLIN HARMONIZE?
RYO-TARO?
SHOW ME WHAT YOU'VE GOT.
I'LL BE YOUR ACCOM-PANIST.

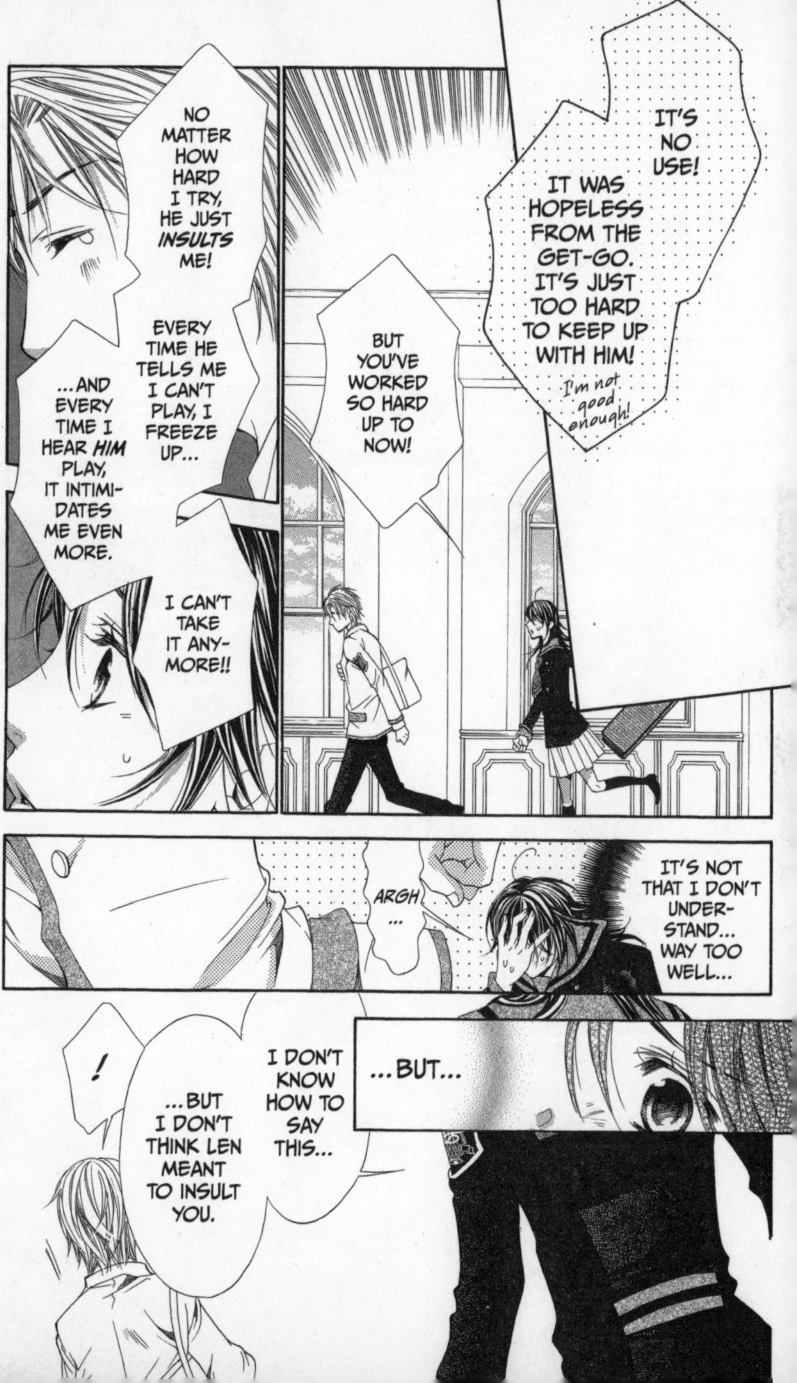
IT'S NO USE!
IT WAS HOPELESS FROM THE GET-GO. IT'S JUST TOO HARD TO KEEP UP WITH HIM!
I'm not good enough!
BUT YOU'VE WORKED SO HARD UP TO NOW!
NO MATTER HOW HARD I TRY, HE JUST INSULTS ME!
EVERY TIME HE TELLS ME I CAN'T PLAY, I FREEZE UP...
...AND EVERY TIME I HEAR HIM PLAY, IT INTIMIDATES ME EVEN MORE.
I CAN'T TAKE IT ANYMORE!!
IT'S NOT THAT I DON'T UNDERSTAND... WAY TOO WELL...
ARGH...
...BUT...
I DON'T KNOW HOW TO SAY THIS...
...BUT I DON'T THINK LEN MEANT TO INSULT YOU.
!

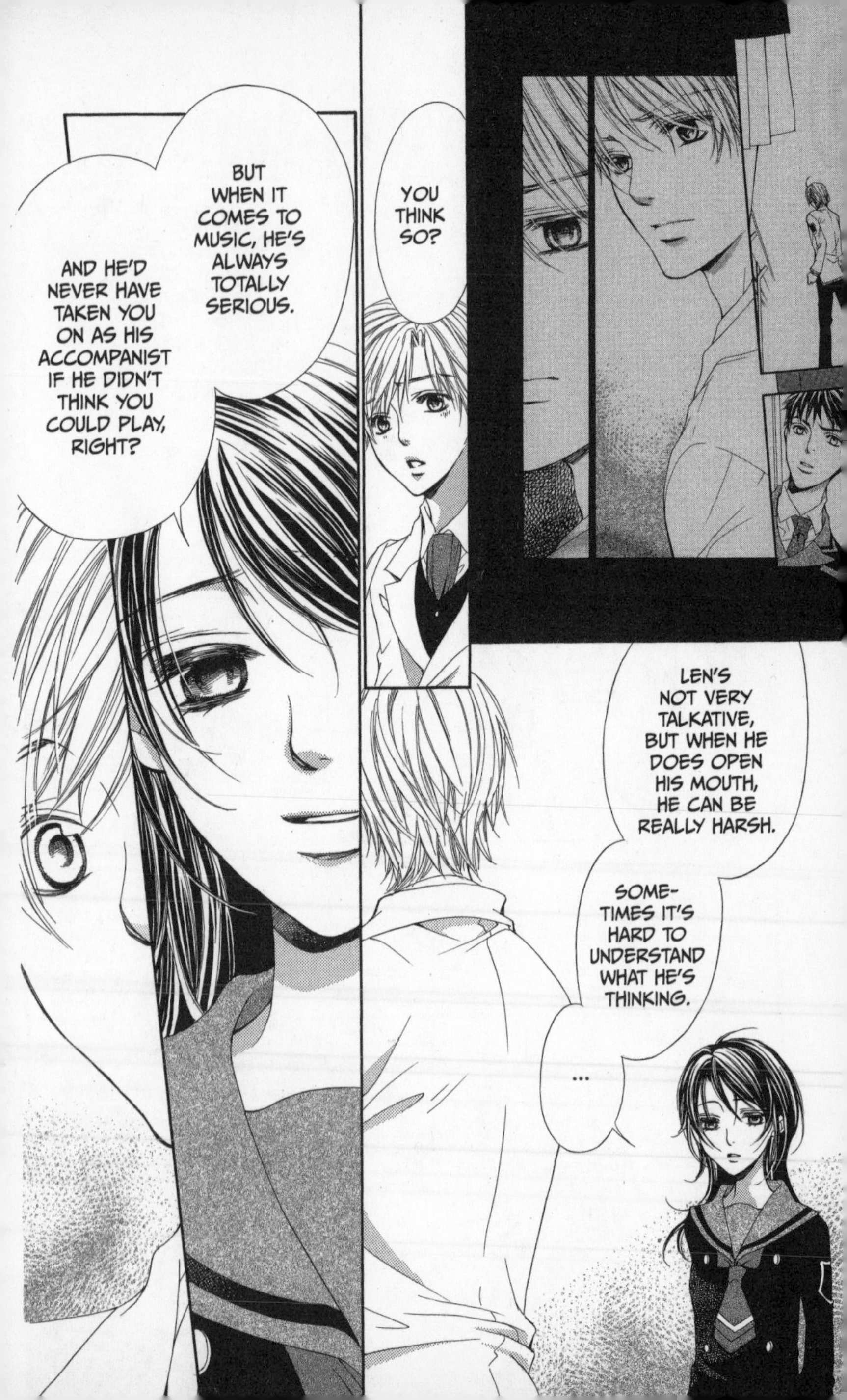
LEN'S NOT VERY TALKATIVE, BUT WHEN HE DOES OPEN HIS MOUTH, HE CAN BE REALLY HARSH.
SOMETIMES IT'S HARD TO UNDERSTAND WHAT HE'S THINKING.
...
YOU THINK SO?
BUT WHEN IT COMES TO MUSIC, HE'S ALWAYS TOTALLY SERIOUS.
AND HE'D NEVER HAVE TAKEN YOU ON AS HIS ACCOMPANIST IF HE DIDN'T THINK YOU COULD PLAY, RIGHT?

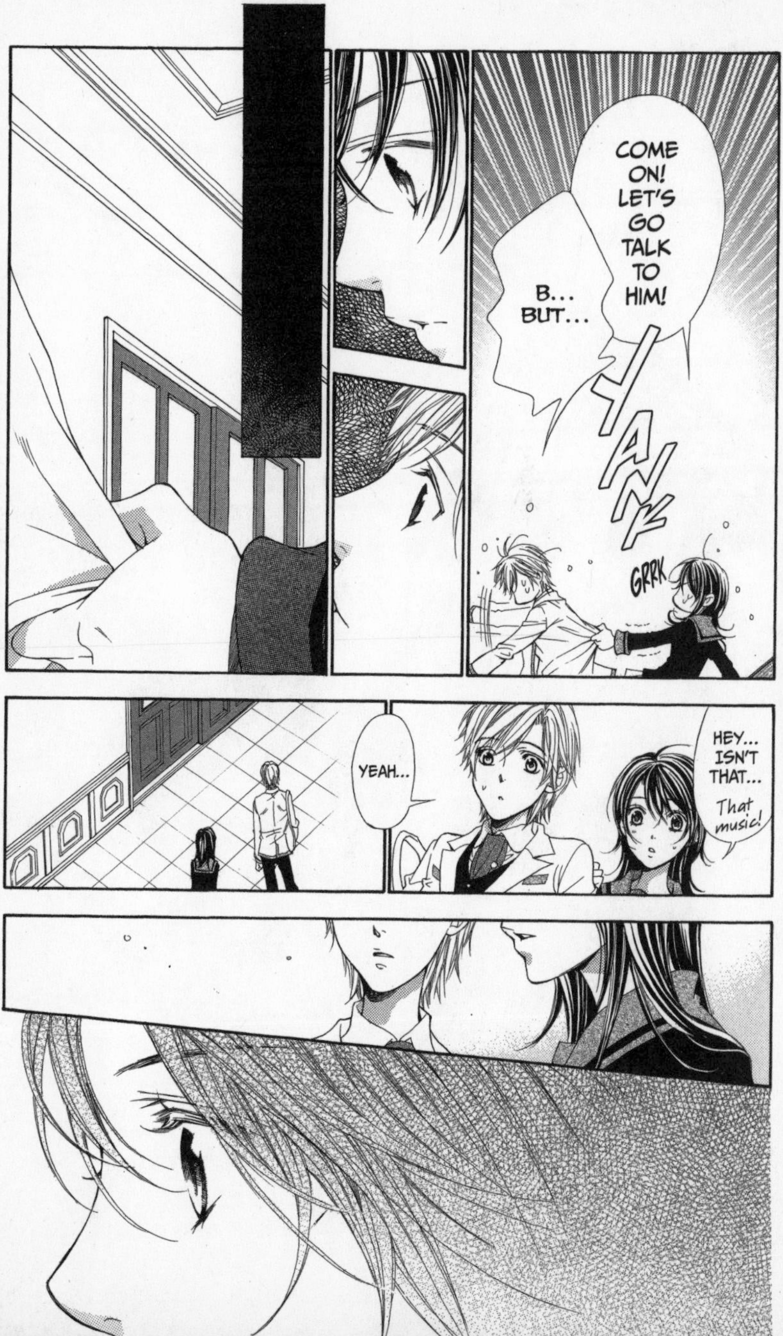
COME ON! LET'S GO TALK TO HIM!
B... BUT...
YANK
GRRK
HEY... ISN'T THAT...
That music!
YEAH...

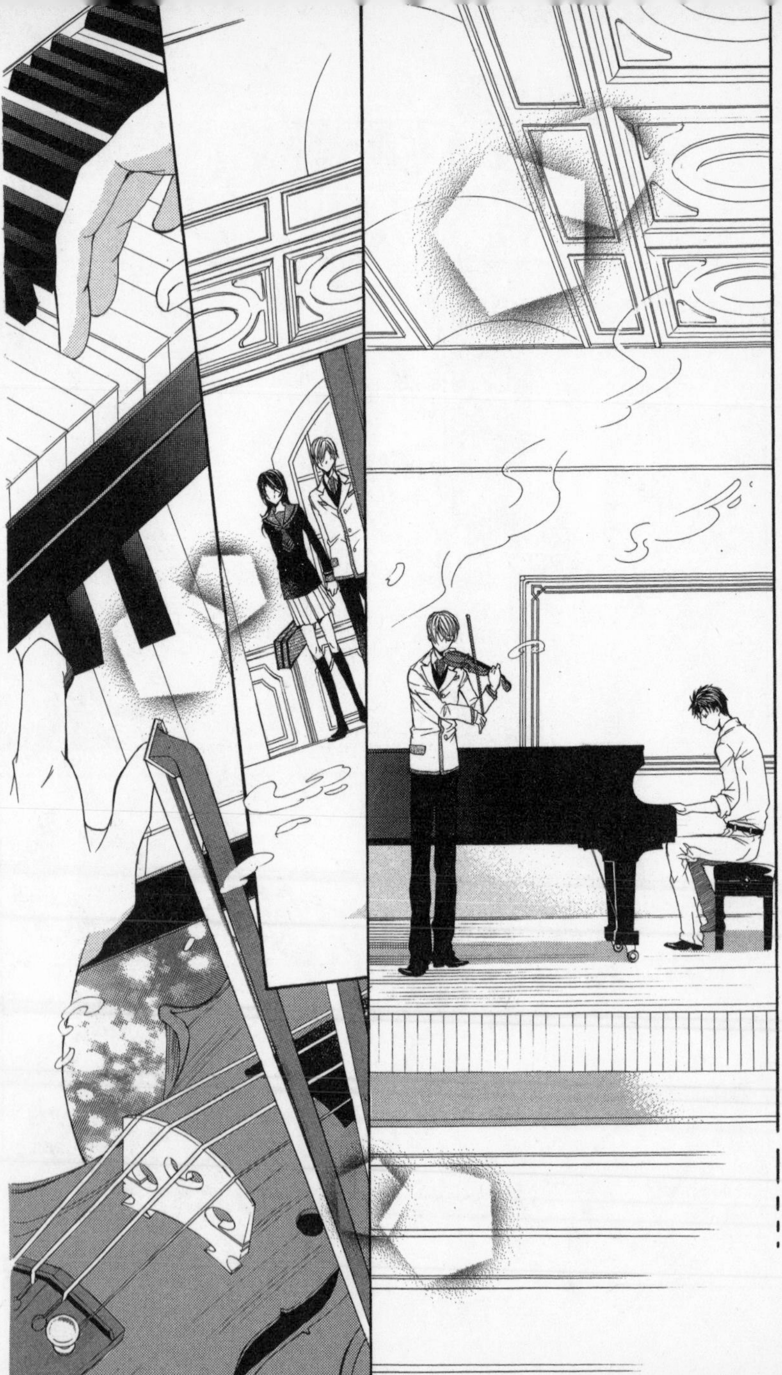

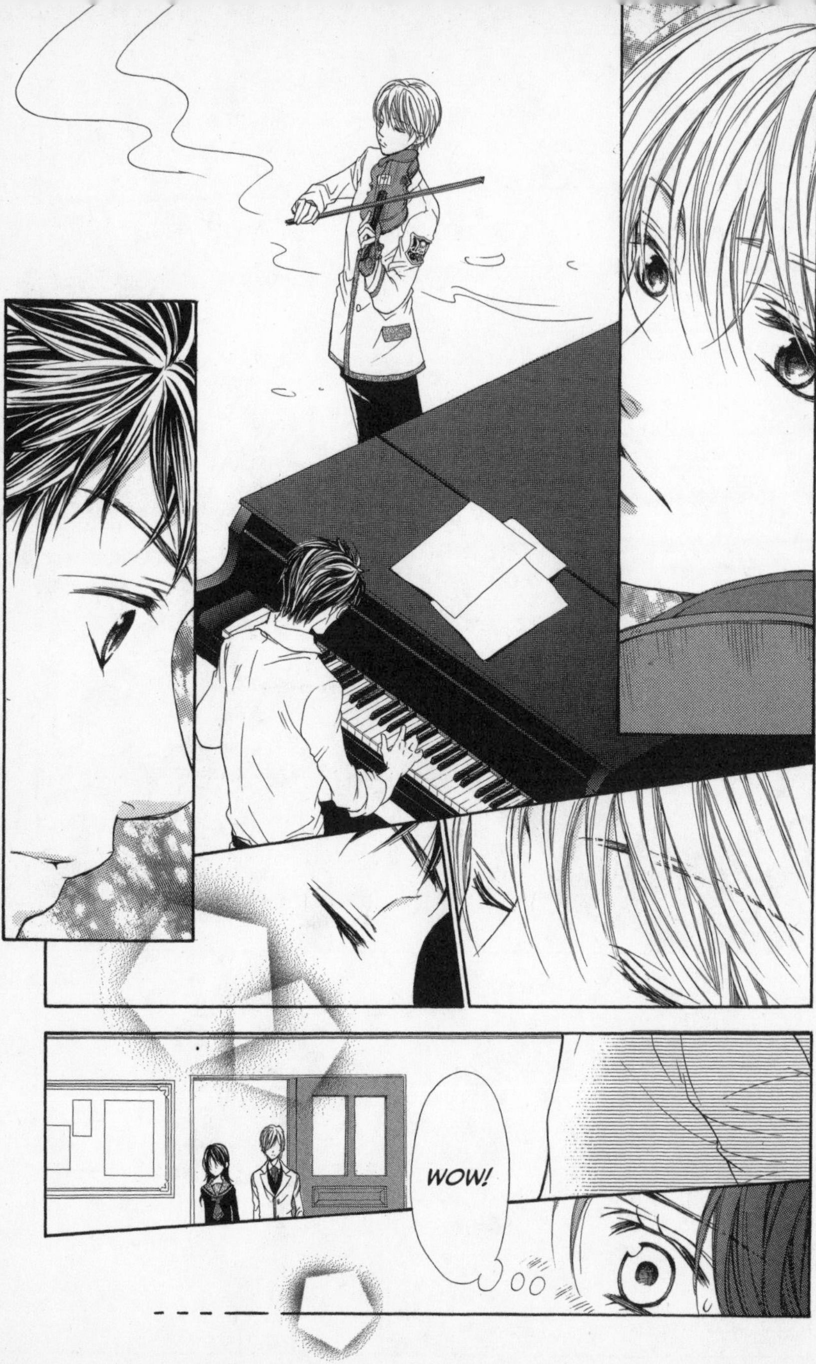
WOW!

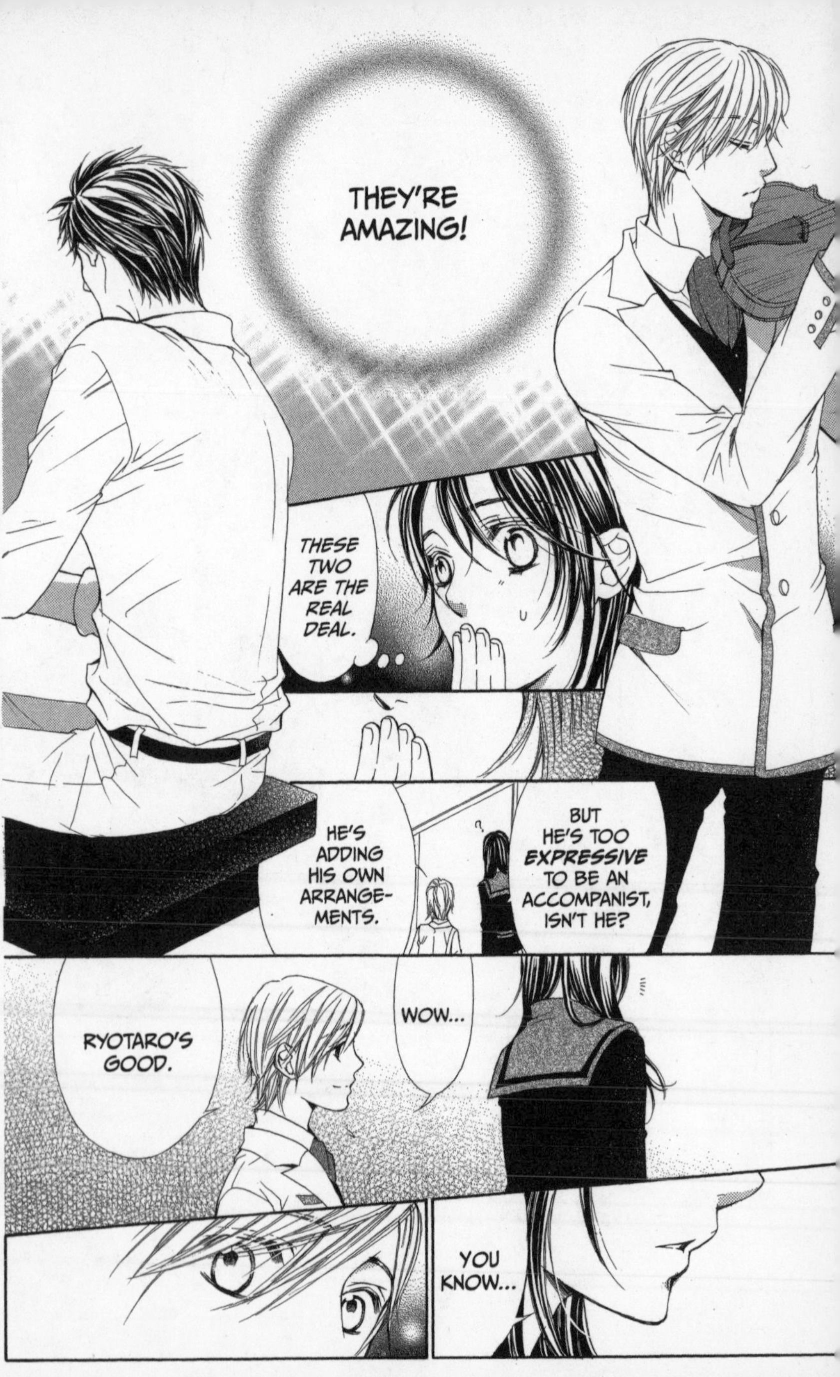
THEY'RE AMAZING!
THESE TWO ARE THE REAL DEAL.
HE'S ADDING HIS OWN ARRANGE-MENTS.
BUT HE'S TOO *EXPRESSIVE* TO BE AN ACCOMPANIST, ISN'T HE?
WOW...
RYOTARO'S GOOD.
YOU KNOW...

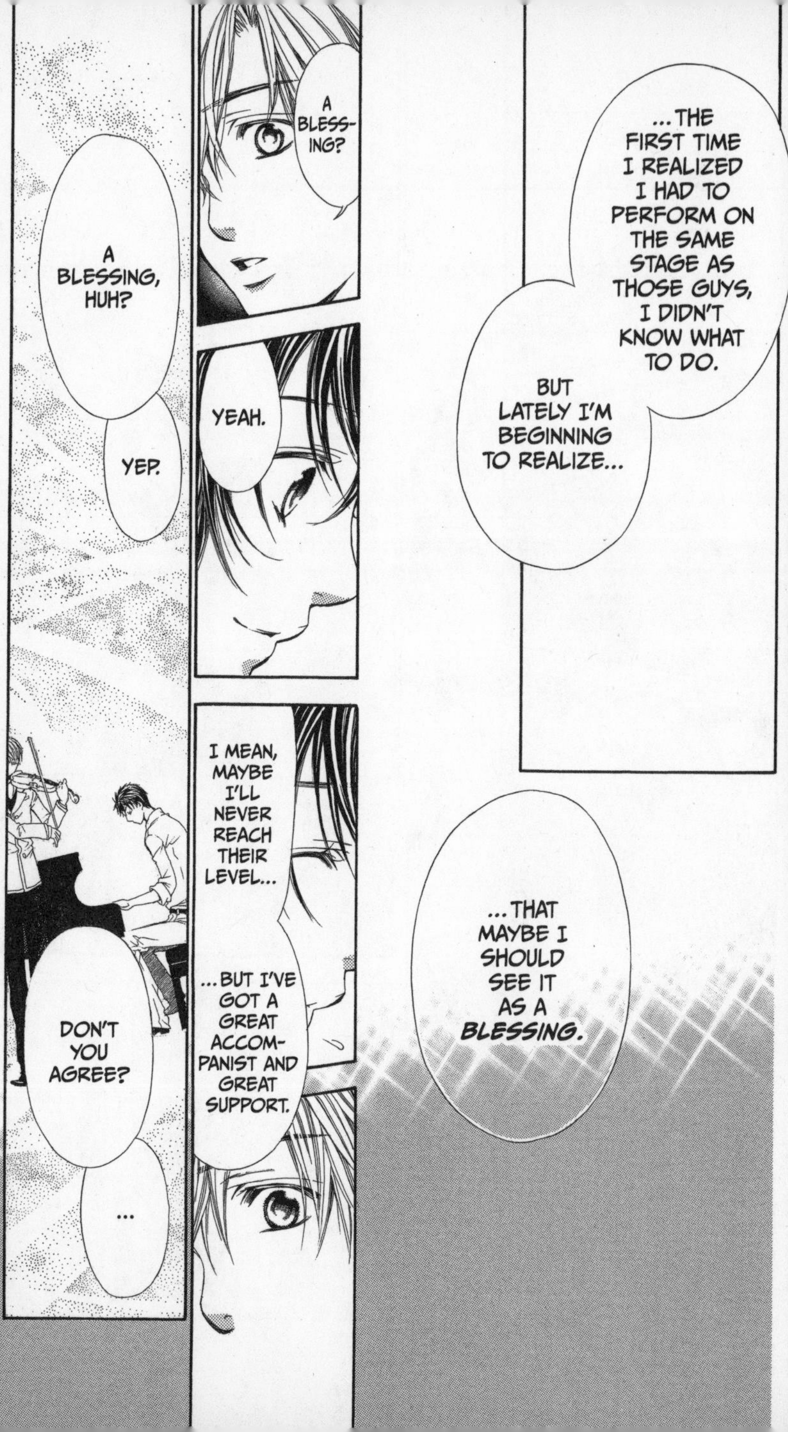
...THE FIRST TIME I REALIZED I HAD TO PERFORM ON THE SAME STAGE AS THOSE GUYS, I DIDN'T KNOW WHAT TO DO.
BUT LATELY I'M BEGINNING TO REALIZE...
...THAT MAYBE I SHOULD SEE IT AS A *BLESSING.*
A BLESS-ING?
YEAH.
I MEAN, MAYBE I'LL NEVER REACH THEIR LEVEL...
...BUT I'VE GOT A GREAT ACCOM-PANIST AND GREAT SUPPORT.
A BLESSING, HUH?
YEP.
DON'T YOU AGREE?
...

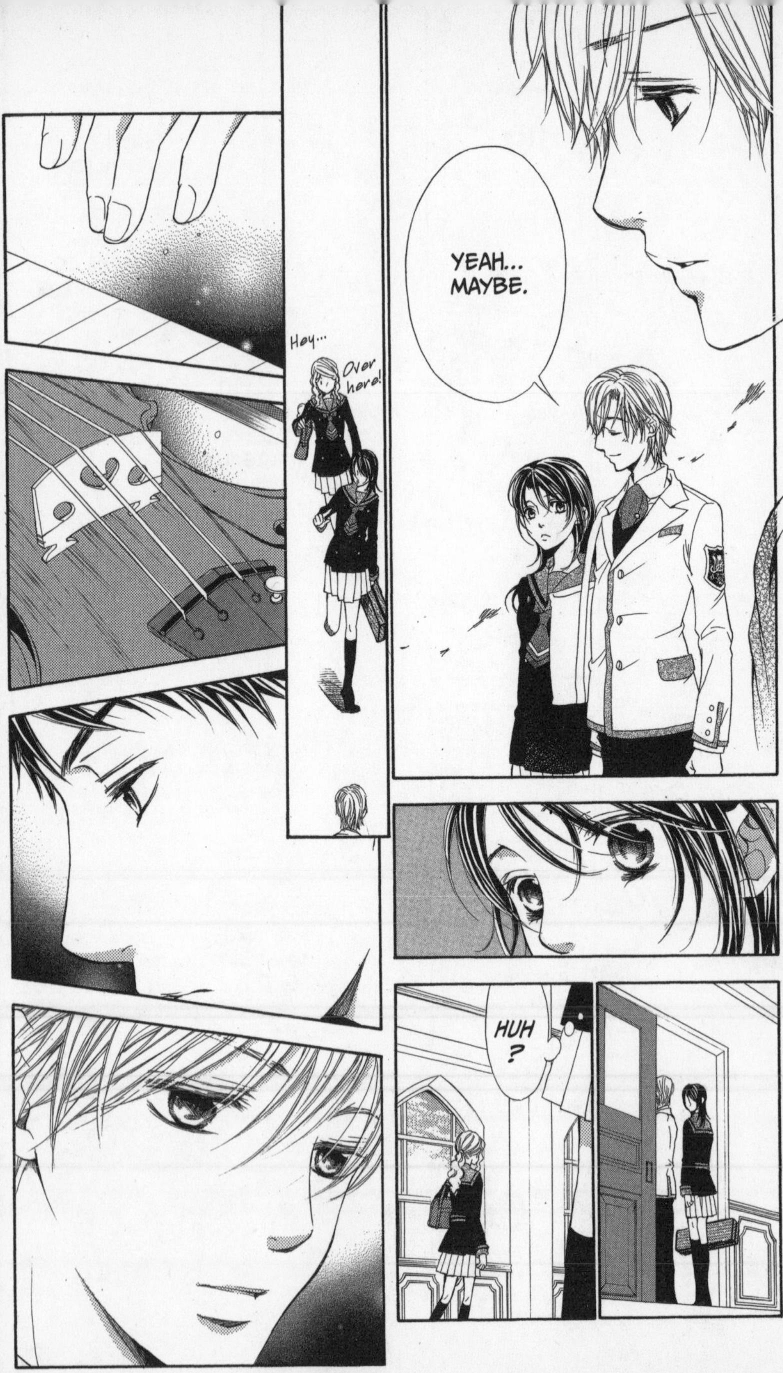
YEAH... MAYBE.
Hey...
Over here!
HUH?

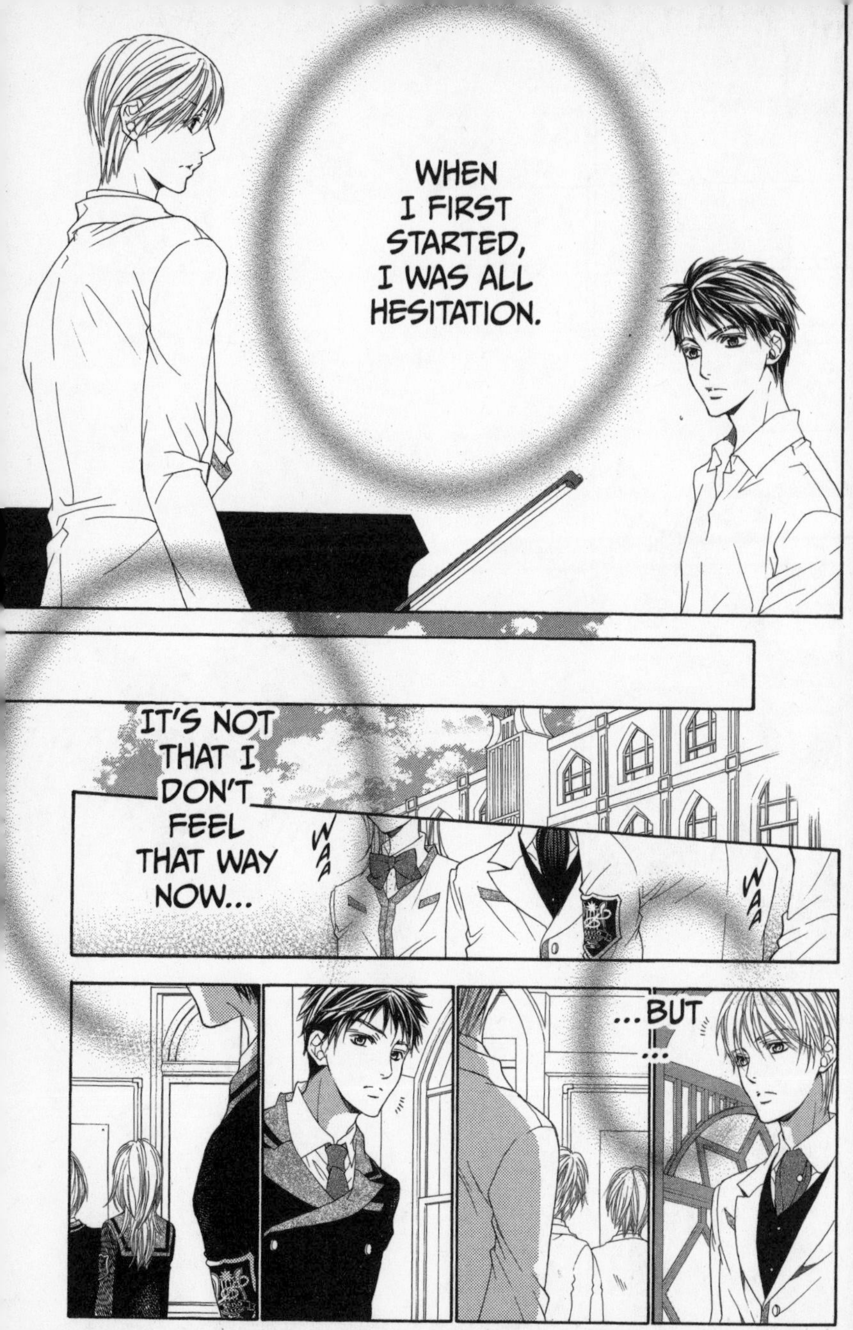
WHEN I FIRST STARTED, I WAS ALL HESITATION.
IT'S NOT THAT I DON'T FEEL THAT WAY NOW...
WAA
WAA
...BUT ...

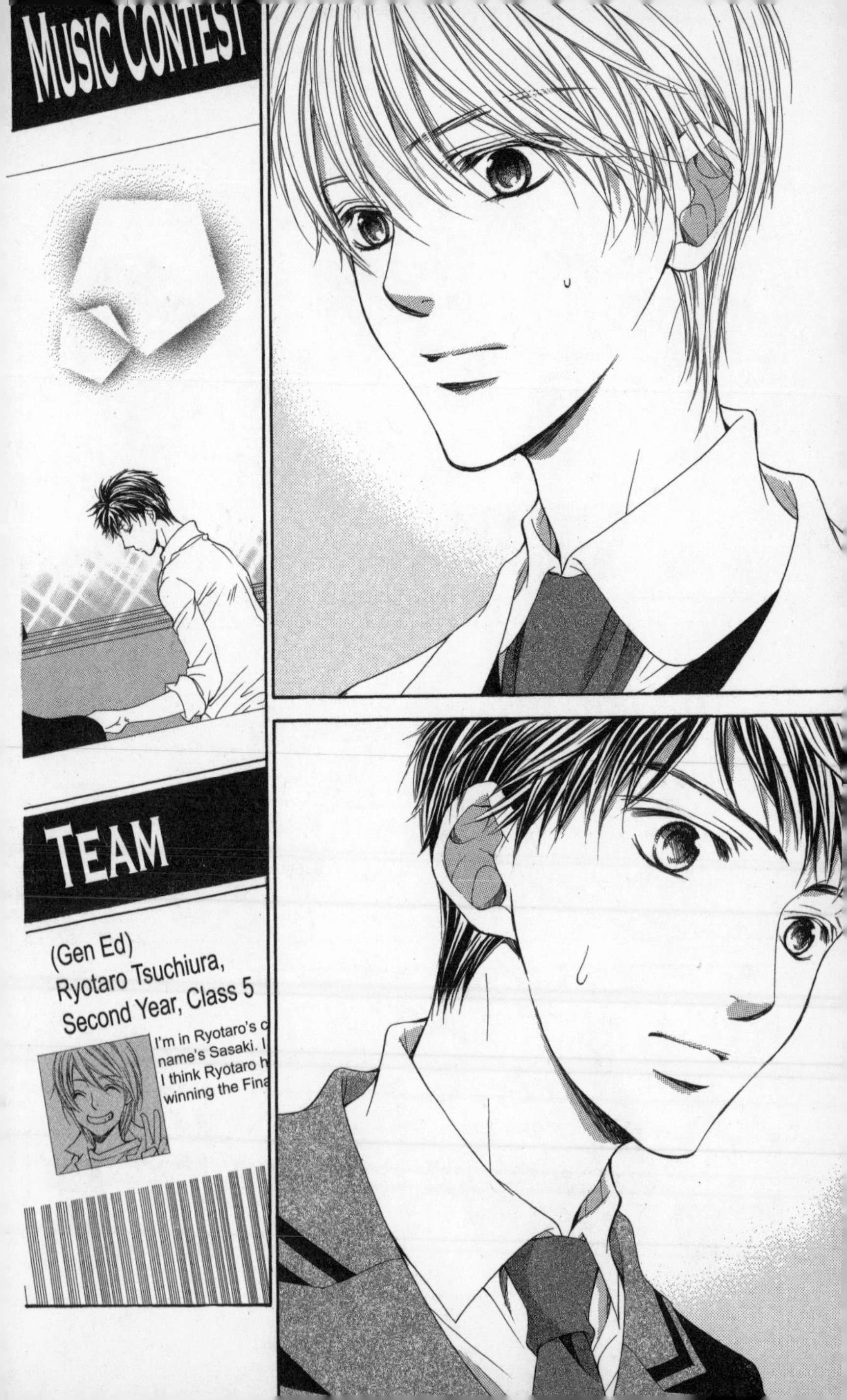
MUSIC CONTEST
TEAM
(Gen Ed)
Ryotaro Tsuchiura,
Second Year, Class 5
I'm in Ryotaro's c
name's Sasaki. I
I think Ryotaro h
winning the Fina

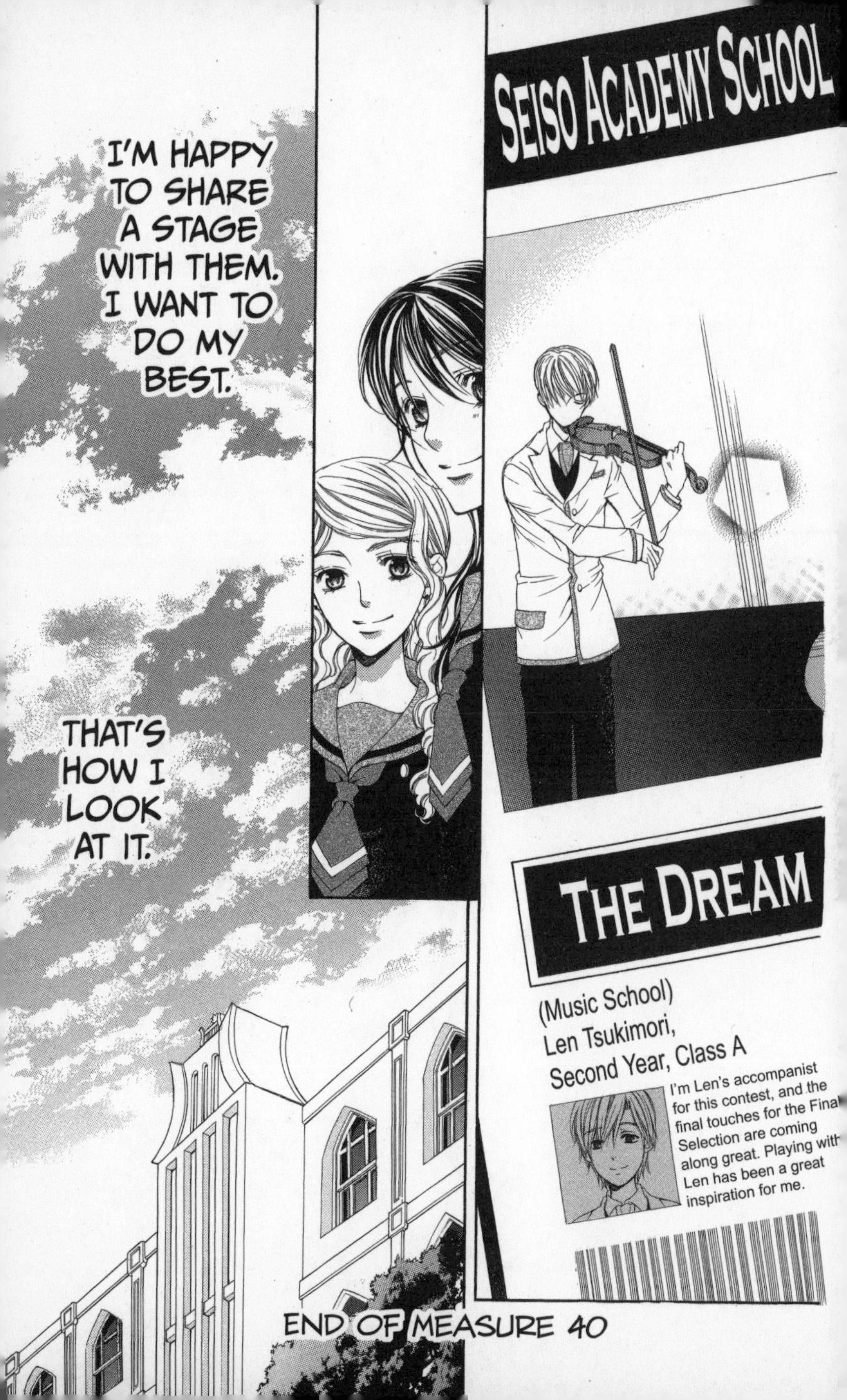
SEISO ACADEMY SCHOOL
THE DREAM
(Music School)
Len Tsukimori,
Second Year, Class A
I'm Len's accompanist for this contest, and the final touches for the Final Selection are coming along great. Playing with Len has been a great inspiration for me.
I'M HAPPY TO SHARE A STAGE WITH THEM. I WANT TO DO MY BEST.
THAT'S HOW I LOOK AT IT.
END OF MEASURE 40

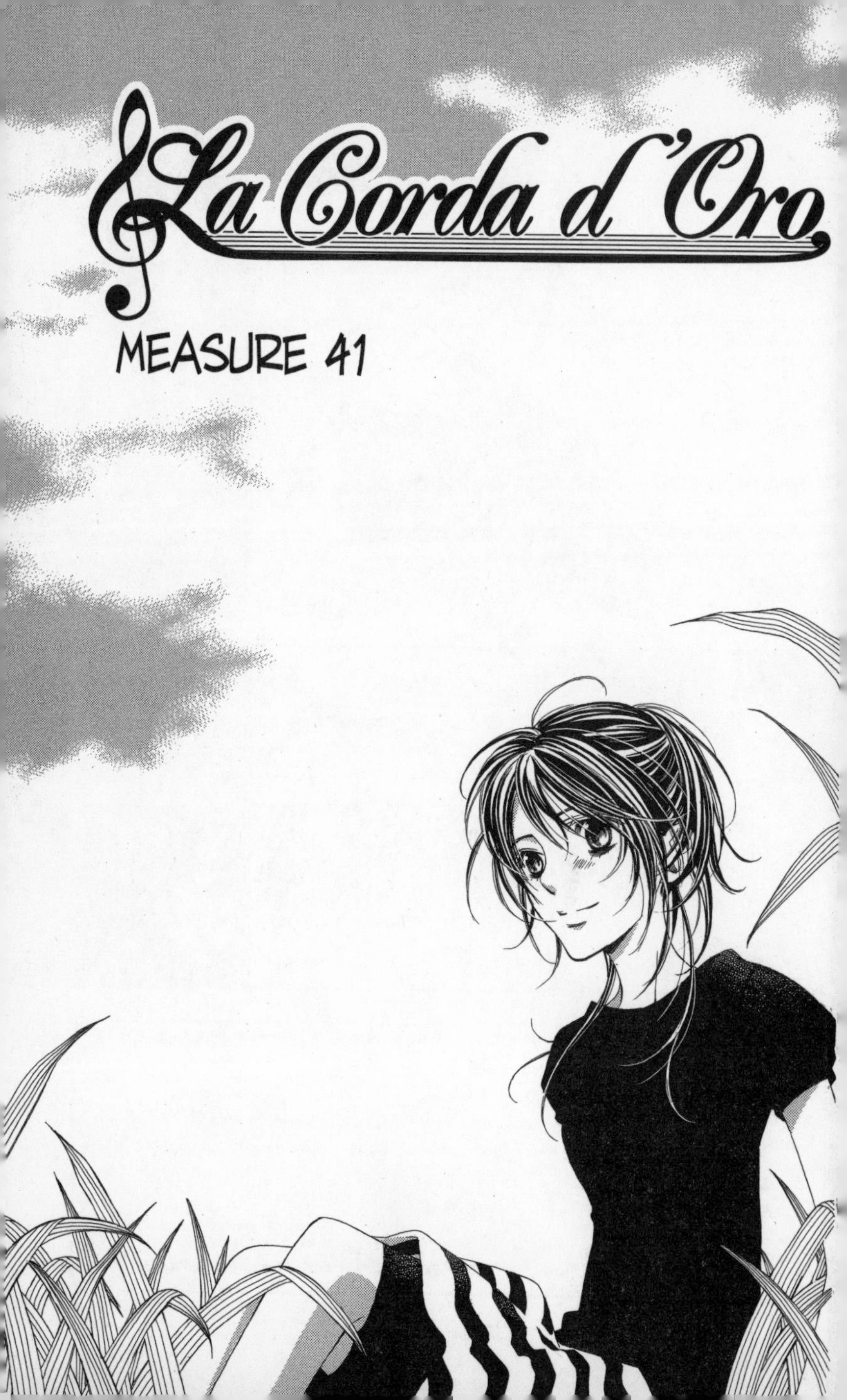
La Corda d'Oro
MEASURE 41

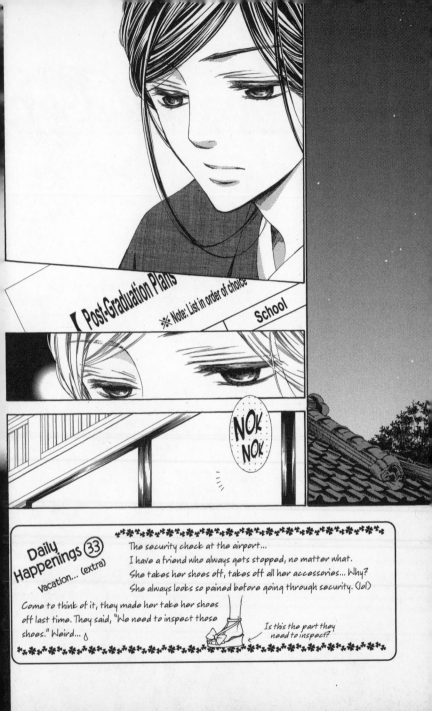

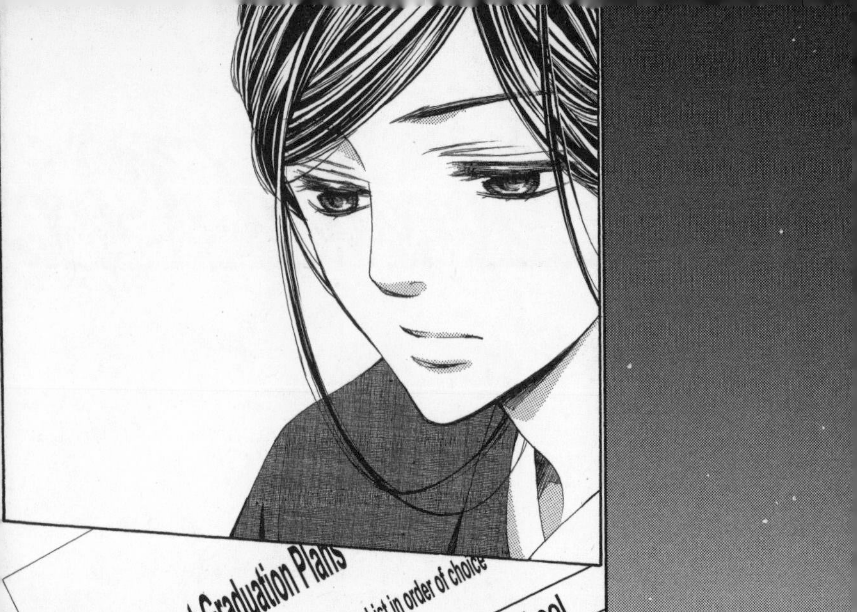
Post-Graduation Plans
※ Note: List in order of choice
School
NOK NOK

**Daily Happenings 33**
Vacation... (extra)

The security check at the airport...
I have a friend who always gets stopped, no matter what.
She takes her shoes off, takes off all her accessories... Why?
She always looks so pained before going through security. (lol)

Come to think of it, they made her take her shoes off last time. They said, "We need to inspect those shoes." Weird...

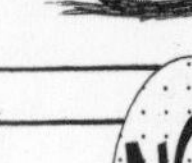
Is this the part they need to inspect?

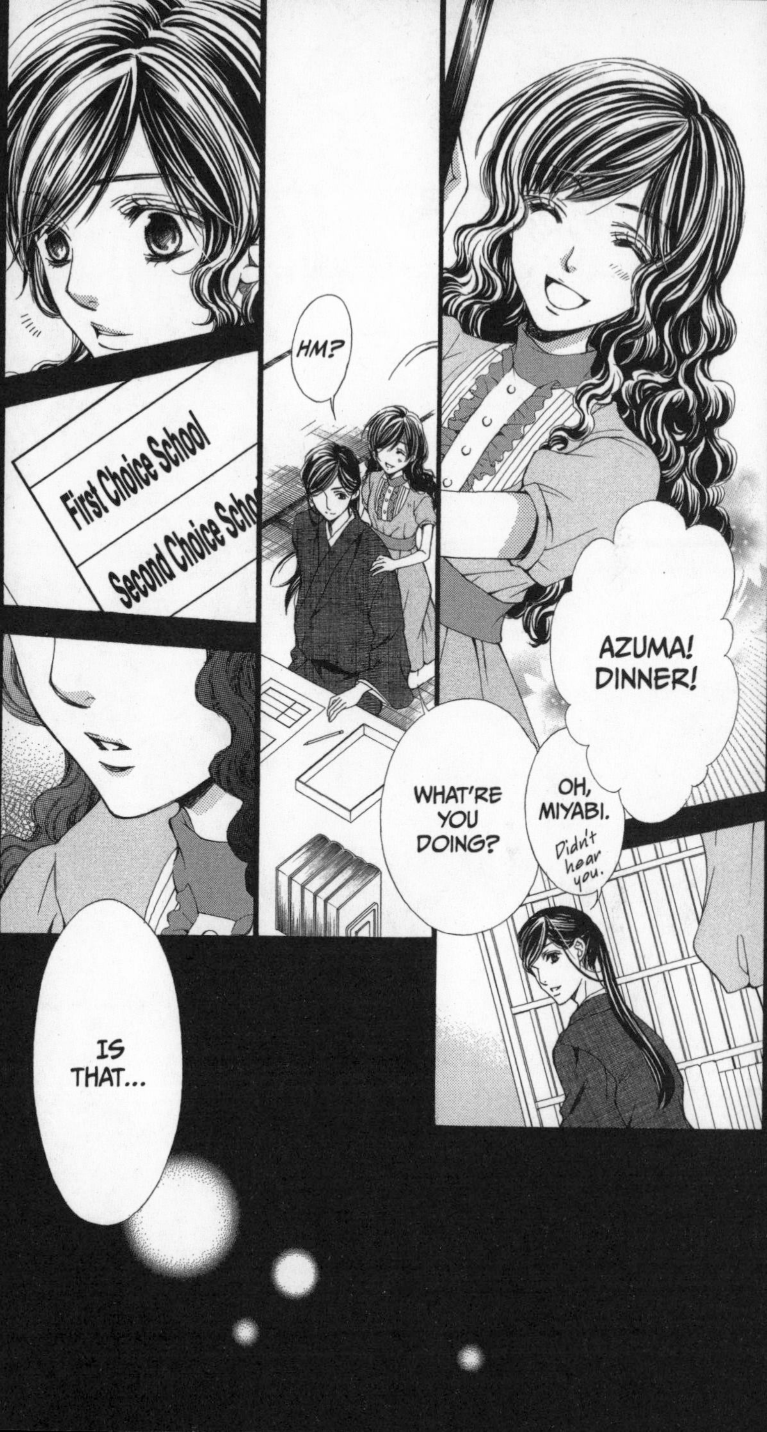
AZUMA! DINNER!
OH, MIYABI.
Didn't hear you.
WHAT'RE YOU DOING?
HM?
First Choice School
Second Choice School
IS THAT...

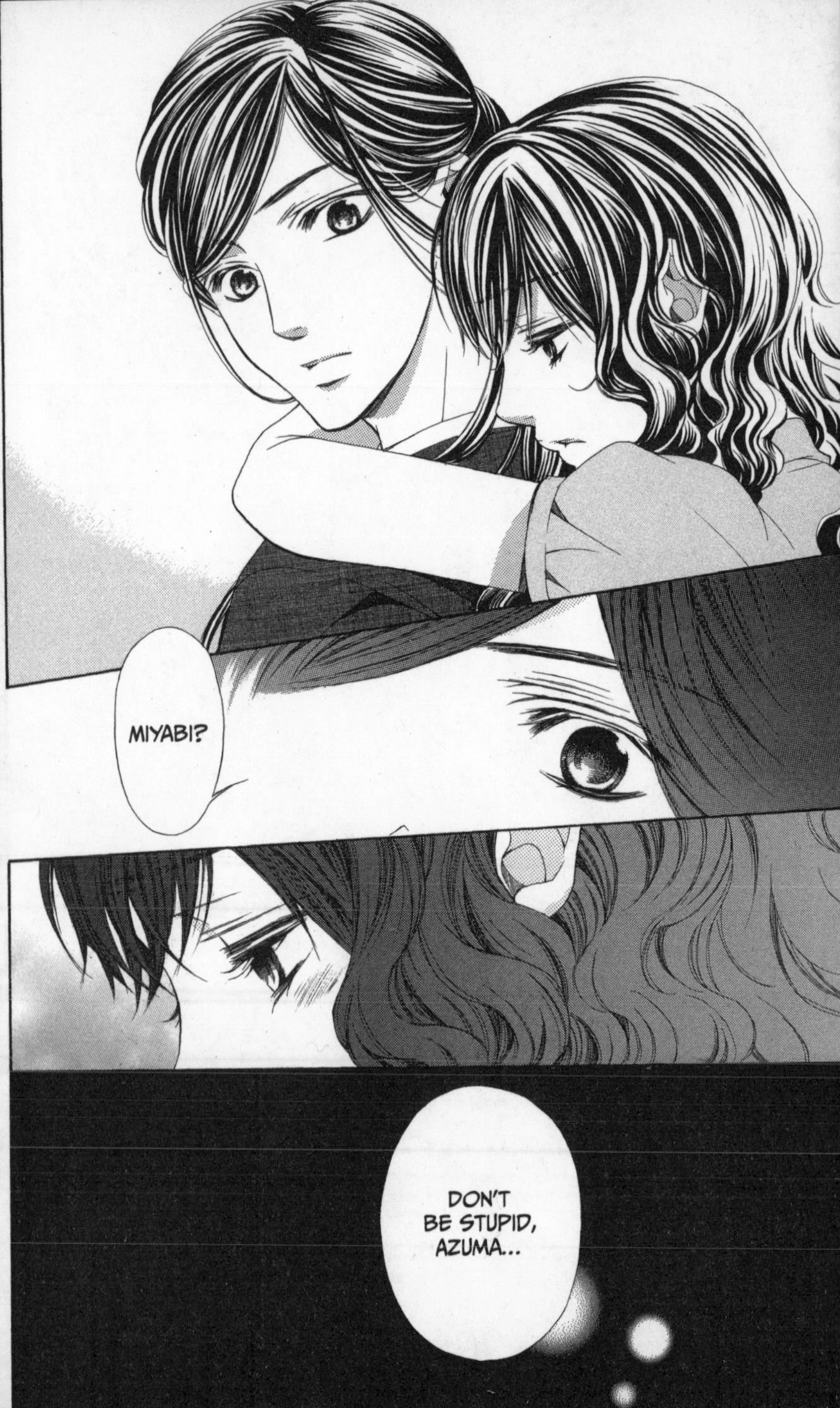
MIYABI?
DON'T BE STUPID, AZUMA...

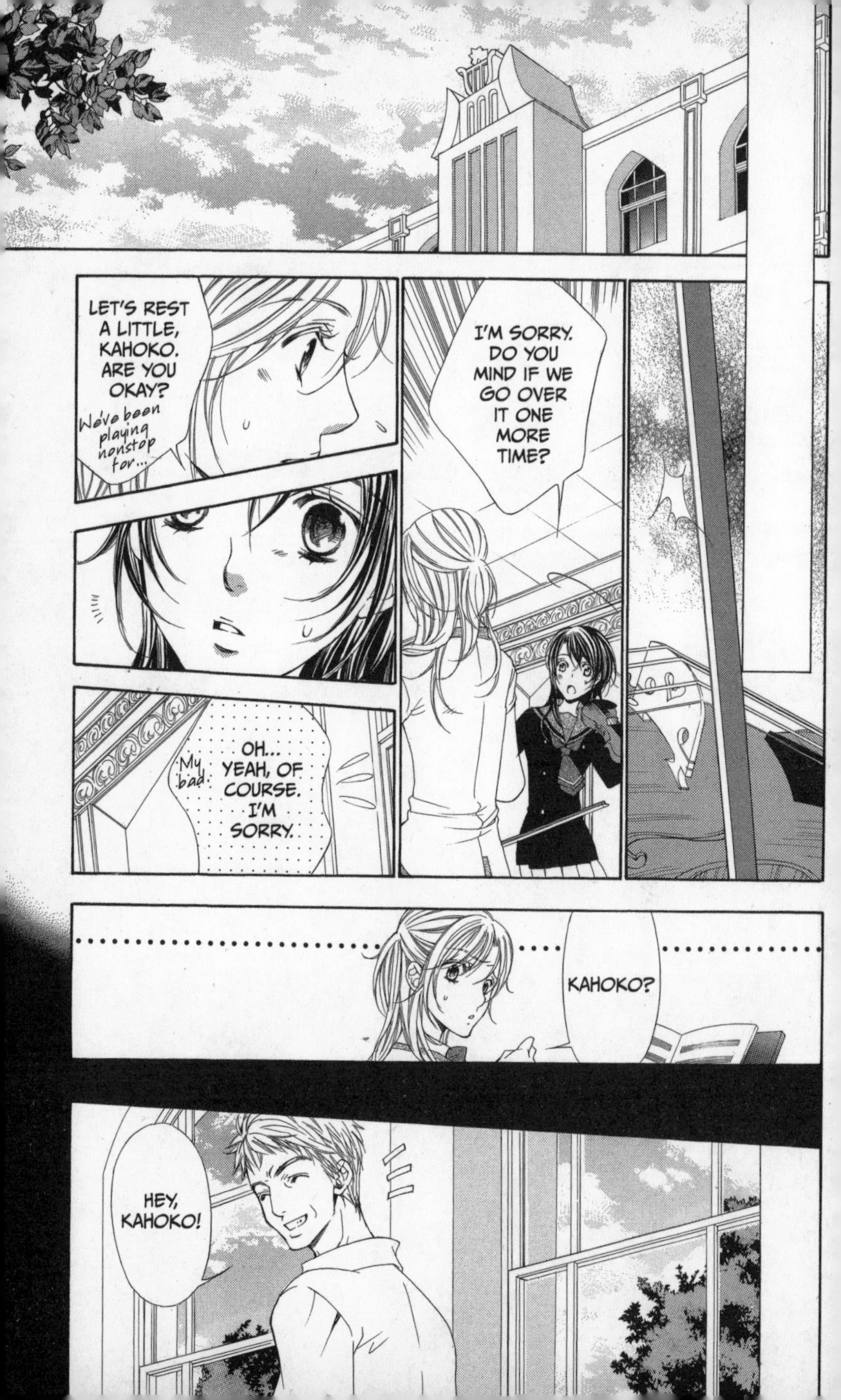
I'M SORRY. DO YOU MIND IF WE GO OVER IT ONE MORE TIME?
LET'S REST A LITTLE, KAHOKO. ARE YOU OKAY?
We've been playing nonstop for...
OH... YEAH, OF COURSE. I'M SORRY.
My bad.
KAHOKO?
HEY, KAHOKO!

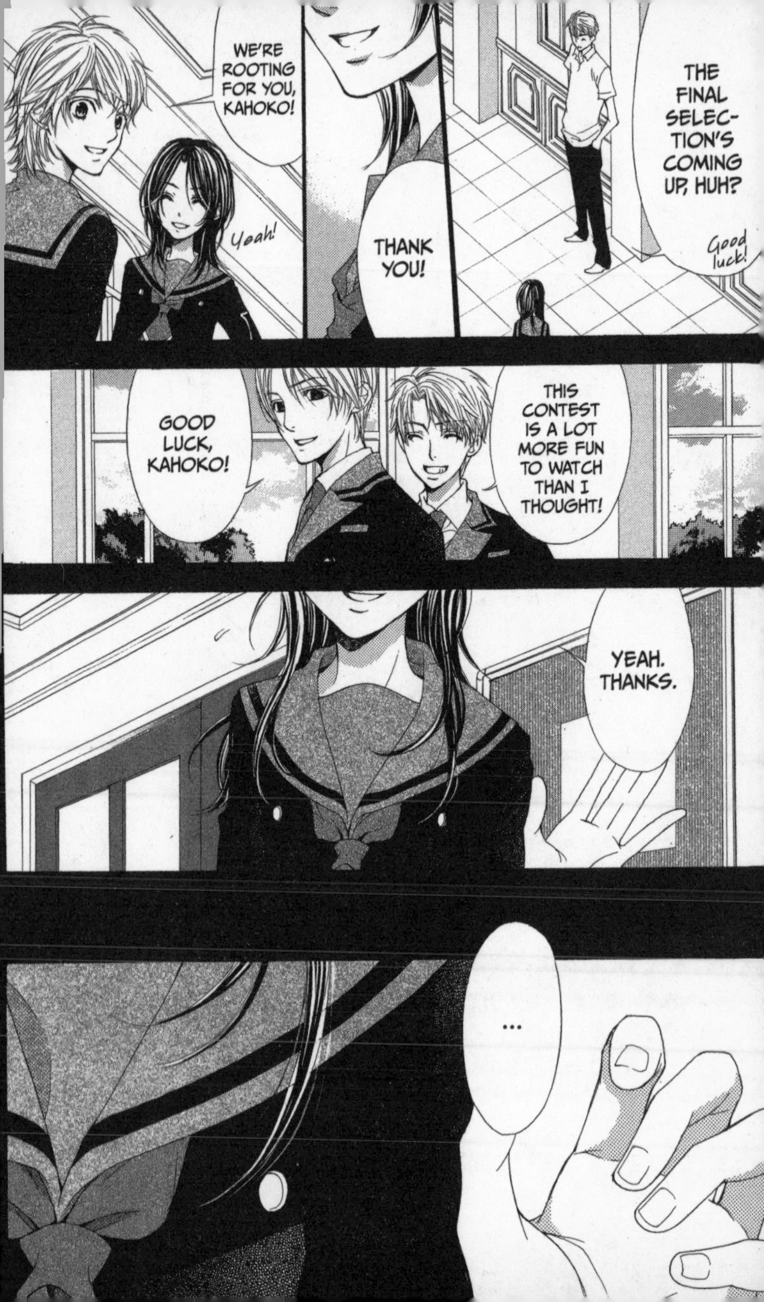
THE FINAL SELEC-TION'S COMING UP, HUH?
Good luck!
THANK YOU!
WE'RE ROOTING FOR YOU, KAHOKO!
Yeah!
THIS CONTEST IS A LOT MORE FUN TO WATCH THAN I THOUGHT!
GOOD LUCK, KAHOKO!
YEAH. THANKS.
...

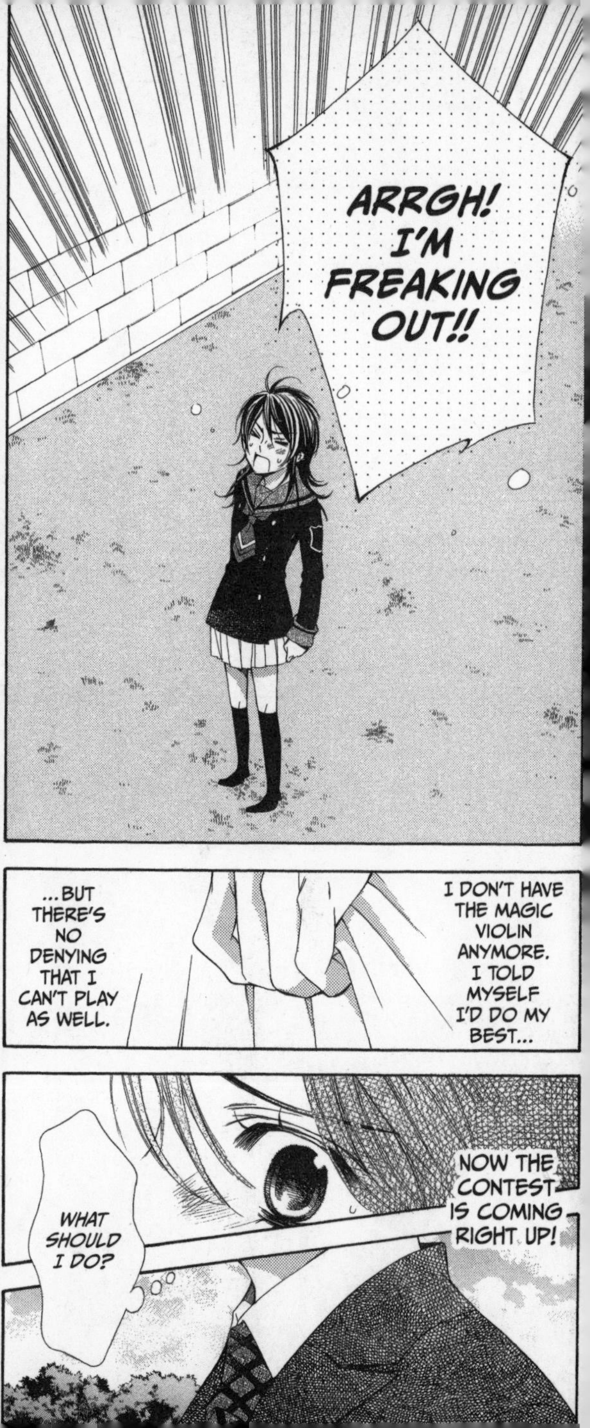
ARRGH! I'M FREAKING OUT!!
I DON'T HAVE THE MAGIC VIOLIN ANYMORE. I TOLD MYSELF I'D DO MY BEST...
...BUT THERE'S NO DENYING THAT I CAN'T PLAY AS WELL.
NOW THE CONTEST IS COMING RIGHT UP!
WHAT SHOULD I DO?

**FIVE**

Thank you so much for reading! It's wonderful to get so much support... I'm just eternally grateful!

And thank you so much for your letters! They're always a great source of encouragement.

Well, I hope to see you again in Volume 10.

(To be continued!)

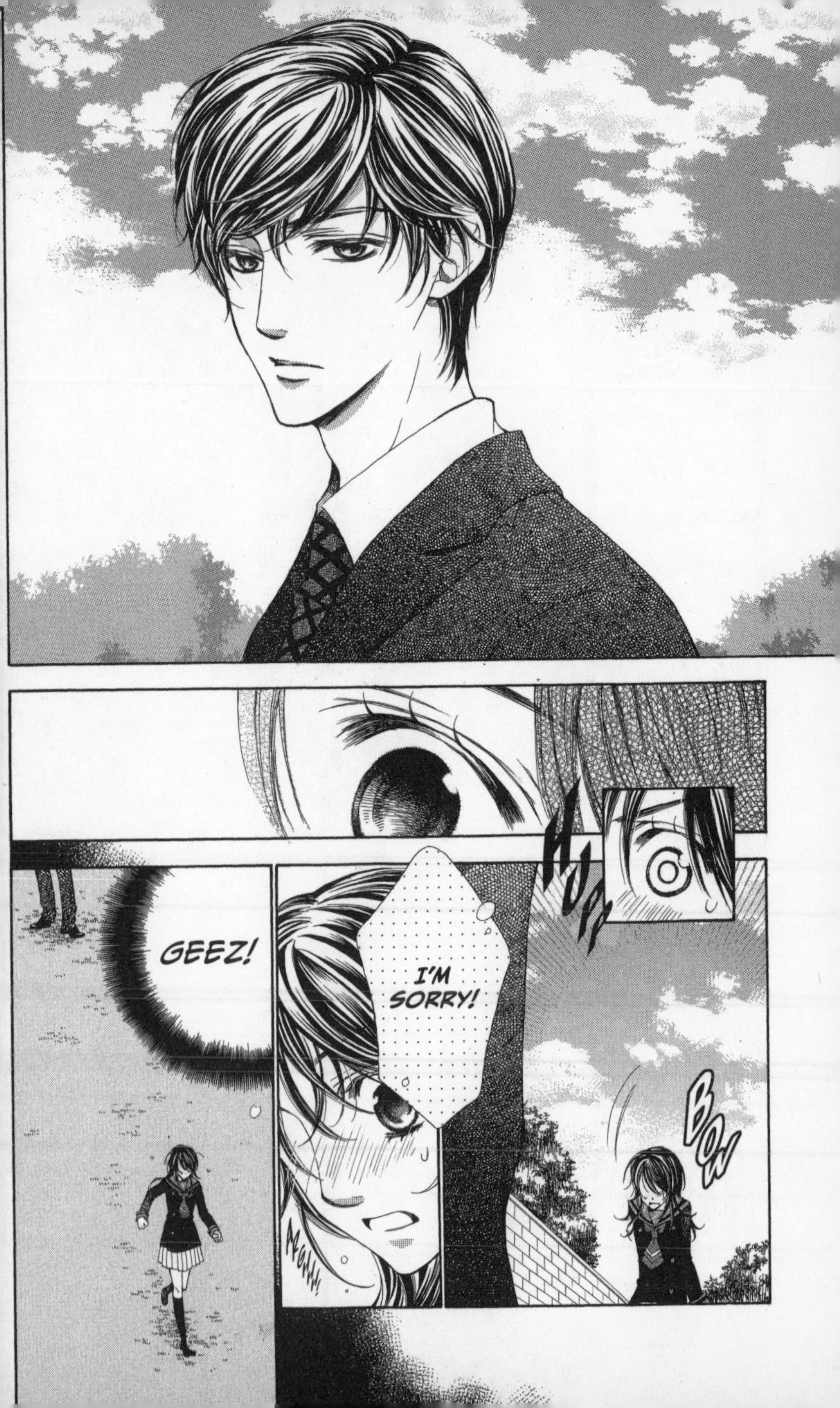
HUP
BOW
I'M SORRY!
ARGHH!
GEEZ!

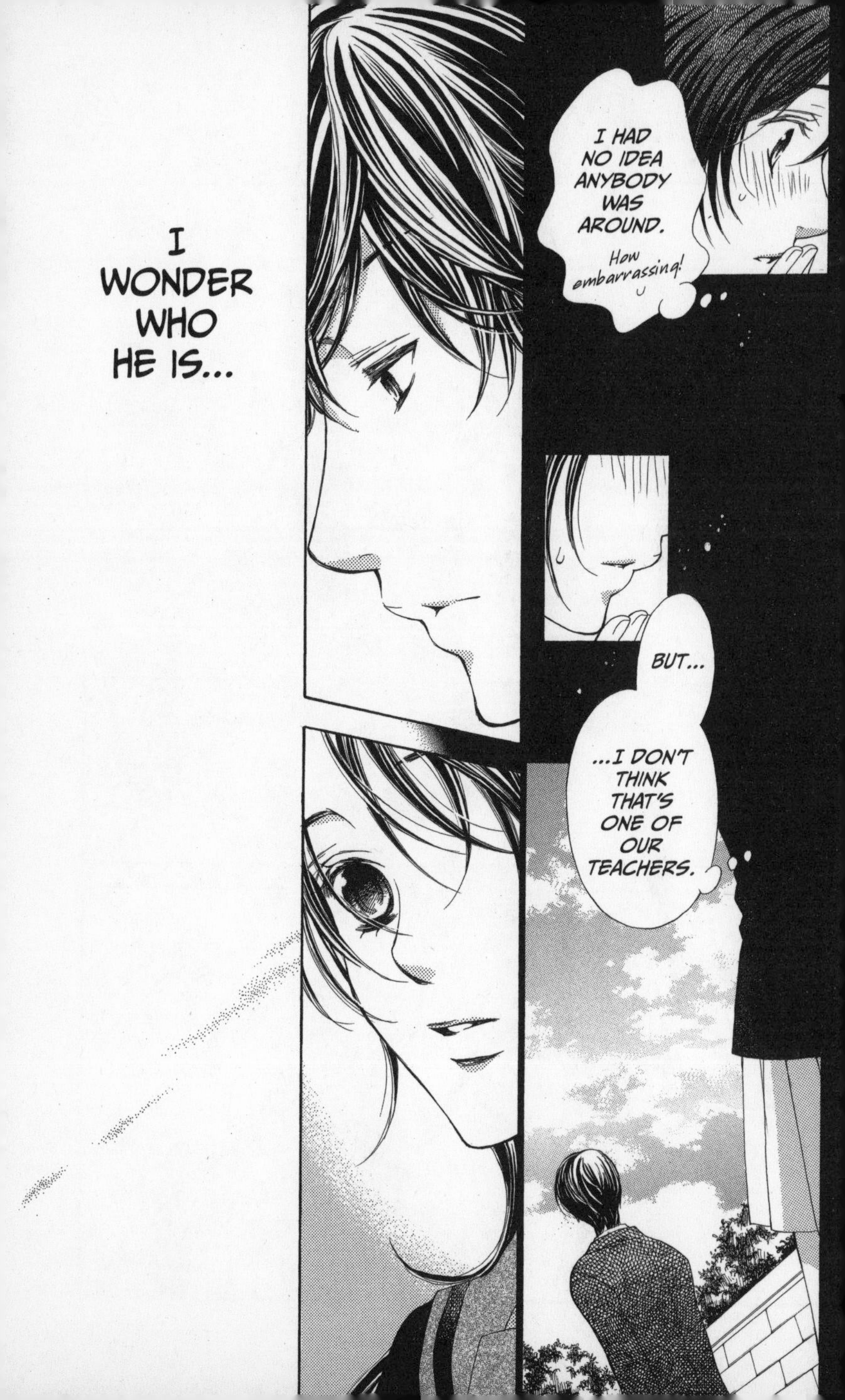
I HAD NO IDEA ANYBODY WAS AROUND.
How embarrassing!
BUT...
...I DON'T THINK THAT'S ONE OF OUR TEACHERS.
I WONDER WHO HE IS...

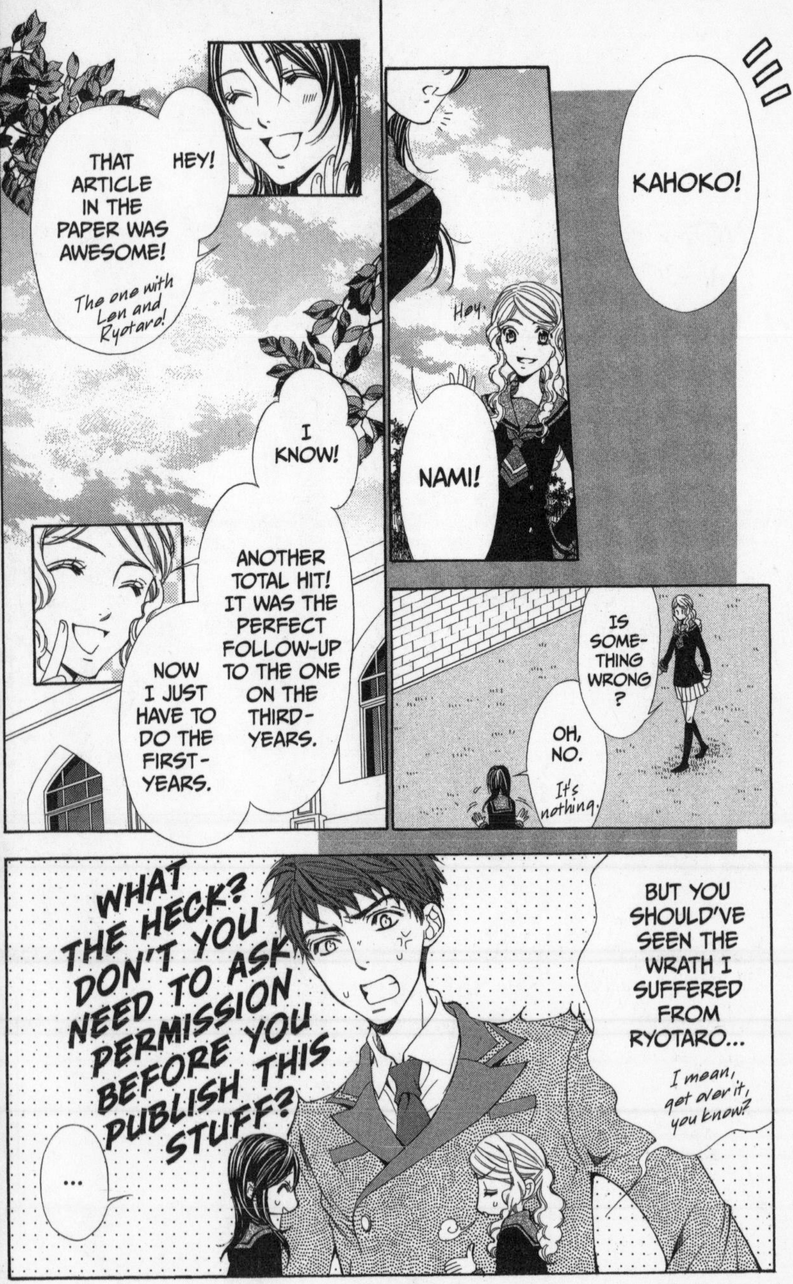
KAHOKO!
Hey.
NAMI!
IS SOMETHING WRONG?
OH, NO.
It's nothing.
HEY!
THAT ARTICLE IN THE PAPER WAS AWESOME!
The one with Len and Ryotaro!
I KNOW!
ANOTHER TOTAL HIT! IT WAS THE PERFECT FOLLOW-UP TO THE ONE ON THE THIRD-YEARS.
NOW I JUST HAVE TO DO THE FIRST-YEARS.
BUT YOU SHOULD'VE SEEN THE WRATH I SUFFERED FROM RYOTARO...
I mean, get over it, you know?
WHAT THE HECK? DON'T YOU NEED TO ASK PERMISSION BEFORE YOU PUBLISH THIS STUFF?
...

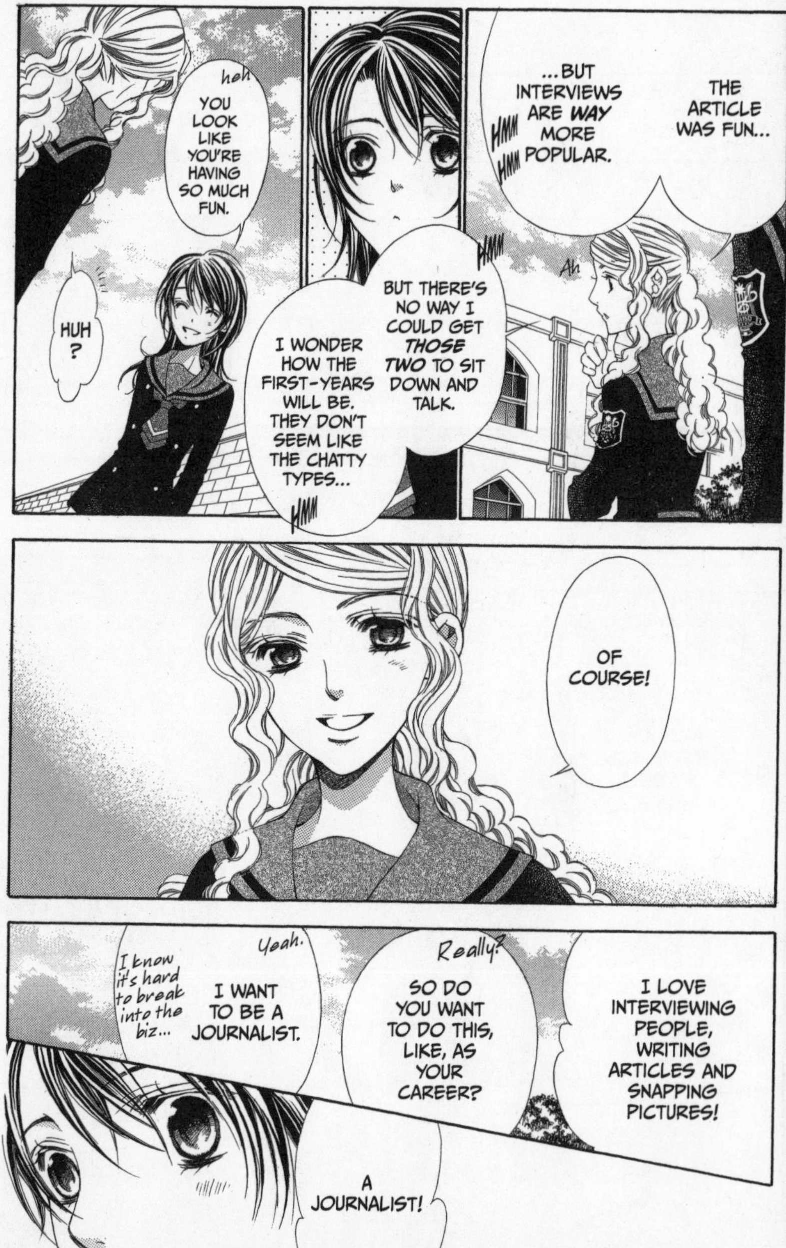
THE ARTICLE WAS FUN...
...BUT INTERVIEWS ARE WAY MORE POPULAR.
HMM HMM
HMM
Ah
BUT THERE'S NO WAY I COULD GET THOSE TWO TO SIT DOWN AND TALK.
I WONDER HOW THE FIRST-YEARS WILL BE. THEY DON'T SEEM LIKE THE CHATTY TYPES...
HMM
heh
YOU LOOK LIKE YOU'RE HAVING SO MUCH FUN.
HUH?
OF COURSE!
I LOVE INTERVIEWING PEOPLE, WRITING ARTICLES AND SNAPPING PICTURES!
Really?
SO DO YOU WANT TO DO THIS, LIKE, AS YOUR CAREER?
Yeah.
I WANT TO BE A JOURNALIST.
I know it's hard to break into the biz...
A JOURNALIST!

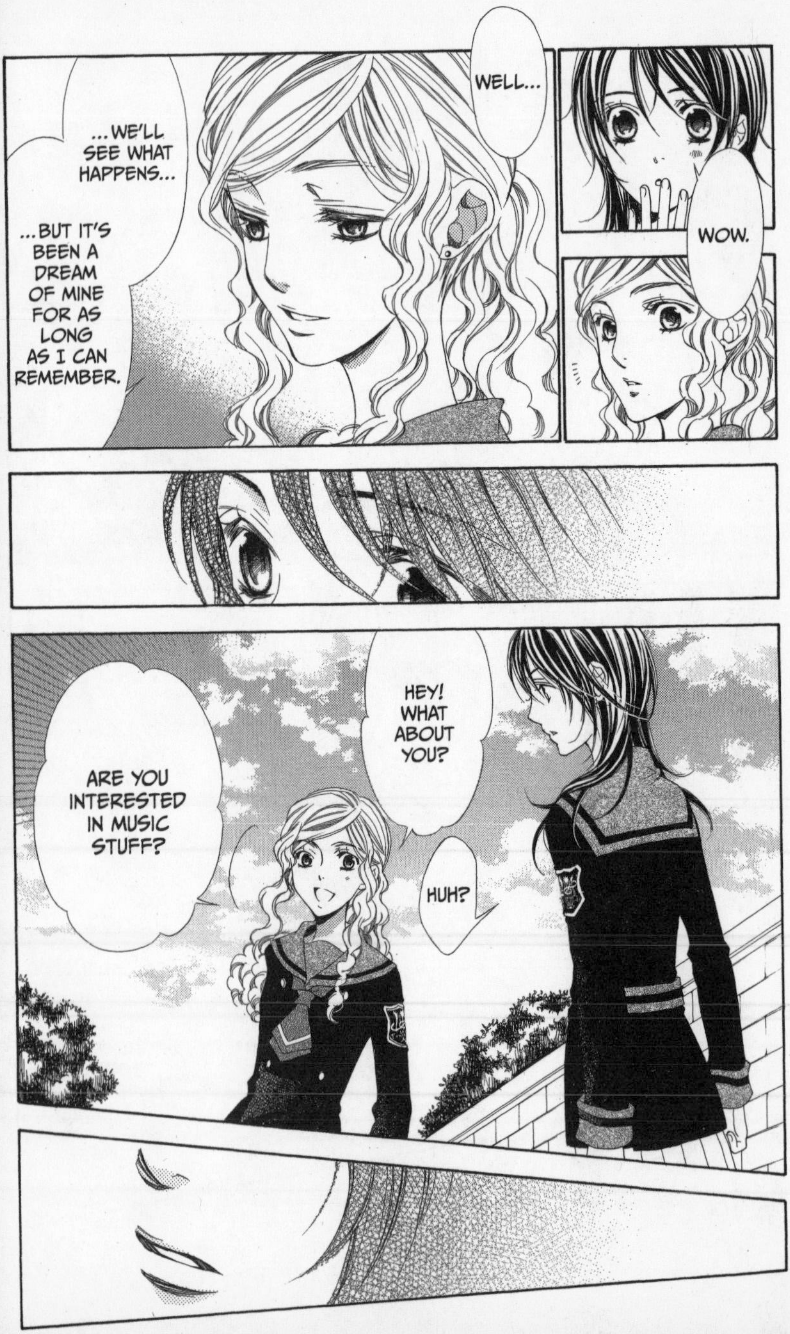
WELL...
...WE'LL SEE WHAT HAPPENS...
...BUT IT'S BEEN A DREAM OF MINE FOR AS LONG AS I CAN REMEMBER.
WOW.
HEY! WHAT ABOUT YOU?
ARE YOU INTERESTED IN MUSIC STUFF?
HUH?

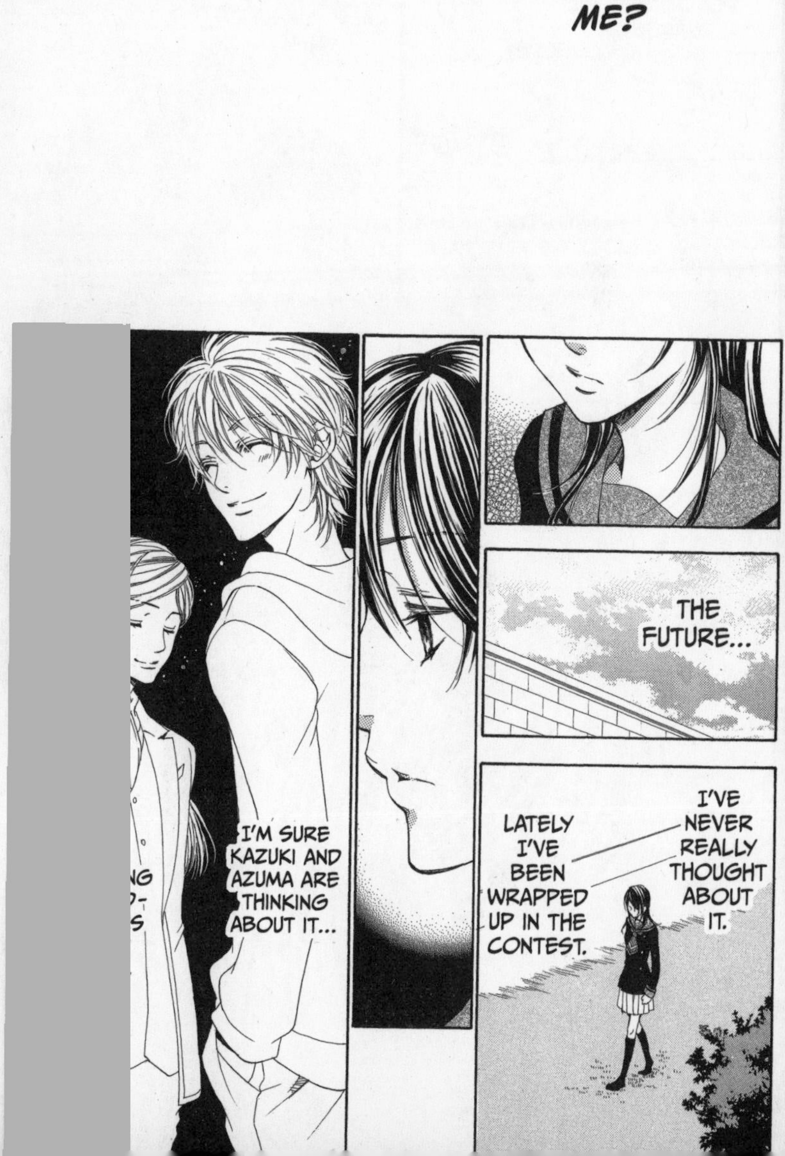
ME?
THE FUTURE...
I'VE NEVER REALLY THOUGHT ABOUT IT.
LATELY I'VE BEEN WRAPPED UP IN THE CONTEST.
I'M SURE KAZUKI AND AZUMA ARE THINKING ABOUT IT...

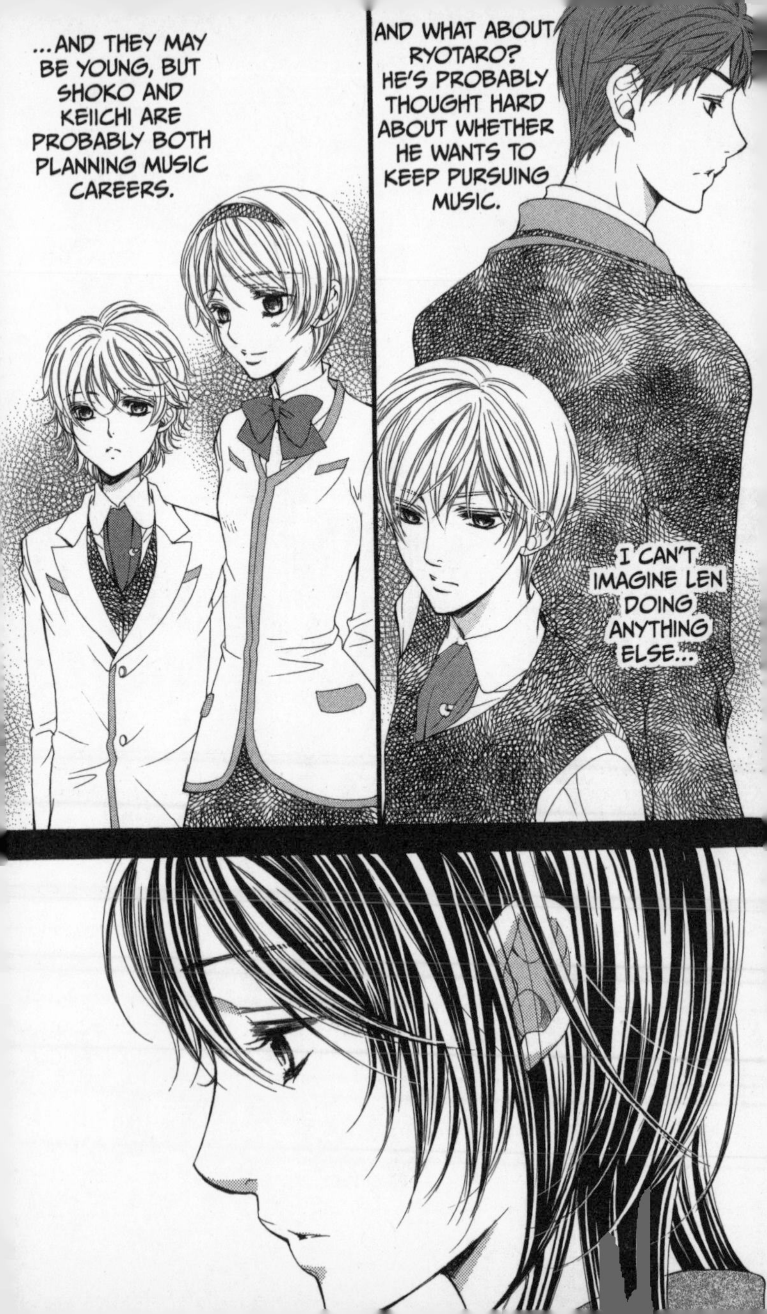
...AND THEY MAY BE YOUNG, BUT SHOKO AND KEIICHI ARE PROBABLY BOTH PLANNING MUSIC CAREERS.
AND WHAT ABOUT RYOTARO? HE'S PROBABLY THOUGHT HARD ABOUT WHETHER HE WANTS TO KEEP PURSUING MUSIC.
I CAN'T IMAGINE LEN DOING ANYTHING ELSE...

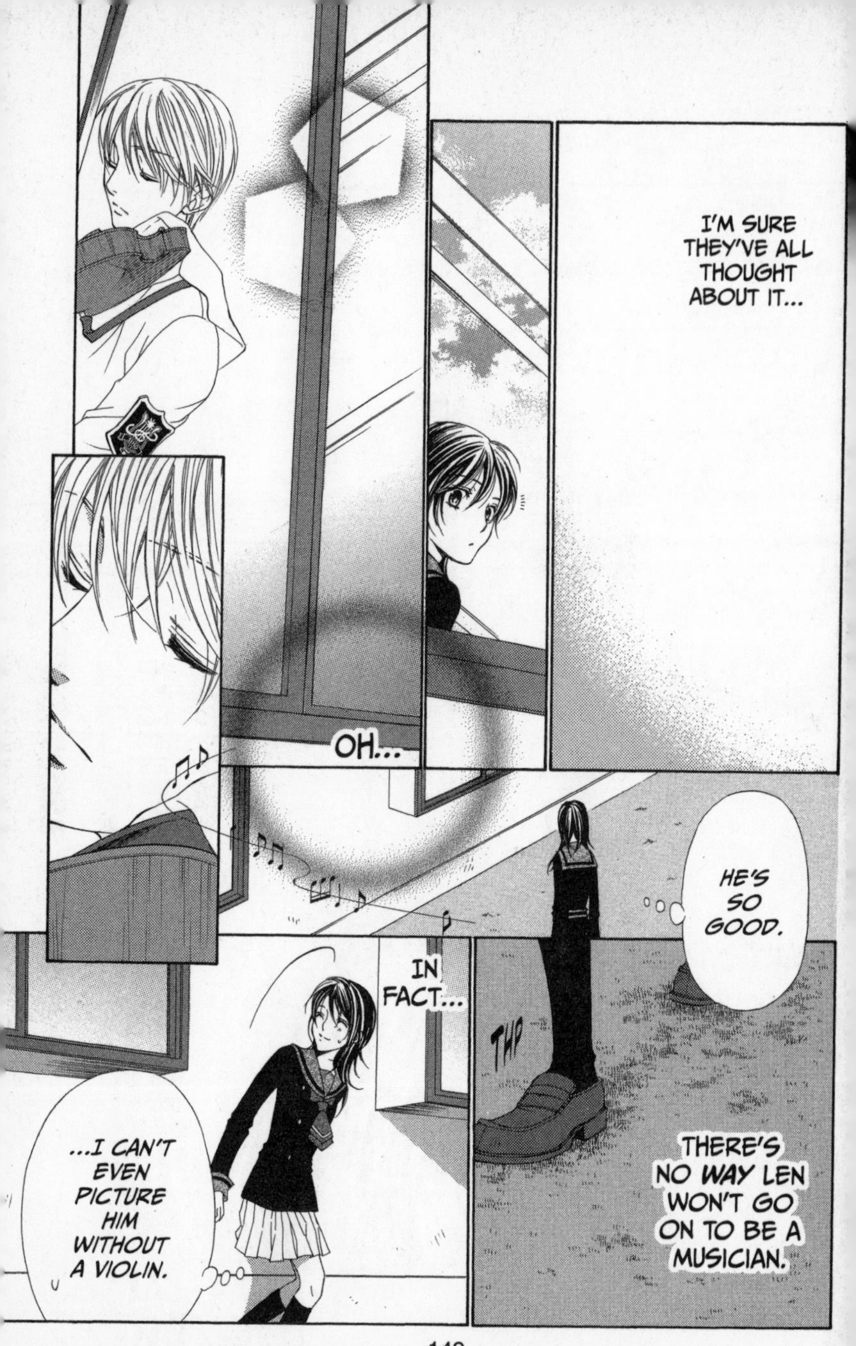
I'M SURE THEY'VE ALL THOUGHT ABOUT IT...
OH...
HE'S SO GOOD.
THP
THERE'S NO WAY LEN WON'T GO ON TO BE A MUSICIAN.
IN FACT...
...I CAN'T EVEN PICTURE HIM WITHOUT A VIOLIN.

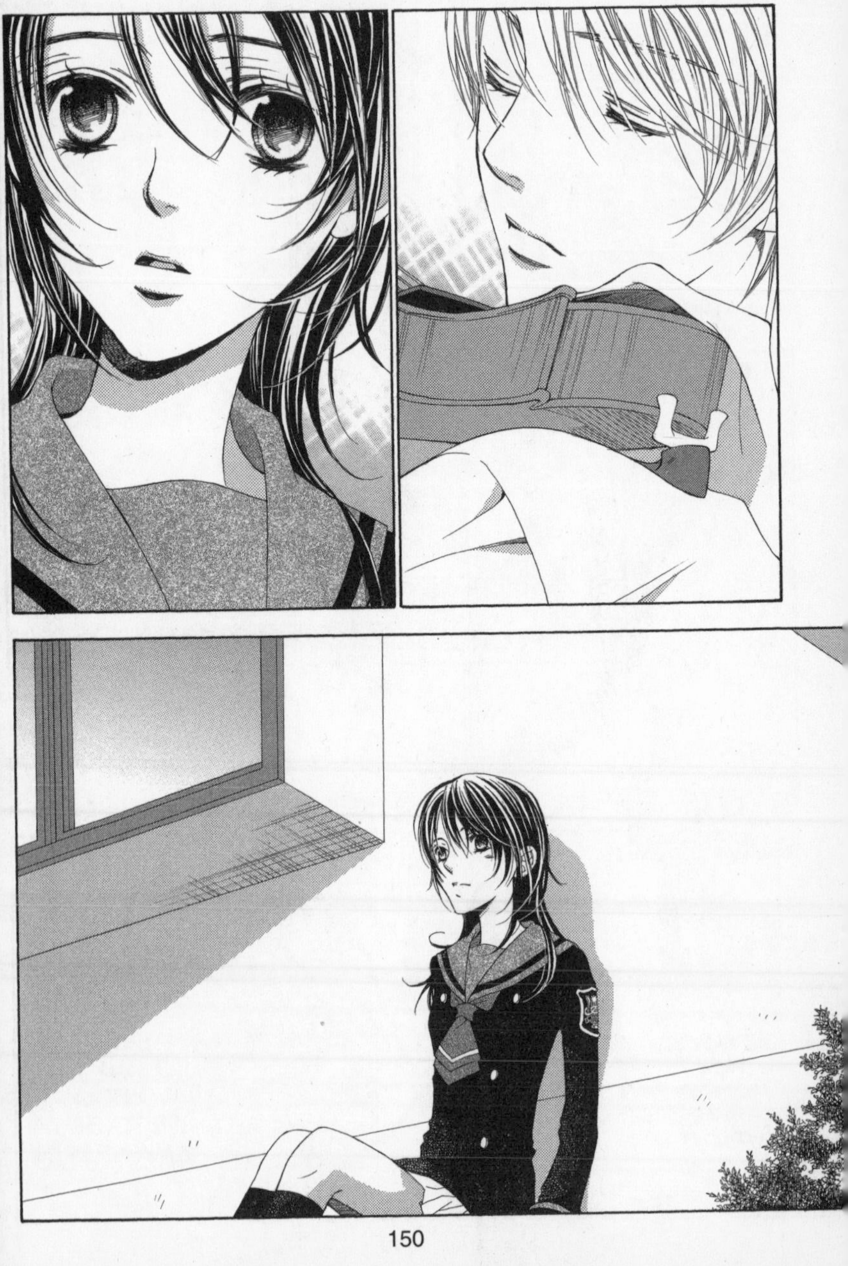

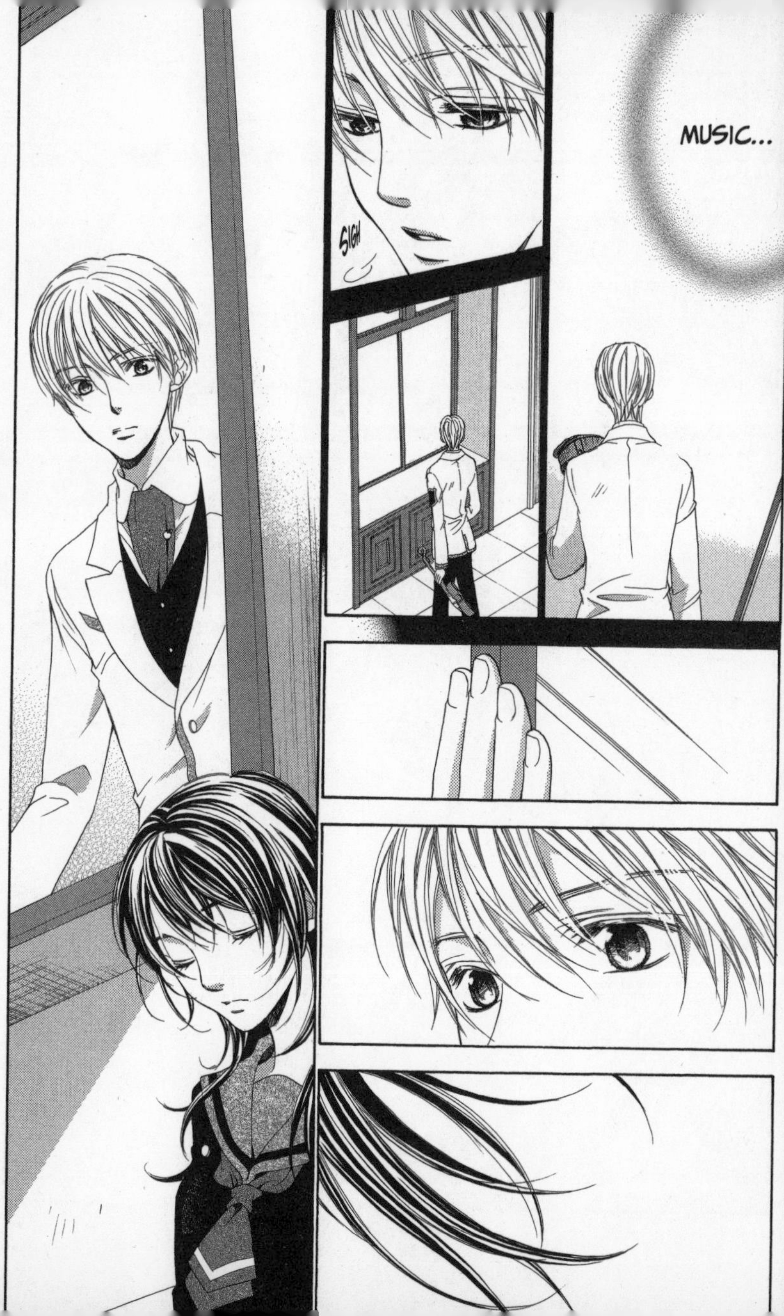
MUSIC...
SIGH

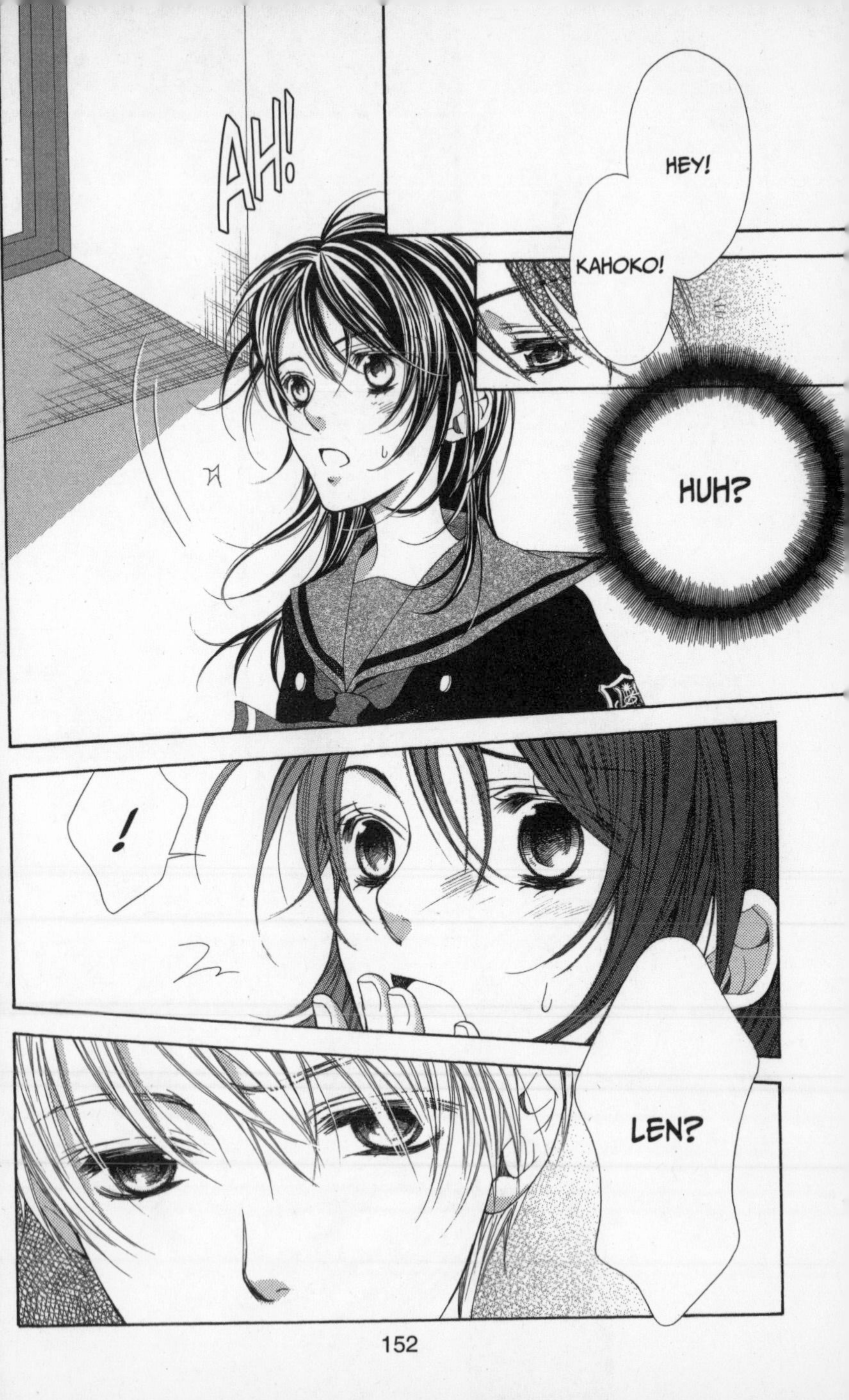
HEY!
KAHOKO!
HUH?
AH!
!
LEN?

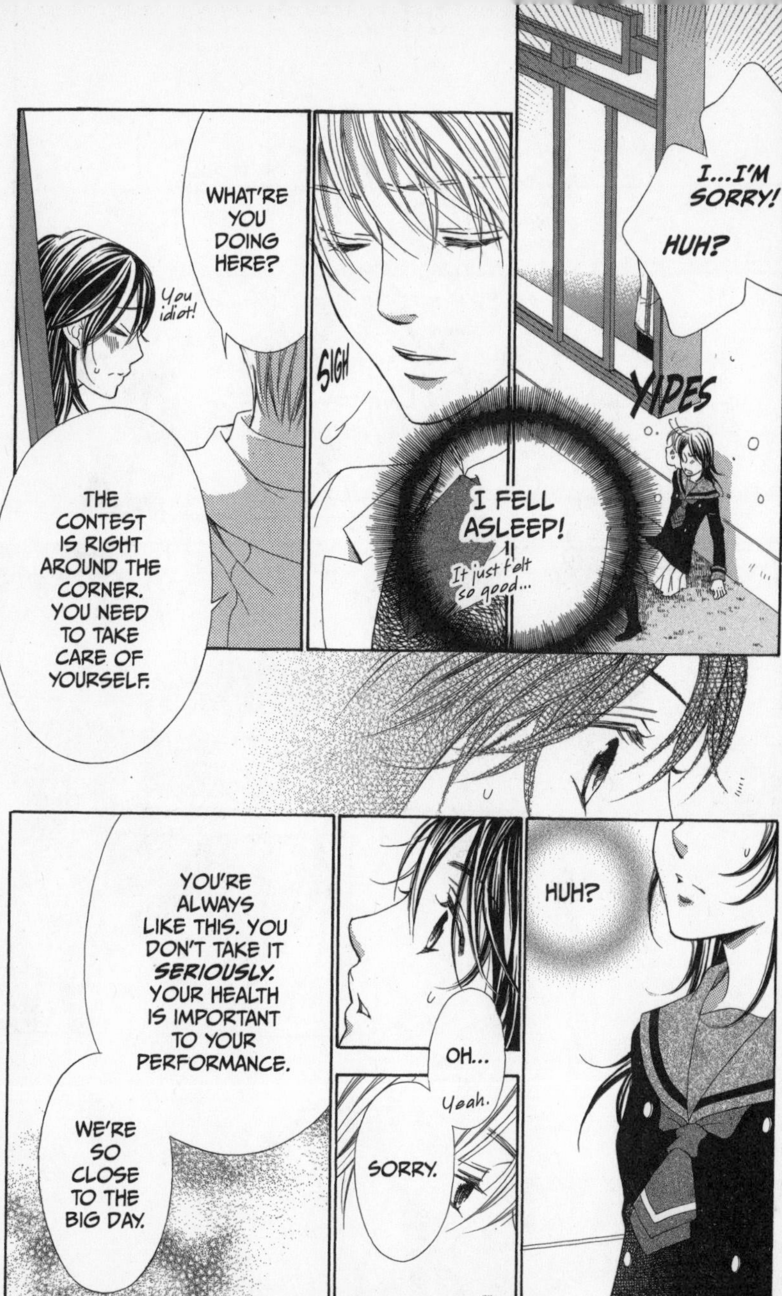
I...I'M SORRY!
HUH?
YIPES
I FELL ASLEEP!
It just felt so good...
SIGH
WHAT'RE YOU DOING HERE?
You idiot!
THE CONTEST IS RIGHT AROUND THE CORNER. YOU NEED TO TAKE CARE OF YOURSELF.
HUH?
OH...
Yeah.
SORRY.
YOU'RE ALWAYS LIKE THIS. YOU DON'T TAKE IT *SERIOUSLY.* YOUR HEALTH IS IMPORTANT TO YOUR PERFORMANCE.
WE'RE SO CLOSE TO THE BIG DAY.

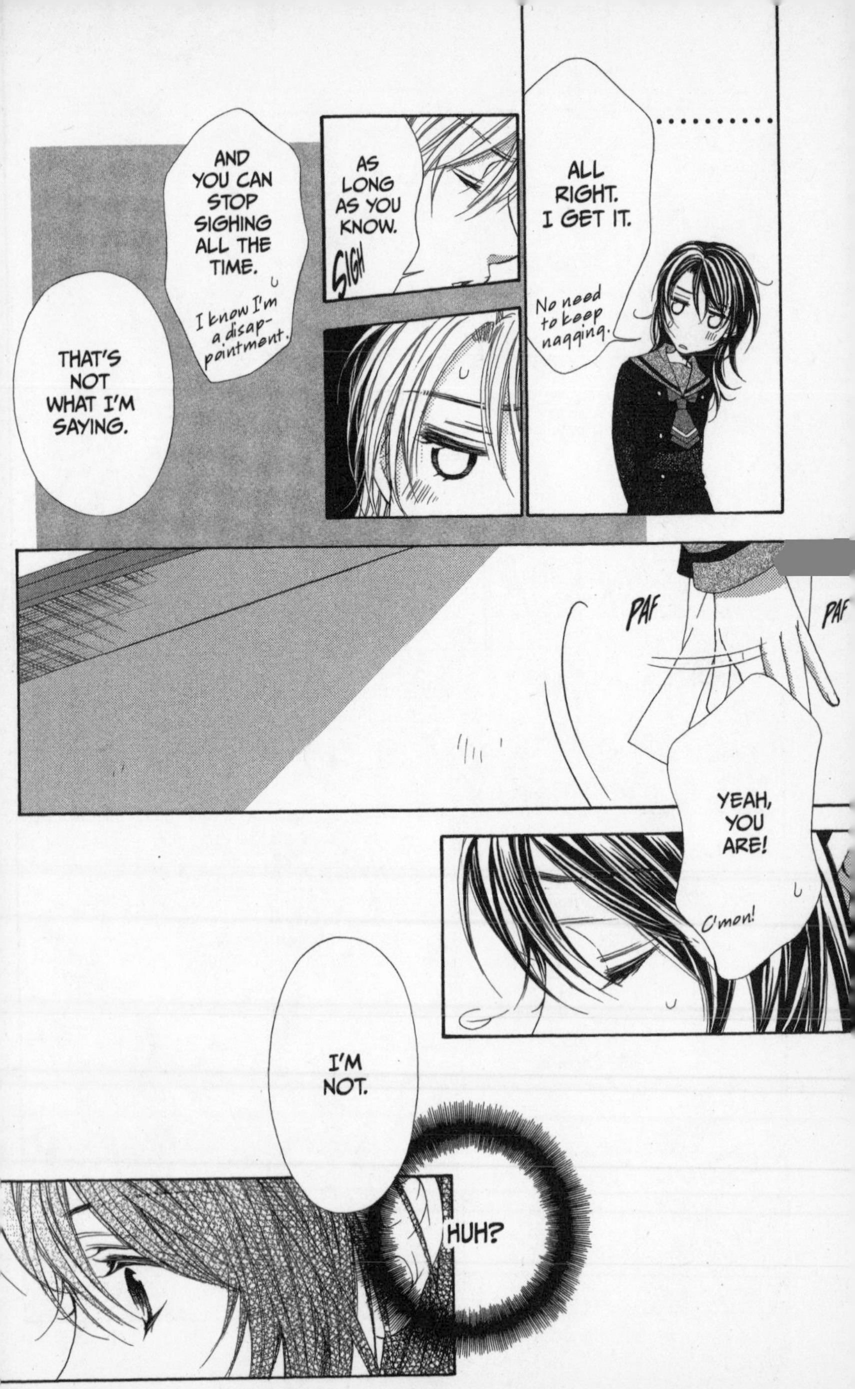

..........
ALL RIGHT. I GET IT.
No need to keep nagging.
AS LONG AS YOU KNOW.
SIGH
AND YOU CAN STOP SIGHING ALL THE TIME.
I know I'm a disappointment.
THAT'S NOT WHAT I'M SAYING.
PAF
PAF
YEAH, YOU ARE!
C'mon!
I'M NOT.
HUH?

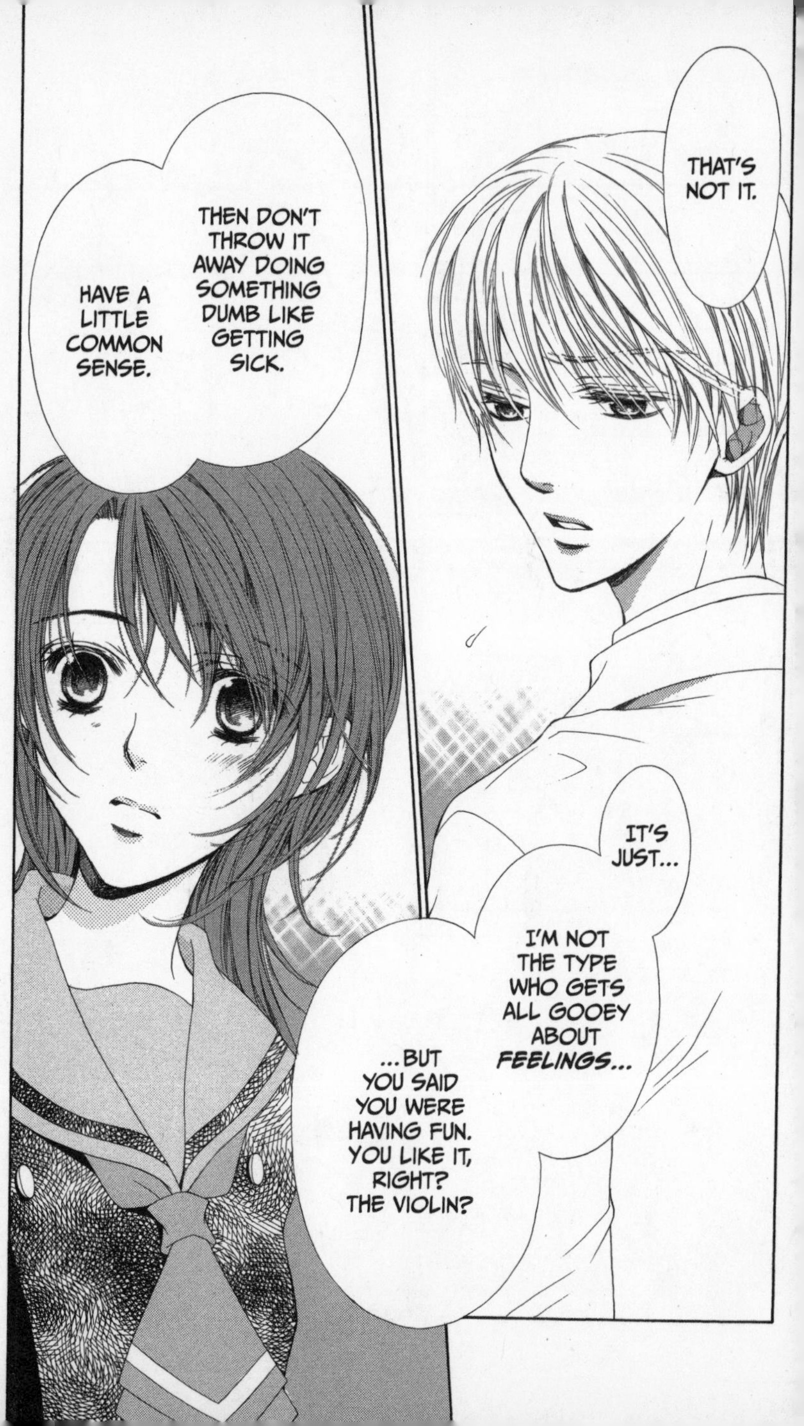
THAT'S NOT IT.
IT'S JUST...
I'M NOT THE TYPE WHO GETS ALL GOOEY ABOUT *FEELINGS*...
...BUT YOU SAID YOU WERE HAVING FUN. YOU LIKE IT, RIGHT? THE VIOLIN?
THEN DON'T THROW IT AWAY DOING SOMETHING DUMB LIKE GETTING SICK.
HAVE A LITTLE COMMON SENSE.

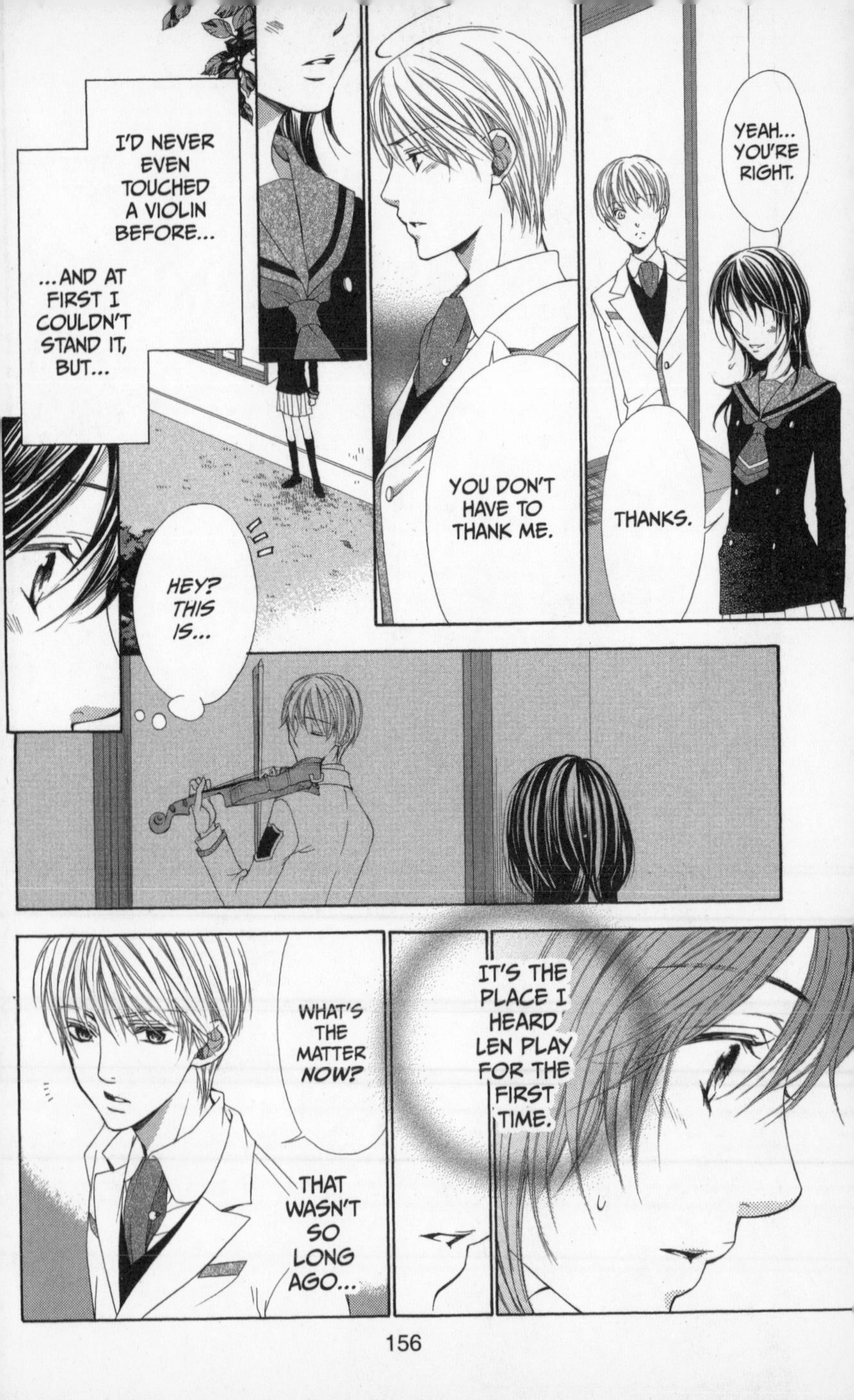
YEAH... YOU'RE RIGHT.
THANKS.
YOU DON'T HAVE TO THANK ME.
I'D NEVER EVEN TOUCHED A VIOLIN BEFORE...
...AND AT FIRST I COULDN'T STAND IT, BUT...
HEY? THIS IS...
IT'S THE PLACE I HEARD LEN PLAY FOR THE FIRST TIME.
WHAT'S THE MATTER NOW?
THAT WASN'T SO LONG AGO...

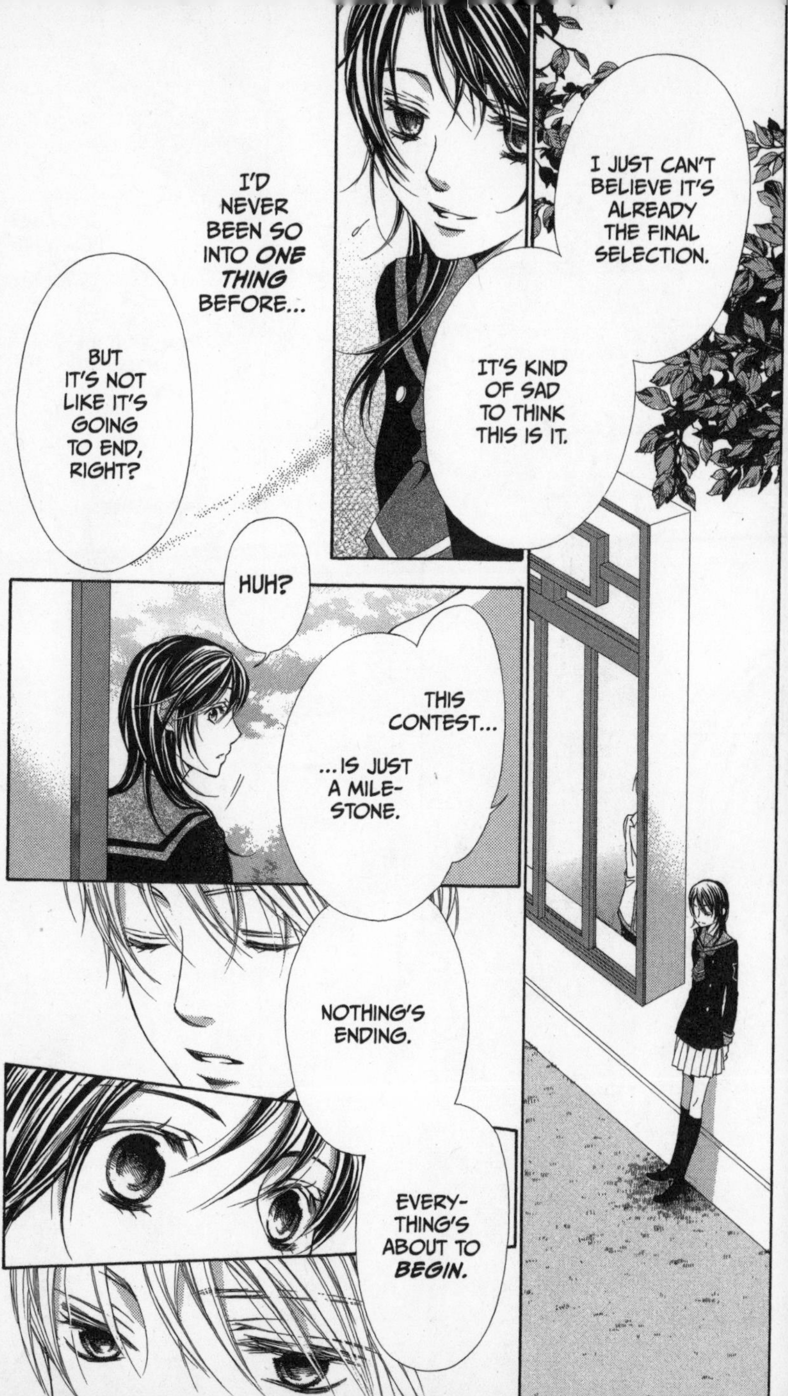
I JUST CAN'T BELIEVE IT'S ALREADY THE FINAL SELECTION.
IT'S KIND OF SAD TO THINK THIS IS IT.
I'D NEVER BEEN SO INTO *ONE THING* BEFORE...
BUT IT'S NOT LIKE IT'S GOING TO END, RIGHT?
HUH?
THIS CONTEST...
...IS JUST A MILE-STONE.
NOTHING'S ENDING.
EVERY-THING'S ABOUT TO *BEGIN.*

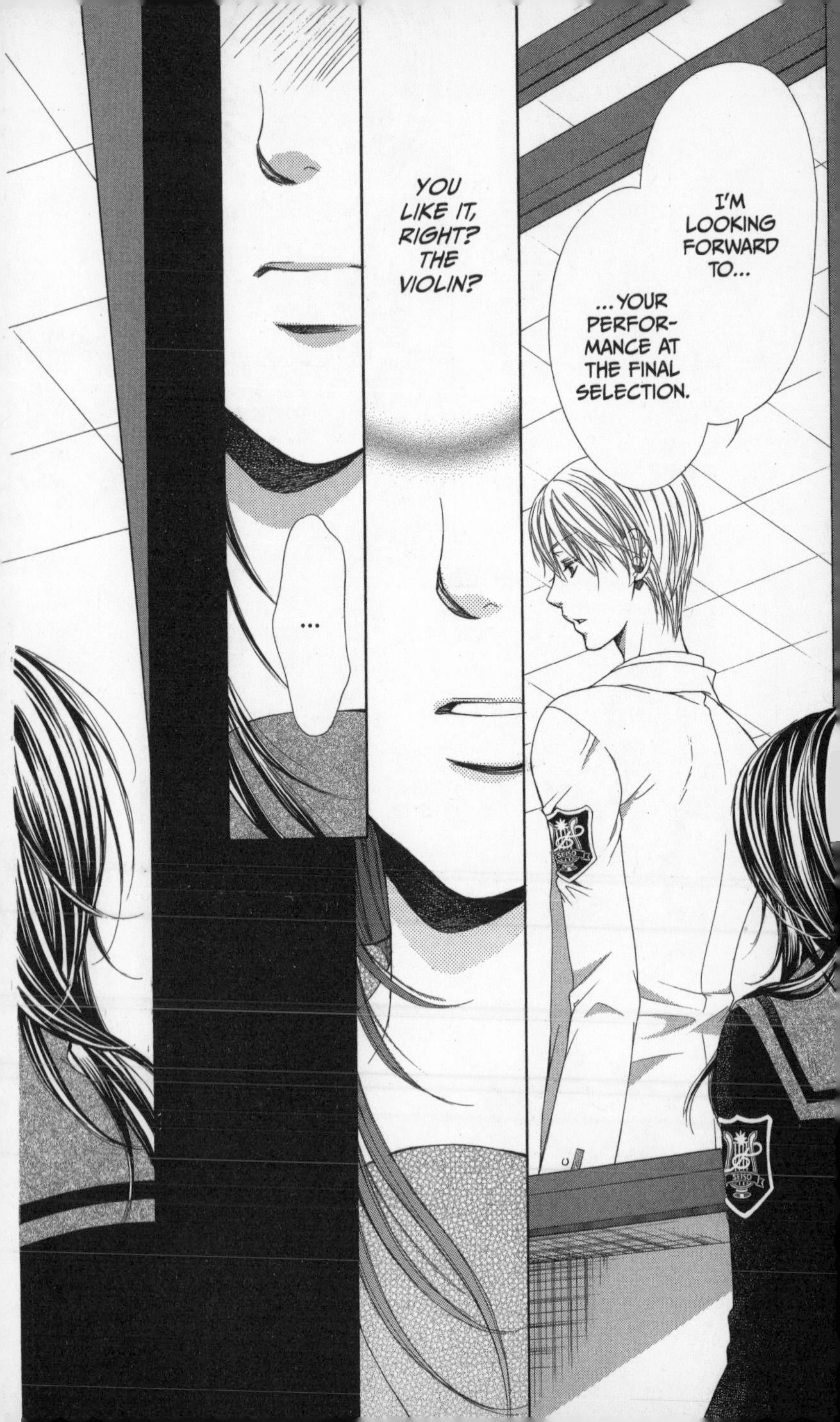
I'M LOOKING FORWARD TO...
...YOUR PERFORMANCE AT THE FINAL SELECTION.
YOU LIKE IT, RIGHT? THE VIOLIN?
...

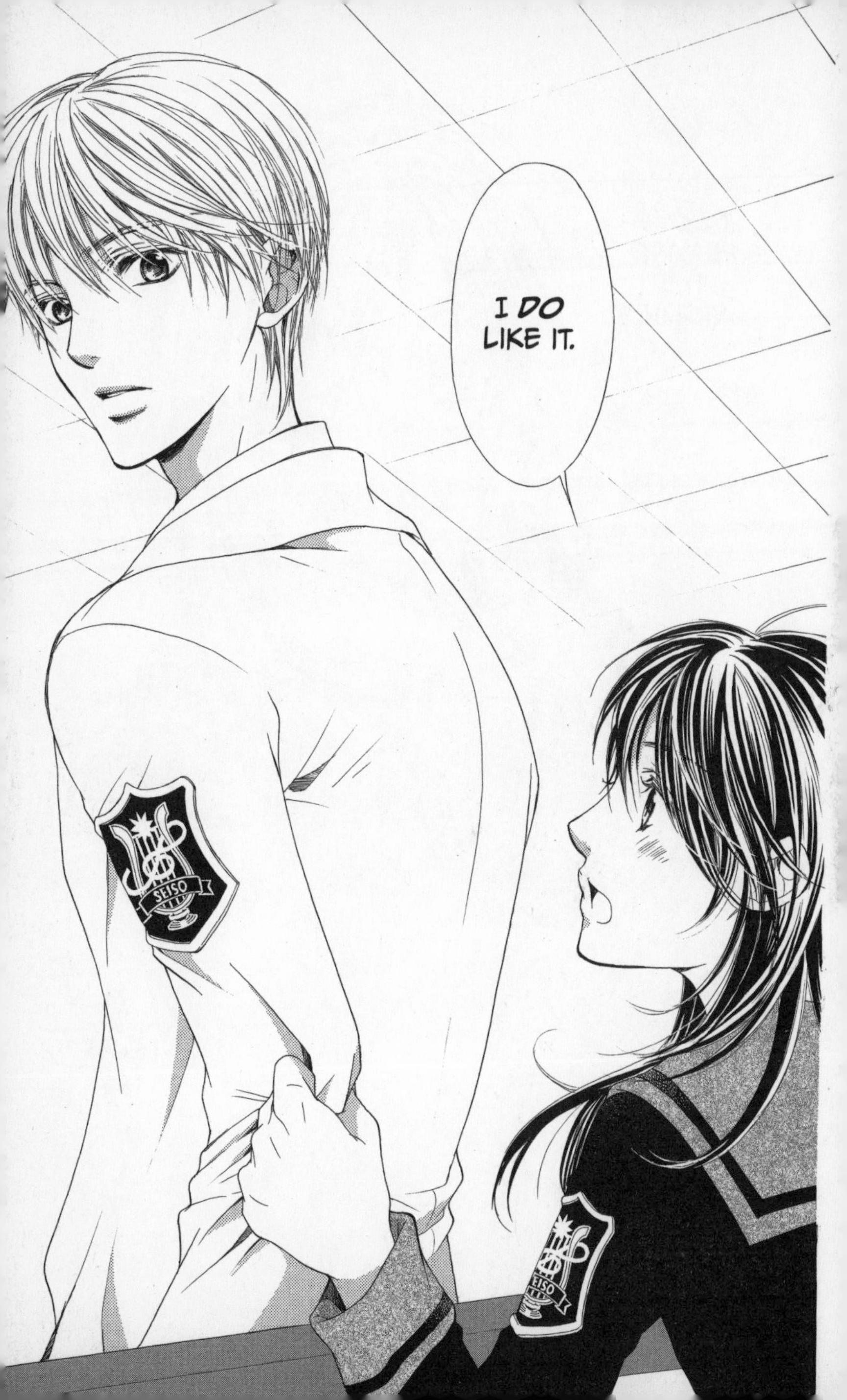
I DO LIKE IT.
SEISO
SEISO

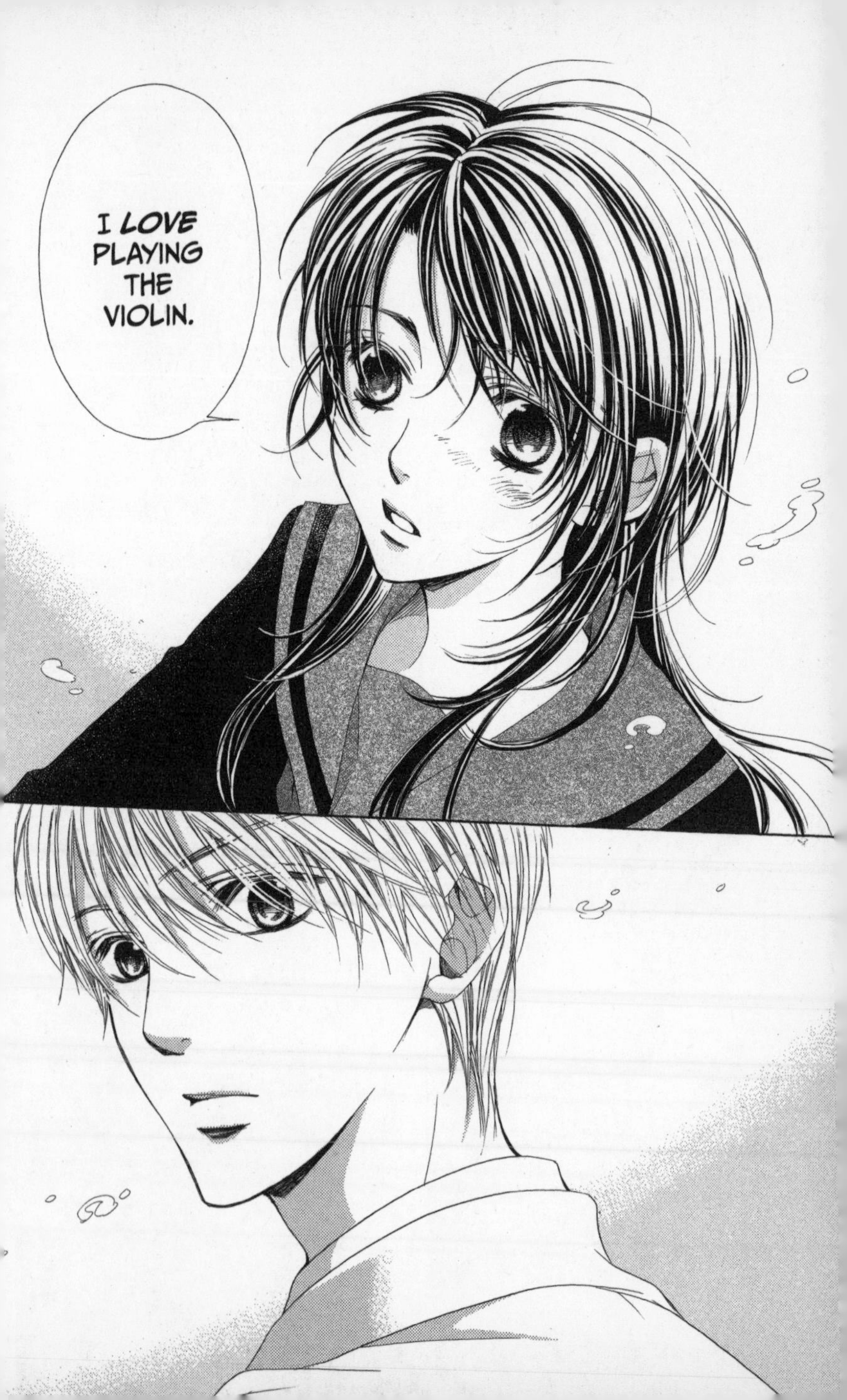
I *LOVE* PLAYING THE VIOLIN.

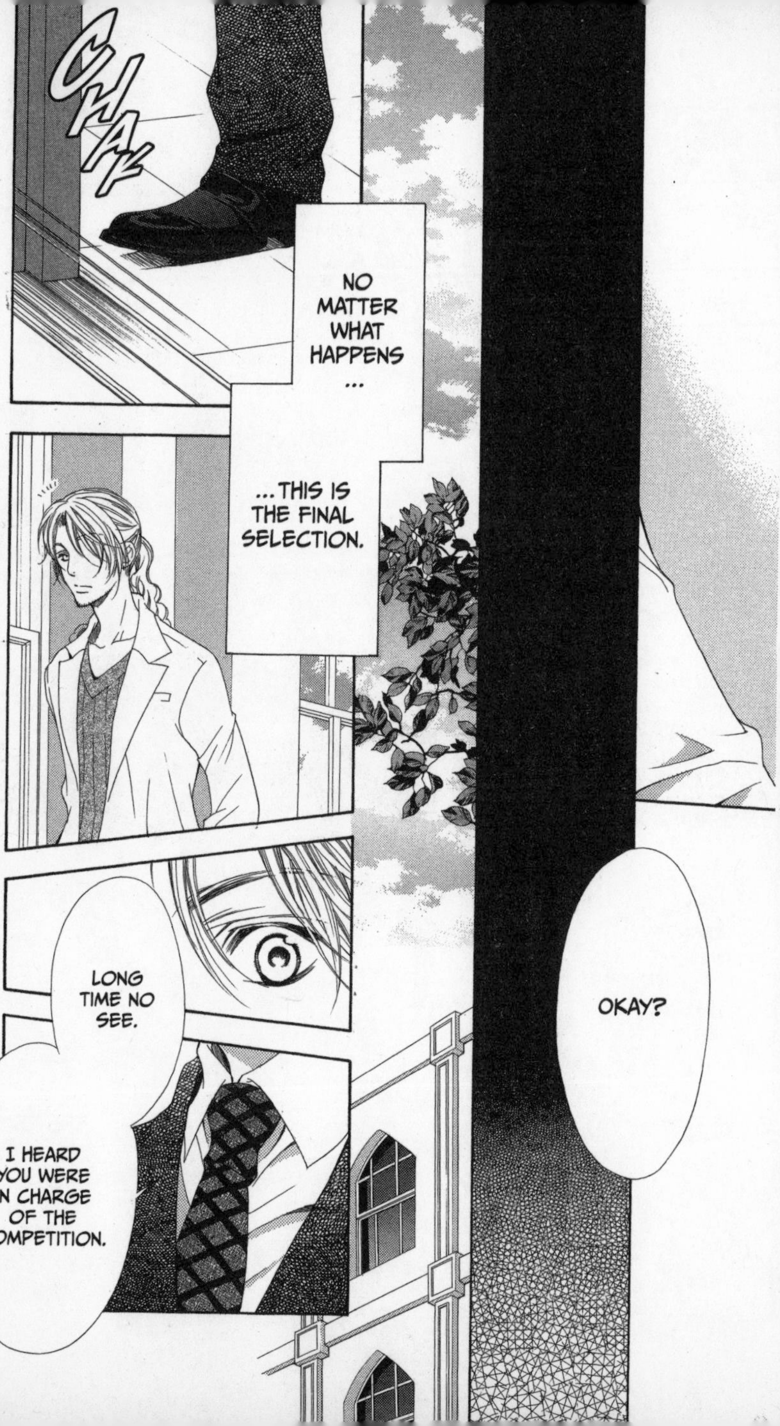
NO MATTER WHAT HAPPENS ...
...THIS IS THE FINAL SELECTION.
OKAY?
CHAK
LONG TIME NO SEE.
I HEARD YOU WERE IN CHARGE OF THE COMPETITION.

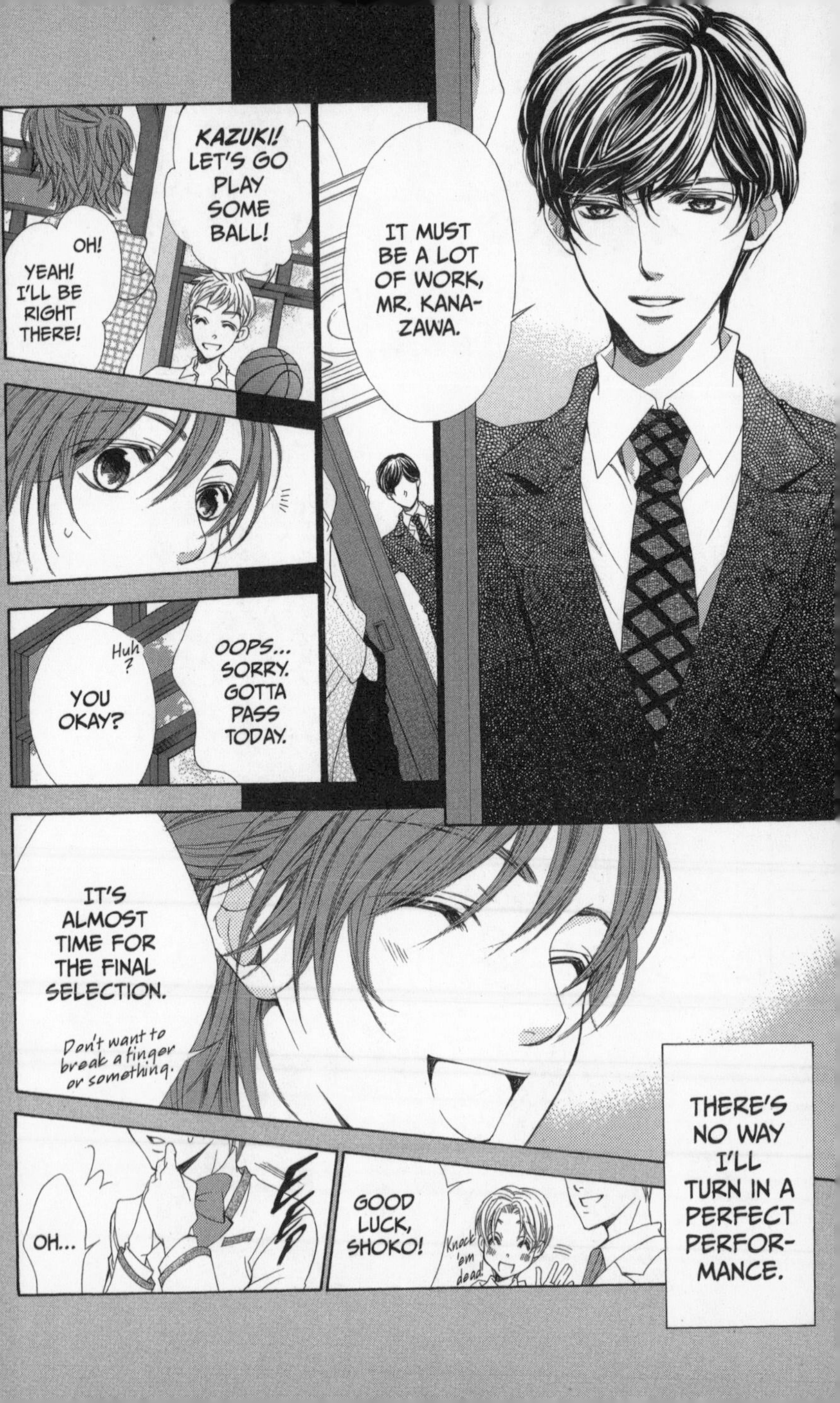
IT MUST BE A LOT OF WORK, MR. KANA-ZAWA.
KAZUKI! LET'S GO PLAY SOME BALL!
OH! YEAH! I'LL BE RIGHT THERE!
OOPS... SORRY. GOTTA PASS TODAY.
Huh?
YOU OKAY?
THERE'S NO WAY I'LL TURN IN A PERFECT PERFOR-MANCE.
IT'S ALMOST TIME FOR THE FINAL SELECTION.
Don't want to break a finger or something.
GOOD LUCK, SHOKO!
Knock 'em dead!
OH...

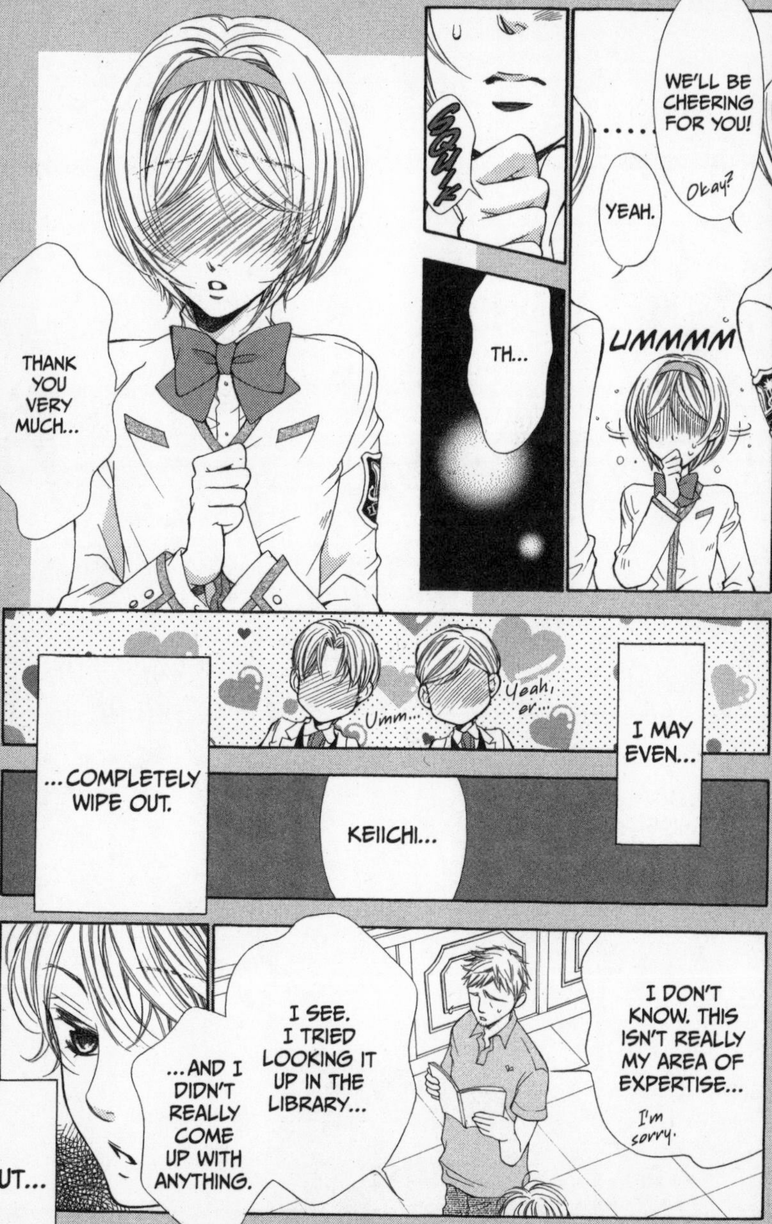
WE'LL BE CHEERING FOR YOU!
Okay?
YEAH.
......
UMMMM
TH...
THANK YOU VERY MUCH...
I MAY EVEN...
Yeah, er...
Umm...
KEIICHI...
...COMPLETELY WIPE OUT.
I DON'T KNOW. THIS ISN'T REALLY MY AREA OF EXPERTISE...
I'm sorry.
I SEE. I TRIED LOOKING IT UP IN THE LIBRARY...
...AND I DIDN'T REALLY COME UP WITH ANYTHING.
BUT...

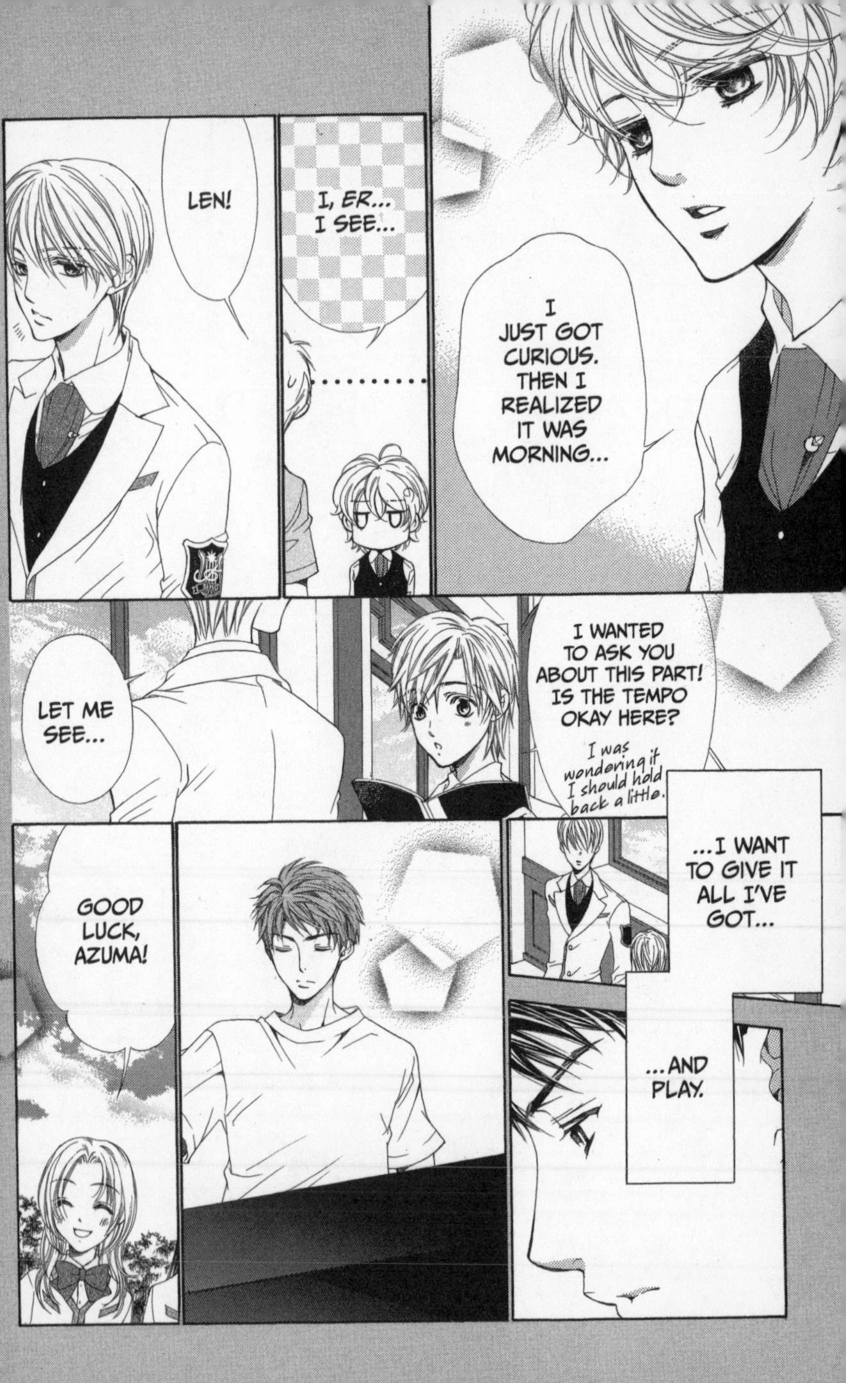
I JUST GOT CURIOUS. THEN I REALIZED IT WAS MORNING...
I, ER... I SEE...
.......
LEN!
I WANTED TO ASK YOU ABOUT THIS PART! IS THE TEMPO OKAY HERE?
I was wondering if I should hold back a little.
LET ME SEE...
...I WANT TO GIVE IT ALL I'VE GOT...
...AND PLAY.
GOOD LUCK, AZUMA!

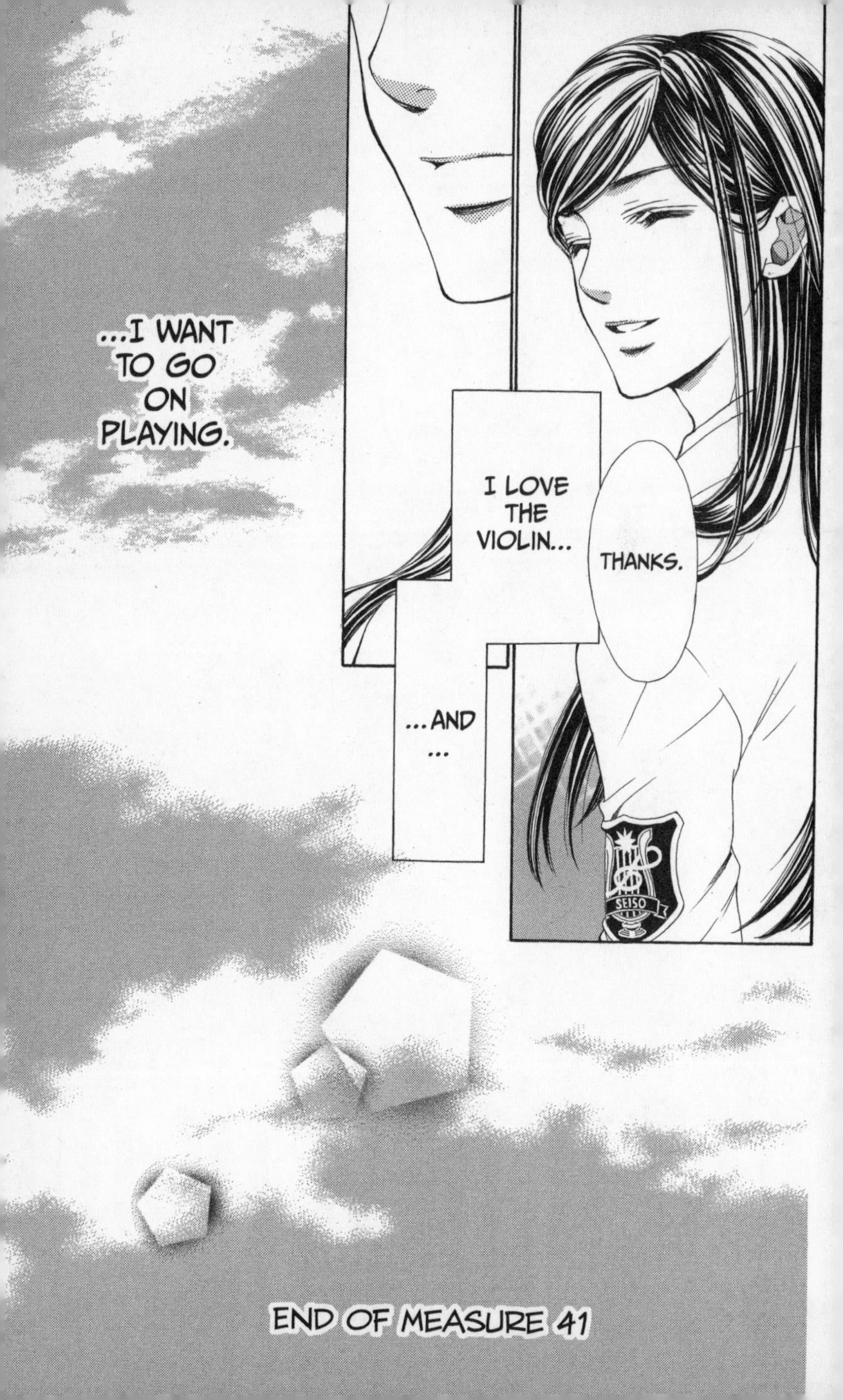
THANKS.
I LOVE THE VIOLIN...
...AND ...
...I WANT TO GO ON PLAYING.
END OF MEASURE 41

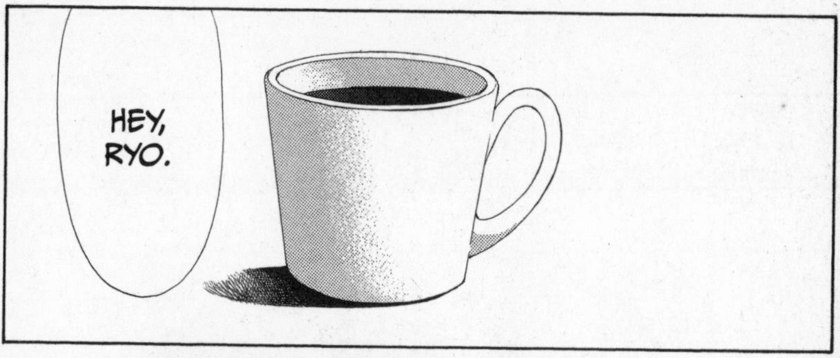
HEY, RYO.

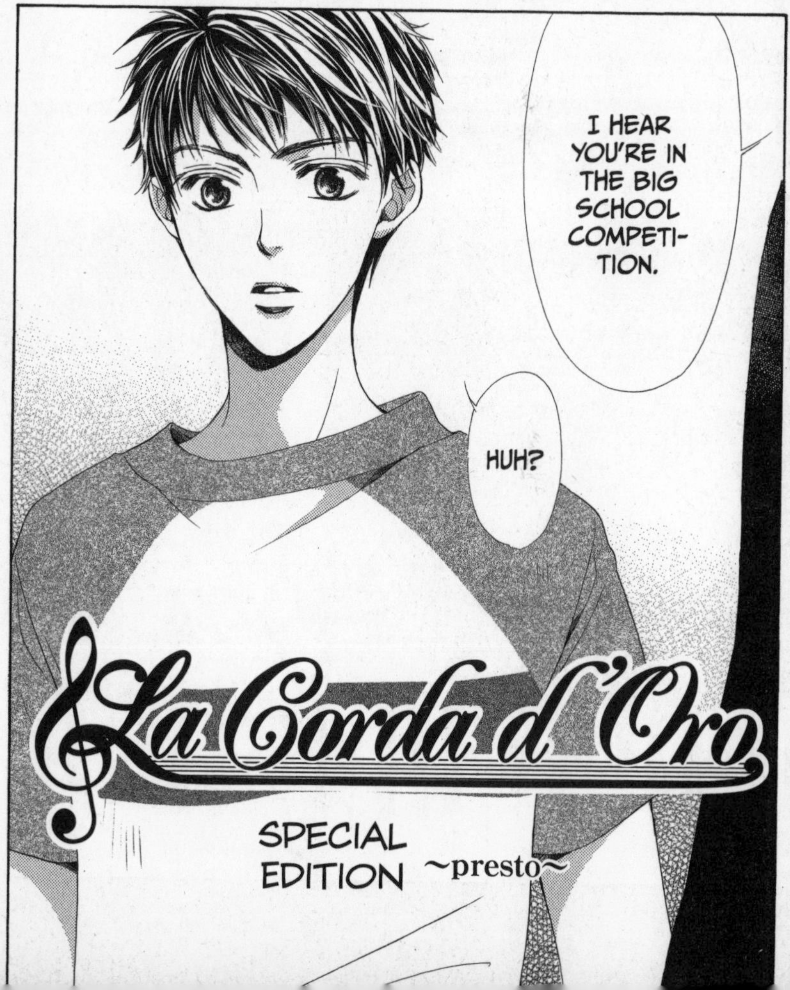
I HEAR YOU'RE IN THE BIG SCHOOL COMPETITION.
HUH?
La Corda d'Oro
SPECIAL EDITION ~presto~

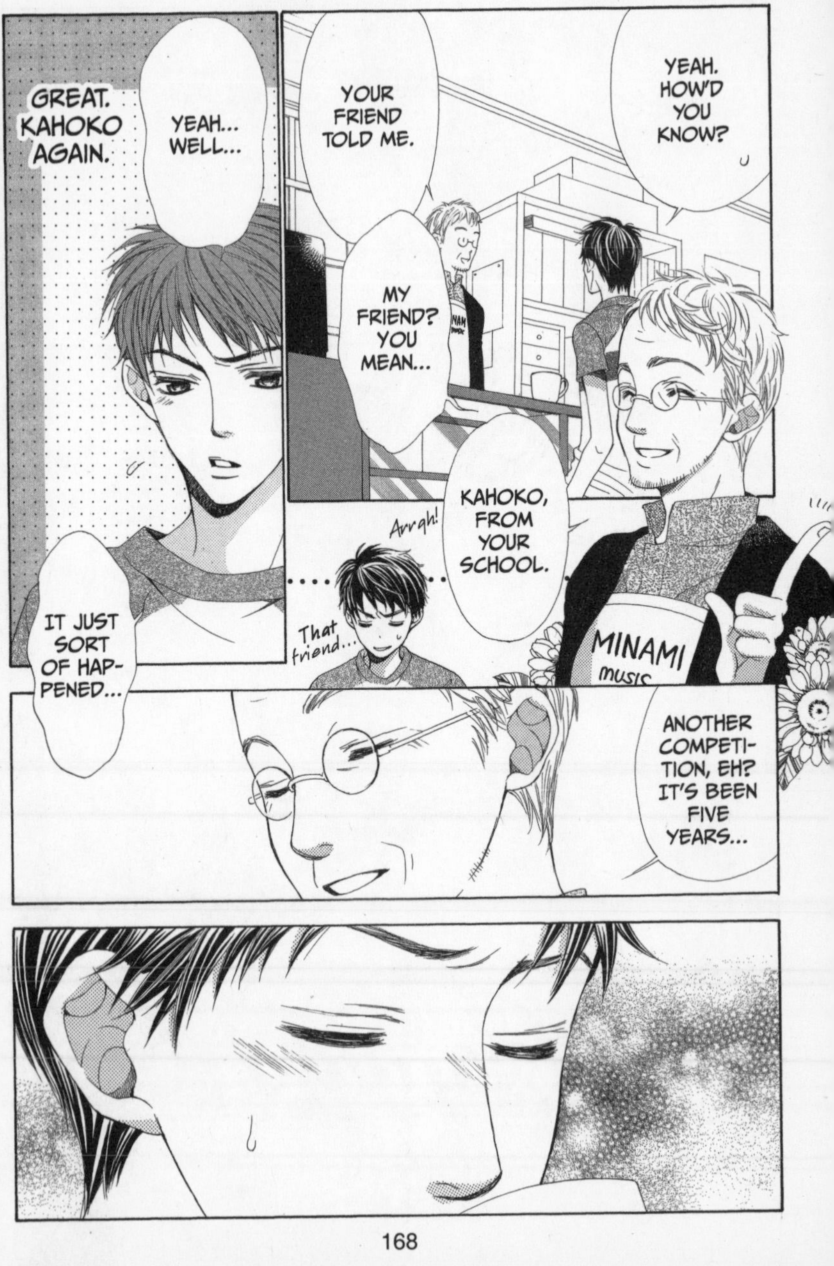

YEAH. HOW'D YOU KNOW?
YOUR FRIEND TOLD ME.
MY FRIEND? YOU MEAN...
KAHOKO, FROM YOUR SCHOOL.
MINAMI
Arrgh!
That friend...
YEAH... WELL...
GREAT. KAHOKO AGAIN.
IT JUST SORT OF HAP-PENED...
ANOTHER COMPETI-TION, EH? IT'S BEEN FIVE YEARS...

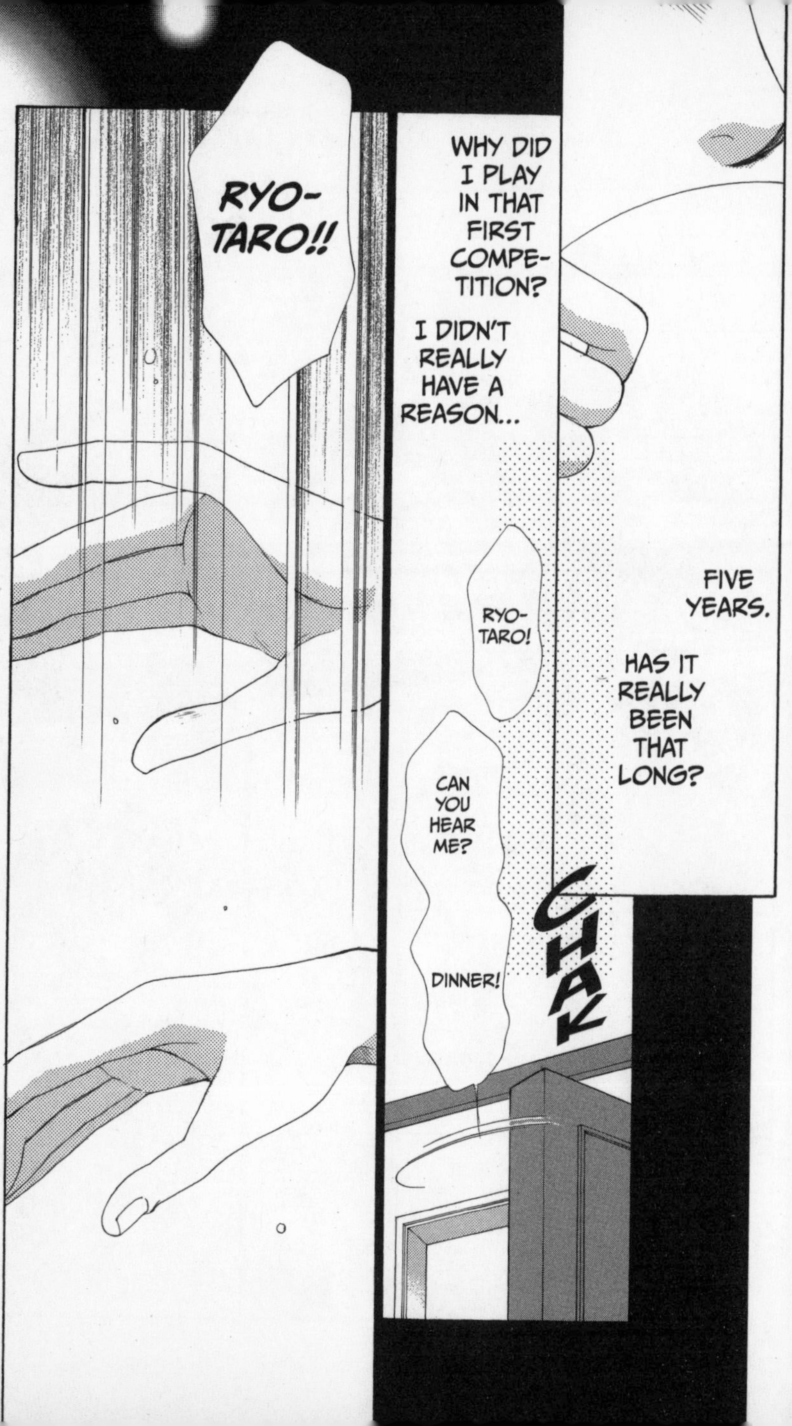
FIVE YEARS.
HAS IT REALLY BEEN THAT LONG?
WHY DID I PLAY IN THAT FIRST COMPETITION?
I DIDN'T REALLY HAVE A REASON...
RYOTARO!
CAN YOU HEAR ME?
DINNER!
CHAK
RYOTARO!!

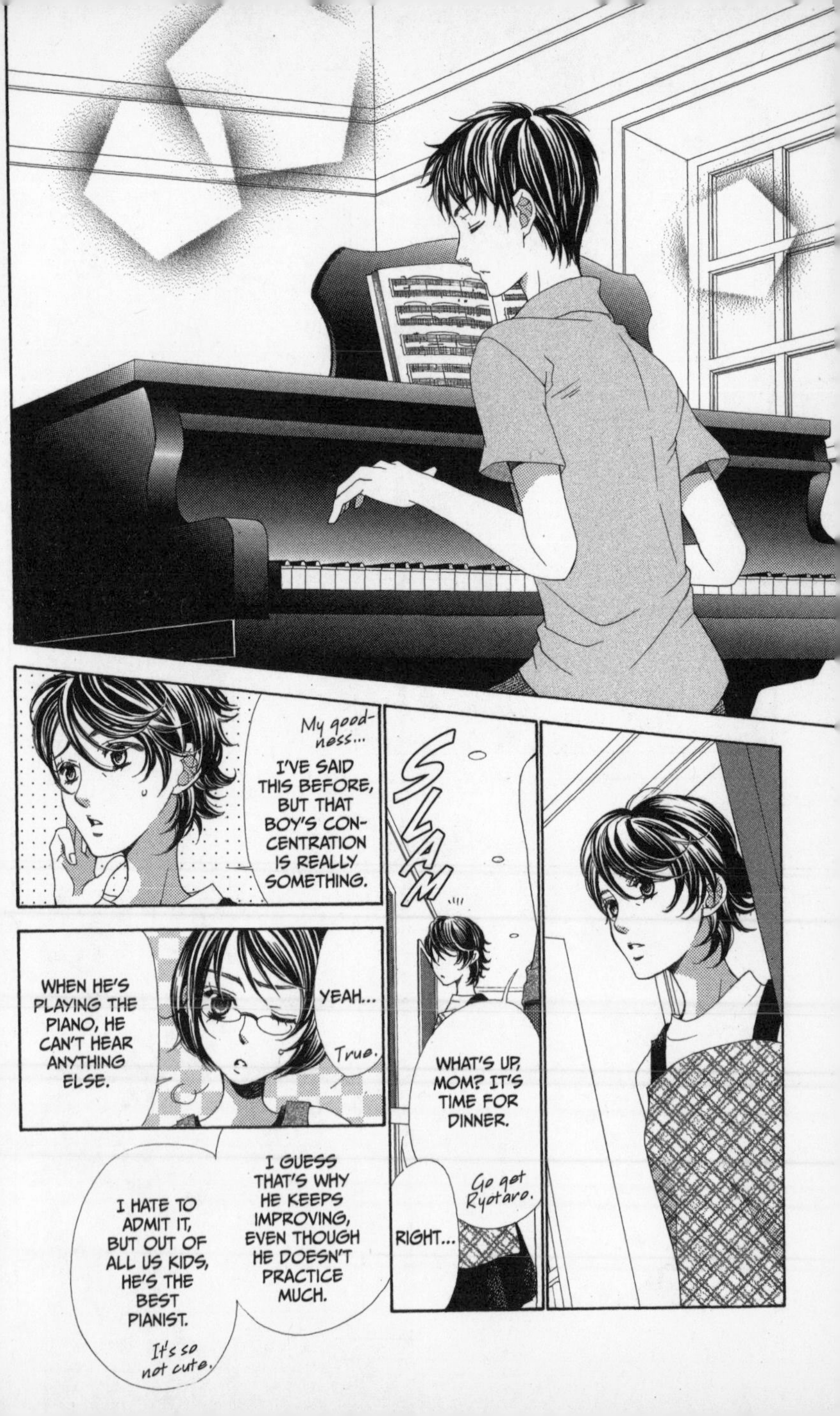
SLAM
WHAT'S UP, MOM? IT'S TIME FOR DINNER.
Go get Ryotaro.
RIGHT...
My goodness...
I'VE SAID THIS BEFORE, BUT THAT BOY'S CONCENTRATION IS REALLY SOMETHING.
YEAH...
True.
WHEN HE'S PLAYING THE PIANO, HE CAN'T HEAR ANYTHING ELSE.
I GUESS THAT'S WHY HE KEEPS IMPROVING, EVEN THOUGH HE DOESN'T PRACTICE MUCH.
I HATE TO ADMIT IT, BUT OUT OF ALL US KIDS, HE'S THE BEST PIANIST.
It's so not cute.

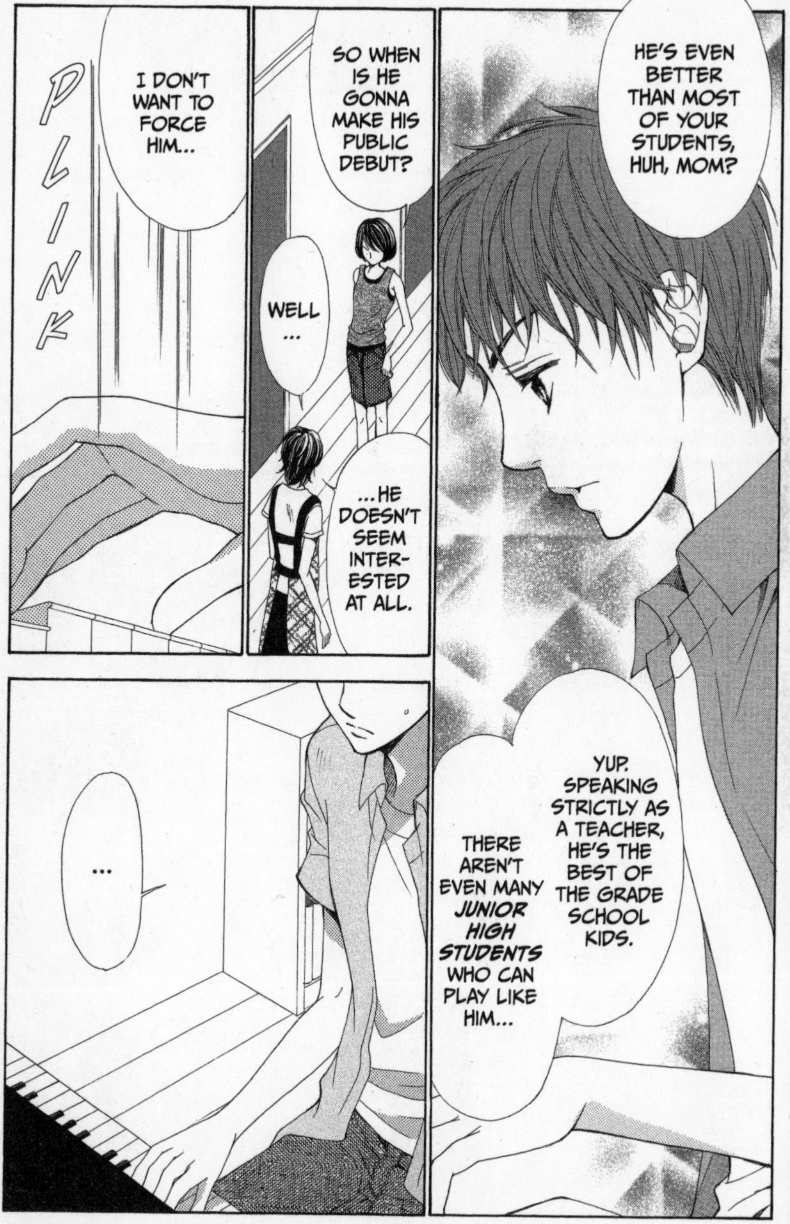
HE'S EVEN BETTER THAN MOST OF YOUR STUDENTS, HUH, MOM?
YUP. SPEAKING STRICTLY AS A TEACHER, HE'S THE BEST OF THE GRADE SCHOOL KIDS.
THERE AREN'T EVEN MANY *JUNIOR HIGH STUDENTS* WHO CAN PLAY LIKE HIM...
SO WHEN IS HE GONNA MAKE HIS PUBLIC DEBUT?
WELL...
...HE DOESN'T SEEM INTER-ESTED AT ALL.
I DON'T WANT TO FORCE HIM...
PLINK
...

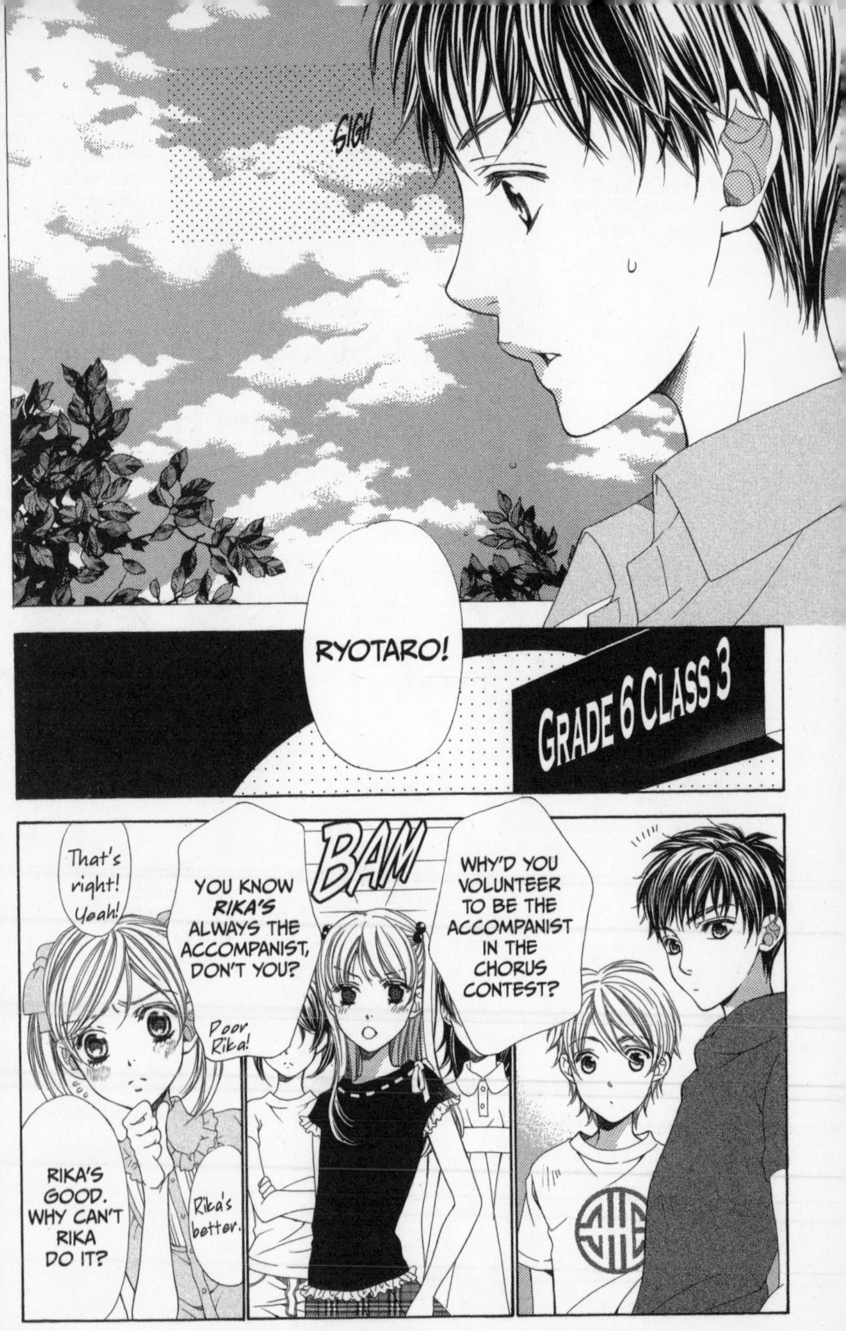

SIGH
RYOTARO!
GRADE 6 CLASS 3
WHY'D YOU VOLUNTEER TO BE THE ACCOMPANIST IN THE CHORUS CONTEST?
BAM
YOU KNOW RIKA'S ALWAYS THE ACCOMPANIST, DON'T YOU?
That's right! Yeah!
Poor Rika!
Rika's better.
RIKA'S GOOD. WHY CAN'T RIKA DO IT?

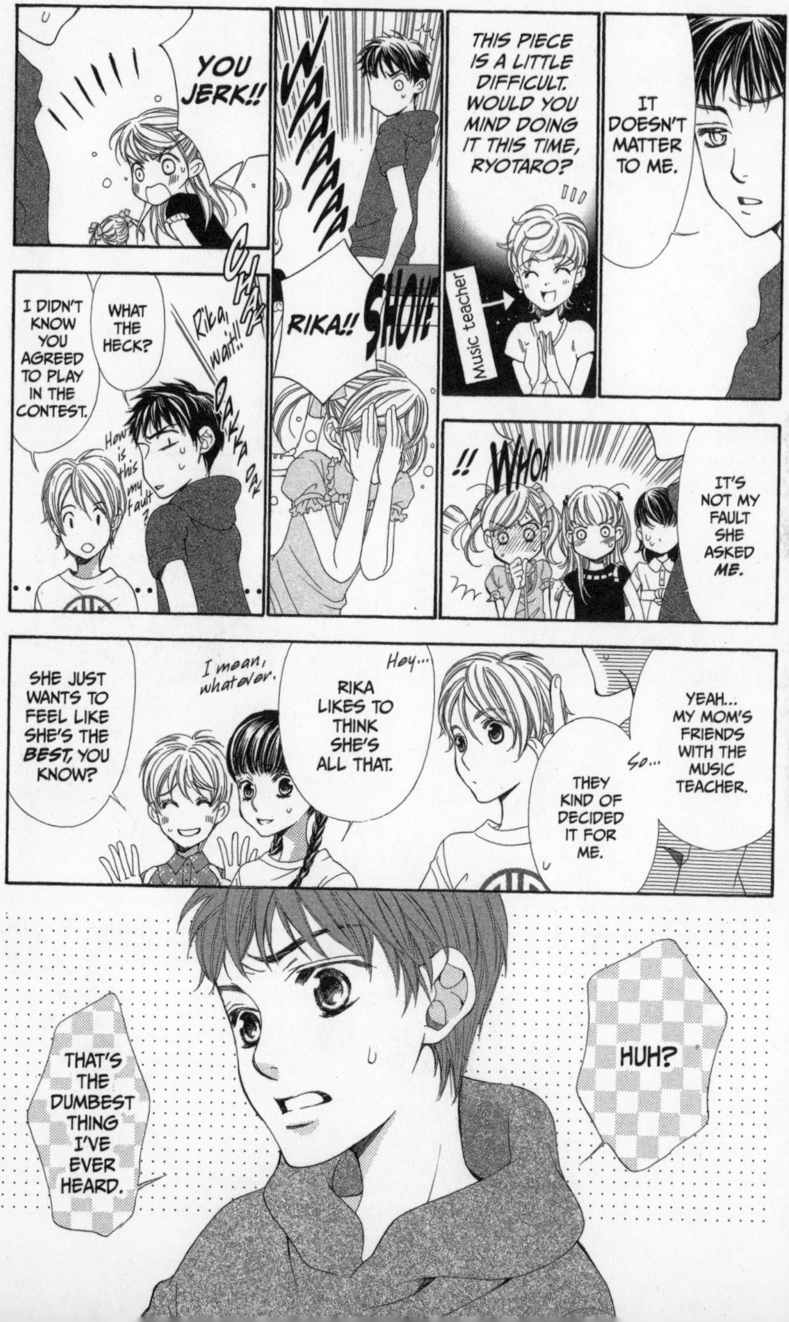
IT DOESN'T MATTER TO ME.
THIS PIECE IS A LITTLE DIFFICULT. WOULD YOU MIND DOING IT THIS TIME, RYOTARO?
Music teacher
!! WHOA
IT'S NOT MY FAULT SHE ASKED *ME*.
SHOVE
RIKA!!
YOU JERK!!
Rika, wait!!
WHAT THE HECK?
How is this my fault?
I DIDN'T KNOW YOU AGREED TO PLAY IN THE CONTEST.
YEAH... MY MOM'S FRIENDS WITH THE MUSIC TEACHER.
So...
THEY KIND OF DECIDED IT FOR ME.
Hey...
RIKA LIKES TO THINK SHE'S ALL THAT.
I mean, whatever.
SHE JUST WANTS TO FEEL LIKE SHE'S THE *BEST*, YOU KNOW?
HUH?
THAT'S THE DUMBEST THING I'VE EVER HEARD.

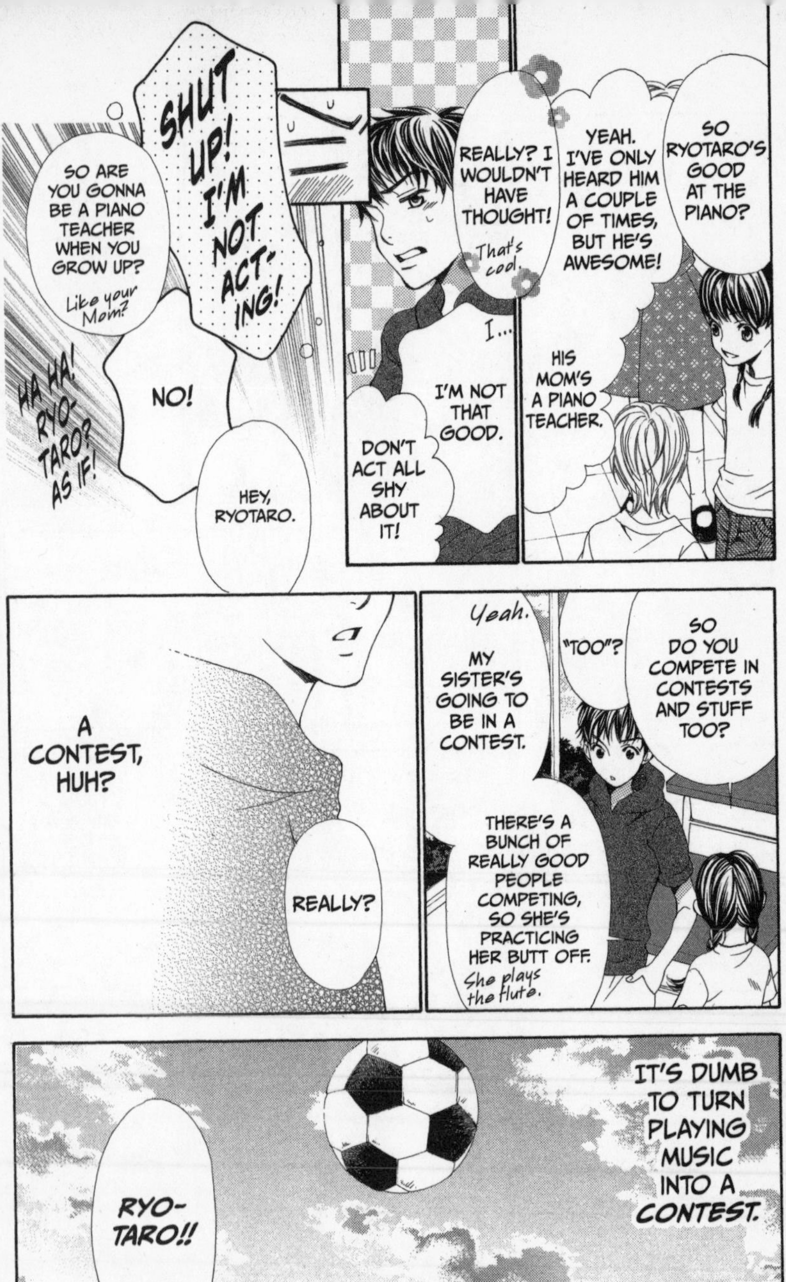
SO RYOTARO'S GOOD AT THE PIANO?
YEAH. I'VE ONLY HEARD HIM A COUPLE OF TIMES, BUT HE'S AWESOME!
HIS MOM'S A PIANO TEACHER.
REALLY? I WOULDN'T HAVE THOUGHT!
That's cool.
I...
I'M NOT THAT GOOD.
DON'T ACT ALL SHY ABOUT IT!
SHUT UP! I'M NOT ACTING!
SO ARE YOU GONNA BE A PIANO TEACHER WHEN YOU GROW UP?
Like your Mom?
HA HA! RYOTARO? AS IF!
NO!
HEY, RYOTARO.
SO DO YOU COMPETE IN CONTESTS AND STUFF TOO?
"TOO"?
Yeah.
MY SISTER'S GOING TO BE IN A CONTEST.
THERE'S A BUNCH OF REALLY GOOD PEOPLE COMPETING, SO SHE'S PRACTICING HER BUTT OFF.
She plays the flute.
A CONTEST, HUH?
REALLY?
IT'S DUMB TO TURN PLAYING MUSIC INTO A CONTEST.
RYOTARO!!

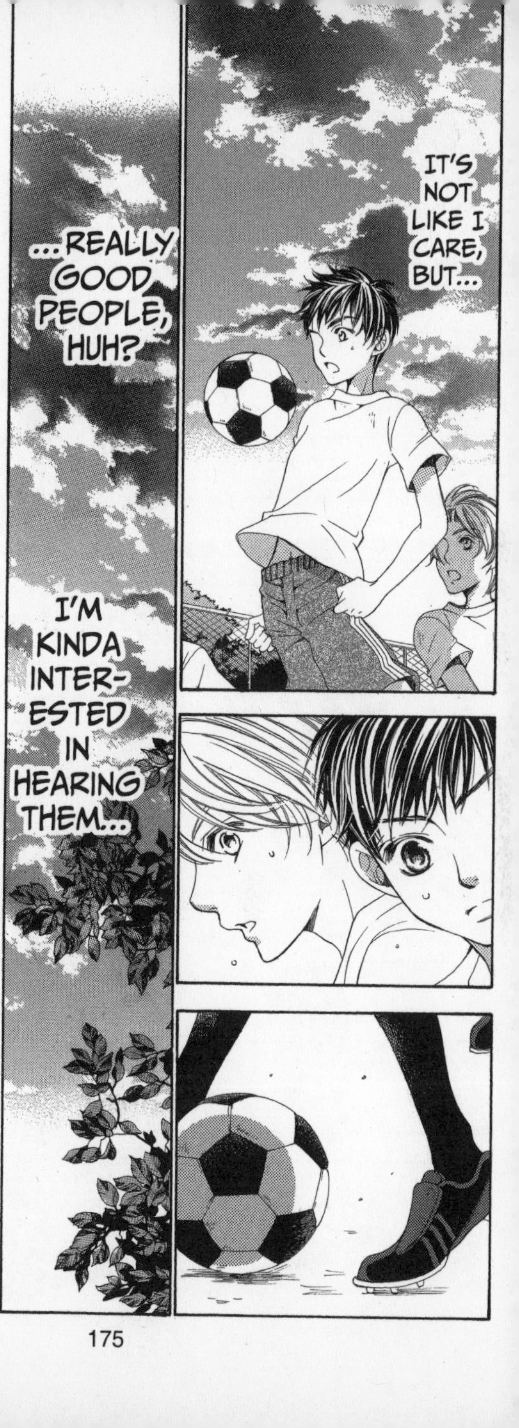
IT'S NOT LIKE I CARE, BUT...
...REALLY GOOD PEOPLE, HUH?
I'M KINDA INTERESTED IN HEARING THEM...

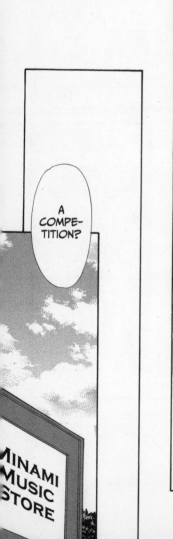

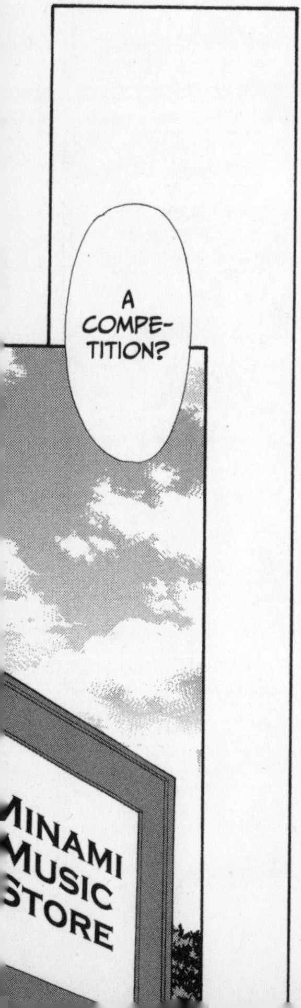
A COMPETITION?
MINAMI MUSIC STORE

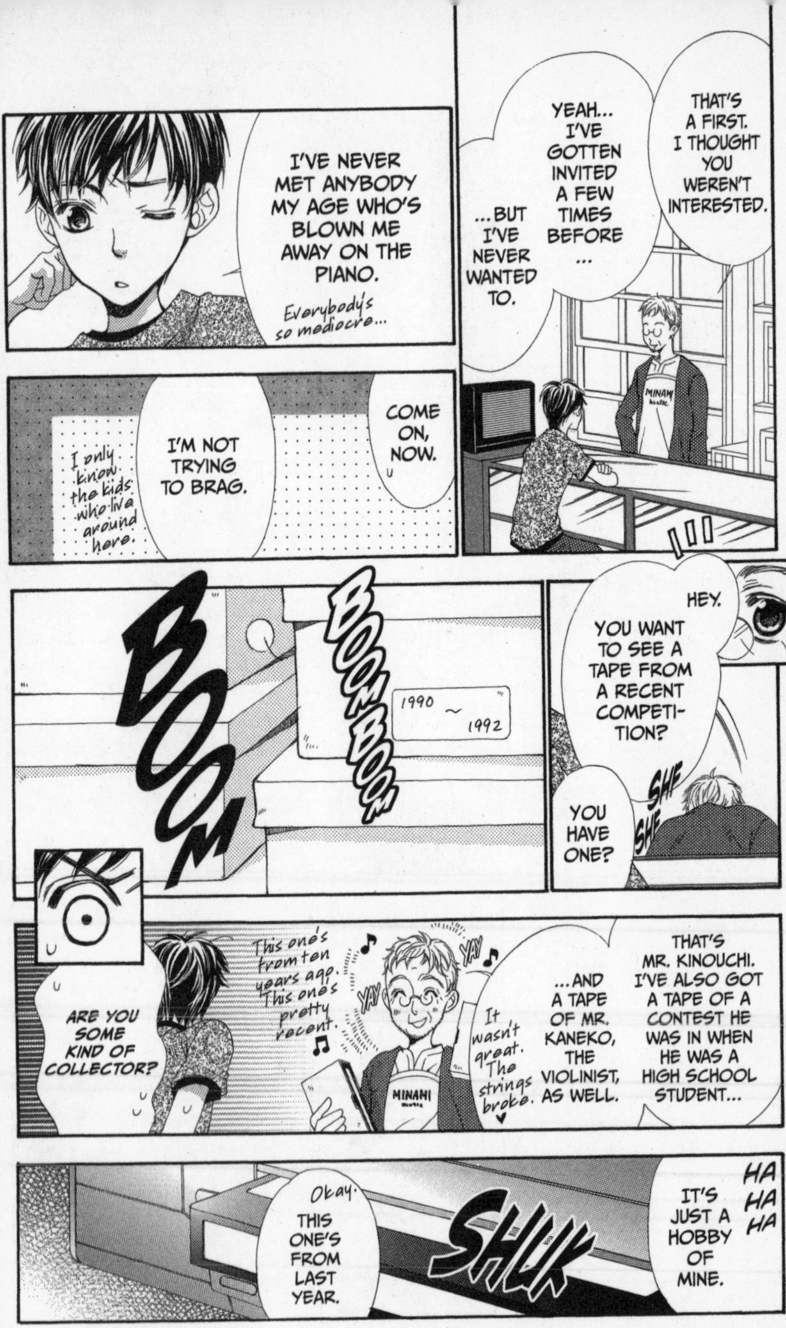
THAT'S A FIRST. I THOUGHT YOU WEREN'T INTERESTED.
YEAH... I'VE GOTTEN INVITED A FEW TIMES BEFORE...
...BUT I'VE NEVER WANTED TO.
I'VE NEVER MET ANYBODY MY AGE WHO'S BLOWN ME AWAY ON THE PIANO.
Everybody's so mediocre...
COME ON, NOW.
I'M NOT TRYING TO BRAG.
I only know the kids who live around here.
HEY.
YOU WANT TO SEE A TAPE FROM A RECENT COMPETITION?
SHF SHF
YOU HAVE ONE?
BOOMBOOM
1990 ~ 1992
BOOM
THAT'S MR. KINOUCHI. I'VE ALSO GOT A TAPE OF A CONTEST HE WAS IN WHEN HE WAS A HIGH SCHOOL STUDENT...
...AND A TAPE OF MR. KANEKO, THE VIOLINIST, AS WELL.
It wasn't great. The strings broke.
YAY
YAY
This one's from ten years ago. This one's pretty recent.
ARE YOU SOME KIND OF COLLECTOR?
HA HA HA
IT'S JUST A HOBBY OF MINE.
SHK
Okay.
THIS ONE'S FROM LAST YEAR.

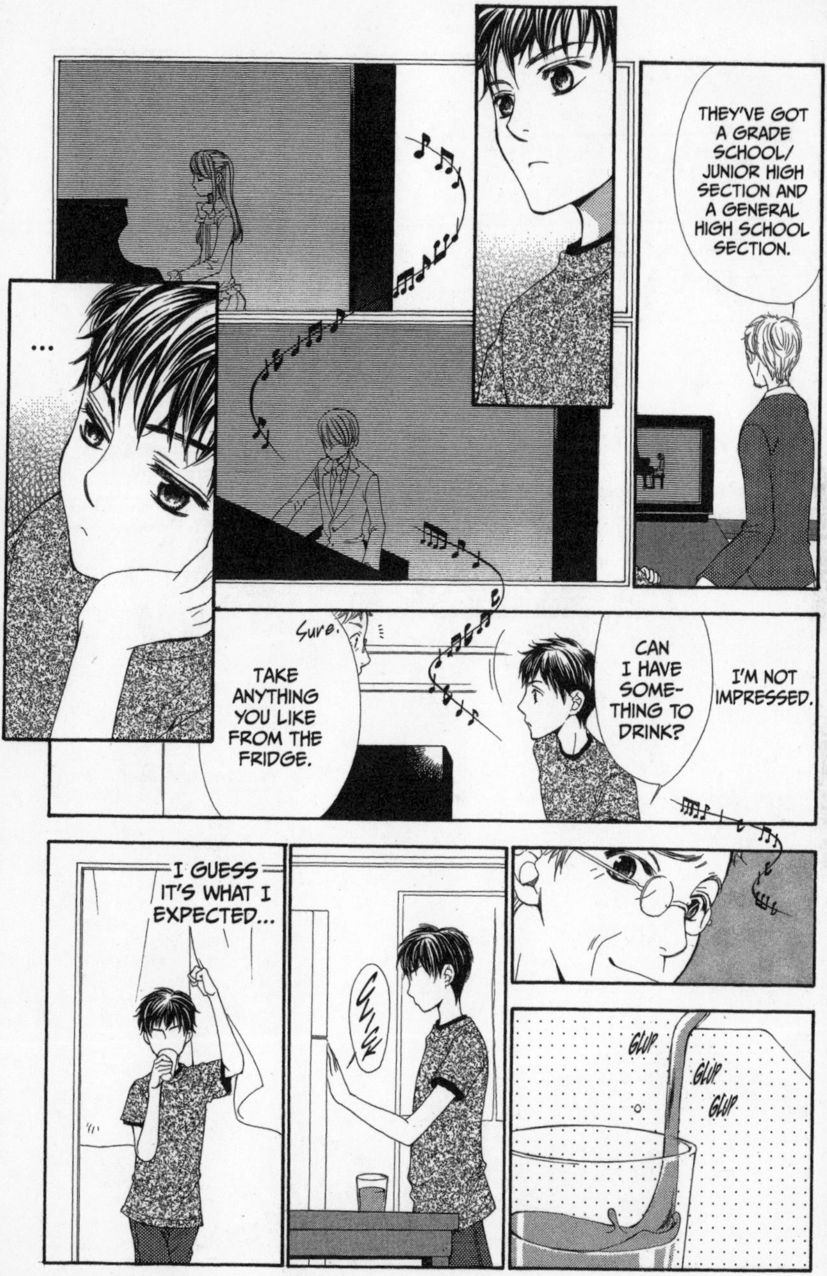
THEY'VE GOT A GRADE SCHOOL/ JUNIOR HIGH SECTION AND A GENERAL HIGH SCHOOL SECTION.
...
I'M NOT IMPRESSED.
CAN I HAVE SOME-THING TO DRINK?
Sure.
TAKE ANYTHING YOU LIKE FROM THE FRIDGE.
GLUP
GLUP
GLUP
CLICK
I GUESS IT'S WHAT I EXPECTED...

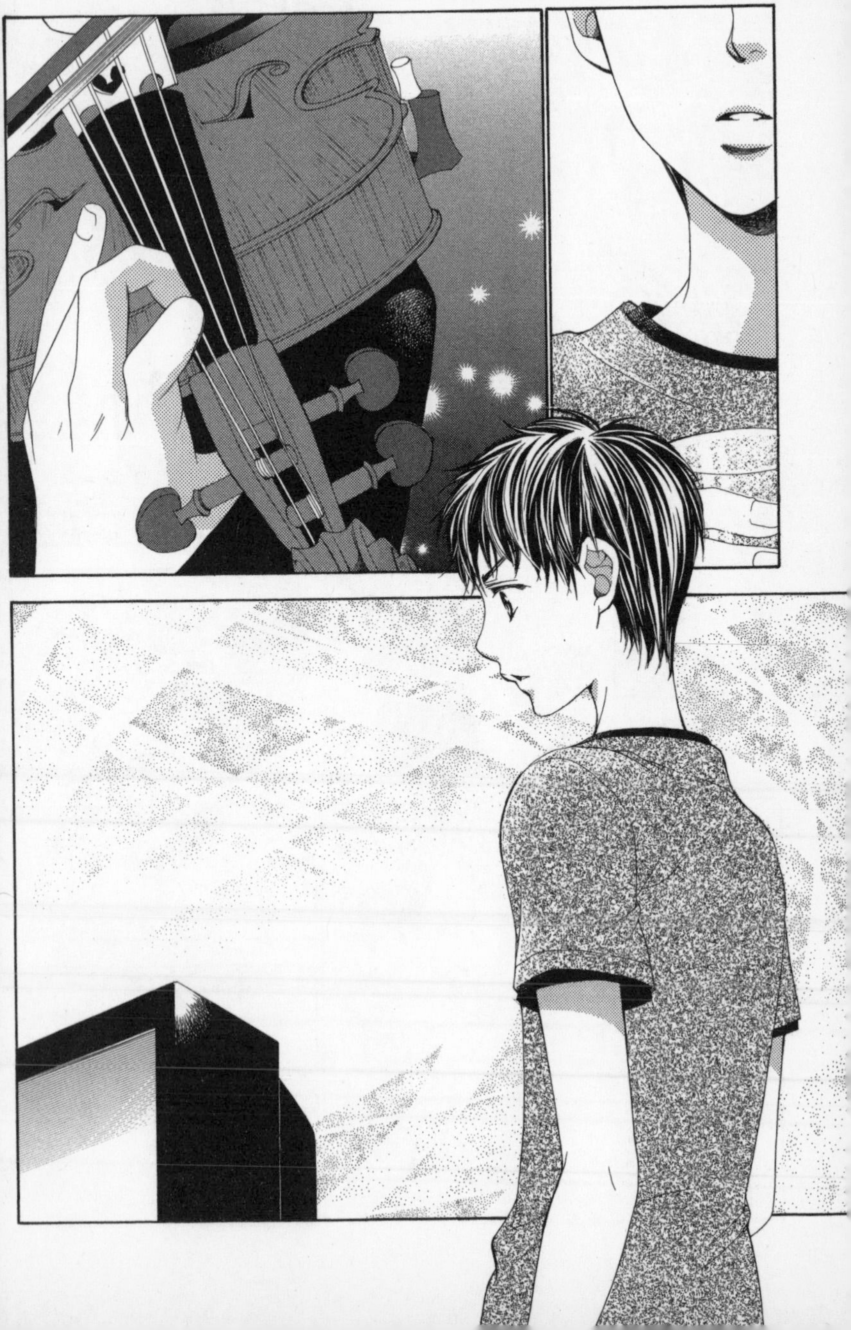

WHAT THE...

THIS KID IS REALLY GOOD!!

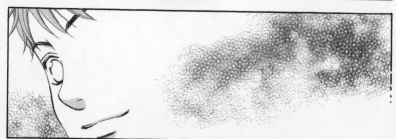

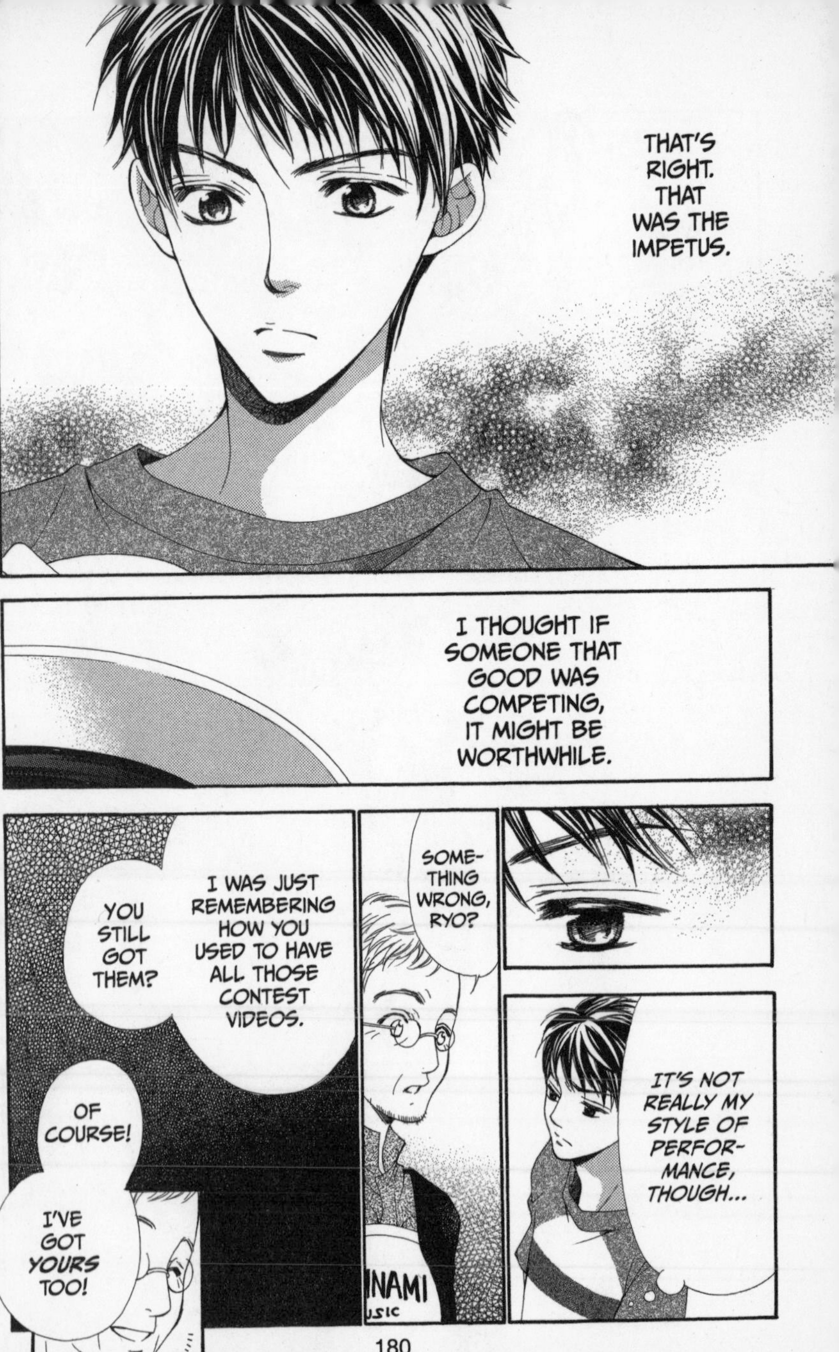
THAT'S RIGHT. THAT WAS THE IMPETUS.
I THOUGHT IF SOMEONE THAT GOOD WAS COMPETING, IT MIGHT BE WORTHWHILE.
IT'S NOT REALLY MY STYLE OF PERFOR-MANCE, THOUGH...
SOME-THING WRONG, RYO?
I WAS JUST REMEMBERING HOW YOU USED TO HAVE ALL THOSE CONTEST VIDEOS.
YOU STILL GOT THEM?
OF COURSE!
I'VE GOT YOURS TOO!

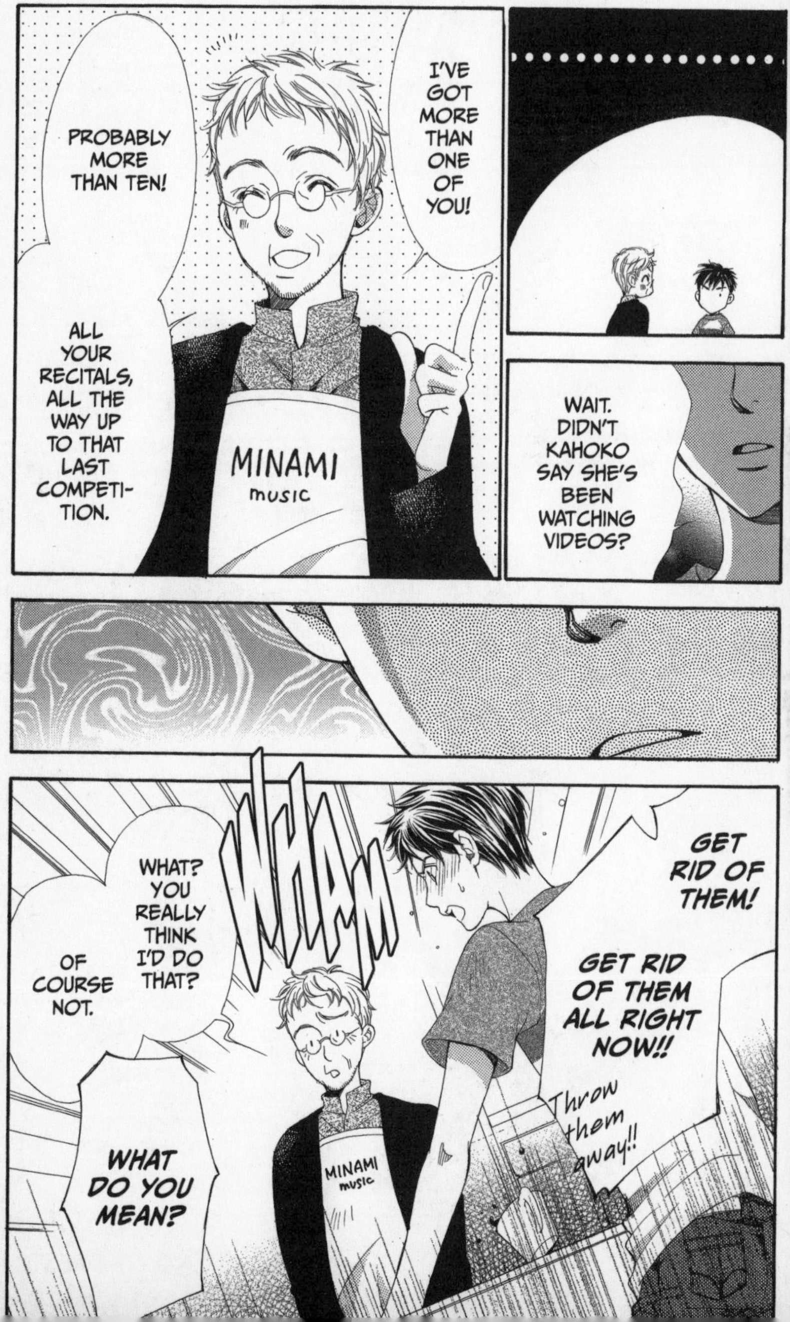
WAIT. DIDN'T KAHOKO SAY SHE'S BEEN WATCHING VIDEOS?
I'VE GOT MORE THAN ONE OF YOU!
PROBABLY MORE THAN TEN!
ALL YOUR RECITALS, ALL THE WAY UP TO THAT LAST COMPETITION.
MINAMI music
GET RID OF THEM!
GET RID OF THEM ALL RIGHT NOW!!
Throw them away!!
WHAM
WHAT? YOU REALLY THINK I'D DO THAT?
OF COURSE NOT.
WHAT DO YOU MEAN?
MINAMI music

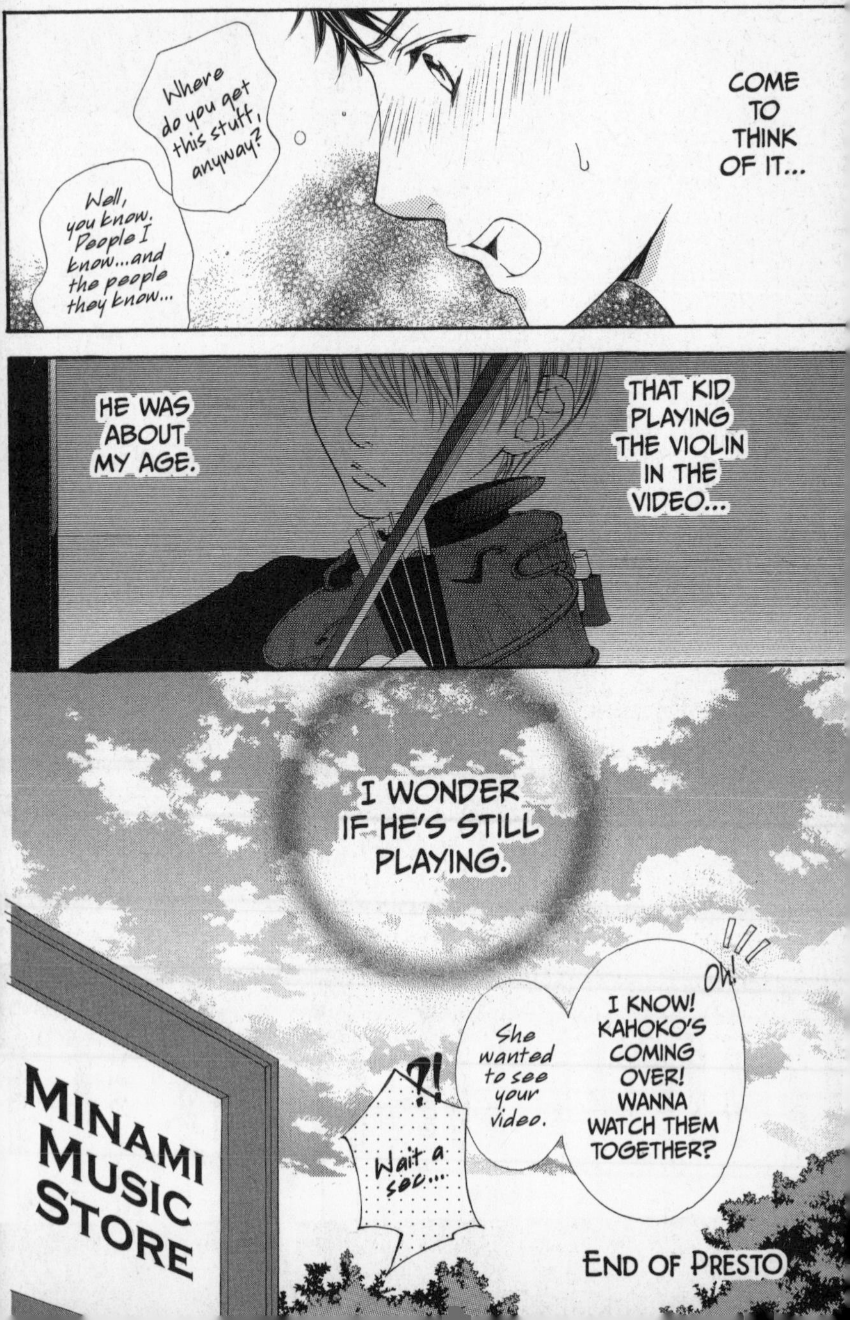
COME TO THINK OF IT...
Where do you get this stuff, anyway?
Well, you know. People I know...and the people they know...
THAT KID PLAYING THE VIOLIN IN THE VIDEO...
HE WAS ABOUT MY AGE.
I WONDER IF HE'S STILL PLAYING.
Oh!
I KNOW! KAHOKO'S COMING OVER! WANNA WATCH THEM TOGETHER?
She wanted to see your video.
?!
Wait a sec...
MINAMI MUSIC STORE
END OF PRESTO

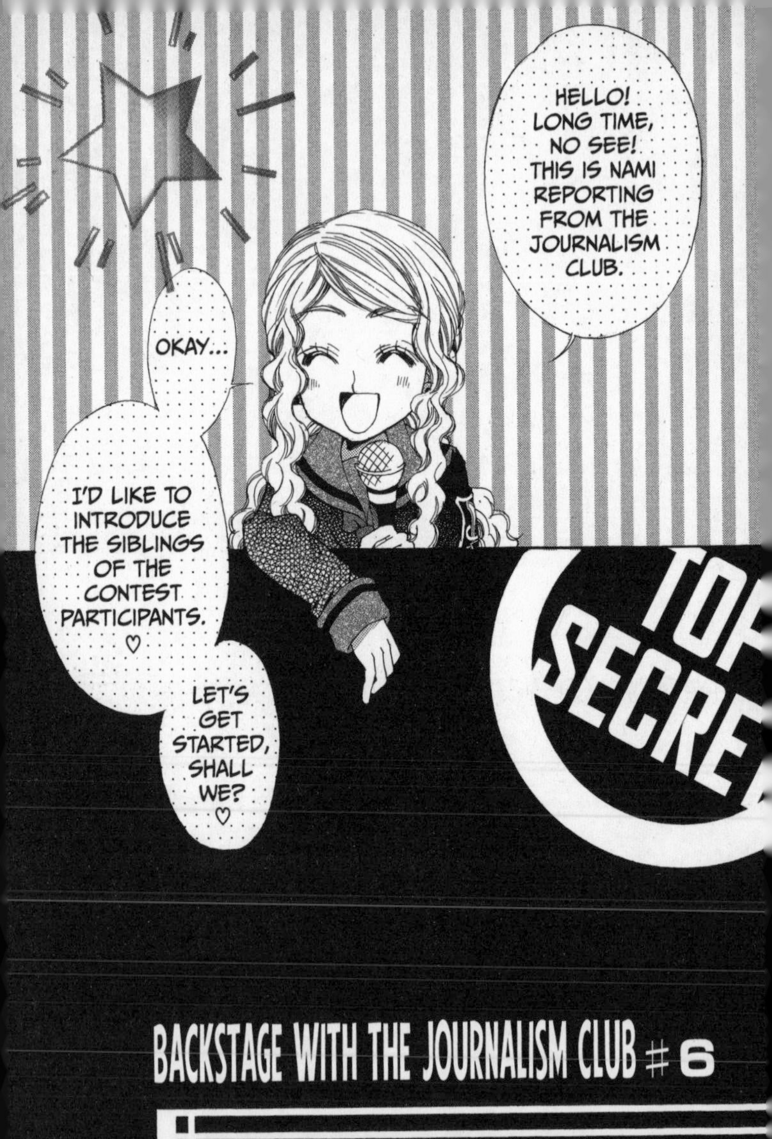
HELLO! LONG TIME, NO SEE! THIS IS NAMI REPORTING FROM THE JOURNALISM CLUB.
OKAY...
I'D LIKE TO INTRODUCE THE SIBLINGS OF THE CONTEST PARTICIPANTS. ♡
LET'S GET STARTED, SHALL WE? ♡
BACKSTAGE WITH THE JOURNALISM CLUB #6

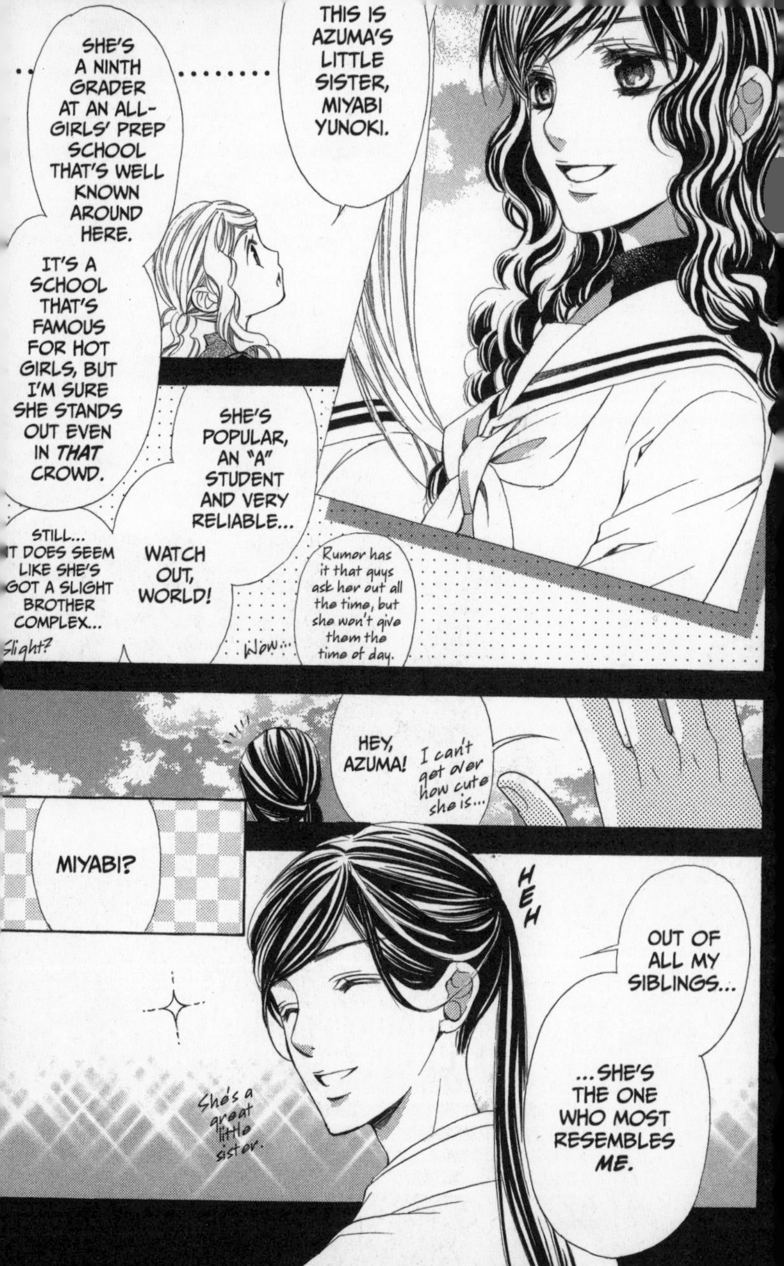
THIS IS AZUMA'S LITTLE SISTER, MIYABI YUNOKI.
........
SHE'S A NINTH GRADER AT AN ALL-GIRLS' PREP SCHOOL THAT'S WELL KNOWN AROUND HERE.
IT'S A SCHOOL THAT'S FAMOUS FOR HOT GIRLS, BUT I'M SURE SHE STANDS OUT EVEN IN *THAT* CROWD.
SHE'S POPULAR, AN "A" STUDENT AND VERY RELIABLE...
Rumor has it that guys ask her out all the time, but she won't give them the time of day.
Wow...
WATCH OUT, WORLD!
STILL... IT DOES SEEM LIKE SHE'S GOT A SLIGHT BROTHER COMPLEX...
Slight?
HEY, AZUMA!
I can't get over how cute she is...
MIYABI?
OUT OF ALL MY SIBLINGS...
HEH
...SHE'S THE ONE WHO MOST RESEMBLES *ME*.
She's a great little sister.

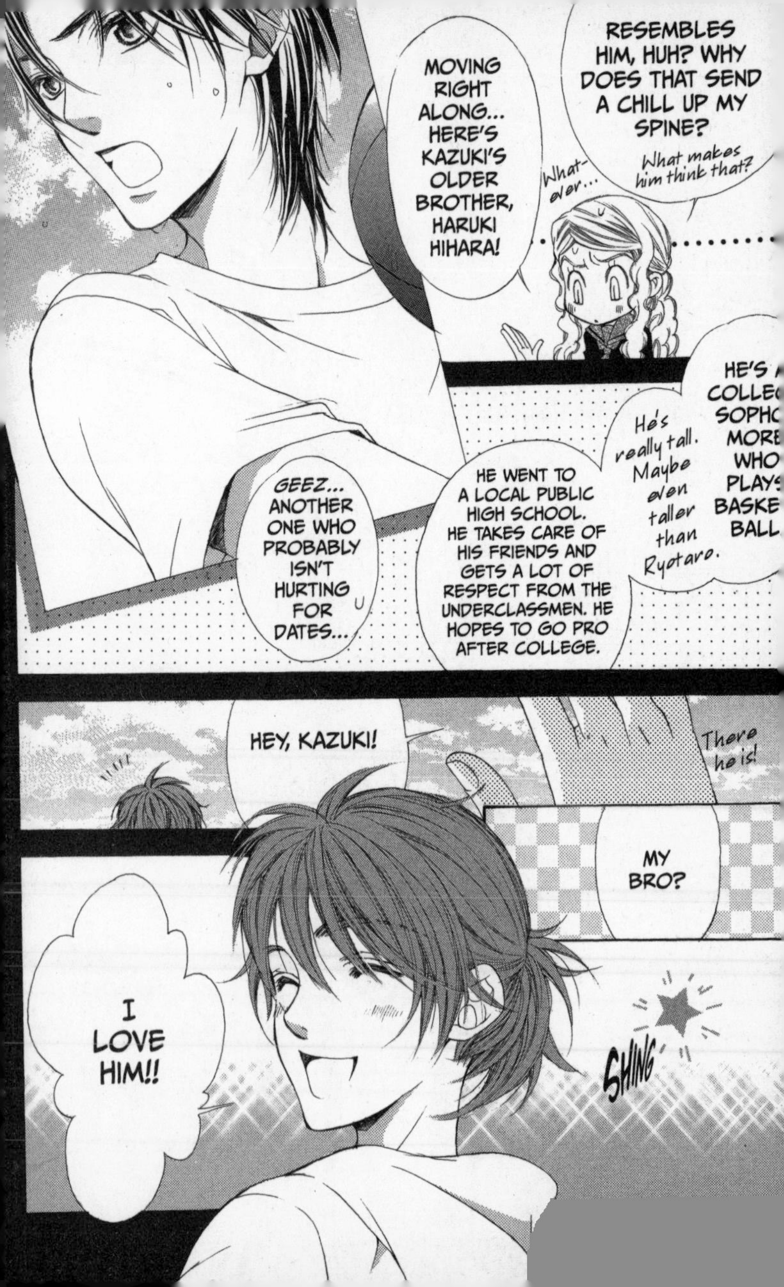
RESEMBLES HIM, HUH? WHY DOES THAT SEND A CHILL UP MY SPINE?
What makes him think that?
Whatever...
MOVING RIGHT ALONG... HERE'S KAZUKI'S OLDER BROTHER, HARUKI HIHARA!
HE'S COLLEG SOPHO MORE WHO PLAYS BASKE BALL
He's really tall. Maybe even taller than Ryotaro.
HE WENT TO A LOCAL PUBLIC HIGH SCHOOL. HE TAKES CARE OF HIS FRIENDS AND GETS A LOT OF RESPECT FROM THE UNDERCLASSMEN. HE HOPES TO GO PRO AFTER COLLEGE.
GEEZ... ANOTHER ONE WHO PROBABLY ISN'T HURTING FOR DATES...
HEY, KAZUKI!
There he is!
MY BRO?
SHING
I LOVE HIM!!

A BIG GRIN AND, "I LOVE HIM!"

WHAT KIND OF HIGH SCHOOL SENIOR *TALKS* LIKE THAT?

I'm at a loss for words...

I GUESS IT'S OKAY.

IT JUST DOESN'T GIVE ME ANY *DIRT*...

I give up...

## SPECIAL THANKS

A.Hagio
A.Kashima
M.Shiino
M.Hiyama
N.Sato
S.Asahina
W.Hibiki
A.Uruno

End of backstage with the Jornalism Club #6

# La Corda d'Oro End Notes

You can appreciate music just by listening to it, but knowing the story behind a piece can help enhance your enjoyment. In that spirit, here is background information about some of the topics mentioned in **La Corda d'Oro**. Enjoy!

**Page 4, Author's Note: Himeji Castle**
A 14th-century castle in Hyogo Prefecture known as one of Japan's "Three Famous Castles." It was declared a World Heritage Site in 1993 and is one of the most visited sites in Japan. Cherry blossom viewing is a traditional Japanese spring pastime; people often turn it into a vacation, traveling up and down the country to see the trees in bloom.

**Page 40, panel 1**
The little seals at the bottom of each photo read "Journalism." Looks like the Journalism Club has been as busy as ever.

**Page 47, Author's Note: *LaLa***
*LaLa* is the magazine in which *La Corda d'Oro* runs in Japan.

**Page 109, panel 3: Brahms' Clarinet Trio, Beethoven's *Gassenhauer*, Bruch, Glinka**
The clarinet was a favorite instrument of the Romantic era, and Romantic composers like the ones Keiichi lists here composed many memorable clarinet pieces. Beethoven's *Gassenhauer*, or "Street Song," is a trio for piano, clarinet and cello. Max Bruch (1838-1920) was a German composer best known for his violin concertos; Keiichi is probably thinking of one of the eight pieces Bruch wrote for piano, clarinet and viola. Mikhail Glinka (1804-1857), one of the first Russian composers to achieve international success, dedicated his career to music celebrating his country's heritage. His "Patriotic Song" was used as the Russian national anthem from 1990 until 2000, when the old Soviet anthem was reinstated with new lyrics.

**Page 167: *presto***
In music notation, *presto* means "faster."

Yuki Kure made her debut in 2000
with the story *Chijo yori Eien ni*
(Forever from the Earth), published
in monthly *LaLa* magazine.
*La Corda d' Oro* is her first manga
series published. Her hobbies are
watching soccer games and
collecting small goodies.

# LA CORDA D'ORO
## Vol. 9
### The Shojo Beat Manga Edition

**STORY AND ART BY
YUKI KURE**

ORIGINAL CONCEPT BY
RUBY PARTY

English Translation & Adaptation/Mai Ihara
Touch-up Art & Lettering/Gia Cam Luc
Design/Izumi Evers
Editor/Shaenon K. Garrity

Editor in Chief, Books/Alvin Lu
Editor in Chief, Magazines/Marc Weidenbaum
VP, Publishing Licensing/Rika Inouye
VP, Sales and Product Marketing/Gonzalo Ferreyra
VP, Creative/Linda Espinosa
Publisher/Hyoe Narita

Printed in Canada

Published by VIZ Media, LLC
P.O. Box 77010
San Francisco, CA 94107

Shojo Beat Manga Edition
10 9 8 7 6 5 4 3 2 1
First printing, October 2008